PRAISE FOR

THE EVER-SHRINKING FIGHTING FORCE

"For more than 40 years, Arnold Punaro has championed bold, innovative ideas for improving the performance of the U.S. military establishment. He has a keen and rare knack for cutting through bewildering detail to precisely identify the heart of a problem. Arnold combines vast energy and insightful intellect to produce profound ideas. He has much of value to say; we must listen."

The Honorable Jim Locher
Former Assistant Secretary of Defense
Principal Staff Architect, Goldwater-Nichols Act

"The national security of the United States is "at risk" given growing security threats, increasing fiscal pressures, bloated bureaucracies, and long-standing business-related challenges. Arnold Punaro has significant experience in three critical dimensions needed to make informed observations and recommendations concerning how to reform the Pentagon. First, he was a Major General in the U.S. Marines Corps (USMC). Second, he was the top staff person on the Senate Armed Services Committee. Third, he has significant experience inside the Pentagon, including many years of experience on the Defense Business Board (DBB). Just as importantly, he is a dedicated patriot who is committed to improving the Pentagon, the Department of Defense, and our country. This book can help the responsible leaders make the needed choices to help create a better future."

The Honorable David Walker
Distinguished Visiting Professor (Crowe Chair), United States Naval Academy
Former U.S. Comptroller General
CEO, Peter G. Peterson Foundation

"Arnold Punaro is one of America's foremost thought leaders on all aspects of defense management. Drawing upon his distinguished service in the military, on Capitol Hill and in industry, he has for decades been an invaluable advisor to Secretaries of Defense, other senior defense officials, and key legislators of both political parties. This book is must-reading for all who recognize the need to reform and modernize the Defense Department as it contends with the challenges of the twenty-first century."

Dr. Dov S. Zakheim
Former Under Secretary of Defense (Comptroller)
Senior Advisor at the Center for Strategic and International Studies

"Whether in uniform, working in the government, or as one of the top thought leaders on national security, Arnold Punaro has invested his life focused on strengthening U.S. national security. When Gen. Punaro speaks, people listen because he is nonpartisan, evidence-based, and thoroughly committed to making sure that the United States military is prepared for the future. This book will change the way you understand the current defense establishment and how you think about the challenges and opportunities ahead for the nation."

Dr. David M. Van Slyke
Dean, Maxwell School of Citizenship and Public Affairs, Syracuse University

"To understand the Pentagon is to understand that it is a place of enduring competition — between America and its adversaries, rival constitutional powers given to the president and the Congress, the tensions of land, sea, air and space in the military departments, and the push of each new generation of technology against the status quo. I have teamed with Arnold Punaro, and at other times sat across the table in House-Senate negotiations, but he has watched it all and is always committed to doing right for the men and women who serve in the armed forces of the United States."

The Honorable Rudy De Leon
Senior Fellow of National Security & International Policy, Center for American Progress
Former Deputy Secretary of Defense
Former Under Secretary of Defense for Personnel and Readiness
Former Under Secretary of the Air Force

"No one has more experience with the Department of Defense in varying roles and capacities than Arnold Punaro. Passionate to protect America, he documents the growing deficiencies of the department. This book is a call to action and a blueprint for reform."

Dr. John Hamre
CEO, Center for Strategic and International Studies
Former Deputy Secretary of Defense & Under Secretary of Defense Comptroller

"In *The Ever-Shrinking Fighting Force*, General Arnold Punaro considers the dilemmas of runaway costs, excessive bureaucracy, and unconstructive politics in America's defense operations – problems that have been decades in the making. Punaro, with his deep leadership experience in the Marine Corps, on the Hill, and in the private sector, has unique vantage points on subjects as disparate as the congressional appropriations process, the doctrine of civilian control of the military, and contracting of military hardware and services. His proposed reforms, grouped into three areas (leadership, legislative, process-oriented) are practicable and well-timed, as the bill for U.S. defense operations approaches three-quarters of a trillion dollars, annually."

Dr. Matthew R. Auer
Dean, School of Public and International Affairs, the University of Georgia

"Arnold Punaro's entire adult life has been dedicated to national security issues, whether in a Marine uniform in Vietnam, in the Senate Armed Services Committee as staff director, or in industry as chairman of the NDIA.

Over 23 years ago, he led a very powerful group of former defense experts in a comprehensive study of the way the Department of Defense is organized and how it spends its immense budget. The study proposed the most complete set of recommendations ever advocated. Had any of the succeeding administrations adopted any or all of the recommendations proposed, the Department of Defense and our country would be in a much better place today and would be doing much more with fewer wasted resources.

Arnold Punaro's second book, also aimed at explaining the problems we face, offers solutions that should be implemented. The incoming administration would do well to pay close attention to his recommendations; they will make the task of providing for our national security much more efficient and more relevant in the face of the 21st-century challenges."

General Jim Jones, USMC (Ret)
Former U.S. National Security Advisor
32nd Commandant of the Marine Corps
Former Commander, U.S. European Command and Supreme Allied Commander Europe

"Arnold Punaro, a retired Marine General and former staff director of the Senate Armed Services Committee, is more devoted and committed to the well-being and effectiveness of our men and women in uniform than anyone I have known. In this valuable book, he warns that our nation's ability to preserve peace through strength is in jeopardy if the current alarming trends continue.

Beyond the battlefield in Vietnam, Punaro has spent tens of thousands of hours on Capitol Hill and in the halls of the Pentagon. He is a southerner, and he knows that kudzu was planted with the lofty goal of preserving the soil but became an overshadowing and smothering noxious weed. He tells us that, like kudzu, well-meaning defense regulations and bureaucracy are smothering the efficiency and effectiveness of our procurement system. With an abundance of facts and figures, Punaro warns that we are producing "an ever-shrinking fighting force."

The Marines, the Senate Armed Services Committee, and the Department of Defense have greatly benefited from Punaro's military experience, his knowledge, his keen insights, his sound judgment and his common sense. This book may be his most important contribution yet to America's security.

In his book, Punaro forgets to tell us how to get rid of kudzu; he does, however, tell us how to get more "bang for the buck" and give our military forces the essential tools they must have to prevent war through our military strength or to fight effectively if required. I recommend this book to all who believe America must spend our dollars wisely while preserving our military strength and capabilities."

Former Senator Sam Nunn
Former Chairman of the Senate Armed Services Committee
Co-Founder and Co-Chair, Nuclear Threat Initiative

Books by Arnold L. Punaro

The Ever-Shrinking Fighting Force (2021)

On War and Politics: The Battlefield Inside Washington's Beltway (2016)

THE EVER-SHRINKING
FIGHTING FORCE

Punaro Press
1313 Dolley Madison Boulevard
Suite 404
McLean, VA 22101

The Ever-Shrinking Fighting Force
Copyright © 2021 by Arnold L. Punaro

All photos are from the author's collection.

ISBN: 978-1-7359114-0-3

Library of Congress Control Number: 2020921106

Printed in the United States of America by IngramSpark

Cover art by VSSL Agency

Layout by Pinkston

THE EVER-SHRINKING FIGHTING FORCE

MAJOR GENERAL ARNOLD L. PUNARO, USMC (RET)

PUNARO
PRESS

McLean, Virginia

"To be prepared for war is one of the most effectual means of preserving peace."

– President George Washington

First annual address to Congress

January 8, 1790

This book is dedicated to the men and women, active duty military, Guard and Reserve, defense civilians, and defense contractors who come to work every day and, in support of the Department of Defense, do the best job they can for our warfighters and taxpayers.

This also includes the dedicated members and staffs of the Senate and House Armed Services Committees, the Senate and House Defense Appropriations Committees, and the Senate and House Intelligence Committees.

They form the cornerstone of our national security capabilities. Their dedication, sacrifice, and hard work on behalf of our country cannot be overstated. Thank you.

Table of Contents

Congressional Reforms

Conclusion

Acknowledgements

An Introduction to Defense Reform

Take a drive through parts of my home state of Georgia, and you can't help but notice the thick vines blanketing the roadside. Known as kudzu, this invasive species has earned nicknames like "the vine that ate the South" for its rapid growth and resistance to any kind of controls. Kudzu grows relentlessly, climbing up telephone poles and creeping across wires, swallowing abandoned buildings and smothering trees and other plants in its shade.

Like so many ideas we now regret, kudzu's introduction to the United States was built on good intentions. In the early 20th century, a government agency called the Soil Erosion Service actually paid farmers to plant kudzu to prevent erosion. Today, the "foot-a-night-vine" covers an estimated 7.4 million acres from Georgia to as far south as Florida, as far west as Texas, and as far north as New England. Less than a century after promoting it, the government added kudzu to the Federal Noxious Weed List.

Bureaucracy is a lot like kudzu. Starting from a place of good intentions, it grows steadily until it begins overshadowing and even smothering the beneficial programs and services it was meant to support. Before we know it, bureaucracy is so ingrained and self-perpetuating that it's almost impossible to root out. Like any government agency, the Department of Defense (DoD) has not been immune from creeping bureaucracy. It is, however, unique among the federal agencies,

1

departments, and bureaus in that its budget and presence, both in terms of people and facilities, dwarf all other parts of the U.S. government. Furthermore, its mission to keep the American people out of harm's way is both a unique and vital function of government.

By any measure, the Defense Department is a leviathan of nearly inconceivable proportions. It is routinely recognized as the largest centrally directed and managed activity on the planet. It should not be surprising that running such an enormous, sprawling, global activity will inevitably present its leaders and those overseeing it with daunting challenges. That does not mean any effort to improve defense management is, by definition, futile; rather, it means that even marginal improvements in the management of DoD will have outsized impacts. Thus, anywhere the department can be more efficiently managed, improved, or streamlined, attempts must be made to do so on a continual basis

A Massive Challenge — and Opportunity

As stated in the Bipartisan Budget Act of 2019, the defense budget for Fiscal Year 2020 (FY20) – which includes the expenses for the Department of Energy's nuclear operations and the expenses for Overseas Contingency Operations (OCO) – essentially the wars in Iraq and Afghanistan – is $738 billion. In FY21, it will increase $2 billion to reach $740 billion. To put DoD spending reform efforts in context, savings of even five percent would equal the annual budget of six of the other 15 cabinet-level departments in the executive branch. Savings of only one percent would more than fund the federal legislative branch and would nearly fund the entire federal judicial branch.

The defense budget is 18 times larger than the combined budgets of the Department of State and the Agency for International Development, the other two main actors of American foreign policy. DoD has a workforce roughly 40 times larger than those two agencies and oversees nearly 20 times more locations. Of DoD's major internal elements, the three military departments of Army, Navy, and Air Force are larger than any other agency of government except for the

Department of Veterans Affairs (VA), an agency devoted to those who served in the nation's armed forces. The VA is a derivation of the nation's defense efforts. This widely disparate allocation of budget distribution across the major sections of government is represented in Figure 1.

FIGURE 1: FY20 BUDGET AUTHORITY ($ IN BILLIONS)

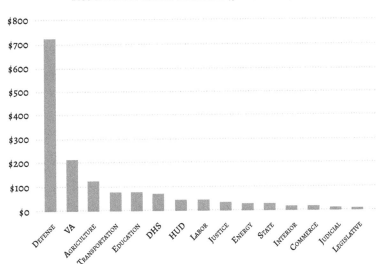

FIGURE 1 ILLUSTRATES THE MAGNITUDE OF DoD'S BUDGET.

The management scope of DoD does not end with its military departments. The department has many other subordinate organizations that it either directs or oversees. On the operational side, it has 11 unified commands run by combatant commanders (COCOMs) who are responsible for vast geographical areas and warfighting domains like space and cyber. These are the entities within DoD that actually conduct combat operations when directed by the National Command Authority. To provide the necessary support to these commanders, DoD supports

28 defense agencies and DoD field activities (DAFAs), providing everything from logistical support through the Defense Logistics Agency to health care via the Defense Health Agency, one of the largest healthcare providers in the nation, serving nearly 10 million beneficiaries. Similarly, DoD operates the four largest organizations within the nation's intelligence community: The Defense Intelligence Agency, the National Security Agency, the National Geospatial Agency, and the National Reconnaissance Office. From its mission to its size, DoD plays a unique role in government.

So, if the Defense Department is not directly comparable with its counterparts, how does it compare to other large organizations that aim for broad but localized presence? Even the world's biggest private company, American retail giant Walmart, is comparatively small. The defense budget is 50% greater than Walmart's annual revenue, and the department employs at least half a million more people, not including government contractors. The only statistic in which they are close is number of facilities – both have roughly 5,000 locations, though DoD's are spread across the globe, with many in hostile locations, taking up hundreds of thousands of acres.

These comments offer just the upper-level view. Considering selected, relevant details about the scope of the empire overseen from the Pentagon may be even more telling:

- It is estimated overall that, in total, DoD has under its wide umbrella nearly 10 million people, including:

- 1.34 million active duty personnel.

- 800,000 members of the Guard and Reserves.

- 751,000 employees in its large civilian workforce.

- 750,000 civilian contractors who support and are paid by the Defense Department but are not considered federal employees.

- 2.3 million retirees (and their survivors) who received approximately $59 billion in pay and benefits from DoD and the Treasury in FY18 – an understandable and expected obligation, but one representing most of DoD's estimated unfunded liability.

- Service family members who also receive housing, education, childcare, and health care.

- DoD employs 34% of all full-time equivalent (FTE) civilian employees of the federal government, by far the largest figure among the executive branch departments.

- DoD operates well over a half-million facilities located on nearly 5,000 sites residing on 25 million acres of land, six hundred of which are located overseas. (By one estimate, DoD has more office space to manage its ongoing operations than the entire office inventory of Manhattan.)

- DoD's enormous capital stock includes over 13,000 aircraft, nearly 300 naval ships, and over 250,000 vehicles for combat operations and ground support.

- The Defense Department is the single largest consumer of energy on the planet. Overall, DoD uses approximately 12 million gallons of fuel per day.

THE "EVER-SHRINKING FIGHTING FORCE"

While the Defense Department has been the largest spender of discretionary funds since it was created after World War II, the ebb and flow of the Cold War and its aftermath have meant that its funding has not always been consistent. In the 1980s, President Ronald Reagan spent much of his two terms in office focused on increasing resources for the Department of Defense to deal with the Soviets and their Warsaw Pact allies. After years of decline because of an unpopular war in Vietnam and disclosures of covert adventurism abroad, the national security apparatus was finally back in the good graces of American political leadership. With the help of allies in Congress like Senator John Tower and Senator Barry Goldwater, and Democratic defense hawks like Senator Henry "Scoop" Jackson and Senator Nunn, President Reagan's calls for reallocation led to increased defense spending and manpower over his eight years in office.

In the 2010s, President Barack Obama also spent much of his eight years increasing DoD resources, though not as unreservedly. The parallels are, nonetheless, strong between the two eras. Reagan was fighting the Cold War against an adversary committed to matching American military capabilities, while Obama was carrying on the Global War on Terrorism, an asymmetric fight against militants who did not need to match America's might in order to do damage. Each conflict in its own right redefined how the U.S. approached its national security, and the presidents leading the nation at the time determined those new definitions. Over their two terms, each saw record levels of defense spending but with dramatically different results. For Reagan, the highest spending years came in the middle of his terms and resulted in more warfighters and capabilities than before. Obama, on the other hand, inherited and initially sustained record defense spending but saw troop numbers decline and readiness levels tumble. During the first two years of his tenure, President Trump added to the budget topline, though it was flatlined in the second half of his term.

In other words, even adjusted for inflation, we are spending more today than at the peak of the Reagan buildup for a substantially smaller military. While we have increased our warfighting capabilities since the 1980s – pouring money into technologies like drones, cyber, and modern aircrafts and ships – that increase is not nearly commensurate with the amount of additional money spent. Despite substantial increases in defense spending over the last decades, the number of warfighters is still declining, a phenomenon that I term the "ever-shrinking fighting force."

The decrease in military manpower since the late Reagan years, and the increased budget authority spent to support it, is visible throughout the department, but nowhere more than in major weapons systems, such as tanks, ships, and aircraft.

During *Operation Desert Storm* in 1991, which occurred five years after the peak of the Reagan military buildup, the Air Force had nearly 10,000 combat aircraft with which to execute the 37-day air campaign preceding the ground war. Today, it has about half that number, despite the fact that in real terms the FY20

Air Force budget was 20% greater than in 1991. Furthermore, almost a quarter of active duty troops aren't warfighters either, instead serving in places like the defense agencies or management headquarters. This is certainly important work, but there are cases where the "tooth-to-tail ratio" – the comparison of warfighters to bureaucrats – needs to significantly improve. This inevitably raises the question, one that has vexed policymakers in both the executive and legislative branches for decades, of why we are paying so much more for so much less.

Fortunately, as illustrated by the 2018 National Defense Strategy, the Pentagon leadership made "reforming the department's business practices for greater performance and affordability" one of its top priorities, along with strengthening alliances and readiness, all with the objective of making our smaller force more lethal. DoD accurately recognizes that the nation needs, especially in the current strategic and fiscal environment, more "trigger-pullers" who increase lethality, and fewer "paper-pushers" who make up back-office management. This applies doubly to areas where a soldier with a gun is not necessarily our best solution, such as cyber warfare, bioterrorism, and conflicts in space. We clearly need to expand our technical capabilities and do so without the bureaucratic growth that accompanied the creation of our current forces. However, we also must understand that even unmanned assets still require manpower to service and operate them, and that smaller, more effective units can still only be in one place at one time.

I have been working on these issues for four decades as a Senate staffer, Marine officer, industry executive, and independent consultant, often switching between multiple hats and using my experience from all sides of the problems to draw attention to them. Over the years, I have been a part of numerous attempts, some of them years in the making, to address the underlying problems of this ever-shrinking fighting force. Very few of the efforts to tame the creeping bureaucracy have successfully altered the tooth-to-tail ratio. I have frequently been asked to provide white papers, presentations, and briefings for each new generation of leaders trying to learn from and improve on the past. So, I decided to consolidate and publish these thoughts and observations from my 40 years in this field into one volume to provide a broadly comprehensive view of the issues, as well as to highlight the enduring problems and scant successes. Most importantly, this book contains my recommendations for improvements going forward.

As some of these materials were written in years past, they have been edited, for form more than content, removing parts of speeches addressed to specific people (e.g., thanking senators for having me testify before their committee or organizations for having me speak at their conventions), streamlining background information that overlaps between memoranda, and bringing statistics from older papers up to date.

Dollar amounts are based on the FY21 president's budget request, the associated national defense budget estimates, or totals in applicable congressional legislation (e.g., bipartisan budget agreements). Most dollars are expressed in terms of current dollars for the year depicted, while some statistics or charts are expressed in terms of FY21 constant dollars that provide a clearer picture of actual purchasing power over time given the impacts of inflation.

We continue to have hard-working and dedicated military and civilian personnel ensuring our nation's security around the clock, but as former Secretary of Defense Bill Perry once told me, "Bad processes trump good people every day," and we have a proliferation of bad processes across government. If I can attribute a theme to my work of many decades, it is the idea of combatting bad processes.

COMMANDER'S INTENT

The first goal of this book is to identify and analyze the significant size, complexity, and cost of the Defense Department's massive overhead and infrastructure. The second goal is to identify options for reducing that overhead and infrastructure both in terms of people and costs so that resources may be redeployed toward executing the compelling 2018 National Defense Strategy.

Let me emphasize that this book is most definitely not a criticism of current or past administrations or Congresses. This is not a report card on individual leaders. These problems have built up over decades, and despite many serious efforts over the years in the Pentagon, the White House, and on Capitol Hill, the firmly entrenched but often antiquated processes of the various bureaucracies have so far proven far more resilient than the large majority of recommended reforms, many championed by some of America's sharpest leaders.

Similarly, this book does not blame either political party. Rather, it addresses a critical need to improve governance and management, whatever party is ruling, for the sake of our country's national security. The growth in the defense back office has been quite similar and continuous through both Republican and Democratic administrations. But the common tendency over the last several decades has been to add rather than subtract. And, as we have added more staff, more layers, and more infrastructure, we have slowed the decision-making process, expanded the number of players, and made the overall system more risk-averse and costly. All of this has continued in an era of strategic and technological change where these conditions indicate we should be moving in the opposite direction – operating more quickly and accepting more programmatic risk.

To borrow a legal analogy, the test for making reductions in both human and physical infrastructure should not be "beyond a reasonable doubt" as it is today, but the lower standard of a "preponderance of the evidence." We need to take some risks in rightsizing, recognizing that some changes may not stand the test of time. But if we wait for certainty, we will have delayed too long and imperiled our war-fighting forces as they wait for us to make decisive changes.

This book is divided into five parts. Part one contains an overview of the problems. Part two addresses policies about people, an important topic for the world's largest bureaucracy. From bloated staffs and some convoluted chains of command to business management and military pensions, there are some things that our great Department of Defense could be doing better. Part three is about money issues and the responsibility of DoD, as the largest handler of discretionary spending, to dutifully dispense taxpayer dollars. This includes its budgets, agencies, and properties, as well as its collaboration with the private sector. Part four looks beyond the Pentagon and back across the Potomac at what the White House and Congress can do to ensure our defense apparatus is operating at full efficiency. Finally, part five contains my recommendations on what the next steps should be for starting and implementing reform.

Finally, I write this as a private citizen; the views expressed herein are mine only. I do not represent the secretary of defense's Reserve Forces Policy Board, which I recently chaired, nor the National Defense Industrial Association, which I currently chair, nor the Defense Business Board, on which I served for many years. I believe, however, that my personal and professional experience is relevant to these matters and has given me a unique perspective on the issues. I served 24 years with the Senate Armed Service Committee, with 14 of those years as the staff director supporting the chairman and the committee, as well as 35 years of commissioned military service in the U.S. Marine Corps, and two decades of defense experience in the private sector, both as a senior executive of a large defense firm and as the head of my own small businesses.

I have chaired multiple task forces and commissions, from the Defense Reform Task Force at the behest of the secretary of defense to the independent Commission on the National Guard and Reserves established by Congress. I am on boards of numerous national security organizations, as well as some of the top public policy schools in the country. For five years as a Marine Major General, I served on the Reserve Forces Policy Board and, after retiring from the Marine Corps, I served as its chairman, as a civilian, under six secretaries of defense. In short, I am no stranger to working with or leading large defense organizations or developing reform recommendations.

It has been and continues to be an honor serving my country in all these capacities, and I hope that my contributions to the defense reform discourse are seen as an extension of that service.

It has been said that "true reform at the Pentagon is glacial in nature. It is only obvious to the most practiced observer." This work seeks to highlight reforms that still require the serious attention of "practiced observers" in leadership across government, to suggest directions they might consider, and with any luck to help everyone else be a more "practiced observer."

Chapter 1: The Ticking Time Bombs of U.S. National Security

This chapter is based on a speech that I originally delivered in April 2011 to the Committee for a Responsible Federal Budget. I identified the major challenges to American national security that were receiving insufficient attention, including the issues of expanding federal deficits, the ever-increasing costs of the Department of Defense's overhead and infrastructure, the all-in life-cycle costs of the all-volunteer force (AVF), the rising costs of the DoD and contractor personnel, and the weaknesses in DoD's acquisition process. I have subsequently updated and used this speech consistently over the years in public, before Congress, and with senior business, industry, and think tank leaders. I have been calling attention to these issues for over a decade, as they have only worsened over time. In 2011, there was little agreement on these problems; however, there is now a strong consensus that all of them must be addressed and solved. This chapter uses updated figures as of August 2020 unless otherwise noted.

Over 50 years ago, as a new second lieutenant finishing the Marine Corps Basic School at Quantico, I rode in a cattle car with my fellow second lieutenants to the Command and Staff College to hear then-Commandant Gen. Leonard Chapman discuss the security challenges we faced as a nation. As newly commissioned officers in 1969, our greatest challenge was that first assignment in combat. That evening, I was certainly more focused on what Vietnam would be like when I got there in two weeks than on the remarks of our now-legendary Commandant.

But with the benefit of a half-century of experience in and outside the Corps, on Capitol Hill, and in the defense industry, I know the national security challenges we face today are much greater than just the pressing issues of the moment, whether that's terrorism, the threats posed by aspiring rival powers, or new domains such as space and cyber – as urgent as they are to the second lieutenants of today. No, our greatest challenge in this dangerous world is getting beat tomorrow because we let our foundations rust away. Unfortunately, that is exactly what we are doing when we try to strengthen the U.S. military to combat daunting external threats in an economy built on the quicksand of deficit spending. I call this and the runaway personnel, acquisition, and overhead costs in the Department of Defense the "ticking time bombs" of our national security posture.

U.S. Fiscal Situation

First, let's talk about ticking time bomb number one: the alarming state of our country's finances, about which organizations like the Committee for a Responsible Federal Budget have been sounding the five-alarm fire bell for almost 40 years.

As my dad used to say, "When your outgo exceeds your income, your upkeep will be your downfall." Sometimes, circumstances necessitate excess spending, such as in response to the coronavirus (COVID-19) pandemic. However, without offsets, the net effect results in increases to both deficits and the total debt. From 2020 to 2025, the projection of outgoing funds exceeding incoming funds is about $11 trillion, adding almost $22 trillion to the total national debt.

A similar example of offset-free excess spending can be found in the aftermath of the 2008 recession. Here, the Obama administration and Congress made a sincere effort to pull the nation's economy out of the ditch, but to do so, they went on a spending spree of gargantuan proportions. This was on top of the early 2000's out-of-control spending and generous tax cuts that preceded the

2008 crisis, compounding the issue. The Budget Control Act (BCA) of 2011 was an effort to find ways to mandate spending controls and avoid the impending fiscal cliff. Despite this effort, annual deficits have continued increasing at alarming rates. Spending more than we have and raising less revenue than we need are among the few bipartisan trends in Washington that continue.

The FY21 budget request projected a deficit of $1.1 trillion, a 41% increase over the $779 billion deficit level in 2018, without taking into account any COVID-19 related stimulus spending. As with most budget request projections, estimates have already changed and worsened, primarily due to COVID-19 related stimulus spending (excluding an additional $1 trillion or more spending expected to be authorized prior to the end of the calendar year). The Center for a Responsible Federal Budget projects a $3.8 trillion deficit for FY20, a number that amounts to 18.7% of our nation's gross domestic product (GDP). Moreover, their projection of total debt could end up equaling or exceeding GDP by the year's end if their projections are realized. These staggering deficit levels are higher than any the fiscal commissions have recommended, and they are significantly worse than projections from just a few years ago.

And, of course, a lot of our debt is owned by China and other foreign countries, a reality that presents its own national security implications. Currently, 30% of the debt is owned outside the U.S., compared to 5% in 1970 and 19% in 1990. Everyone, from former Chair of the Federal Reserve Janet Yellen to former Director of National Intelligence Dan Coats, has underscored the unsustainable nature of American deficits, and most agree we need to get them back under 4% of GDP as soon as possible.

Part of the annual deficit calculation is the amount of spending to pay for the interest due on the national debt. The FY21 budget request projects that the payment due for interest on the debt will be $376 billion for FY20 and is only set to increase each year through 2030. The Federal Reserve can and has taken actions to help reduce total interest payments on the debt by lowering the interest rates, but rate decreases have been outpaced by deficit spending increases. At the rate we are progressing, it is not unrealistic that at some point in the future, the net interest on the debt could exceed the defense budget.

David Walker, the former comptroller general of the Government Accountability Office, sought to champion fiscal responsibility both while in office and now. In 2007 he said, "Continuing on this unsustainable fiscal path will gradually erode, if not suddenly damage, our economy, our standard of living, and ultimately our national security. Let me repeat – ultimately our national security." In his book published in 2020 he states, "The U.S. has lost control of its finances, especially since 2003. The plain and simple truth is that America's future is at risk. The greatest threat to our collective future does not come from beyond our borders, but from within."

Because of this reality, fiscal responsibility and deficit spending has rightfully risen to the top of political dialogue. There is now a keen awareness that this is one of the toughest challenges facing the DoD, as it touches everything, from preserving the right balance of combat structure, readiness, technological edge, to taking care of our troops and their families, and the budget, deficit, and debt realities. Solving this issue is of the utmost immediate importance. We cannot build and sustain a strong defense on an economy dependent on deficit spending. It is long overdue to put our fiscal house on a sounder foundation.

DEFENSE: HIGH COSTS FOR LOW OUTPUT

Now, let's focus on the defense budget topline – what we get for what we spend and the adverse trends in discretionary versus mandatory spending.

Once upon a time in the 1960s, discretionary spending made up two-thirds of the federal budget. In that era, decision makers in the executive and legislative branches would adjust close to 70% of total spending in a given year to address current and emerging priorities.

Today, as Figure 1 illustrates, it is the exact opposite. Discretionary spending now accounts for a little more than a third of total federal spending, and mandatory spending – popularly called entitlements, and this includes interest on the debt – accounts for two-thirds of the total outlay.

The discretionary wedge continues to get proportionally smaller. The projections for spending in the FY21 president's budget request show that the trend continues. Here, FY20 mandatory spending is estimated at $3.35 trillion, while discretionary outlays are estimated at $1.44 trillion (only 30% of total spending). Within the totals for FY20 in the FY21 budget request, defense outlays are projected at $713.6 billion (14.9%), and non-defense agency outlays are projected at $724.7 billion (15.1%).

The projections for FY25 show that non-defense discretionary spending will decrease to be 11.7% of projected outlays (down 3.4% from FY20's projected 15.1%) and defense discretionary spending will decrease to 14.5% of total outlays (down 0.4% from the FY20 projection of 14.9%).

Further, 73.8% of all the outlays in the budget is projected to be mandatory spending in FY25, an increase of 3.8% over the 70% proportion expected in FY20. Figure 1 illustrates the historical trends of mandatory and discretionary spending allocations by the Bureau of Economic Analysis category. Decision makers today practically have no control over the mandatory spending, which is on autopilot and has severely limited the ability to address today's issues.

Note: These projections only represent a baseline and do not include the COVID-19 related spending increases approved after the budget request was released.

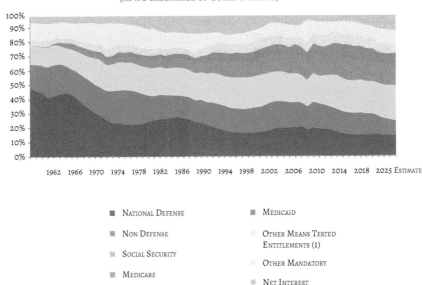

FIGURE 1: DISCRETIONARY AND MANDATORY OUTLAYS BY BEA CATEGORY, 1962-2025
(AS A PERCENTAGE OF TOTAL OUTLAYS)

- NATIONAL DEFENSE
- NON DEFENSE
- SOCIAL SECURITY
- MEDICARE
- MEDICAID
- OTHER MEANS TESTED ENTITLEMENTS (1)
- OTHER MANDATORY
- NET INTEREST

FIGURE 1 ILLUSTRATES THE GROWTH OF MANDATORY SPENDING AND THE DECREASE IN DISCRETIONARY SPENDING OVER TIME.

As outlined in Figure 2, for FY20, the total defense discretionary budget authority measures a total of $713.5 billion. This number includes the DoD base budget request ($633.3 billion) and Overseas Contingency Operations (OCO) funding ($79.2 billion).

In order to control defense spending, Congress instituted budget caps, effective January 2013. The caps required a $1 trillion spending reduction over 10 years, resulting in a $50 billion annual reduction from DoD's future plans over the next decade. Additionally, if the sequester was triggered, DoD would lose an additional $50 billion a year. While a poor public policy and destructive approach to spending restraints, the established budget caps represented a reduction to previously projected budget requirements found in the president's FY12 Future Years Defense Program (FYDP) budget.

While the DoD budget experienced real reductions under the sequester from FY13 through FY16, Congress usually provided additional base budget funding and utilized OCO as a method to allow increases in total defense spending levels from the prior year. While this provided DoD with additional funding, it also diminished the restraint of the budget caps.

FIGURE 2: DoD DISCRETIONARY BUDGET AUTHORITY (FY21 DEFENSE BUDGET ESTIMATES)

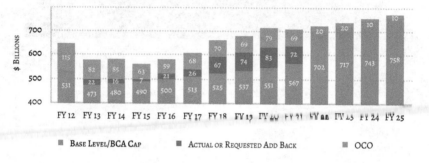

FIGURE 2 DETAILS THE BREAKDOWN OF DoD DISCRETIONARY FUNDING.

By any measure, we have to recognize that the base defense budget is huge, even prior to the large additive amounts in the OCO fund. I am reminded of the *Capitol Steps'* parody of *My Fair Lady's* "The Rain in Spain" during the Reagan administration entitled "Immense Expense is Mainly in Defense." That remains true.

Yet hidden below the "immense expense" toplines is an even more startling trend. The costs per active service member have risen astronomically since the inception of the AVF in 1973 in all areas, from personnel and compensation to the ever-increasing operation and maintenance budgets, to costly acquisitions. Actual combat forces are much smaller than in previous timeframes, even with the current larger budgets – the defining feature of "the ever-shrinking fighting force." So, we need to do more than just focus on total amounts. We need to look at how that money is spent. As defense supporters and as a nation, we have to ask ourselves, "What are we getting for the money we spend?" Figure 3 illustrates the costs of active service members.

FIGURE 3: COST PER ACTIVE SERVICE MEMBER BY TITLE

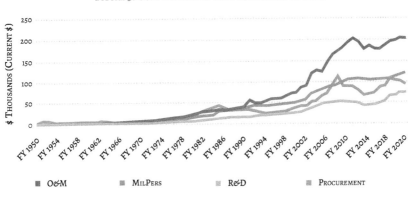

FIGURE 3 BREAKS DOWN THE RISING COSTS ASSOCIATED WITH AN ACTIVE SERVICE MEMBER.

On one hand, our financial input results in the best military in the world by any measure. This is largely thanks to the people in DoD, industry, Congress, and public policy centers who served, continue to serve, and work to improve the system.

However, DoD and Congress have historically aimed much of their focus on the top line – specifically to large accounts like procurement or research and development (R&D). There has been less focus on the output and specifically on examining the results we are getting for the money we spend. Hardly anyone is asking, much less answering the question, "Are our warfighters and taxpayers getting enough bang for the buck for what we are spending?"

In my view, the answer to that question is no. This is ticking time bomb number two – we are not maximizing the value of our dollars being invested; therefore, our advantages and margins are decreasing. Why is that?

There are three primary reasons for this. First, is the excessive amount of money and personnel tied up in DoD's massive and inefficient overhead. Second, is the growing "all-in" or "fully-burdened" costs of the support structure for the AVF, which includes retirement, healthcare, fringe benefits, and deferred compensation. Third, is the substantial costs of DoD's acquisition framework, a place where the expenses increase while the quantities decrease. Congress and the Department have a very poor track record in addressing these expenses.

DoD Overhead

DoD overhead is a prime area of concern. Here, we are spending more and getting more, but this is an adverse trend in that we should not want to increase our overhead costs.

In order to assess overhead, one can examine the number of personnel assigned to activities that are inherently commercial, rather than governmental or war fighting, in nature.

Based on the DoD's latest Inherently Government/Commercial Activity Inventory report in FY15 (this is no longer updated on an annual basis, which I suspect relates to the unimpressive results), the overhead workforce is made up of roughly 775,000 civilian employees and about 320,000 uniformed personnel in commercial roles. This means that the total overhead workforce measures greater than the population of eight U.S. states. Moreover, this number does not consider the impact of contractors, for whom there are wide variations in estimates across DoD.

Another way to assess overhead involves examining the number of military, civilian, and contractor personnel serving in HQ activities. These statistics are provided annually in the Defense Manpower Requirements Report (DMRR) and, in some cases, provide visibility to contractor counts. In the FY20 report, military and civilian personnel, including those in the Office of the Secretary of Defense (OSD), the defense agencies and DoD field activities (DAFAs), the Joint Staff, combatant commands (COCOMs), and service HQs, number over 250,000 people. When adding this number to the estimated contractor workforce, the total number becomes nearly 1 million people. The directly related costs for just the DoD Headquarters, DAFAs, and Joint Staff/COCOM organizations exceed $137 billion. Figure 4 illustrates the breakdown of DoD and service personnel.

Figure 4: FY20 Headcounts for DoD HQ and Service HQ Activities

Organization	Military	Civilian	Contractor	Total
Total DoD Headquarters & Agencies	28,893	163,550	78,428	270,871
Joint Staff & Combatant Command Totals	19,666	16,097	11,131	46,894
Service Headquarters and Field Activities	15,257	21,821	547,655	584,733
Aggregate DoD HQ Count	63,816	201,468	637,214	902,498

FIGURE 4 PROVIDES INSIGHT INTO THE NEARLY 1 MILLION PERSON WORKFORCE AT THE DoD HQ AND SERVICES HQ.

OSD itself serves as a microcosm of these trends. In 1997, when Secretary Cohen requested the Defense Reform task force, on which I served as chairman, to examine these issues in detail, the Director of Administration and Management reported OSD consisted of 2,000 employees. However, our task force discovered an additional 1,000 people, raising the size of the office by around 50%. After learning of these results, Secretary Cohen decided to reduce his organization back to the advertised level of 2,000.

By FY10, howevever, the OSD staff had once again ballooned to 2,708 people. Additionally, when including full-time reservists, detailees, and what OSD estimates to be the number of contractors, the staff count measured over 5,000.

It included 2,636 government civilians and military, about 76 full-time reservists, 381 over staffs or detailees, and over 2,000 contractors.

OSD spends approximately $5.5 billion a year, some toward R&D and systems costs for OSD-run programs. Understanding that this number was unnecessarily high, Secretary Gates attempted to freeze the budget and institute reductions. Unfortunately, cuts were disproportionately smaller and insufficient when compared to reductions in the fighting forces.

At FY19 levels, the "advertised" size of OSD is 4,134 military, civilians, and contractors. DoD acknowledges that "bookkeeping" entries have made the OSD staff look smaller than it really is. For example, the Office of the Inspector General is not included in the total count, nor is the Washington Headquarters Service, the group that operates the Pentagon and National Capital Region facility operations. Because of this, it is understood that the actual size of OSD is much larger than the publicized 4,134 headcount.

FIGURE 5: SIZE OF OSD (EXCLUDES CONTRACTORS)*

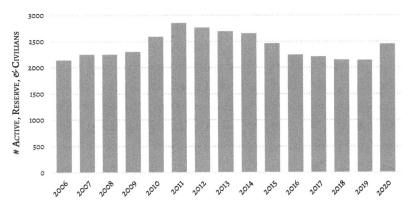

*DATA COMES FROM THE FY20 DMRR AND PRIOR YEAR EDITIONS

FIGURE 5 DEPICTS THE TRENDS IN OSD PERSONNEL GROWTH FROM 2006-2020.

MILITARY DEPARTMENT INFRASTRUCTURE

Despite the importance of personnel and costs within OSD, DAFAs, and COCOMs, the military departments account for the overwhelming majority of DoD's overhead. When examining personnel and costs here, overhead totals measure at least 70%. Hundreds of thousands of personnel work within areas related to installations, central logistics, training, personnel administration, management HQ, and acquisition systems. Because of its massive size, the military departments are clearly a target-rich environment that would significantly benefit from reforms that promote efficiency and effectiveness.

When considering the size and costs associated with all of these different DoD components – OSD, DAFAs, COCOMs, and military departments – it becomes even more clear exactly how much there is to be dealt with. This component serves as ticking time bomb number three – DoD's massive, layered, and inefficient overhead.

CONTRACTOR AND ACTIVE WORKFORCE

There is another alarming personnel-related issue: No one seems to be able to answer the question, "How many contractors work for DoD?"

It is impossible for any leadership team to control costs and effectively manage personnel if there is not a clear understanding of their workforce size. Many groups – both inside and outside government – have attempted to identify the number of DoD contractors, both as a total and by specific categories. Additionally, many have sought to determine the cost of these contractors. However, there seem to be no precise answers, frustrating everyone – the DoD included.

In July 2010, then-Under Secretary for Acquisition, Technology and Logistics (AT&L) Ashton Carter released a document that estimated the number of contractors to be approximately 766,000 at a cost of about $155 billion. This number exceeded the 750,000 civil service workforce in the U.S. (which itself has grown by 100,000 people since 2000) and does not include contractors working for intelligence organizations. Additionally, Carter noted that the 766,000 contractor estimate was not a "high confidence" figure.

Since this 2010 report, the DoD aggressively instituted a DoD-wide audit. Despite this improvement there are still no concrete or updated answers regarding the size and cost of DoD contractors.

This reality constitutes ticking time bomb number four – too many of DoD's most precious and expensive assets – most namely the active duty military – are in the "rear with the gear" versus being at the "tip of the spear."

MILITARY PERSONNEL COSTS ARE RISING

Rising personnel costs for the active duty (roughly 1.3 million) and retired service members (roughly 2.4 million) are consuming an ever-increasing percentage of the DoD budget.

In the last 20 years, the average fully burdened cost for a mid-career individual on active duty has gone from $80,000 per year to $160,000 at the end of the Bush administration, to current estimates of close to $400,000 today. These rapidly rising costs provide some explanation as to why the active duty force size has stayed relatively constant since 2000 – the cost of adding more members is simply too high. Additionally, the $400,000 fully burdened cost can be misleading, as DoD uses a composite rate strictly for budgeting purposes. The Department should accurately report the real all-in personnel costs.

Typically, advocates for military pay and benefits focus on the individual's paycheck and those items funded in the military personnel budget account. However, solely counting the military personnel account ignores the long-term, fully burdened costs of our uniformed members and also excludes total personnel costs to run the Defense Department. Costs for the military are much higher because of the support structure we provide the service members and their families, such as the cost to recruit them and provide skill training, the military health program, a taxpayer-subsidized grocery chain, military dependents' schools, a childcare system, and more.

When all these costs are added, they consume a significant portion of the DoD budget. For FY16, the military-related items totaled over $186 billion, or 35% of the total DoD base budget. If the cost of civilian personnel ($73.7 billion) were added to the military total, then almost half of the total DoD base budget is spent on personnel-related costs. Additionally, costs of contractors are estimated to exceed $130 billion. If these are accurate, this further increases the DoD personnel total to consume over 70% of the DoD base budget. Even more concerning, these data points exclude over $58 billion in retirement payments to military retirees and their survivors paid each year by the Department of Treasury. They also exclude the costs of over $160 billion in discretionary and mandatory payments to veterans by the Department of Veterans Affairs.

DoD once had another calculation they used, called "Taking Care of People," and put these costs in the FY10 budget at $245 billion, or 50% of DoD's base budget. While official records of this calculation are no longer published – likely because of the sticker shock – most indicators point to the percentage having grown to 60%. A few specific functions appear to shoulder an outsized amount of blame.

In the next chapter, I reference the Reserve Forces Policy Board (RFPB) study on the fully burdened and life-cycle costs of military personnel. The study proved that not only were personnel costs underestimated at the time, but also that the real numbers were unsustainable. There has been a real reluctance to debate these trends publicly, so there first needs to be a recognition of just how much these costs are. From there, the nation's leaders in the Pentagon and Congress need to determine if they will put their hands on the helm or just leave it on autopilot. The RFPB recommended to the Secretary of Defense that as a matter of policy, DoD should start calculating, tracking, and using fully burdened and life-cycle costs in their decision processes.

There are unique aspects to being in the military. I spent 35 years in uniform, and I know firsthand the sacrifices the military and their families make. Americans know that we could never match with a paycheck the sacrifices they make in wartime.

Yet, we must recognize that the costs are significant and that most of the management policies and strategies for personnel, pay systems, and compensation are being questioned more and more by those inside and outside the department. There are questions, not only about their affordability but whether or not they will produce the force that is required to meet future threats.

We are talking about the force of tomorrow – it takes 18 years to prepare a battalion commander and slightly less time for a battalion first sergeant – meaning we must think from a long-term perspective. Recruiting and retaining the force of the future will not be successful with WWII personnel policies enshrined in the Personnel Management Acts of the late 1970s.

Further complicating the problem is DoD's antiquated military pay system, which is based on time-in-grade and longevity versus skills and performance. Additionally, the department retains a pre-all-volunteer force (AVF) military retirement system established when life expectancy was 66. This system encourages our military to leave after 20 years – despite the fact that this is when they are the most productive and experienced – and then pays them, their families, and their survivors for another 40 years. During this time, they receive benefits including a monthly salary with annual cost-of-living increases, full health care, and other taxpayer-funded benefits. All in all, we pay them for 60 years to serve for 20 years while not even maximizing on their full potential.

Thomas Gates, the chairman of the commission in 1970 that recommended moving from a draft-based force to the AVF, concluded that the AVF would not be affordable over time unless you eliminated the 20-year retirement cliff, changed pay and compensation from time in grade to skills and performance, and toned down the up-or-out promotion system. Of these recommended changes from 1970, we only just started moving away from the up-or-out personnel system in 2018 and have increased the benefits of the cliff-retirement system. Meanwhile, the other issues remain unaddressed despite their continued importance.

The Government Accountability Office (GAO) has questioned whether the "increasingly costly military compensation system would be affordable, sustainable, and fiscally sound over the long term," concluding that it is "unlikely." Based on all the analyses I have seen, coupled with my personal experience, I agree with the GAO's assessment.

This is ticking time bomb number five – the fully-burdened costs of an AVF with outdated personnel management, compensation, and retirement programs.

HEALTH CARE COSTS ARE RISING

Nowhere are the rapid cost increases more evident than with health care. DoD's FY20 costs to run the Defense Health Program are approximately $45 billion per year when including Medicare-eligible health care fund receipts. Like all health care costs, military health costs were increasing and have only recently started to settle. According to the Congressional Budget Office (CBO), "Between 2000 and 2012, the cost of providing health care to service members, retirees, and their families increased by 130%." The reasons were an increased number of eligible service members, expanded benefits, increased utilization, and medical inflation.

The largest increase in health care costs has been for retired personnel, not active duty, the latter group being much smaller in size. Including dependents, 5.6 million people make up the retiree population, while only 2.6 million (including dependents) constitute the active duty beneficiary population. In 2009, Secretary Gates highlighted the "need to lay out for the Congress how health care is eating the department alive." Yet every time he tried to do something about it, Congress and the military associations blocked him. Fortunately, in 2018, Congress finally ushered in some very important changes that introduced cost controls to cover some of the out-of-control spending.

These measures need to be implemented. According to a 2017 report by the CBO on DoD support funding since 1980, per-service member costs of central medical programs and back-office management have grown by an astounding 318% and 180%, respectively. Most of that growth came in the last 20 years, as Figure 6 shows.

FIGURE 6: FUNDING FOR SELECT SUPPORT FUNCTIONS PER SERVICE MEMBER, 1980 TO 2016 (2016 DOLLARS, THOUSANDS)

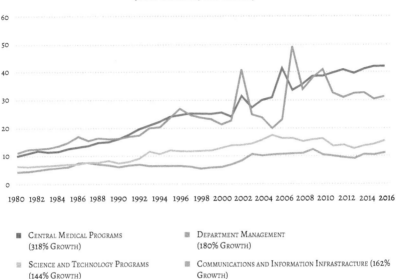

CENTRAL MEDICAL PROGRAMS
(318% GROWTH)

DEPARTMENT MANAGEMENT
(180% GROWTH)

SCIENCE AND TECHNOLOGY PROGRAMS
(144% GROWTH)

COMMUNICATIONS AND INFORMATION INFRASTRACTURE (162% GROWTH)

FIGURE 6 DEPICTS COSTS OVER TIME OF DIFFERENT SERVICE MEMBER SUPPORT FUNCTIONS.

This is ticking time bomb number six – the out-of-control health care costs provided by a highly duplicative medical infrastructure.

MILITARY RETIREMENT COSTS ARE RISING

The costs of military retirements follow the same trend of rising total costs. Because of this, we need to examine whether this system is the best system for the future military recruits, while recognizing that the vast majority of those who serve in uniform do not ever share in these hugely expensive noncontributing benefits. Almost 80% of those who serve in the military never qualify for the 20-year retirement. Moreover, for those that do, 75% of those retire at career year 23 or earlier.

In 1986, Congress recognized military retirement as the largest unfunded liability of the federal government. At that point in time, total retiree expenditures totaled $17.6 billion. During that time, there was concern that the entire system might get the ax, especially within the Gramm-Rudman-Hollings "cut environment" of the era. There was also a recognition that we needed to incentivize our most experienced people to serve longer.

Consequently, Congress reformed military retirement on a delayed schedule, grandfathering everyone for 20 years. The military retirement system was also put on an accrual basis. However, in 2006, when the new system was about to go into effect and save substantial sums of money and, more importantly, keep our most experienced people longer, Congress reverted to the system that originated in the 1950s, based on prodding by the Joint Chiefs and the military lobby.

While there had been no adverse impact on recruitment or retention since 1986, the uniformed military argued that it would be unfair for those who had been under the new system for almost 20 years, and they should be allowed to retire under the more generous system.

Essentially, all attempts at reform were disrupted, and any projected savings were lost. As of the FY19 Statistical Report on the Military Retirement System, expenditures for retired pay total $60.4 billion, up $42.8 billion from when reform measures were initially discussed. Just a few years earlier, Congress had also added TRICARE for Life (TFL) for military retirees and their dependents. This is one of the most expensive health care benefits ever and further compounds the financial problem. Figure 7 illustrates Congress' impact on rising health care in greater detail.

There has been a change to the military retirement system that went into effect for personnel entering the military on or after 1 January 2018 called the Blended Retirement System. This new system is significantly different than the prior military retirement system, which previously allocated a pension measuring a minimum of 50% of base pay to qualified service members at the time of their retirement. In contrast, the new Blended Retirement System more closely mirrors retirement plans found within civilian 401K plans, as the defined benefit plan is combined with the defined contribution plan. The extent to which this change will impact future costs for retirees remains to be seen, but common sense says it will cost more, as it kept the previous 20-year retirement system and added a retirement for those who do not stay for 20 years.

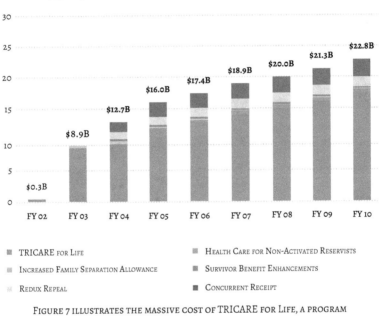

FIGURE 7: CONGRESSIONAL ACTIONS SHAPE THE COMPENSATION BILL

FIGURE 7 ILLUSTRATES THE MASSIVE COST OF TRICARE FOR LIFE, A PROGRAM INTRODUCED BY CONGRESS.

While programs like TRICARE for Life come from well-meaning intentions, these decisions add up and often carry massive future costs that are rarely considered at the time. If you were to examine all of the Congressional records concerning TRICARE for Life, you would be hard-pressed to find any serious debate on the program, and especially on its huge cost.

In 2018, the federal government spent $58 billion on retired service members' pensions and that amount did not include health care costs or other benefits, illustrating the astronomical total costs. That was more than the budgets of every state except New York and California.

Today, we have over 2 million retirees – up 600,000 since the end of the Cold War. Out of this total, who is receiving these noncontributory retirement payments? Not most of those who served in World War II, Korea, Vietnam, the Cold War, nor the current wars in Iraq and Afghanistan. Nearly 80% of those who joined our military during those periods never receive a nickel in retirement because they didn't stay for 20 years. Only about 17% of those who join the military ever achieve 20 years of active service, a reality further illustrated by Figure 8.

FIGURE 8: RETIREE POPULATION RECEIVING PAY BY YEARS OF SERVICE (FY18 POPULATION)

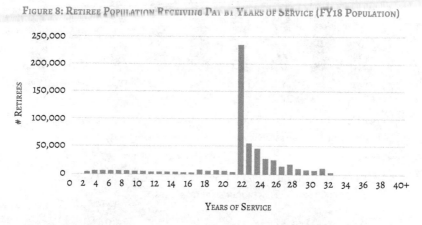

FIGURE 8 ILLUSTRATES THE NUMBER OF YEARS SERVED BY RETIREES RECEIVING PAY.

For the small percentage of service members who remain in the armed services for 20 or more years, they often enter into new careers once reaching their forties – an age when they are very productive and experienced. After reaching their 20 years of service, they're able to draw retirement pay, receive health care for life, and enjoy other benefits like subsidized commissaries for another 40 years, adding up to an unsustainable trend. Correcting this is not about the people who served with distinction and earned this retirement at 20 years of service. Rather, it's about an antiquated system that incentivizes service members to leave when they are the most productive and experienced. (Note – I didn't start earning a reduced reserve retirement until age 60, and I served for 35 years, not 20).

Any changes in these areas of personnel, healthcare, and retirement will be long-term fixes that require discipline and the development of a comprehensive transition plan to address the complex and interrelated issues. We should not postpone the inevitable, especially given the fact these expenses are mortgaging the current and future war fighting force. While we should grandfather all current military members into the current system, implementing these reforms would result in substantial future savings (especially in the accrual of funds) that measure hundreds of billions of dollars.

There were some solid proposals out there to fix this, such as economist Tim Kane's idea of a retirement account, structured such that it will "create an asset that will be *more* highly valued by the veteran retiree than the status quo defined benefit lifetime income stream, meanwhile saving the government $1.3 million per retiree." Combined with other personnel reforms to improve retention and lateral entry for highly skilled workers, his concept could go a long way toward fixing the Pentagon's retirement and talent management problems. Recently, Congress did add a benefit for those who serve less than 20 years.

In a flat or declining budget environment, the alternative to the status quo for these mandatory DoD expenses is a significantly smaller active duty military force, smaller procurement and R&D budgets, less for operations and maintenance, or decreases in all categories. No responsible policymaker should be faced with Hobson's choice. We need to get back to the old slogan of "praise the Lord and pass the ammunition" versus "praise the Lord and pass the benefits."

This is ticking time bomb number seven – a military retirement system that is long past its prime.

DoD Acquisition System is Broken

The DoD does not employ proven business practices and processes when it comes to huge expenditures for goods and services, supplies, and equipment, despite the fact that American industry has proven conclusively that significant savings are possible. In total, the most current federal procurement data reports that DoD spends $320 billion on contracts – 51% on goods, 41% for services, and 8% for R&D – a total sum that measures more than all the other government agencies combined. This cost alone consumes about 8% of the federal budget. Other estimates put the total annual spending in these areas well over $400 billion, including prior year obligations.

Over the last 40 years, there have been close to 100 studies conducted and numerous laws enacted with hopes to "fix" the way DoD purchases goods and services, supplies, and equipment. However, it has proven very resistant to change. The DoD acquisition process is further hampered by negative factors, including gold-plated requirements that are frequently changed; failure to meet schedules, performance, and quantities; significant cost overruns; and consistently poor management. In addition, DoD is suffocating under massive layers of bureaucracy as well as layers upon layers of rules and regulations. Figures 9 and 10 illustrate the disparity between what the acquisition system could be and how the acquisition system actually functions right now.

The Defense Business Board, after a year of analysis for a study that I led, made eight recommendations designed to link and streamline the defense requirements, acquisition, and budget processes. The recommendations in April 2012 were well received and approved by both the senior civilian and military leaders in the building at all levels. Years later, they are still "studying them," and few have been fully implemented.

While the acquisition leaders in both the Obama and Trump administrations, including Ash Carter, Frank Kendall, Ellen Lord, and others, attacked these problems and implemented positive changes, it is not how far we have come but how far we still have to go.

FIGURE 9: DEFENSE ACQUISITION SYSTEM: IN THEORY

FIGURE 9 ILLUSTRATES THE THEORETICAL PROCESS OF THE DEFENSE ACQUISITION SYSTEM, ONE THAT CHAMPIONS EFFICIENCY AND EFFECTIVENESS.

FIGURE 10: DEFENSE ACQUISITION SYSTEM: IN REALITY

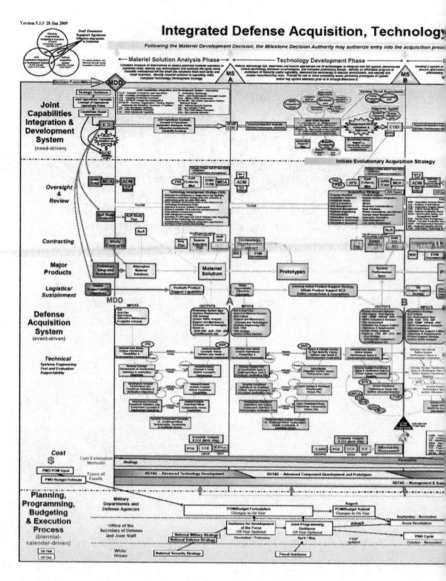

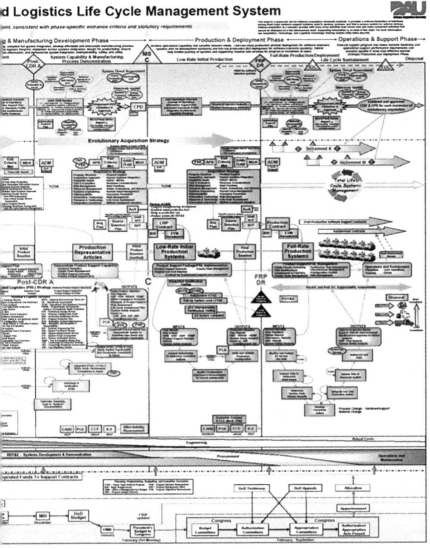

FIGURE 10 ILLUSTRATES THE ACTUAL PROCESS OF THE DEFENSE ACQUISITION SYSTEM, ONE WHOSE HUGELY COMPLEX BUREAUCRACY HAMPERS ANY ATTEMPTS AT EFFICIENCY.

This is ticking time bomb number eight – a broken acquisition system that costs more, takes longer, and produces less, despite the Herculean efforts of the recent leaders cited above to improve it.

TOUGH STRATEGIC DECISIONS

Now, let's examine some of the major policy questions we face. What do we need our military to be ready for in the years and decades to come? Should our military focus more on near-peer competitors? Homeland defense? Missile defense? Counterinsurgency? Stability and reconstruction? How about cybersecurity? Space?

All of the above? None of the above?

According to the latest National Defense Strategy (NDS), our focus for the near future consists of great power competition with other states and an expansion of cyber and space operations. In both Iraq and Afghanistan, we have emphasized helping friendly militaries train their forces to cope with their security problems instead of us doing it for them. During his time in office, President Trump shifted the emphasis from helping them to letting them stand on their own, a sentiment shared by President Biden.

These are not the wars of decisive outcomes that we fought in the past. Secretaries Gates and Mattis advocated for more resources for the State Department because they understood the military is not equipped or intended to handle all aspects of every conflict. Rather, we need to be prioritizing technological innovation, force modernization, and alliance building, as outlined in the current NDS. However, as the senior military and civilian leaders in the Pentagon indicated, the projected flat defense budgets are insufficient to implement the NDS, meaning changes are necessary.

WARFARE/TECHNOLOGICAL CHANGES

The nature of warfighting is also evolving in important ways. Today we have space, cyber, asymmetric, and non-linear warfare; systems-of-systems; and joint and coalition operations. Tomorrow we will see warfare influenced by artificial intelligence, the proliferation of unmanned systems, and how societies, increasingly dependent on technology, are vulnerable in new ways. Each one of these raises questions about how front-line decisions are made as the front line itself becomes harder to define.

Some people say the answer is not in superior technology. Rather, they say we have to invest in smart, adaptable people, believing that people will trump technology. Some say we need the right balance of both. Because of the budget situation, we will be forced to choose. Should it be billions for weapons or billions to retain experienced mid-level officers and NCOs? One thing is certain, we cannot do it all, so we will have to make hard choices and avoid wasting resources on capabilities whose values are diminishing.

Another question we have to answer is whether the current DoD organizations and processes will deliver the decisions we need – or, to put it another way, we need to ask, is each organization up to the tasks?

However, if the department and Congress do not substantially reform the acquisition process, shrink overhead costs, overcome bureaucratic inefficiencies, and get a grip on the rising personnel and benefits costs, then we will be looking at the trade-offs of a much smaller active duty military, little or no modernization, or significantly less investment in research essential to maintaining our technological edge.

These efforts will require the full participation and support of the national security community. In particular, we need support in Congress, which historically has led the way in pushing needed changes in the executive branch. In recent years, however, Congress has been not much more than an interested bystander and has adopted a strategy of alternating between an adding machine or a machete. Congress needs to be a full partner in providing the changes in law and budgets to support the fundamental shifts that must occur.

CONCLUSION

To defuse all these ticking time bombs, the nation will need leaders with profound wisdom, courage, and determination.

Change will require significant sacrifices on all fronts and in all spending categories – mandatory and discretionary, domestic and defense – sacrifices that are essential if we are to return to the promise of a better quality of life and more promising future for our children and grandchildren, as well as to continue to be a beacon of hope to thousands and thousands in a troubled world.

It would be naïve to think these kinds of difficult choices will or should exempt the Department of Defense, the largest repository of discretionary spending that contains some of the more expensive entitlements in government. We clearly need to think smarter – not richer.

CHAPTER 2: DEFENSE OR DISARMAMENT: THE URGENT NEED TO REFORM DoD OVERHEAD

This chapter is based on my testimony before the Senate Armed Services Committee (SASC) in November 2015 during a hearing on obstacles to management reform in both DoD and the national security apparatus at large. Like the previous chapter's origins, this testimony was the culmination of years of analysis and alarm-raising that was synthesized to show the true scope of the problems. It has also been similarly updated and redistributed at the request of additional national security leaders. As recognition of these challenges grew, so did the calls for reform. Congress and the Pentagon have since made a number of these recommended changes, for which they deserve much credit. What matters in reform, however, is not how far we have come, but how far we have to go.

The United States has the strongest military in the world today, but recent advances from Russia and China threaten to diminish that superiority. If their gains are not matched by equal or superior American commitment to address the threats of the future, the U.S. risks losing its military supremacy. In order to avoid this, the DoD needs to be as agile as possible in redefining its mission, especially as technological innovations and new domains (i.e., space) change the nature of warfare. But the Pentagon is currently overburdened with the bureaucratic weight of its support structures. Today, the major problem in defense is the composition of the defense budget, specifically how the internal PAC-MAN of growing costs in personnel, acquisition, and overhead are consuming our warfighting forces.

According to DoD's FY20 Defense Manpower Requirements Report, DoD's overhead represents 43.6% of its total workforce. When this ratio is applied to the total annual DoD budget, overhead costs total over $309 billion. If these numbers represented a country's gross domestic product (GDP), it would rank 56th in the world. DoD's overhead, including the number of people working in the department, totals almost 1.3 million personnel, which is more than the entire population of the state of Rhode Island. Yet somehow, as the defense budget increases, nearly every output measure declines, as seen in Figure 1.

Figure 1: Defense Trends Over Time

Category	End of Carter 1980	End of Reagan 1988	End of Bush 1992	End of Clinton 2000	End of GW Bush 2008	End of Obama 2016	Latest Enacted 2020	Change 1980 to 2020	Change 1988 to 2020
Total Budget Authority ($B -- Constant $)	$463	$619	$542	$470	$487	$537	$657	42%	6.2%
Total Budget Authority ($B -- Current $)	$143	$284	$282	$291	$849	$664	$722	406%	154.2%
Supplementals ($B)	$0	$0	$4	$0	$187	$59	$79		
Active Duty Personnel (K)	2,063	2,209	1,880	1,449	1,474	1,378	1,427	-30.8%	-35.4%
Reserve and Guard Personnel (K)	851	1,158	1,135	865	843	811	801	-5.9%	-30.8%
DoD Civilian Personnel (K)	991	1,090	1,006	698	707	755	807	-18.6%	-26.0%
Active in Commission Ships	521	573	471	341	282	285	293	-43.8%	-48.9%

Army Divisions (Active)	19	20	20	10	10	10	10	-47.4%	-50.0%
AF Fighter / Attack (Total Active Inventory)	2,789	3,027	2,000	1,666	1,521	1,141	1,513	-46%	-50.0%

FIGURE 1 PROVIDES INSIGHT INTO DEFENSE SPENDING LEVELS FROM 1980-2020.

As Figure 1 illustrates, despite the fact we have continued to spend more on defense – even surpassing historically high levels – each dollar supports a significantly smaller active duty military end strength. The $700 billion we spent on defense in 1952—a draft era force—supported 3.6 million troops. In the all-volunteer force (AVF) era at the peak of the Reagan buildup, $600 billion supported 2.2 million active troops. Today, $700 billion supports less than 1.3 million active duty personnel—approximately $100 billion more for one million fewer active forces.

We see this trend for three major reasons. The first is the all-in costs for the AVF and its support structure, as well as the costs of the retired force to DoD that is increasing with wars in Afghanistan and Iraq. The second is the $400 billion we spend annually on goods and services, supplies, and equipment, which can best be described as "spend more, take longer, and get less," and has also increased as the department has continued to buy legacy systems. Finally, the DoD's massive overhead and infrastructure is weighing it down, with defense-wide spending going from just 5% of the budget to almost 20% of the budget. Additionally, the combined Office of the Secretary of Defense (OSD), Joint Chiefs of Staff (JCS), defense agencies and DoD field activities (DAFAs), combatant commands (COCOMs), and other headquarters with over 270,000 people cost $137 billion a year, further illustrating why these problems are only growing. Figure 2 depicts this trend in further detail.

FIGURE 2: DoD BUDGET AUTHORITY OVER TIME

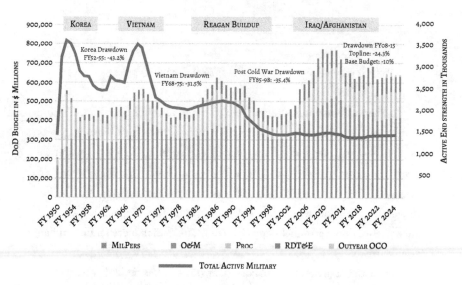

FIGURE 2 BREAKS DOWN THE HISTORY OF DoD'S BUDGETS FROM 1950-2024.

In short, we are not realizing the full potential of our defense capacity for the dollars we spend. If this trend continues uncorrected, we will not have the military capabilities we need to deter and, if necessary, defeat near-peer adversaries in the years ahead.

FULLY BURDENED COSTS

It is of utmost importance that an organization as large as DoD maintains the necessary capabilities to have an accurate balance sheet. Currently, the DAFAs and services document their costs in an incredibly convoluted and inefficient way. For example, they sometimes duplicate reports, while at other times, certain reporting requirements may omit vital information.

Reining in the "outgo," or the costs, will require updating and standardizing these reports to provide a more comprehensive picture of Pentagon spending.

Nowhere is this more applicable than in the case of the fully burdened costs for personnel. Typically, this category includes some factors such as base pay, expenses, and other commonly documented expenditures. However, it needs to include the full range of benefits paid for by the U.S. government if we are to actually calculate the total cost. Figure 3 illustrates the different types of costs that are frequently, sometimes, and rarely included in these calculations.

FIGURE 3: INCONSISTENT USE OF COST
ELEMENTS IN MILITARY PERSONNEL COST
ANALYSES IN DoD

Broadly Recognized Costs

Basic Pay

Basic Allowance for Housing (BAH)

Basic Allowance for Subsistence (BAS)

Incentive Pays

Special Pays

Allowance - Uniform Clothing

Allowance - Station Allowance Overseas

Allowance - CONUS COLA

Subsistence in Kind

Family Subsistence Supplement Allowance

Social Security & Medicare (Employer Contribution)

Permanent Change of Station - All but
Separation Travel

Retired Pay Accrual

Separation Payments

Education Assistance (GI Bill)

Unemployment

Death Gratuities

Survivor Benefits

Other

Medicare - Eligible Retiree Healthcare Fund
(MERHCF)

~ $130 Billion

$605B in costs to the US Government can easily go uncounted!

Occasionally Considered Costs

Allowance - Family Separation

Allowance - Personal Money Allowance, Gen & Flag Offers

Permanent Change of Station - Separation Travel

Other Military Personnel Cost - Adoption

Other Military Personnel Cost - Partial Dislocation

Other Military Personnel Cost - Transport Subsidies

Family Housing Construction & Operation

Military Construction

Health Care

Discount Groceries / Commissary Costs

Child Day Care Facilities

Training

Recruitment Advertising, Etc.

DoDEA and Family Assistance

Child Education (Department of Education Impact Aid)

Operation & Maintenance

Procurement

~ $315 Billion

+

Overlooked Costs

Veteran Employment and Training

Treasury Contribution to Retirement

Treasury Contribution to Concurrent Receipt

Treasury Contribution to MERHCF

Treasury Contribution to Survivor Benefits

Veteran Benefits (Cash and In-Kind)

DoD Research Development Test and Evaluation

Military Construction

~ $290 Billion

=

$605 Billion

FIGURE 3 CATEGORIZES PERSONNEL COSTS BY THEIR LEVEL OF RECOGNITION IN ANALYSES.

In 2013 while I was serving as chairman, the Reserve Forces Policy Board (RFPB) conducted a year-long study as a Federal Advisory Committee. During this time, RFPB deliberated in open sessions, coordinated within the department, and worked with outside experts like the Government Accountability Office (GAO) and Congressional Budget Office (CBO) to ultimately produce a lengthy report containing six recommendations for the secretary of defense. In the study, RFPB found glaring discrepancies in what was reported versus actual total costs. We concluded that once these total costs were taken into account, the reserve component (RC) troops provide a true bargain for taxpayers. In 2019, the RFPB released an update showing increased costs across the board, but especially in the active component (AC). In terms of per capita costs to the U.S. government, AC costs had increased over four times as much as the RCs — roughly $57,000 versus $14,000. While the costs for both RC and AC troops are increasing, the AC costs are increasing faster, and the RCs still maintain their significant cost advantage of being more than 71% cheaper than their AC counterpart. Figures 4 and 5 illustrate the AC and RC cost differences.

FIGURE 4: OMITTING BENEFIT COSTS IGNORES 20% OF DoD COMPENSATION

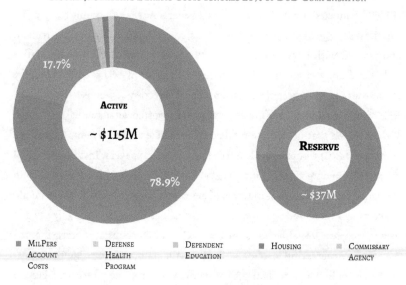

FIGURE 4 ILLUSTRATES THE DISPARITY IN AC AND RC TOTAL COSTS.

FIGURE 5: FY 2018 FULLY BURDENED PER CAPITA COST TO THE U.S. GOVERNMENT

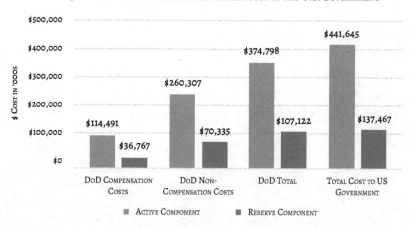

FIGURE 5 FURTHER DETAILS THE OVERALL COST DIFFERENCES BETWEEN AC AND RC.

Without a consistent set of criteria across all services and agencies, DoD is blind to several facts, not least that hundreds of billions of dollars per year were unaccounted for, but also that troops on active duty stationed in the U.S. cost the government roughly three times as much per year as reserves. Having a more accurate picture of costs could affect important policy decisions about how and where to base troops. In short, having data that is as complete as possible and consistently organized can uncover major opportunities for cost savings.

Conversely, ignoring or overlooking this data means continuing on an unsustainable path, as the RFPB's 2019 update confirmed. The report gives examples of DoD elements committing to upgrading their calculations to meet the "fully burdened" standard and then, even after several years, failing to meet that commitment. In particular, the report highlights the need for the director of Cost Assessment and Program Evaluation (CAPE) to take the lead on this, something he pledged to do in early 2013; in the seven years since, CAPE has addressed only four of the six recommendations and only in part. If the next seven years follow the same trend, the department will eventually find itself in a funding crisis of its own making based on a refusal to account for the real estate, facilities, utilities, infrastructure, training, and other costs required to support personnel who are on active duty 365 days per year. In other words, the problem is avoidable, but it requires immediate attention. Fortunately, in 2020 Deputy Secretary Norquist approved the 2019 RFPB recommendations, and CAPE and the Comptroller are directed to use fully-burdened costs when doing personnel analysis. However, only time will tell if the department fully implements this essential approach.

CIVILIAN VS. ACTIVE DUTY: EMPLOYMENT DISPARITIES

Another major cause of the "ever-shrinking fighting force" is active military working in commercial activities. As shown in the RFPB study, these soldiers, sailors, Marines, airmen, and other warfighters are by far the most expensive personnel DoD has, whether from a recruiting, training, and retaining standpoint or from a lifecycle perspective. While a civilian responds to a job posting, service members join through the department's elaborate recruiting methods – which costs money. There are expected to be nearly 375,000 uniformed members joining the military in FY20, and the services anticipate spending $10.4 billion to recruit them and impart the skills they will need. Civilians are hired for skills and, subsequently, do not incur the same training costs nor the delay in the start time, meaning there is neither that delay nor the cost to train them.

When new contractors come on base to begin a job, there are virtually no hiring costs, which enables them to start and finish work in a timely, efficient manner. In contrast, new armed forces recruits have to spend months training to become lethal and effective arms of our national security. While this is necessary, it also costs money. Active duty service members can also retire decades before their civilian counterparts, meaning they receive government pensions for an extra 20 years compared to the civilian who stays to the normal retirement age of 65—this costs, yet again, more money. With military retirement available after 20 years on active duty, 75% of those who earn it leave at career-year 23 or sooner. Average retirement age for active enlisted is 42, for officers is 46. If they live to age 85, that's 40 years with a cost of living adjustment (COLA) pension and free health care for life. Over the course of a lifetime, the government spends up to 75% more on active duty service members than on civilians performing similar roles.

With all that investment, one would expect the active military to be at the tip of the spear—after all, they are the only ones who are specifically trained for combat-related roles. However, if we review the numbers, we find that that is not the case. Of the 1.3 million people serving on active duty, approximately 220,000 are stationed overseas or forward deployed on a daily basis in the Middle East, Afghanistan or other locations. So, what are the other one million doing?

While some active military are just getting back from deployments and some are getting ready to deploy, the latest DoD Federal Activities Inventory Reform (FAIR) Act inventory report from 2016 showed over 320,000 active duty military personnel—our most expensive personnel asset by far—are working in jobs that could be done by civil servants or contractors. There are several hundred unique descriptions for commercial activity positions in the FAIR inventory reports (i.e., budget support, commissary operations, ambulatory care services, contract administration, finance and accounting operations, and stateside supply services). Basic combat training is not a prerequisite for these positions, so why fill them with someone who spent months learning to fight? This is another area the Congress and the department must correct.

Furthermore, freeing up the uniformed personnel makes them available for the inherently governmental and military activities that cannot be performed by non-uniformed personnel. By some estimates, removing even 10% of the 322,975 active duty personnel from this category could free up $5.2 billion per year. Some of this total would pay for the civilians assuming that role, but the rest could be reallocated for combat purposes. This estimate is based on the programming figure for active personnel, which fails to account for health insurance, pensions, and other benefits. If we use the fully burdened annual costs for that same 10%, we would save the Pentagon over $10 billion per year.

Other estimates aren't as generous but still make the same case, such as the CBO's 2015 assessment that converting 80,000 military jobs into civilian positions could eventually save the federal government $3.1 billion to $5.7 billion per year. Regardless of the savings, we need to act soon; like the "ever-shrinking fighting force," this trend does not appear to be significantly improving. There are roughly the same number of active duty military personnel working in commercial activities in this most recent report as in the previous one.

Fixing this is the smart thing to do for defense spending and the right thing to do for national security, but can only be done with accurate numbers. As a first step, DoD must update the 2016 FAIR report to reflect the current situation. We should have our most capable and expensive military at the tip of the spear, not in the rear with the gear.

HUMAN INFRASTRUCTURE AND OVERHEAD

When it comes to defense infrastructure, we simply don't know how big it actually is. Likewise, we don't know what it actually costs. In some areas, we have the data but disagree over the definitions; in other areas, we agree on definitions but don't have the data. Getting to the bottom of this problem merits intense study and the close attention of DoD's senior managers, especially the deputy secretary of defense. We must better understand why it appears we do not have the modernized and required Army Brigade Combat Teams, Air Force Tactical Fighter Squadrons, Navy Battle Force Ships, Marine Infantry Battalions, and cyber and space units, yet we can afford larger management staffs and agencies within the Pentagon than ever before. In fact, DoD established a new defense agency as this book was being written: the Space Development Agency (SDA). While we can debate the merits of individual agencies and field activities, the current overhead growth follows a long history of positions and arrangements swelling ad infinitum, far beyond how they were originally imagined.

Let me elaborate briefly using one example. When Congress passed the National Security Reorganization Act of 1947, it created the framework for the department of today. Among the organizational structures created was the Joint Staff, and legislation capped the staff at 100 officers. The 1949 Amendment, which created the Office of the Chairman of the JCS, more than doubled the Joint Staff manpower to 210. The DoD Reorganization Act of 1958 doubled the Joint Staff again to 400. So, what do we have in Joint Staff numbers today?

As Figure 6 shows, the Joint Staff today, including the separately reported office of the chairman, numbers over 5,000 military, civilians, and contractors. Since 1958, the size of the Joint Staff has increased by a factor of 10. When Secretary Gates disestablished the Joint Forces Command in 2010, the military assigned there—over 2,000—were reassigned to the Joint Staff. This is a staple of the Pentagon playbook in all administrations when directed by Congress to reduce overhead; when one agency goes down, another one is created to absorb the shock.

Figure 6: Headcounts for the Joint Staff and Combatant Commands

Organization	Military	Civilian	Contractor	Total
The Joint Staff (JS)	1,368	1,384	1,703	4,455
Chairman of the Joint Chiefs of Staff (CJCS)	354	772	0	1,126
North American Aerospace Defense Command (NORAD)	275	104	0	379
North Atlantic Treaty Organization (NATO)	2,381	69	0	2,450
US Africa Command (USAFRICOM)	696	457	596	1,749
US Central Command (USCENTCOM)	1,041	425	408	1,874
US Cyber Command (USCYBERCOM)	441	474	129	1,014
US European Command (USEUCOM)	1,503	443	304	2,250
US Northern Command (USNORTHCOM)	739	855	223	1,817
US Pacific Command (USPACOM)	2,242	589	328	3,159
US Southern Command (USSOUTHCOM)	802	612	427	1,841
US Special Operations Command (USSOCOM)	4,193	6,651	6,014	16,858
US Space Command (USSPACECOM)	349	268	184	801
US Strategic Command (USSTRATCOM)	1,220	1,749	696	3,665
US Transportation Command (USTRANSCOM)	1,784	1,135	0	2,919
US Forces Korea (USFK)	308	110	119	537
Joint Staff & Combatant Command Totals	19,666	16,097	11,131	46,894

Sources: Table 2-4 and 2-6 from FY20 DMRR, OP-5's from DW, OMA, OMN, and OMAF

FIGURE 6 ILLUSTRATES GROWTH OVER TIME IN THE JS AND COMBATANT COMMANDS.

Similar to the kudzu-like growth in the tail of DoD—overhead, agencies, HQ, and layers of management—the COCOMs and their service components have also increased staffs and bureaucracy. Historically, the chain of command was convoluted and overly-bureaucratic. During the terrorist bombing of the Marine barracks in Beirut, Lebanon, in October 1983, this inefficient system contributed to the 241 service personnel deaths. While U.S. European Command (EUCOM) Commander Bernard Rogers, an Army general, was the de facto leader of those troops and later took personal responsibility for their deaths, it was generally recognized that the Marines and the Navy in the region received their marching orders from numerous rear-echelon offices in the Pentagon, bypassing EUCOM.

The Long Commission, which reviewed the incident, recommended a streamlining that became one of the key tenets of the 1986 Goldwater-Nichols reforms: strengthening the warfighting commands and allowing them to establish modernized subordinate structures. Unfortunately, bureaucratic creep has occurred in what should be lean and mean, tip-of-the-spear organizations.

When we look at the staffing of the COCOMs, the total number of those assigned to joint billets is over 40,000—yet another increase by a factor of 10. The COCOMs have expanded from lean warfighting headquarters to sprawling mini-Pentagons with thousands of staff members. We have added two more COCOMs in recent years: Cyber Command and Space Command. Like the DAFAs, we can debate the individual merits of each COCOM, but we rarely, if ever, trim them, despite the fact that some have been in existence for 70 years. They no longer fight wars themselves but instead create new joint task forces to accomplish that mission.

Many of the regional COCOMs have evolved into political-military ambassadors who focus heavily on peacetime engagement. Given the inability of other parts of our government to fulfill their proper role, this is a very important mission, but if we rely too heavily on it, we undermine the ability of those other agencies to do their work. Yet Goldwater-Nichols specifically resisted the notion of adding requirements to the combatant commanders, such as budgeting and acquisition, so they would not lose focus on their primary duty—waging war. The proper role and size of the COCOMs, their service component commanders, and the standing ad hoc joint task forces should be the subject of careful review.

Shifting over to the civilian employees in the Pentagon, we see a similar issue of ever-increasing staff and management layers. Let me draw particular attention to the more than 4,000 people employed in the Office of the Secretary of Defense (OSD), as seen in Figure 7. We can all agree that serving as the secretary of defense in the current world is an incredibly difficult and demanding undertaking, but we must ask ourselves if the SecDef truly needs a staff of over 4,000 people.

In the early 1960s, when DoD had 2.8 million active duty personnel and 1.6 million reservists, there was one deputy, no under secretaries, and only three assistant secretaries. Today, with about half as many total military personnel, there is still one deputy, but six unders, and 13 assistants with a proliferation of deputy unders, deputy assistants, principal deputies, and so on. And GAO says they do not have confidence in the size of OSD as carried on DoD's books.

What we need is a firm baseline that DoD cannot constantly amend. This baseline needs to be the "all-in" count, including active, Guard, and reserve military, as well as defense civilians, contractors, and personnel from Federally Funded Research and Development Centers (FFRDCs). Unfortunately, the all-in count does not exist today, further obscuring the actual size of departments. For example, there are some estimates that OSD could be higher than 8,000 personnel. Figure 7 differentiates between OSD, the Office of the Inspector General (OIG), the Pentagon Force Protection Agency (PFPA), and Washington Headquarters Service (WHS)—all which could arguably be defined as part of OSD. Altogether, this would put the count over 11,500.

Figure 7: FY20 Headcounts for Defense Agencies & DoD Field Activities

Organization	Military	Civilian	Cont.	Total	Budget
Office of the Secretary of Defense (OSD)	558	1,893	1,972	4,423	6,987,357
Office of the Inspector General (OIG)	31	1,721	114	1,866	363,499
The Joint Staff (JS)	1,866	1,384	1,703	4,953	1,279,731
Civil Military Programs (CMP)	0	0	0	0	165,707
Defense Advanced Research Project Agency (DARPA)	15	179	2,796	2,990	3,427,049
Defense Commissary Agency (DeCA)	0	4,432	296	4,728	634,971
Defense Contract Management Agency (DCMA)	705	11,250	175	12,130	1,478,320
Defense Legal Services Agency (DLSA)	206	459	185	850	34,632
Defense Logistics Agency (DLA)	1,051	26,530	10,864	38,445	38,419,523
Defense Security Cooperation Agency (DSCA)	106	423	80	609	713,941
Defense Security Service (DSS)	0	1,806	200	2,006	912,103
Defense Threat Reduction Agency (DTRA)	889	1,354	621	2,864	1,334,871
Pentagon Force Protection Agency (PFPA)	14	1,272	709	1,995	598,200
Missile Defense Agency (MDA)	120	2,183	1,031	3,334	9,385,907
Defense Human Resources Activity (DHRA)	95	1,268	2,118	3,481	944,911
Defense Media Activity (DMA)	880	580	246	1,706	213,753
Defense POW/MIA Accounting Agency (DPAA)	274	332	75	681	495,475
Defense Technical Information Center (DTIC)	0	212	330	542	63,743
Defense Technology Security Administration (DTSA)	29	127	20	176	35,626

Defense Test Resources Management Center (DTRMC)	3	28	0	31	0
DoD Education Activity (DoDEA)	0	12,501	12	12,513	2,933,546
Office of Economic Adjustment (OEA)	3	37	11	51	59,513
Defense Health Agency (DHA)/DHP	717	9,190	16,729	26,636	32,994,685
Washington Headquarters Service (WHS)	153	1,336	669	2,158	325,508
Space Development Agency (SDA)	20	30	40	90	149,750
Defense Acquisition University (DAU)	43	705	95	843	180,250
Uniformed Services University of Health Science (USUHS)	982	659	178	1,819	0
US Court of Appeals for the Armed Services	0	59	0	59	0
Defense Information Services Agency (DISA)	1,803	4,144	12,124	18,071	11,423,791
Other Communications and Classified Activities (not DISA)	14,109	46,672	15,637	76,418	4,310,307
Special Operations Command (USSOCOM)	4,193	6,651	6,014	16,858	9,441,603
Cooperative Threat Reduction (CTR)	0	0	567	567	338,700
Chemical, Biological, Radiological, Nuclear, and Explosives (CBRNE)	0	0	0	0	1,363,843
Total DoD Headquarters & Agencies	**28,893**	**163,550**	**78,428**	**270,871**	**137,028,115**

Sources: 1) DMRR/OP-5/PB-22/PROC/R&D, 2) DMRR/OP-5, 3) DMRR/OP-5/PROC/R&D, 4) OP-5, 5) DMRR, DW R&D/FY17 ICS, 6) DMRR/DWCF DeCa/FY17 ICS, 7) DMRR/OP-5/PROC/R&D, 8) DMRR/OP-5/PROC/R&D, 9) DMRR/DWCF DW/FY17 ICS, 10) DMRR/OP-5/FY15 ICS, 11) DMRR/OP-5/DWWCF&PROC/FY17 ICS, 12) DMRR/OP-5, 13) DMRR/OP-5+OHDCA, 14) DMRR/OP-5, 15) DMRR/DW Funds/FY15 ICS, 16) DMRR/OP-5/MDA R&D/PROC, 17) OP-5, 18) OP-5, 19) OP-5, 20) DMRR/DTIC R&D/FY15 ICS, 21) DMRR/OP-5, 22) DMRR, 23) DMRR/OP-5/FY17 ICS, 24) DMRR/OP-5, 25) DMRR/DHP PB-11A/FY17 ICS, 26) DMRR/OP-5, 27) DMRR/OP-5, 28) DMRR/OP-5, 29) DMRR/FY15 ICS, 30) DMRR, 31) DMRR/OP-5/DWCF DW PROC/R&D/FY17 ICS, 32) DMRR/O&M Summary/Prior estimates, 33) DMRR/OP-5, 34) OP-5, 35) CBDP R&D/PROC, 36) FY20 PB Request/DMRR/FY17 ICS

Note: Personnel counts use end strength or FTE from either the DMRR or OP-5 whichever is higher. Military includes reserve personnel where reported, civilian personnel count includes direct and indirect hires plus foreign nationals when reported, contractor personnel count is derived from contract data reported in the FY15 or FY17 inventory of contacted services or OP-5 exhibits, whichever is higher. Budget totals are sum of O&M, Procurement, R&D, WCF and include OCO if reported, DHA total includes all of DHP costs but only DoD HQ headcount.

FIGURE 7 PROVIDES INSIGHT INTO THE NUMBER OF PERSONNEL WORKING AT DAFAS.

Business as Usual is Not Good Enough

In his 1984 autobiography, Lee Iacocca, the legendary CEO of Chrysler Corporation who successfully turned that company around from the brink of extinction in the late 1970s, noted that he had a very small headquarters staff at Chrysler—much smaller than he had as a senior executive at Ford. But Iacocca argued that with a smaller staff, the headquarters was forced to focus on the big issues; they did not have time to micromanage, and his staff could not present him with a decision to be made with any greater than 80% certainty. Iacocca felt that it was his job to provide, with his experience and intuition, the remaining 20%. At Ford, he stated that senior management used its much larger staff to provide 95% certainty. Iacocca argued that achieving such certainty meant sacrificing speed and increasing the cost of overhead, and with a company that was initially in serious financial distress, he could not afford the cost burden of additional overhead.

That experience is worth some serious consideration. One could strongly argue that the current management structure in the Pentagon is too large, too complex, too layered, and too heavily invested in overseeing processes that are, in general, too slow. In terms of just the number of personnel in OSD, the JCS, the COCOMs, and the DAFAs, there are over a quarter-million—270,000 people—and this does not include some of the very large contractor counts. The costs for these people are $137 billion. These organizations have shown consistent growth since 2000. Secretary Gates, in his overhead reduction efforts, subsequently supported by Secretary Panetta, identified these areas for reductions. Congress even passed laws in line with Gates's vision, but the bureaucracies have time and again dodged attempts by the most powerful and focused heads of DoD at reining them in. Figure 8 provides a snapshot of the size of each infrastructure category.

FIGURE 8: INFRASTRUCTURE CATEGORY DISTRIBUTION FOR FY20

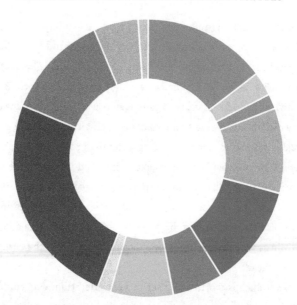

- FORCE INSTALLATIONS, **15%**
  PEOPLE: **155.9 THOUSAND**

- COMMUNICATIONS & INFORMATION, **3%**
  PEOPLE: **29.8 THOUSAND**

- SCIENCE & TECHNOLOGY PROGRAM, **2%**
  PEOPLE: **18.9 THOUSAND**

- ACQUISITION, **10%**
  PEOPLE: **105.7 THOUSAND**

- CENTRAL LOGISTICS, **12%**
  PEOPLE: **127.2 THOUSAND**

- DEFENSE HEALTH PROGRAM, **6%**
  PEOPLE: **64.2 THOUSAND**

- CENTRAL PERSONNEL ADMINISTRATION, **7%**
  PEOPLE: **80 THOUSAND**

- CENTRAL PERSONNEL BENEFITS PROGRAMS, **2%**
  PEOPLE: **17.6 THOUSAND**

- CENTRAL TRAINING, **25%**
  PEOPLE: **267.9 THOUSAND**

- DEPARTMENTAL MANAGEMENT, **12%**
  PEOPLE: **132.6 THOUSAND**

- OTHER INFRASTRUCTURE, **5%**
  PEOPLE: **57 THOUSAND**

- CADETS/MIDSHIPMEN, **1%**
  PEOPLE: **12.8 THOUSAND**

FIGURE 8 ILLUSTRATES THE PERSONNEL SIZE AND TOTAL PERCENTAGE OF INFRASTRUCTURE CATEGORIES.

It is often pointed out when one suggests that DoD needs to significantly improve its management chain of command that the Pentagon is not a business. This is correct; the department is not a profit-generating enterprise. But there are world-class business practices that are definitely applicable to government, as outlined in Figure 9.

Figure 9: World-Class Business Practices		
World-Class Business Practices	**OSD Today**	**OSD Application**
Balance between leadership and management	Traditional leader role focused on management	Increase attention to leadership
Unifying vision for the future	Unarticulated, competing visions	Develop and communicate a unifying vision
Focused on core functions	Diffused work effort	Define and focus on core functions; Divest other activities
Flat, flexible structures	Layered, rigid structure	De-layer, Consolidate
Widely shared information and knowledge	Little information/ knowledge-sharing	Powerful CIO focused on promoting information and knowledge-sharing
Sustained high-level attention to human resource management	Haphazard human resource management	Leader-driven fundamental reforms
Process-centered in cross-functional teams	Some use of integrated process teams	Establish cross-functional teams for key processes
Performance goals used to achieve results	Few performance goals	Establish a performance management system
Tight control over overhead personnel	Few, ineffective controls	Establish an effective control system

FIGURE 9 SUGGESTS BETTER BUSINESS PRACTICES OSD COULD MORE FULLY ADOPT TO IMPROVE EFFICIENCY.

Figure 9 lists certain world-class business practices that are applicable to DoD, how OSD stacks up against those practices, and how they could be applied to OSD. This list is consistent with multiple studies that have been done in this area over the decades. Many of the points above I touched on in my own testimony before the Senate Armed Services Committee (SASC) in 2015, such as the need to focus on core functions, reduce layers, tightly control overhead personnel, and use performance goals to incentivize change, are underscored here. Getting the right people in place to make these adjustments will be an essential first step to making them stick. In some of the larger defense agencies, replacing active duty military leaders with civilian private sector leaders tethered to performance goals and incentives would be a great way to begin to change the business culture for the better.

Not all of these changes will stick, and there are definitely some ways that DoD should not run like a business—it is a government department after all—but despite being a unique organization, it must learn from the private sector. Defense infrastructure costs are higher than the GDP of all but 50-odd countries, but there are private firms that also have large scale enterprises, such as Walmart; diverse international operations, such as Exxon; and extensive supply chains supporting highly distributed product lines, such as Trader Joe's. The DoD needs to learn from these organizations, which have to compete in the global economy, keep costs low, and deliver products on time and on cost. Several years ago, a senior Army general asked his head logistician what the order-to-ship time for a repair part was. The logistics officer proudly announced it had been reduced to 15 days, to which his superior replied, "General Motors' time is 15 hours. Why can't we do that?" Although the incentive structures between the public and private sectors are much different, performance objectives in similar functions should produce positive results.

A LONG WAY TO THE TOP

We have also known for years that the military structure of DoD institutionalizes layers of management. With so many senior personnel, more layers follow. For example, the top person in a layer, the "head dawg," will have a "deputy dawg" and the "deputy dawg" will have a "deputy, deputy dawg" and so on. DoD needs to cut out some of these management layers—by some accounts, there are 28 layers from the action officer in the military department to the secretary of defense. This drives huge staffs and support personnel that continue to increase. This has proliferated across the board, with excess layers popping up between OSD, the Joint Staff, service secretariats, military staffs, the COCOMs and their staffs, and the various standing groups and committees, such as the Joint Requirements Oversight Council (JROC) and the commander's action groups (CAG). Figure 10 — developed in 1997 when I chaired Secretary Cohen's reform task force—is but one example of a defense-wide issue. Twenty-plus years later, despite numerous efforts to curtail this, the strata are all still there.

FIGURE 10: DoD LAYERS ON A LONG TRIP TO THE TOP

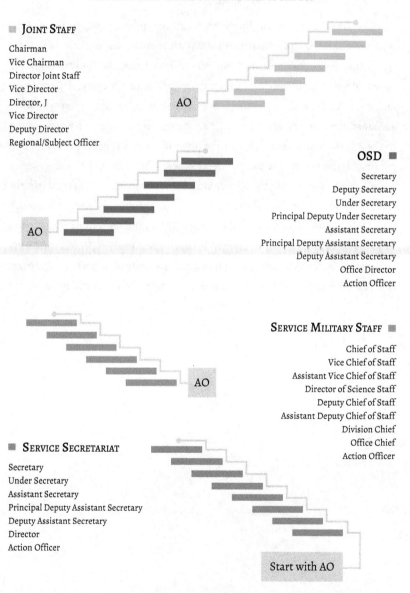

JOINT STAFF

Chairman
Vice Chairman
Director Joint Staff
Vice Director
Director, J
Vice Director
Deputy Director
Regional/Subject Officer

AO

AO

OSD

Secretary
Deputy Secretary
Under Secretary
Principal Deputy Under Secretary
Assistant Secretary
Principal Deputy Assistant Secretary
Deputy Assistant Secretary
Office Director
Action Officer

SERVICE MILITARY STAFF

Chief of Staff
Vice Chief of Staff
Assistant Vice Chief of Staff
Director of Science Staff
Deputy Chief of Staff
Assistant Deputy Chief of Staff
Division Chief
Office Chief
Action Officer

AO

SERVICE SECRETARIAT

Secretary
Under Secretary
Assistant Secretary
Principal Deputy Assistant Secretary
Deputy Assistant Secretary
Director
Action Officer

Start with AO

FIGURE 10 DEPICTS THE SEVERAL LAYERS OF BUREAUCRACY FOUND WITHIN OSD ALONE.

There are far too many management tiers populated by well-meaning officials and officers who feel they have a major role in any issue, large or small. In general, with such rich staffing, there is a natural tendency toward micromanagement where macromanagement is required. The trend in the private sector, conversely, including the major players in the defense industry, is to move toward small corporate staffs that provide the oversight and guidance that can only come from the top, with a transfer of basic management authority to line units.

On the battlefield, the services have learned that modern conflict requires the authority and responsibility to be pushed down to lower levels. They call it "powering down." This practice needs to be implemented more widely in the Pentagon. At a minimum, we ought to put a statutory limit on the number of deputy, under, and assistant secretaries in OSD and in the services; collapsing the service staff would remove some duplication. Any increases must be offset by decreases.

Furthermore, there are numerous places in the Pentagon where we have significant duplications of effort, most obviously between OSD and the Joint Staff. For example, there is overlap between OSD Policy and J-5 on the Joint Staff, as well as other areas, including personnel, communications, budgets, and requirements. In addition, there is the common view that the formal requirements process takes too long. Creating the JROC was an aspiration of the Goldwater-Nichols Act, but, in my view, it is one of those areas where we did not get it quite right, despite serious efforts by recent vice chairpersons to improve it.

DEFENSE COMMISSION DÉJÀ VU

I have personally been involved in some of the efforts to manage these redundancies and other problems. After I left the SASC in 1997, I was asked by Secretary of Defense Bill Cohen to chair the Defense Reform Task Force, a dream team chosen from some of the defense and congressional staffs' most experienced analytical talent. Secretary Cohen wanted to bring world class business practices to the management side of the Pentagon.

After eight months of review, we reported to him that DoD needed to focus on core functions, reduce multiple layers of management, eliminate the duplication between OSD and the JCS, control the headcounts in the headquarters, and streamline the DAFAs, among other recommendations. Secretary Cohen was delighted with our results, saying that this was exactly what he was looking for. But I pointed out to him these were actually the conclusions of a commission set up by President Eisenhower in 1956.

Our Task Force came to the same conclusions they had some 40 years earlier and presented Secretary Cohen with five major studies and recommendations to reduce the size and duplication in OSD and the JCS, reducing the number of senior personnel and multiple layers of management, streamlining the defense agencies and installing performance-based management, and divesting or eliminating noncore activities. More than 20 years after the work we did for Secretary Cohen, and more than 60 years after the work Henry Kissinger did for President Eisenhower, the management chain of command in DoD still requires significant improvements, since the tooth is getting smaller while the tail is getting larger and more expensive.

WE GET WHAT WE PAY FOR

Part of the tail is the amount of money spent on contractors to support DoD's activities. Many people will guess correctly that the largest organization getting money from the DoD is Lockheed Martin, Boeing, or one of the other large prime contractors. Three points are important to understand when contracted dollars are concerned. First, commercial businesses receiving contracts are subject to market forces, and as such, must continuously evaluate their cost structures to remain competitive. Second, a large portion of contracts fund the research and development and purchase of equipment and supplies that directly support the warfighting mission and not overhead activities. And third, DoD's own agencies are substantively large enough to equate to the major prime contractor organizations.

In fact, eight of the top 20 organizations in terms of DoD dollars are DoD's own agencies. For example, look at the Defense Logistics Agency (DLA). DLA does over $38 billion a year in business with DoD, second only to Lockheed Martin's $47.1 billion. In the top 10 largest businesses, four out of 10 are the department's own agencies, not including the large intelligence agencies. Eight top defense organizations on the list spend $111 billion. Most of the defense agencies would rate at least in the Fortune 250, and several would be in the Fortune 50. Yet they are not managed as businesses—even though they are essentially a grocery chain, a worldwide communications provider, a global supply chain, and one of the world's largest and most expensive health care providers. Figure 11 better depicts the size and scope of DoD's defense agencies.

Figure 11: Defense Agencies are Big Business

Rank	Defense Agency/Defense Contractor	Agency Budget/ Contract Awards ($B)
1	Lockheed Martin Corp	$47.1
2	Defense Logistics Agency (DLA)	$38.4
3	Defense Health Program (DHP)	$33.0
4	Boeing Co	$26.3
5	General Dynamics Corp	$16.5
6	Raytheon	$15.6
7	Northrup Grumman	$14.2
8	Defense Information Systems Agency (DISA)	$11.4
9	Missile Defense Agency (MDA)	$9.4
10	United Technologies Corporation	$9.3
11	Office of the Secretary of Defense	$7.0
12	Humana Inc	$6.7
13	Huntington Ingalls Industries, Inc	$6.6
14	BAE Systems PLC	$6.2
15	L3Harris Technologies, Inc	$6.1

1 6	Defense Commissary Agency (DeCA)	$4.6
1 7	Other Communications/Classified Activities (not DISA)	$4.3
1 8	Defense Advanced Research Project Agency (DARPA)	$3.4
1 9	General Atomic Technologies Corps	$3.3
2 0	Analytic Services Inc	$3.3

Source: FY20 Presidents Budget Request, FPDS-NG report of FY19 Top 100 Contractors (DoD obligations).

Note: Contractor totals may not include impact of recent merger, acquisition, and divestiture activity.

FIGURE 11 ILLUSTRATES THE MASSIVE BUDGETS AND CONTRACT AWARDS ASSOCIATED WITH DoD'S LARGEST DEFENSE AGENCIES.

If one looks at the staffing of the various defense agencies that have been established over time, the trend is similar to OSD and Joint Staff. Today, the various defense headquarters and agencies have a headcount of over 270,000 active duty military, defense civilians, and contractors. To put this in perspective, the manpower of these support activities is appreciably more than the active duty size of the entire United States Marine Corps.

The number one reason these defense agencies should be managed more as businesses is that their total expenditures are in excess of 18% of the entire defense budget. Worse yet, they are largely supervised by OSD civilian political appointees whose day-to-day jobs do not provide them with ample time for management and leadership. These entities lack strong, disciplined business leadership and performance management systems, and several perform functions that are nonessential to the DoD missions. In 2020, Secretary Esper pushed for major savings and reforms in the DAFAs. He was determined that his efforts would not end up in the dustbin of history, as did similar efforts of several of his predecessors. As of early 2021, it is still too early to determine the results.

The DAFAs have grown in number, scope, and costs. They are not just defense agencies; these are very large business enterprises and should be managed accordingly.

MILITARY ENTITLEMENTS

Discretionary spending is just the tip of the iceberg. The rising all-inclusive costs of personnel over the last 30 years have gone up 270%, and in just the last 10 years, they have risen almost 100% for a slightly smaller force.

The Military Compensation and Retirement Modernization Commission, in its oft-overlooked 2014 interim report on what programs actually cost, included a chart that showed that the total cost for pay, benefits, health care, and retirement was over $400 billion a year. Additionally, this chart also highlighted the presence of a $1 trillion unfunded liability over the next 10 years in the military retirement fund, which is not included in any budget. The commission challenged the notion that military compensation represents 30% of the budget and is, therefore, not a concern. The commission said:

> The fact that military compensation costs [as carried in the military personnel appropriations accounts] consistently represent roughly one-third of the DoD budget does not provide evidence of fiscal sustainability… The commission considers the growth rate in GDP to be the maximum rate at which compensation funding, holding force size constant, can grow while representing the same share of national income.

When they looked at this comparison from 1998 to 2014, growth in military pay, quality of life, retired pay, VA and DoD health care far exceeded both the GDP and the Employment Cost Index. This is why four former secretaries of defense—Gates, Panetta, Hagel, and Carter—have said publicly that this cost growth is unsustainable. DoD leadership in the Trump administration also expressed similar concerns.

ACQUISITION

Our approach to acquisition requires major improvements. A byproduct of the Pentagon's culture of risk aversion and the prohibitively complicated way DoD acquires new technology and services from the private sector makes it needlessly difficult for companies to do business with the government. And even when projects have been started or prototypes delivered, there are so many steps to get new equipment from the lab to the field that it is likely to be outdated by the time it arrives. Since technology advances exponentially, this will only get worse going forward.

On top of that, cost overruns on large projects are rampant and reports abound that products aren't being delivered on schedule. Delayed and on-time projects alike are often exorbitantly expensive, especially the updates to major weapons systems: Current light and medium tactical vehicles cost roughly twice as much as what they are replacing, and each new *Ford*-class aircraft carrier is three times more expensive than its predecessor, the *Nimitz*-class. Furthermore, the department often starts copious major weapons projects they ultimately cancel, such as the Comanche helicopter, Crusader artillery, and the Expeditionary fighting vehicle. The disaster initiatives and enterprises, like the Future Combat Systems and DIMHRS, which, after 12 years and over $3 billion trying to put the military under a single payroll and personnel records system, came to nothing, and no one was held accountable.

Fixing this requires increased accountability, which, in turn, will lead to increased cost controls. Congress has been aware of the problem for some time and began taking steps to amend the process with the FY17 and FY18 National Defense Authorization Acts (NDAAs), the former pushing more acquisition authority to the service chiefs and the latter splitting the duties of Under Secretary of Defense for Acquisition, Technology, and Logistics into two distinct entities. One of these positions focuses on pursuing cutting-edge technologies needed to fulfill the national strategy, while the other specializes in improving DoD purchasing outcomes.

Locations and Logistics

Another source of wasteful spending is on unused or underused facilities. DoD maintains one of the largest property books in the world, worth over $880 billion—over 562,000 facilities, on more than 4,800 sites, in all 50 states, seven U.S. territories, and 40 foreign countries. The annual cost to operate and maintain these facilities is estimated at over $30 billion a year, but GAO has stated that there is significant room for improvement. DoD estimates that 22% of its facilities are excess.

The executive branch used to be able to close such properties at will, but since bases are enormously important to local communities and such losses can be devastating, the people whose job it is to look out for such constituencies stepped in. The Base Realignment and Closure (BRAC) process came about in the late 1970s when President Jimmy Carter closed bases without giving Congress any role. Consequently, Congress passed a measure tying the hands of future presidents and secretaries of defense.

Since then, the process requires empaneling a BRAC commission that investigates and weighs the value of bases in question. Throughout the first five rounds of BRAC, no president or Congress has rejected the recommendations of the commission.

Despite the fact that the last BRAC round in 2005 resulted in $15 billion in savings over 20 years, there is significant congressional opposition to even the mention of any new rounds. Thus, the Pentagon has formally dropped its request and quit asking, though it believes offloading today's unneeded facilities could save it about $2 billion per year.

Another area ripe for review is the overall activity in logistics. DoD operates one of the largest logistics enterprises in the world. Its annual cost is over $170 billion, including supply, maintenance, and transportation. DoD has over 100,000 suppliers, $96 billion in inventory, and is supported by 18 maintenance depots, 25 distribution depots, and over 49,000 customer sites. The logistics enterprise does provide a real warfighting advantage, a fact that must be kept in mind.

Despite many efforts to bring DoD's logistics enterprise up to the level of today's world-class business practices, it has a long way to go, as evidenced by the 2018 revelations that the Defense Logistics Agency (DLA) lost track of $800 million for construction projects.

This is not something that would occur with a 21st-century logistics enterprise. Private citizens have multiple online options to buy a product, know what it will cost, and when it will arrive—not just by the day, but sometimes even the exact hour. When supply clerks in a military office go to the DLA to order a part, they don't know if the part is in stock, how much it will cost, or when it will arrive. DLA is still in the Stone Age compared to private sector logistics practices.

WAR SPENDING AND FINANCIAL ACCOUNTABILITY

Logistics is an enormous task when multiple wars are raging on the other side of the world, and our warfighters serving overseas deserve the best efforts from supporting functions. Those best efforts should also include wise dispensing of funds, which means better oversight to prevent further misuse of taxpayer dollars on things like luxury cars and nepotism. As with the DLA, this waste was discovered by an internal audit limited to just that agency.

DoD needs to put the rest of its organizations under a similar microscope. Fortunately, in 2018, the department completed the first ever audit of all facets of the organization. This is one of the most important developments in terms of reining in costs because it is difficult—nigh impossible—to come up with lasting solutions to problems we don't fully understand, let alone ones we have yet to identify.

Headlines about the completed audit got caught up on the word "failure," but this was a misrepresentation of DoD's work. Expecting an organization with $2.7 trillion in assets to get a clean bill of health on their first audit is unrealistic, and the auditors' inability to grant a clean opinion stemmed from record-keeping inconsistencies across DoD, not because of widespread fraud or corruption.

For defense insiders, the main takeaways of the audit included the importance of standardized recordkeeping. Following the audit, then Undersecretary of Defense Comptroller David Norquist emphasized the importance of implementing corrective actions, for even incremental progress will generate significant benefits.

Beyond the Pentagon

Bureaucratic sprawl is not just a problem in DoD, whose reforms must also be coupled with changes in White House procedures. It must reduce the proliferation of executive offices and staffs, and establish controls on a National Security Council (NSC) that has become widely known over the years to have trouble distinguishing between its coordination role and the operational functions of Cabinet officers. In other words, NSC staff are micromanaging decisions that are supposed to be made in the standalone departments.

We need to return the NSC to the model laid down by Andrew Goodpaster under President Eisenhower and Brent Scowcroft under President H.W. Bush, both in approach and size. Under their direction, the NSC had a smaller staff that focused on coordinating policy, not directing or micromanaging it. It eschewed the operation role that characterized Iran-Contra and the Reagan years and, instead, focused on providing timely, objective analysis to the president.

Much of this can be attributed to the fact that the staff has ballooned in recent decades, from 40 staffers under H.W. Bush to 400 under Obama. For a body with enormous influence on American foreign policy, that's far too large to have no Congressional accountability. Not one of those staff positions requires Senate confirmation, and their policy deliberations are protected by executive privilege. Such opacity makes it susceptible to the groupthink and wildly irresponsible decision-making that led to the Iran-Contra scandal.

Fortunately, the 2017 NDAA capped the NSC staff at 150, though this may still be too much, since it needs to go back to coordinating between bureaucracies and not being one itself. Before the expansion, it cooperated better with Cabinet and other officials than the modern NSC, and most importantly, its members shunned the spotlight, preferring to work behind the scenes, making it more effective at coordinating policies across multiple departments.

The Office of Management and Budget (OMB) likewise needs to spend more time on government-wide management and much less time on budget micromanagement, which is more prevalent for the domestic agencies than DoD, though the White House has, at times, been known to hold the Pentagon on a shorter leash than is prudent.

Of course, these problems are not the sole responsibility of the Pentagon, nor even the executive branch. Any reforms in the latter will be insufficient without serious reforms in the Capitol as well. Both bodies are drowning in budget detail and duplicative processes. Congress should consider reestablishing the Joint Committee on the Organization of the Congress (JCOC), which has produced major recommendations three times in the past, most recently in 1993. However, no serious reform has yet occurred.

Intending to modernize the legislature for the coming millennium, the JCOC focused on the committee system, trying to resolve inter-jurisdictional disputes. A new joint committee should have the similar presumption of reducing the size of Congress's staffs and support agencies as well. In the last century, congressional staff numbers rose significantly as federal authority grew and America took on a larger role in the world. After a dip in the mid-1990s due to the JCOC, they continued to rise until 2010 but have since declined slightly, as seen in Figure 12.

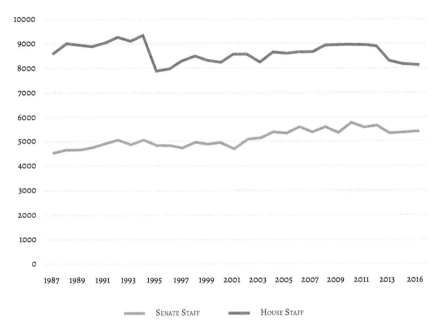

FIGURE 12: LARGE CONGRESSIONAL STAFF

SENATE STAFF   HOUSE STAFF

FIGURE 12 SHOWS THE SIZES OF CONGRESSIONAL STAFFS IN BOTH THE HOUSE AND SENATE
OVER TIME.

As these trends are somewhat haphazard and are likely to reverse again, consideration should be given to managing congressional staff size with more intent. In a world where events move in nanoseconds, DoD needs significantly more flexibility from Congress in how it spends its money to adjust to changing circumstances. That means streamlined staffs.

Congress fundamentally does the same thing three times a year—budget, authorize, and appropriate. It should consider reducing the separate processes to two steps by combining the authorization and appropriations steps. If Congress authorized and appropriated in the same bill, it would save the time and attention of its members, valuable commodities on the Hill, and avoid the possibility of actions being authorized but not funded and vice versa—a source of gridlock on the Hill and frustration in the executive branch.

Essentially, this would mean breaking up the appropriations committees into their respective parts and giving that power to the authorizing committees. For example, the SASC and its counterpart, the House Armed Services Committee (HASC), would together constitute authorizer and appropriator for defense issues, so once the NDAA is passed and signed, that would be it; the military would know its spending levels. There would be no need to make its case before a separate committee, no more need to fight for money for things already authorized. Furthermore, these authorizing committees are more specialized—they deal with these issues more regularly and are the ones providing oversight—so they are the best situated to know what an appropriate level of funding is and when to use their power of the purse to bring the executive branch back under the control of the people's representatives. This is a clear-cut case where having stronger committees means a stronger democracy.

This appeal for reform would be remiss if it did not involve the Appropriations Committees' cousin: The Budget Committees. Created by the 1974 Congressional Budget and Impoundment Control Act, the House and Senate Budget Committees are tasked with laying out a framework for spending that is meant to guide later appropriations. Their budget resolutions, which are not law and are not signed by the president, set spending targets and deficit levels prior to the authorization and appropriations processes and put in place controls and roles to restrict deviations from the approved levels. In the 45 years since the passage of the law, Congress has failed to pass a budget resolution 10 times. All of these failures have occurred in the last 20 years. Clearly, something needs to change.

To streamline the process, budget committee membership should change, too. The new budget committees would still set the overall control totals for the next two years: the amount of revenue to be raised, the discretionary spending levels, and the amount of the deficit. The change is that the chairs and ranking members of the authorizing committees, now imbued with appropriating power, should automatically constitute the budget committees. That way, there is no daylight between the front and back ends of the government funding process, and the committees are stacked with members who have shown considerable devotion to working on the topics.

Finally—and it's a testament to the current hyper-partisan climate to have to say this—Congress needs to complete its work on time. Since 1843, the government fiscal year started on July 1. By the mid-1900s, Congress never met that deadline, so the 1974 Budget Act moved it to October 1. History has proven that Congress cannot do its job in six months, so now it has nine months to the beginning of the fiscal year—and Congress is still behind.

Over the last 30 years, DoD has spent an average of 55 days—roughly two months—per fiscal year under a continuing resolution (CR). That's five presidents and 16 Congresses, and only the 108th Congress and George W. Bush were able to avoid throwing the department into budgeting limbo; all they did was get the Defense Appropriations Act signed before the end of the fiscal year twice in a row.

Consideration should be given to pushing the start of the fiscal year back to January 1 to line up with the calendar and business tax years. However, the budget for the next fiscal year would still be submitted on February 1; that way, Congress has nearly a full year to deliberate. For example, in this system, the president would submit his FY21 budget on February 1, 2020, and Congress has until January 1, 2021, to hammer out the combined authorizations and appropriations bills, which should cover the calendar year.

Yet the most impactful change Congress could make would be to move to a two-year budget system. The first year would be spent making decisions on the request, and the second year would be reserved for extensive congressional oversight and fact-of-life changes. This could improve both processes, because members and committees could devote ample time to each.

In laying out Congress's powers, Article 1, Section 8 of the Constitution even mentions a two-year appropriations timeline for national security. When I was staff director of SASC in the early 1990s, we did this with the defense authorization bill, and it made the process much smoother; but the appropriations committees refused to adapt with us, and subsequent Congresses dropped the requirement. An effort should be made to return to this model on all fronts.

Absent these major structural reforms, which would bring with them years of planning and fierce debate, the SASC could also look inward and streamline its own affairs. In the final chapters of this book, I lay out how the committee could optimize itself by reorganizing its subcommittees, returning to issues of grand strategy, and discarding its budget micromanagement mindset. There's plenty that can be done now without having to wait for external initiative.

Sequester and Reform Incentives

One of the biggest reasons to fix the budget process is to avoid another disastrous sequester. Former Chairman of the Joint Chiefs of Staff Adm. Mike Mullen called the nation's long-term deficits our number one national security threat. Admiral Mullen was right when he said this back in 2010, and the situation is worse today, as recently outlined by then-National Security Advisor John Bolton. Absent any sustainably bipartisan (and sadly unlikely) compromise, the interest on our debt will be larger than defense spending by 2024. Yet we cannot take the same approach as the Budget Control Act (BCA) of 2011; we need to learn from that experience.

The idea was to get control of the deficit through a high-stakes, taxpayer-funded game of chicken. The risk of not coming to a compromise was supposed to be so great and the cuts so painful that it would be political suicide to let them go into effect. In the BCA, capping discretionary spending was the first step. The joint committee was tasked with coming up with revenue increases and entitlement reductions to reduce the deficit as well—essentially, finding $1 trillion in savings from a $41 trillion pot over 10 years—but it was unsuccessful and, unlike previous instances of Congress kicking the can down the road, this one came with immediate consequences. With no compromise reached, the military budget, along with those of numerous other programs, was slashed.

Fortunately, the last few Defense Appropriations bills have rolled back those cuts and set national security spending at levels that both the administration and the budget and defense committees indicated. With Congress setting aside artificial spending caps and finally allowing DoD to escape the threat of sequestration—an approach to budget control that had few merits and even fewer advocates—the increased resources flowing to defense will have a near-term, positive impact on readiness, modernization, and quality of life. Now, leaders on Capitol Hill should focus on creating lasting solutions through compromise. To credibly reform the Pentagon, Congress needs to fix the way it does business as well.

THE NECESSARY STEPS TOWARD REFORM

1. Define

The legendary Senator Russell Long had a saying: "You should not solve a problem for people before they know they have one." Well, I've outlined the problems that will be discussed in detail in the coming chapters. Consider yourself notified.

To begin tackling these issues, we must first establish a definitional agreement on what defense overhead actually is, including headquarters and management layers. Many will argue that some of those problem areas mentioned previously are actually tooth, not tail. Others, like Business Executives for National Security (BENS), will argue the infrastructure is much larger than DoD admits. We need consensus on what is counted as infrastructure and overhead. Having addressed the definitional challenge, we then need to determine where it all resides. In other words, where do the people work? And it needs to include active military, defense civilians, Guard and Reserves, defense contractors, and FFRDC personnel.

A particular challenge to this exists in determining total contractor personnel in overhead and infrastructure. Here, we are referring to contractors in direct support of DoD, not those who build major weapons systems or parts. Currently, there is not a data source that fully and accurately captures the exact numbers of contractors or where they work. While some data exist, contractors are typically paid from operations and maintenance (O&M) accounts. Therefore, their exact numbers are not as easily derived as military personnel—with their own appropriations, and civilian full time equivalents (FTEs)—who are paid through the Defense Finance and Accounting System.

The fact that no DoD-wide register of expenditures exists complicates all efforts for overhauling the system. This was a much-cited lesson of the Pentagon's first audit, that the department needs to improve its internal tracking databases and IT processes to accurately reflect real-world changes in real time. This is especially true for contractors. According to David Norquist: "What [the audit] found is the error rate in inventory held by contractors is higher than the inventory errors that we had in the services." Fixing the overall problems identified in the audit goes hand in hand with the issues with the current manner of tracking contractors.

2. Collect

After determining who and what comprises infrastructure and overhead and determining with much higher confidence where they work, we then need to know what they cost. Not just salary; we need to understand the fully burdened and life-cycle costs of active military, government civilians, Guard and Reserves, contractors, and the FFRDC personnel supporting these activities. It is imperative that we reach an agreement on what constitutes the fully burdened and life-cycle costs of the AVF, taking into account all cost elements, including education, health care, and future retirement costs.

Of equal significance is the fact that the defense retiree population is growing and is now at 2.4 million people. Retirees are living longer, and their health care costs are growing. Under the current system, their retirement income is inflation-indexed. This means that it will be difficult to afford the force of tomorrow as we continue to pay large amounts for the force of yesterday. DoD does not know and does not track the fully burdened and life-cycle costs of its full personnel as listed above. Some say because it is too difficult—and it is difficult—but others suspect that DoD does not want to do the calculations to reveal the actual costs because of the sticker shock. This was also an alleged factor behind resistance to the department-wide audit. The 2013 RFPB study and its 2019 update on the fully burdened costs are but one example of why necessity overrides those concerns.

3. Decide

Once we have agreed upon definitions, determined work locations, and calculated full costs, we have one more number-crunching step before taking action. Since one of the goals here is right-sizing, we need to determine what the actual right size is for the various activities. This is difficult, and we might not get it right the first time, but it is not enough to just study the issue.

Part of becoming more risk acceptant is being willing to make incremental progress. With headquarters size, we need to make the same tough decisions about how much is enough, just like with force structure. Certainly, we should all agree that we cannot allow the status quo to continue. There are too many people—active duty, defense civilians, Guard and Reserves, FFRDCs, and contractors—working in OSD, JCS, the COCOMs, and the DAFAs. Once we can show exactly how many, we can decide what constitutes too many, and where to draw that line.

4. Act

After taking the steps above to establish definitions, identify infrastructure, and agree upon metrics, costs, and size, it will be time to act. Along with building a broad base of support and mobilizing a coalition of backers in key positions, a number of steps should follow, which will be laid out in subsequent chapters. They will cover the specific areas of defense budgeting, management reform, the Goldwater-Nichols Act, and revisions for the future, acquisition, defense industries, personnel reform, and how all of it ties in with congressional oversight.

Once the plausibility of such changes is determined, the next step is laying out who can make them. Can the president do it by executive order? Can the departments change their own policies on simpler issues? What reforms are so big that they require legislation? In short, who can make which changes?

Reforming the national security apparatus will be no easy feat, but Secretary Gates said it well when he summed up his reform efforts before leaving office: "My hope and expectation is that, as a result of these changes over time, what had been a culture of endless money, where cost was rarely a consideration, will become a culture of savings and restraint."

WE'VE DONE IT BEFORE; WE'LL DO IT AGAIN

Former Secretary of Defense Mark Esper and Maj. Gen. Arnold Punaro, USMC, Ret. stop for a photo together in January 2020 before delving into their discussion on key challenges affecting the department.

I know America's national security leaders are willing to take up such a daunting challenge. They follow in the footsteps of esteemed visionaries that came before them, leaders who made the sweeping changes that created the Department of Defense from the separate Departments of the Navy and Army after World War II, addressed its problems in 1956, shifted the military from the draft to the all-volunteer force (AVF) in 1973 and then saved the AVF when it needed reforms in the late 1970s, passed Goldwater-Nichols and Special Operations legislation, and continued to tackle the problems with the acquisition process. We know from history that large institutions like DoD cannot make significant organizational and process reforms from within. The SASC, HASC, and the Senate and House Appropriations Committees have an enviable history in solving major defense problems. They will need to be the battering ram of reform once more, but they do not need to struggle alone.

After a long and distinguished career in the Marines, President Trump's first Secretary of Defense James Mattis was clear-eyed about the difficulties the department faced and his stated priorities showed this. Not only did he talk about shifting resources to prize readiness and lethality, but he also sought to bring business reforms to the DoD to make it more flexible and efficient, a goal which I obviously support wholeheartedly. His successor, Mark Esper, spent decades on all sides of these issues, both inside and outside government, which proved useful in hastening reform. Others in leadership have also begun to repeat the well-established mantra of the business world, "fail early, fail cheap."

We must distinguish between working hard and working well. With the fiscal pressures we face, with new strategic challenges erupting all around us, and with the operational demands accumulating on the force, we can no longer afford the luxury of a growing imbalance between what we must field operationally and what we can field managerially. We need to generate more units—with more combat power—from our military end strength and the fiscal resources associated with it, not fewer. And today we are fielding fewer.

I want to close this chapter by reiterating that none of my comments are meant as criticism of the dedicated, patriotic people who come to work every day across the Department of Defense with the intention of doing their part to keep the country safe. One senior officer recounted that, on September 12, 2001, hundreds of military and civilian employees reported to work at the Pentagon, even though the building was still on fire. They went to their offices to salvage what they could, gather up classified materials that had been scattered about by the explosion, and as we say in the military: Charlie Mike – continue mission.

I am so proud that such people serve the nation. As a 24-year Senate staffer, I know this dedication is mirrored in the congressional offices as well, and my 20 subsequent years in the defense industry showed me that sentiment is there too.

Along with defense civilian and military leadership, I also want to applaud the Senate and House Armed Services and Defense Appropriations Committees for their continued bipartisanship when taking a hard look at these problems. We must continue exerting this same diligence and commitment to problem-solving.

Chapter 3: National Security in Divided Government

This chapter, distributed as a white paper in the aftermath of the 2018 midterm election, was designed to help calm the waters roiled by uncertainty and concern that important national security programs would be terminated due to partisan considerations. In the executive branch, in industry, and on the Hill, there were many who had not previously served in divided government, furthering concern. I was the staff director of the Senate Armed Services Committee during many years of divided government and gained firsthand experience ensuring needed legislation and programs got approved. This paper was provided to leaders in DoD, Congress, and industry in November 2018. Not long after, the annual defense bills confirmed my predictions that national security legislation and key programs would be approved on a bipartisan basis, despite the tense rhetoric – the FY20 and FY21 NDAAs are proof positive. While this paper has been updated with the results of the 2020 election, it primarily focuses on national security in divided government as of 2018.

In the first two years of the Trump administration, the Republican party controlled the executive branch and both houses of Congress. On many defense issues, the new administration followed traditional Republican orthodoxy. However, after the Democratic party regained control of the House of Representatives in the 2018 midterm election, there was broad concern that clashes between the White House and the new majority in the House could create policy and process problems for the national security establishment.

What are the implications of divided government for the U.S. defense establishment and its supporting industrial base? What does it mean for the way government could work both now and in future periods of split control? Is there anything to be learned from past periods of divided government that would successfully guide federal agencies and their leaders, especially in the national security field?

WHAT HISTORY TELLS US ABOUT DIVIDED GOVERNMENT

Between 1965 and 2021, divided government was the dominant form of government, prevailing for 36 of the last 56 years, with unified government in the remaining 20 years. In fact, the election of President Clinton ended the longest sustained period of divided government in the history of the Union. The 2018 election added two more years of divided government to that total, though the 2020 election and subsequent 2021 Senate runoff race resulted in unified Democratic control. However, this result is the exception – not the norm. Figure 1 provides an in-depth look to the history of divided government.

Figure 1: President, Senate, and House Control (from 1965-2021)					
Congress #	Year	Admin.	POTUS	Senate	House
89	1965	Johnson	D	D*	D*
89	1966	Johnson	D	D*	D*
90	1967	Johnson	D	D	D
90	1968	Johnson	D	D	D
91	1969	Nixon	R	D	D
91	1970	Nixon	R	D	D
92	1971	Nixon	R	D	D

92	1972	Nixon	R	D	D
93	1973	Nixon	R	D	D
93	1974	Nixon	R	D	D
94	1975	Ford	R	D*	D*
94	1976	Ford	R	D*	D*
95	1977	Carter	D	D*	D*
95	1978	Carter	D	D*	D*
96	1979	Carter	D	D	D
96	1980	Carter	D	D	D
97	1981	Reagan	R	R	D
97	1982	Reagan	R	R	D
98	1983	Reagan	R	R	D
98	1984	Reagan	R	R	D
99	1985	Reagan	R	R	D
99	1986	Reagan	R	R	D
100	1987	Reagan	R	D	D
100	1988	Reagan	R	D	D
101	1989	Bush I	R	D	D
101	1990	Bush I	R	D	D
102	1991	Bush I	R	D	D
102	1992	Bush I	R	D	D
103	1993	Clinton	D	D	D
103	1994	Clinton	D	D	D
104	1995	Clinton	D	R	R
104	1996	Clinton	D	R	R
105	1997	Clinton	D	R	R
105	1998	Clinton	D	R	R
106	1999	Clinton	D	R	R
106	2000	Clinton	D	R	R
107	2001	Bush II	R	D / R	R
107	2002	Bush II	R	R	R
108	2003	Bush II	R	R	R
108	2004	Bush II	R	R	R

109	2005	Bush II	R	R	R
109	2006	Bush II	R	R	R
110	2007	Bush II	R	D	D
110	2008	Bush II	R	D	D
111	2009	Obama	D	D	D
111	2010	Obama	D	D	D
112	2011	Obama	D	D	R
112	2012	Obama	D	D	R
113	2013	Obama	D	D	R
113	2014	Obama	D	D	R
114	2015	Obama	D	R	R
114	2016	Obama	D	R	R
115	2017	Trump	R	R	R
115	2018	Trump	R	R	R
116	2019	Trump	R	R	D
116	2020	Trump	R	R	D
117	2021	Biden	D	D	D

FIGURE 1 PROVIDES HISTORICAL PERSPECTIVE INTO DIVIDED GOVERNMENT OVER THE LAST 50+ YEARS.

In *Federalist Paper* No. 47, James Madison wrote, "The accumulation of all power, legislative, executive, and judiciary, in the same hands, whether of one, a few, or many, and whether hereditary, self-appointed, or elective, may justly be pronounced the very definition of tyranny." Further, in *Federalist* No. 51, he wrote:

In order to lay a due foundation for that separate and distinct exercise of the different powers of government, which to a certain extent is admitted on all hands to be essential to the preservation of liberty, it is evident that each department should have a will of its own ... It may be a reflection on human nature, that such devices should be necessary to control the abuses of government.

In general, down through the generations, Americans have been wary of too much accumulation of power by any one group, be it political, economic, or social. This explains why divided government tends to be the rule, not the exception, within American politics.

On the one hand, divided government has meant more partisanship and gridlock, maintaining the well-documented trend in recent years. On the other hand, it can sometimes also result in major legislative accomplishments. In fact, Senate Majority Leader Mitch McConnell's view, as expressed in a meeting with the *New York Times* in 2011, is that divided government is a perfect time to do big things. However, this belief stands in contrast with his approach during the Obama administration when Republicans worked to block almost all of the president's agenda. The Democratic House took a similar approach to most of President Trump's agenda.

Legislative accomplishments, however, do occur in divided government, as seen through the analysis of Yale political scientist David Mayhew. He identified 267 important laws enacted by Congress between 1947 and 1990 to determine which periods were most productive, and found that under unified government, each two-year Congress enacted an average of 12.8 important laws. Under divided government, each Congress enacted only one fewer, 11.7, a figure understated by counting the sweeping budget and tax cuts of 1981 as just two laws. In the 1960s and early 1970s, for example, Congress passed numerous laws on civil rights, social policy and environmental protection. Much of this happened under two Republican presidents, Nixon and Ford, whose administrations were productive legislatively, notwithstanding divided government. Then, during the 1980s, a conservative wave induced a Democratic Congress to work with President Reagan on a series of major policy changes in a more conservative direction, including:

- Overhaul of Social Security in 1983 negotiated by President Ronald Reagan and Speaker Tip O'Neill.

- Changes to the tax law enacted in 1986 (Reagan was president; Democrats still controlled the House).

- Domestic spending reductions and a defense buildup in the 1980s under divided government with Reagan and a Democratic Congress.

Democrats had near solid control of both houses of Congress since Franklin Roosevelt's election in 1933, with the exception of the 80th and 83rd Congresses. That trend was broken by Republican's capture of the Senate for the first time since 1955 when Reagan was elected president in 1980. Democrats' hold on the House remained unbroken until 1995.

When President Clinton assumed the presidency, he had a unified government for two years, but lost it for the remaining six years of his term. Yet, it was in 1996 when Republicans controlled both houses of Congress that he reached a major welfare reform agreement with Capitol Hill.

Major policy changes have occurred when national conditions or the public mood demanded them. They have not necessarily required a unified government. However, the last two decades have produced some of the least productive Congresses in the country's history, with many observers noting that recent years, under both divided and unified governments, compare unfavorably with even the famous "Do Nothing Congress" of the Truman era.

In 2018, we entered another one of these common periods of divided government. It was difficult to determine precisely what the implications of this would be, as we were in a period where many of the traditional and conventional expectations and practices of both government and politics were themselves in flux. The 2016 presidential election and the subsequent Trump administration realigned some traditional party positions, such as the Republican stance on deficit spending and free trade. A trend of increasing partisanship has only kept growing, and many members of the 2018 congressional class were more hardline in their views than their predecessors.

One trend that has emerged is a clear shift of power from one end of Pennsylvania Avenue to the other. Any legislation that the president requests and any that reaches his desk will require support from majorities in both houses of Congress, and with different parties controlling the chambers,

Congress's bargaining power substantially increased. Unfortunately, there have been commensurate challenges in accomplishing some of the basic functions of government, as evidenced by the difficulty of passing effective and timely authorization and appropriation bills and especially the prolonged reliance on continuing resolutions (CRs) to fund the government. Given all of this turbulence, the record from divided governments of the past provides needed insight on national security in the future.

Historical Trends in Defense Policy

In the domain of national security, the role of Congress can be defined within three broad categories: budgetary decisions, strategic policy, and war powers. First, the budgetary role of Congress relates to its constitutionally enumerated responsibility for the allocation of resources that allows it to raise armies, maintain a navy, and provide the rules and governance thereof. But this role, by nature, extends into such areas as military facilities and base infrastructure, weapons procurement, and personnel policies. The second role – strategic policy – has more to do with strategy reviews, which work to define the purpose and costs associated with our national military objectives. It includes the administration's approach to defense and foreign policy. Finally, Congress also has the sole power to declare war—which it has not exercised since World War II. Congress has largely ceded this authority to the executive branch, which has used its authority to send troops abroad on numerous occasions in that same time frame. In some circumstances, congressional authorization was provided via resolutions, such as in the first Gulf War and through the Authorization for the Use of Military Force (AUMF) post 9/11.

In the past, Democrats and Republicans have differed in their approaches to each of these three areas. Going back to the Nixon administration, several trends emerge on defense policy in divided government, specifically during Republican administrations and Democratic Congresses. Figure 2 depicts the defense funding averages in various periods of government control.

Figure 2: Defense Appropriations Averages, 1950-2019 (in millions $)[1]

Admin	House	Senate	House vs. Request	Senate vs. Request	Total vs. Request
R	R	R	-984	-1,894	1,336
D	D	D	-1,699	-1,269	-1,285
R	D	R	-11,506	-5,557	-8,771
R	D		-6,887	-4,526	-4,932
R			-4,976	-3,510	-2,996
D			-2,196	-2,952	-2,913
	D		-4,789	-3,210	-3,458
		D	-3,847	-3,507	-3,945
R		D	-5,036	-3,921	-3,597
	R		-1,810	-3,618	-2,139
		R	-3,886	-3,256	-1,384
D	R		-2,983	-5,616	-5,489
D		R	-1,363	-2,558	1,125

[1]This chart shows the average differences between the president's budget request, the House and Senate appropriations bills, and the final bill during different periods of unified and divided government. The 4th column, for example, represents all years of a Republican administration and a Democratic House, regardless of Senate control. The 5th column represents all years of Republican administrations, regardless of Senate or House control.

FIGURE 2 DEPICTS THE DEFENSE APPROPRIATIONS AVERAGES IN PERIODS OF DIVIDED GOVERNMENT.

As a general trend, Democratic majorities—especially in the House—have supported lower defense spending than requested by Republican administrations, though the final passed budget has usually been closer to the Senate number than the House. In 1970, President Nixon's first year in office, Congress authorized the largest defense cuts since 1954. Nixon had proposed a $2.5 billion cut from Johnson's original budget, while the House passed $5.3 billion in cuts. The final budget for FY70 was $5.6 billion below the Nixon request, despite the still ongoing Vietnam War. In FY76, a Democratic Congress further lowered defense spending by $7.4 billion below the requested level despite Secretary of Defense Schlesinger's strong warning that the cuts would put U.S. forces at a disadvantage against the Soviet Union.

The Reagan era saw the largest difference between administration requests and passed budgets. Between FY84 and FY88, the passed budget was an average of $18.6 billion lower than the administration request, with the largest cut in FY87 of $25 billion. It is important to note that during this time, year-over-year growth was still increasing—just at a lower pace than the Reagan administration requested. Democrats were increasingly concerned with growing defense budgets in the face of growing deficits and Reagan's unwillingness to raise taxes or boost domestic spending. Despite the reductions, the Reagan buildup is still referred to in glowing terms, though few remember the number of Reagan budget requests approved at a lower level.

In FY91, a Democratic Congress enacted a $17 billion budget cut from the previous year—$18.3 billion below President Bush's request—as a result of the end of the Cold War and a signal to the administration that it needed to change its defense strategy.

In terms of specific programs and policies, arms control and nuclear issues, major weapons systems, social and environmental issues, strong oversight, and opposition to overseas operations have been major areas of tension between Republican presidents and Democratic Congresses.

Nuclear weapons have always been a contentious topic between the two parties. Republicans, in general, have supported weapons increases and tended to distrust arms control efforts, while Democrats have been much the opposite. Between FY71 and FY76, Congress restricted Nixon's and Ford's antiballistic missile expansion plans and pushed back on the multiple independently targetable reentry vehicle (MIRV) missiles. This trend was especially evident during the Reagan administration, when Democrats were skeptical of Reagan's commitment to arms control. The House voted and passed a symbolic nuclear arms freeze in 1983. There was also strong opposition to Reagan's Strategic Defense Initiative, MX missiles, and antisatellite (ASAT) missile development, with Congress seeking to limit funding to all those programs throughout his administration.

Democrats also tended to be more skeptical of major weapons systems, mostly due to their massive cost overruns. They were skeptical of building additional nuclear-powered aircraft carriers in 1970 and later rejected the administration's FY77 plan to build six new warships to counter the Soviets. In the late 1970s, a number of the more liberal members attacked the Army's Big Five programs, but they were fully supported by large bipartisan majorities. During the Reagan years, Democrats charged that Reagan was sacrificing readiness (ammunition and training time) for major weapons systems, and made procurement their biggest target for finding DoD savings. Democrats have also pushed back on the B-2 bomber and other major weapons systems, the Army's Future Combat Systems, and various missile systems.

Democrats have also strongly upheld the Armed Services Committees' tradition of oversight of the Pentagon, specifically on the issues of cost overruns, headquarters staff, and personnel policies. Beginning in 1974, Congress demanded stronger oversight of CIA activities, resulting in major investigations by the Church and Pike committees into the intelligence community in 1975. This resulted in the shift of intelligence oversight from the defense committees to the newly-created intelligence committees. The year 1983 saw the beginning of stronger procurement oversight of DoD that led to the Packard Commission and its acquisition reforms. Democratic Reps. Jack Brooks and John Dingell also launched aggressive oversight investigations into the Pentagon from the House Government Operations and Energy and Commerce Committees, respectively. Strong oversight of the Pentagon within the committees of jurisdiction is, however, a bipartisan issue, with both Democrats and Republicans leading investigations into the executive branch—regardless of the party in power— throughout the years. These included Desert One, the 1983 Beirut barracks bombing, academy and recruiting scandals, the USS *Iowa* turret explosion, Somalia, and many more. The Pentagon should expect the same level of scrutiny with the new Congress, including from outside the traditional defense committees.

In line with their domestic agendas, Democrats try to pass more social and environmental changes affecting the Defense Department. In 1974, a Democratic Congress successfully overrode President Ford's veto of H.R.12628, expanding vocational and educational benefits for Vietnam veterans. In 2008, a Democratic Congress passed the largest expansion of the GI Bill since WWII in that year's Overseas Contingency Operations (OCO) funding bill. Several other social issues championed by Democrats include opening combat roles to women beginning in 1991 and "Don't Ask, Don't Tell" and its repeal. Democrats have also sought to ensure that DoD is a responsible steward of the environment, such as with the 1986 Defense Environmental Restoration Program and with several environmental cleanup issues passed in FY91.

Another major area of contention has been Democrats' opposition to overseas operations, showing Congress's enduring but partial interest in its war powers authority. In 1973, Congress overrode Nixon's veto of H.J.Res. 542 to limit the president's powers to commit U.S. forces abroad without congressional approval. The War Powers Act has been a continuing source of tension between the legislative and executive branches ever since. During the Vietnam War, Congress sought to limit in scope the Nixon administration's actions, including a ban on ground troops in Laos and Thailand in FY70, limits on aid to Vietnam, Laos, and Cambodia in FY71, and reductions in foreign aid to Vietnam and a reduction in troops overseas in FY75. Democrats were also opposed to a large troop presence in Europe after the end of the Cold War. And though both authorizations ultimately passed, many Democrats voted against the Persian Gulf War resolution in 1991 and the Iraq War resolution in 2003. In 2007, Democrats opposed Iraq and Afghanistan funding unless it was accompanied by policy changes and withdrawal dates from the Bush administration. Most recently, Democrats (along with Republicans) passed a resolution to limit President Trump's ability to use force without Congress's approval—specifically in Iran and Yemen—and House Democrats passed a resolution to repeal the 2002 AUMF, which was not taken up by the Republican Senate.

We saw some of these policy differences continue in the 116th Congress, with nuclear weapons, arms control, and overseas operations being the major areas of concern. However, the HASC and SASC have always operated in a bipartisan approach, and I fully expect this to continue into the future.

THE USE OF PRESIDENTIAL VETOES IN DIVIDED AND UNIFIED GOVERNMENTS

One of the strongest levers of power possessed by the president is the veto. Before using it, the White House usually tries to determine whether or not enough votes can be mustered to sustain a veto, either 146 votes in the House or 34 votes in the Senate.

In signaling to Congress its displeasure with a bill, the White House uses three gradations of veto threats. First, the strongest veto threat is that the "president will veto the bill if passed." Second, the intermediate threat is that "the president's senior advisors" or "the president's advisors" will recommend a veto. Finally, the weakest form of a veto threat is that one or more "cabinet secretaries will recommend a veto." The executive branch signals these threats to the Congress both informally through the White House Office of Legislative Affairs and through formal communications known as statements of administration policy (SAP). After the issuance of one of these SAPs, behind-the-scenes discussions take place to see if offending provisions can be modified or changed before its passage. If not, the Constitution requires that the president return a vetoed bill to Congress within 10 days of its receipt at the White House with an explanation of his objections in a veto message. If the veto threat is not at the presidential level, it is often the case that the president ultimately signs the bill but, again, the White House Office of Legislative Affairs works with Congress to make the objectionable provisions more acceptable. Often, the cabinet secretary and the White House closely coordinate on these efforts. While presidents have succeeded in vetoing certain provisions out of bills, they cannot veto provisions into bills.

If Congress has adjourned, a president may "pocket veto" a bill since he cannot return it to Congress. In recent administrations, this has rarely happened.

Recent presidents have generally been able to sustain their vetoes, which makes the veto threat an effective tool. Between the Kennedy and Trump administrations (1961 to 2021) there were 384 vetoes but only 39 successful overrides by Congress.

Appropriations bills have been vetoed 43 times since 1960, with four of those vetoes overridden. Though several of these vetoes were continuing resolutions that would have included defense funding, the Defense Appropriations Bill itself has never been vetoed. The White House has only vetoed the National Defense Authorization Bill six times since 1961, the most recent being in 2020 during the Trump administration. Not all six vetoes occurred during periods of divided government. President Carter vetoed the defense authorization bill for FY79 (H.R. 10929), passed by a Congress in Democratic control, because he objected to the bill's authorization of almost $2 billion for a nuclear-powered aircraft carrier. After the House sustained the veto, the Congress passed a second FY79 authorization bill that did not authorize funding for the carrier, and the president signed the bill into law on October 20, 1978.

President Reagan vetoed the FY89 NDAA (H.R. 4264) over Congress's cuts to his Strategic Defense Initiative program, ballistic missile submarines, and ICBM modernization programs. He described these cuts as "unilateral concessions on arms control [to the Soviet Union]." Almost two months later, Reagan signed the updated NDAA (H.R. 4481) with those provisions removed.

In the case of the bill vetoed by the Obama administration in 2015, the NDAA (H.R. 1735) would have authorized essentially the total amount requested by the president for defense-related spending but without changing the current budget caps. The bill would have avoided breaking the cap on defense base budget spending by shifting roughly $38 billion of the total requested into the OCO budget, which was exempt from the budget caps. The president objected to effectively lifting the spending cap on defense without providing the same degree of relief for non-defense discretionary spending and, accordingly, vetoed H.R. 1735.

The impasse was resolved by the enactment on November 2, 2015, of P.L. 114-74, the Bipartisan Budget Act of 2015 (BBA). It raised the discretionary spending caps for both defense and non-defense programs in FY16 and FY17 and also set nonbinding "targets" for discretionary OCO appropriations in both the defense and non-defense categories, the latter falling within the budget function for international relations. The OCO target cap for defense exceeded the president's defense-related OCO budget request by $7.9 billion. Thus, the net effect of this was to allow (within the revised budget caps for FY16) total defense-related discretionary appropriations amounting to $606.9 billion, which was $5 billion less than the president requested (counting both base budget and OCO funding).

President Trump's veto of the FY21 NDAA in December 2020 was mostly the result of his displeasure that the bill excluded a provision to modify the liability shield for big tech companies. The legislation – Section 230 of the Communications Decency Act – was not within the jurisdiction of the defense committees nor included in either the House or Senate versions of the bill. Trump also opposed provisions to rename military bases named after Confederate generals and limit the withdrawal of troops from overseas without Congressional approval.

The president signed five of the six vetoed defense authorization bills, with or without modified provisions that had previously been veto issues. The president signed them despite the fact that the veto did not convince Congress to add the requested provisions. The Trump veto was the first time a veto of the NDAA was overridden by Congress, resulting in none of the president's objections being addressed. This reflects how committed the defense authorization committees and the Pentagon are to making sure they get a bill enacted every other year, now going on 60 years straight. Many other agencies do not consistently receive an annual authorization bill the way defense does—during periods of both unified and divided governments.

EMERGING PARTISAN VIEWS ON DEFENSE IN THE 116TH CONGRESS

On the nuclear issue, the debate has already begun. At the time this chapter was first published as a white paper, the most recent edition of *Foreign Affairs* asked on its cover "Do Nuclear Weapons Matter?" Inside, six essays by accomplished scholars explored this provocative title, offering arguments essentially covering the spectrum from nuclear weapons do not matter to they do, and we would be downgrading or dismissing them at our peril. At the same time, one of the major expenses for DoD is the cost of replacing or modernizing the nuclear deterrent force.

All three legs of the nation's nuclear triad require modernization. The existing ballistic missile submarine fleet (Ohio-class ships) is quickly reaching the end of its operational life. Simultaneously, the Minuteman III land-based missiles require serious upgrading, especially in regard to its command-and-control network and procedures. The bomber fleet has its own aging issues. In addition, the Trump administration withdrew from the 1987 Intermediate Nuclear Forces (INF) Treaty, an agreement that eliminated an entire category of land-based nuclear weapons. Withdrawal from the INF Treaty has led DoD to begin research and development into this previously banned class of missiles.

Representative Adam Smith (D-WA), who became chairman of the House Armed Services Committee (HASC) in 2019, has constantly signaled his disagreement with the Trump administration's nuclear weapons funding and programs. He believes that the Nuclear Posture Review calls for more nuclear weapons than he or most Democrats think are needed. In his view of the larger budget picture, nuclear weapons are not the best investment. Resistance against increased nuclear weapons funding was further underscored when several Democrats introduced bills aiming to limit the production and use of low-yield submarine-launched ballistic missiles (SLBMs). But, regardless of the number of nuclear weapons, the funding requirements for just maintaining and refurbishing the existing nuclear infrastructure are daunting and will cause difficult funding tradeoffs between nuclear and non-nuclear programs. This approach is entirely consistent with previous times Democrats have controlled the HASC and caucus in the era of Speakers Tip O'Neill, Tom Foley, and Nancy Pelosi.

Rep. Smith also differed with the Trump administration on military engagement, believing that the U.S. should draw down from places that do not serve our best interests. He believes that the administration is stretched too far across the world with too many missions in a wide range of countries. In his view, Congress should become more involved in making decisions about military operations overseas. This again is a historical norm for Democratic chairs and caucuses.

In particular, the Trump administration's support of Saudi Arabia in Yemen was a contentious issue. After the murder of Saudi journalist Jamal Khashoggi, lawmakers of all stripes – from progressives like Bernie Sanders and Chris Murphy to conservatives Mike Lee and Jerry Moran – voiced their support for new measures to rein in the Kingdom's activities. Senator Reed, the senior Democratic leader on the SASC, also came out with new conditions in U.S. support of the Saudis – ending the refueling of their planes and limiting weapons sales to defensive ones. Most of President Trump's vetoes have been of bills that would have restricted arms sales to Saudi Arabia and the UAE and limited funding for the use of force in Yemen and Iran.

Time will tell how such differences will affect future appropriations or defense authorization bills under President Biden and the 117th Congress; there were other, deeply controversial issues that sucked up much of the oxygen in public discourse. In particular, the Trump White House was adamant about funding the wall at the southern border, a central Trump campaign promise, and in 2019 began repurposing defense spending for this task. Democrats in the House roundly rejected this, setting up high-profile clashes over both authorizations and appropriations, and more vetoes by the president. These events, along with the history of how Democratic majorities mark up the defense bills, suggest further areas where Congress will differ on policy or resource distribution.

WHAT DIVIDED GOVERNMENT MEANS FOR THE DEFENSE TOPLINE

Given the hyperpartisan nature of the country at the moment, divided government may well lead to more partisanship and gridlock, particularly on domestic priorities. But is defense hurt by such an electoral outcome? For example, what has divided government meant for the defense topline? Not as much as many expected. Previous periods of divided government show that both the president and Congress have ultimately worked together when it came to how much money to spend on defense, even though they would communicate and advertise their policy differences up to the last moment.

Reagan submitted requests to Congress called Future Years Defense Programs (FYDP) showing higher defense growth than appropriated by Congress. Yet, Reagan signed the lower appropriations bills, which in some cases were significantly lower than he requested. In the six years where there was a Republican administration, a Republican Senate, and a Democratic House, the defense base budget increased an average of $25 billion per year. The defense base budget could similarly increase should the recent initiatives to move OCO to base be approved in FY22 or later years. During the same six-year period, the average amount appropriated for defense was $8.7 billion lower than the amount requested (or -3.9%), with the Senate level being $5.6 billion lower and the House level being $11.5 billion lower. Final appropriations were delayed by an average of 68 days from the beginning of the fiscal year (ranging from a low of 12 days to a high of 90 days).

In the 1990s, the Clinton administration repeatedly projected lower defense spending in its FYDPs than Congress ultimately appropriated. However, President Clinton signed the appropriations bills. Similarly, the Obama administration repeatedly projected higher defense budget requests than appropriated by Congress—even with a Republican House and Senate—which adhered to the Budget Control Act on the defense budget. Yet again, the Obama administration signed those bills.

The pattern of accommodation suggested above may be because the spending differences between the executive branch and Congress were never of such significant magnitude to merit bigger political fights. Also, getting defense money appropriated and available for obligation always becomes imperative due to its ties to national security and the significant number of government, civilian, and contractor jobs provided. Figure 3 illustrates potential patterns of future spending.

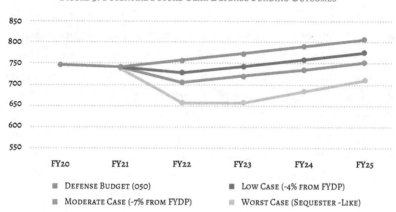

FIGURE 3: POTENTIAL FUTURE YEAR DEFENSE FUNDING OUTCOMES

FIGURE 3 ILLUSTRATES THE POTENTIAL PATH FOR FUTURE DEFENSE SPENDING OVER THE NEXT
FIVE YEARS.

The bottom line for defense budget funding projections will depend on the Biden administration and 117th Congress. The existing Trump future year funding profile projections start with the existing Future Years Defense Program in the FY21 budget request – which is relatively flat – with the alternative scenarios both representing declines in future spending. Given the historical pattern of House reductions to the topline, reduced projections start with the highest number possible. In today's circumstances, the $741 billion for FY21 is the recommended starting point.

Given that that there is an agreed-upon bipartisan budget agreement that sets FY21 defense spending levels at $741 billion already in place, spending will mostly likely match the FY21 requested level. Democrats are also signaling some constraint for future years. Asked specifically if $716 billion was the right number for defense in FY20 and whether future budgets will stay at that level, Rep. Adam Smith said at the second annual Defense News Conference, "I think the number's too high, and it's certainly not going to be there in the future." Defense News reported Smith argued that the debt and deficit situation has to be seriously addressed. It is important to remember, though, that 67.5% of House Democrats and 85% of Senate Democrats voted in favor of the $716 billion for defense in 2019—pretty significant majorities and a considerable testament to the Pentagon leadership.

FIGURE 4: DEBT HELD BY THE PUBLIC UNDER THE PRESIDENT'S BUDGET (PERCENT OF GDP)

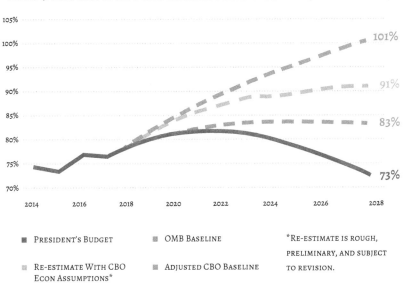

FIGURE 4 ILLUSTRATES THE LEVELS OF PUBLICLY-HELD DEBT UNDER THE PRESIDENT'S BUDGET.

Ballooning deficits are also going to be a major concern in years to come. During the mid-1980s, when deficits were believed to be out of control, Congress passed the Gramm-Rudman-Hollings Balanced Budget Act (GRH BBA), which included control mechanisms to keep spending deficit neutral. This was also the Republican House position during all of the Obama administration. We now have deficits that dwarf the conditions for GRH BBA, and the House Freedom Caucus is likely to eventually return to their roots and lose their amnesia on deficits they acquired at the beginning of the Trump administration. Any deal they would support is unlikely to get Democratic support in the House or get to a 60-vote margin in the Senate. In 2018, Senate Republicans increased their majority but did not get to 60, and they were not willing to remove that 60-vote requirement for policy or spending bills. It does not appear the 60-vote requirement will change in the 117th Congress.

The difficulties cited above were further complicated by the Trump administration's apparent failure to spend domestic discretionary funding at the levels agreed to. For example, FY18 domestic outlays were $72 billion, or 2.3%, lower than the agreed levels. The underspending is greater than the increases agreed to—$60 billion in FY18.

Despite these complicating factors, an agreement on funding—while more difficult to achieve than in the first two years of the Trump administration— did occur. Senate Republicans had 22 seats up for reelection in 2020 and the congressional body politic understood that a functioning government is better than a non-functioning one. After sizable increases in defense spending over the last few years, defense resources will likely be constrained in the immediate future, though the Bipartisan Budget Agreement struck in late 2019 sounded the death knell for the sequester, a definite improvement. Considering the massive amounts of public spending for COVID-19 relief bills, Congress's concerns over deficits are even more likely to resurge and hamper significant defense increases.

How should the Secretary of Defense Respond to Divided Government?

On a positive note, while the 2020 election exhibited a nation that is still sharply divided, it is not split by any antipathy toward the military, as was seen in the 1970s. As Robert J. Art noted in a 1985 *Political Science Quarterly* article, "both the disillusionment with the 'imperial presidency' and the anti-defense mood of the country after Vietnam pushed Congress into ever more detailed scrutiny." If anything, the strains and sacrifices demanded of the military during the past 19 years make defense spending less controversial than it has been in the past. However, deciding on necessary defense spending levels and determining where cuts must be made elsewhere will still involve a spirited debate.

The role of the secretary becomes more important in a budget constrained environment, especially building or maintaining relationships across the aisle with new authorization and appropriations committee heads. Taking a constructive and pragmatic approach to policy discussions on the Hill should further cement such relationships. While not undermining the White House, the secretary's relationships can serve in a critical way to move the process along, be it appropriations or authorization bills or policy issues before other committees. The secretary can serve as a link between congressional committees, the White House Office of Legislative Affairs, and the National Security Council when they might have equity in a particular issue.

The White House tends to have more relationships at a very senior level in Congress, as opposed to committees where the secretary can play the major role. If the White House tends to be more ideological or partisan, the secretary can and should play the role of broker to ensure that national security equities are understood and acceptably met. For example, in cases of veto threats from the White House, the secretary can play an important role in helping resolve issues with the bill. Or, if the veto does occur, the secretary can work with Congress and the White House on a new bill that resolves the issues.

Finally, while the secretary must first and foremost advocate for DoD's equities, they must also recognize that domestic and defense spending are linked, as has been reflected in previous statutory changes to the caps. This does not require a dollar-for-dollar match. The secretary should also ensure an advantageous relationship with the new majorities and leaders and closely coordinate with both the chairmen and ranking members, especially in the Senate. History shows the stronger conference position is one that has both the SASC and Senate support. In conclusion, the positive results for national security in divided government for the past 36 of 55 years will continue for the next two, as long as both the defense and congressional leaders adhere to the bipartisan playbook.

Chapter 4: History of OSD: 1947 to Present

This chapter originates from a paper I wrote in 2010, providing an analytical basis for Secretary of Defense Robert Gates to streamline the Office of the Secretary of Defense (OSD), reduce DoD overhead, and implement needed management reforms. I have updated it multiple times since, including versions for the incoming administrations in 2016 and 2020.

This chapter stresses the historical importance of OSD and its critical role in national security decision-making. At the same time, it illustrates the substantial growth in the size and scope of the functions in OSD since its inception. To enable timelier and more relevant decision-making capabilities, OSD needs a more streamlined approach to avoid what former Under Secretary of Defense for Policy Michèle Flournoy calls "the tyranny of consensus."

This chapter provides observations, details past and recent trends, and offers some suggestions about reducing the managerial overhead of OSD, particularly pertaining to the numbers of Under Secretaries of Defense (USD); Deputy Under Secretaries (DUSD); Assistant Secretaries (ASD); Principal Deputy Assistant Secretaries (PDASD); Deputy Assistant Secretaries of Defense (DASD); Directors of Defense Research and Engineering (DDR&Es); Deputy Comptrollers; Directors for Defense Intelligence (DDIs); and Presidentially Appointed, Senate Confirmed (PAS) roles and Principal Staff Assistants (PSA) and other positions established in law or by discretion of the secretary of defense. Simply enumerating these management labels illustrates the scale of OSD's structure and the resulting staffs and processes that support it.

Since the establishment of the DoD in 1947, the structure and focus of OSD have changed, driven by factors including the focus of the administration in office and the geopolitical circumstances, with the ever-growing staffs to support these real and imputed functions. Numerous discussions and studies have argued for greater narrowing of the functions OSD oversees, i.e., the elimination of lower-priority functions, or a switch to oversight rather than direct management of programs. It is also important that OSD maintains the appropriate relationship with the Joint Staff to ensure civilian control, as there have been periods since the Goldwater-Nichols Act (GNA) of 1986 where that relationship has been tilted too much toward the military. OSD and the JS are not equivalent headquarters. They have distinctly different functions, and the JS is a subordinate office to OSD. Former Chairman of the Joint Chiefs (CJCS) Martin Dempsey, USA (Ret), has pointed out that the JS's specific function is to provide support for the CJCS's independent military advisory role and should not duplicate OSD functions.

A Brief History of OSD Staff Growth

On July 26th, 1947, President Truman signed the National Security Act, legislation that set the foundation for the modern organization of the country's national security apparatus. The 1947 Act founded the National Security Council (NSC), consolidated the War and Navy departments to form the National Military Establishment (NME), which would be led by the secretary of defense, and recognized the U.S. Air Force as an independent service from the U.S. Army. In the intelligence community (IC), the 1947 Act formalized the post of the Director of Central Intelligence (DCI) and transformed the Central Intelligence Group (CIG) into the Central Intelligence Agency (CIA), the nation's first peacetime intelligence agency. Initially, the three secretaries of the military departments – War, Navy, and Air Force – ranked at the quasi-cabinet level. However, 1949 amendments to the original National Security Act established these positions as subordinate to the secretary of defense. Additionally, the 1949 amendments renamed the NME as the Department of Defense.

The 1949 amendments also provided for a deputy secretary of defense (DSD) and stipulated that one of the existing assistant secretaries be designated as the comptroller of the DoD, thus beginning the efforts of OSD to coordinate and unify the entire defense budget. These 1949 amendments to the original National Security Act were all made under the jurisdiction of the newly-established Senate Armed Services Committee (SASC).

THE TRUMAN ADMINISTRATION

Secretary Forrestal formed the first OSD staff with 45 staff officials and three special assistants from the Navy. By January 1948, the OSD staff grew rapidly, increasing first to 173 and then 347 a year later. Until the start of the Korean War, the number in the secretary's immediate office ranged between 350 and 400 employees, of whom 15%-20% were "on loan" from the military. Overall, when including the 1,200 civilians and military assigned to the Joint Staff, three statutory boards (the Armed Forces Policy Council, the Munitions Board, and secretary's organization) numbered about 1,600 total by the end of 1949.

Forrestal originally intended OSD to be an oversight and policymaking organization, while execution and line management would be left to the military departments, the Joint Staff, and the unified and specified commands. It is worth noting that the 1949 National Security Act did not identify "unified and specified commands," which were informal titles. In fact, some of those commands dated back well before the seven in existence then. For example, the Caribbean Defense Command traces its roots to a Marine detachment established in 1905 to guard the Panama Railroad. Today, this is the U.S. Southern Command (SOCOM). The GNA required the combatant commands (COCOMs) to be separate DoD components and identified in law as the unified and specified commands. However, Forrestal quickly realized that OSD could not remain the small policymaking office he originally envisaged, nor could he rely on the military services to cooperate and coordinate voluntarily, as they preferred to resist or evade OSD control. The services' perceived self-interests demanded as much autonomy as possible, and they fought hard to maintain it.

Accordingly, the senior leadership positions on the OSD staff began to steadily expand (as shown in Figure 1). What began as three special assistants, selected by Forrestal during the Truman administration, became the statutorily required positions called Assistant Secretaries of Defense (ASDs). ASDs were the principal staff officials until the establishment of Under Secretaries of Defense (USDs) in 1977. Today, the USDs serve as the most senior type of principal staff officials and most ASDs report to a USD, though this is a more recent arrangement. In 2020, the OSD PAS positions total 32, and 34 if including the secretary of defense and deputy secretary of defense. If you add in all PDASDs and DASDs, the number is considerably larger. There are 250 senior executive service personnel in the OSD senior leadership and usually about nine senior general and flag officers serving in OSD.

FIGURE 1: UNDER AND ASSISTANT SECRETARIES OF DEFENSE IN SELECT ADMINISTRATIONS

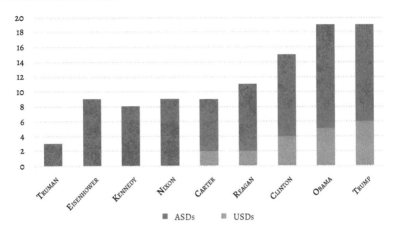

FIGURE 1: UNDER AND ASSISTANT SECRETARIES OF DEFENSE IN SELECT ADMINISTRATIONS

FIGURE 1 PROVIDES A LOOK INTO THE NUMBER OF ASDS AND USDS PER ADMINISTRATION SINCE THE DOD'S INCEPTION.

Since its beginning, staffing at OSD has been adjusted to some degree by nearly all subsequent administrations as strategic, political, and technological conditions changed. The major structural changes made by subsequent administrations are worth a brief review.

THE EISENHOWER ADMINISTRATION

Given his military background and the controversies of the Korean War – including the nation's unpreparedness to fight and the dismissal of General Douglas MacArthur for openly challenging the president – it was not surprising that President Eisenhower entered office with firm ideas about the structure of DoD. Interestingly, Eisenhower also had lingering concerns about the ability of the Joint Chiefs of Staff (JCS) to provide opinions and options to the president that were not significantly muted by the need for service consensus.

Outgoing Defense Secretary Robert Lovett sent a letter to President Truman offering a pragmatic and thoughtful set of recommendations to deal with what he considered a defective organization. Eisenhower agreed with Lovett's views. He believed that the secretary's powers over the military departments and the Joint Staff should be made more explicit and that the secretary should have a military staff in OSD to provide assistance when necessary.

Accordingly, in February 1953, Eisenhower's newly installed defense secretary, former General Motors CEO Charles Wilson, appointed a review committee chaired by future Vice President Nelson A. Rockefeller to review the existing defense organization. The three major problems addressed by the Rockefeller committee were the same ones that had been the focus of the 1949 amendments: the powers of the secretary, the inflexible board structure that was left from WWII, and the functions of the Joint Staff.

The Rockefeller committee agreed to clarify the authority of the secretary over all elements of the department and presented their recommendations to the president as "Reorganization Plan 6." This plan became the basis of the OSD staff restructuring of 1953—approved by Congress—that abolished the Research and Development Board, the Munitions Board, the Defense Supply Management Agency, and the Office of the Director of Installations, instead investing their functions in OSD. Significantly, to assist the secretary in carrying out his new responsibilities and authorities, the 1953 law provided for nine ASDs instead of three and established the general counsel of the DoD as a PAS position.

Following the launch of *Sputnik* by the Soviets in 1957, President Eisenhower announced another defense reorganization during his annual State of the Union Address. Defense Secretary Hugh McElroy started the review, which led to the Defense Reorganization Act of 1958. This act gave Eisenhower much of what he had asked for, mostly centralizing and unifying the structure under the secretary (which included greater control over the service departments).

Other major changes resulting from the act included elevating the status of the Chairman of the JCS (CJCS) and allowing this position to vote in JCS decisions, almost doubling the size of the Joint Staff, prescribing the establishment of unified and specified commands by the president, and reducing the number of assistant secretaries from nine to seven by folding the ASD for Research and Engineering and the ASD for Applications Engineering into the newly-created Director of Defense Research and Engineering (DDR&E). During this period, the OSD and Joint Staff grew nearly 30%, mostly driven by the establishment and expansion of the DDR&E.

THE KENNEDY AND JOHNSON ADMINISTRATIONS

During the Kennedy administration, somewhat surprisingly, there were not many changes made to the structure of the OSD staff, with the notable exception being the establishment of the ASD for Systems Analysis. The major changes that took place during the Kennedy and Johnson years, driven primarily by Defense Secretary Robert McNamara, included the establishment of numerous defense agencies to capture functional synergies. These included the Defense Intelligence Agency (DIA), the Defense Communications Agency (DCA), the Defense Supply Agency (DSA), and the Defense Contracts Audit Agency (DCAA). By the time Secretary McNamara stepped down in 1967, there were seven defense agencies. Today, there are a total of 20 defense agencies and 8 DoD field activities.

With the Vietnam War raging, there was less consideration given to structural changes in OSD. Nonetheless, with the establishment of the ASD(SA), Secretary McNamara and his defense comptroller, Dr. Charles Hitch, took strong steps to exercise greater control over service planning, programs, and budgeting, creating a system that became the Planning, Programming, Budgeting, and Execution (PPBE), a process that survives to the present. McNamara and Hitch used this process to create a much more integrated and structurally common defense budget, despite strong service objections to retain their independence that President Eisenhower had sought to eliminate.

THE NIXON ADMINISTRATION

Following the lead of many past administrations at the start of their term, President Nixon and Defense Secretary Melvin R. Laird commissioned a study in July of 1969 focused on defense organization. This study became known as a Blue Ribbon Defense Panel and included 16 businesses and a variety of professional experts who sought to focus on the structure and functioning of the department. One year later, the panel presented a 237-page report that contained 113 recommendations, of which 15 pertained to defense organization.

The major recommendation affecting OSD grouped the functions of DoD into three categories headed by three deputy secretaries of defense: military operations (including operational command, intelligence, and communications); management of personnel and material resources; and evaluation functions (including financial controls, weapon testing, cost analyses, and the force structures' effectiveness). Additionally, assistant secretaries were to be given to assist the three new deputy secretaries. The study recommended replacing the Joint Staff and operational staffs of the services with an operational staff in OSD under a senior military officer. The commission also advised consolidating all military forces into three unified commands—strategic command, tactical command, and logistics command—under the full control of their commanders and with component commanders serving as deputies.

Very few of these recommendations were ever carried out, but at Laird's request, Congress authorized a second DSD in 1972, although, interestingly, Laird never filled the position. It remained open until filled briefly between December 1975 and January 1977 by Secretary Donald Rumsfeld, who named Robert F. Ellsworth to the position, though his role was limited to coordinating intelligence within the Pentagon. The post was abolished in 1977, giving way to the establishment of the first USDs. Given the complexity and size of today's department, the issue of a second deputy secretary, in some form, has been advocated by the Government Accountability Office (GAO) and a number of other studies.

Congress authorized an increase of ASDs back to nine in December 1971. This change permitted the appointment of Assistant Secretaries for Health and Environment and for Telecommunications. In addition, Laird appointed an Assistant Secretary for Intelligence, replacing the Assistant Secretary for Administration, who was re-designated a Deputy Assistant Secretary and placed under the ASD (Comptroller). This initiated a process in which frequent changes to the assistant secretary roles happened more often as the rank of particular functions increased or decreased and as circumstances and the wishes of the secretaries dictated.

The Carter Administration

When Secretary Harold Brown came into office in January 1977, he entered office with almost eight years of DoD experience, having formerly served as DDR&E and as Secretary of the Air Force. Brown brought with him ideas for streamlining the organization. He felt that the secretary, with 29 major DoD offices and eight unified commands reporting to him, had far too broad a span of control. Both OSD and the military department headquarters were too large and engaged in too many activities that could be handled at lower organizational levels. His past experiences strongly suggested to him that the weapon system acquisition, research, and engineering processes needed closer integration.

In March 1977, after only two months in office, Secretary Brown eliminated the positions of Assistant Secretary for Intelligence and the Director of Telecommunications and Command and Control Systems and merged those functions into the Assistant Secretary for Communications, Command, Control, and Intelligence, ASD(C3I). The intelligence function was later split out by Secretary Rumsfeld, who created the Under Secretary for Intelligence and Security and supporting organization and the ASD for Networks and Information Integration (NII), which would be dual-hatted as the Chief Information Officer (CIO) of the DoD. In another important merger of functions, Brown combined the Office of the Assistant Secretary for Manpower and Reserve Affairs and the Office of the Assistant Secretary for Installations and Logistics.

Brown received congressional approval for a defense reorganization order in April 1977, effectively reducing the number of assistant secretary positions from nine to seven. Following this, Brown asked for legislation to eliminate the second deputy secretary and create two under secretaries—one for research and engineering (assuming the responsibilities of the DDR&E) and one for policy. When this legislation was enacted in October 1977, Brown described the reorganization as intended to "eliminate confusion regarding the distribution of authority below the secretarial level" and "clarify the role of the remaining deputy secretary as the single principal assistant and alter ego to the secretary in all areas of defense management." Note that Secretary Brown viewed the deputy secretary's job as the alter ego for management oversight and not military and operational policy. It should be noted that all management is implemented through the establishment of policy.

These changes settled the role of the deputy secretary and established the role of the new under secretaries of defense, which entailed advising the secretary on functions of military and operational policy and acquisition policy. Brown would be assisted by Deputy Secretaries Charles Duncan—a former President of the Coca-Cola Company who later became Secretary of Energy—and Graham Claytor, who stepped up from his position as Navy Secretary. As for the under secretary positions, President Carter named William J. Perry as Under Secretary for Research and Engineering, and Stanley Resor, a former Army Secretary, as Under Secretary for Policy. The courtly Resor served for two years and was succeeded by the often-assertive Robert Komer.

THE REAGAN AND BUSH I ADMINISTRATIONS

Defense Secretary Caspar W. Weinberger, who spent much of his tenure leading an enormous Cold War-era buildup of armed forces, believed that OSD's organization was essentially sound and required little or no change. The changes he made on his own initiative during his tenure were chiefly in OSD management and processes. However, Congress and the president ushered in fundamental changes through their own initiatives, such as the Goldwater-Nichols DoD Reorganization Act (GNA) of 1986 and the implementation of recommendations from the Packard Commission. These changes were approved by President Ronald Reagan and included in the authorization bills and the separate GNA. These were the most fundamental changes in the organization and power centers in DoD since the National Security Act of 1947 and 1949 and were put in place predominately over Secretary Weinberger's and the then-uniformed military leaders' objections.

Weinberger did usher in some changes during his tenure, including the addition of four assistant secretaries by law and a reshuffling of functions between some of the existing assistant secretaries. One significant change, to accommodate a new appointee, Richard Perle, transferred responsibility for handling European, NATO, and Soviet Union matters from the Assistant Secretary of Defense for International Security Affairs (ISA) to a new Assistant Secretary of Defense for International Security Policy (ISP). Congress enacted explicit statutory requirements for two other positions related to reserve affairs and intelligence, neither of which exist today as ASDs. These functions are today covered by the ASD for Manpower & Reserve Affairs and the Under Secretary for Intelligence and Security.

During this period, Congress and President Reagan implemented a wide variety of new positions. One is the Under Secretary for Acquisition and Technology, which would later become the Under Secretary for Acquisition, Technology, and Logistics in 1999. They also redesignated the USD for Research and Engineering back to the DDR&E and established the ASD for Special Operations and Low Intensity Conflict ASD(SO/LIC). The creation of ASD(SO/LIC) was included in the NDAA – not the GNA – as is commonly reported. The creation of ASD(SOLIC) was included in the NDAA – not the GNA – as is commonly reported. The Reagan administration ended with two under secretaries and 11 assistant secretaries of defense.

There were several major changes to the senior level management of OSD during the administration of President George H. W. Bush in addition to the consolidation of the changes mandated by the GNA – specifically, the expansion of the authority of the chairman of the JCS and the increased size and independence of the Joint Staff. The PAS USD (P&R) and the PAS DUSD (P) – which is sometimes referred to as the PDUSD (P) – were added. However, the Bush administration's Defense Department was largely focused on *Operation Just Cause* in Panama, *Operations Desert Shield* and *Desert Storm* in the Middle East, as well as leading the initial efforts to reduce DoD's size after the collapse of the Soviet Union in 1991.

THE CLINTON ADMINISTRATION

The Clinton administration implemented statutes mandating several senior management changes in the Pentagon – the most significant change was shifting to four USDs and the addition of two more ASDs. Congress approved the creation of the Under Secretary for Personnel and Readiness (P&R) with the National Defense Authorization Act (NDAA) of 1994 and the redesignation of the Defense Comptroller as a USD in the 1995 NDAA.

THE BUSH II AND OBAMA ADMINISTRATIONS

In response to the 9/11 terrorist attack, President Bush's administration established the ASD for Homeland Defense and removed the intelligence function from the ASD(C3I) to create a fifth USD for Intelligence (USD(I)), which was intended to be an office of no more than 100 people. However this office expanded somewhat during the Obama administration. The USD(I) structure was focused on operating agencies such as the Defense Intelligence Agency (DIA), the National Reconnaissance Office (NRO), the Defense Security Service (DSS), the National Geospatial-Intelligence Agency (NGA), and the

National Security Agency (NSA), as well as the coordination required with the new position of Director of National Intelligence (DNI) created from the 9/11 Commission recommendations. The USD(I) was renamed the USD for Intelligence and Security during the Trump administration when the Defense Counterintelligence and Security Agency (formerly the Defense Security Service) was formed and when the security clearance function was brought back to the DoD from the Office of Personnel and Management.

In 2012, Secretary Gates would disestablish the ASD(NII) in an effort to streamline OSD. However, as the CIO position is statutorily required, the majority of the office would be retained under the CIO "hat." Congress would emphasize the importance of the position by establishing, in 2019, a requirement for a PAS CIO. The 2019 law also added additional authorities for the CIO to set IT standards for the DoD and to scrutinize the $40 billion IT budget.

After presenting former Secretary of Defense Leon Panetta with the National Defense Industrial Association's 2015 Eisenhower Award, Maj. Gen. Arnold Punaro, USMC, Ret. then moderated a discussion with Secretary Panetta on the role of the Office of the Secretary of Defense and national security issues.

THE TRUMP ADMINISTRATION

The major DoD organizational changes in the Trump administration were the establishment of the U.S. Space Force (USSF), the Space Development Agency, and the elevation of CYBERCOM and SPACECOM to full combatant commands (COCOMs). In addition, the 2017 NDAA broke the USD (AT&L) into an Under Secretary for Acquisition and Sustainment (A&S) and an Under Secretary for Research and Engineering (R&E) and created the Chief Management Officer (CMO), all effective on February 1, 2018. The FY21 NDAA disestablished the CMO and added two ASDs. Currently, the senior management within OSD is composed of the SD, DSD, six USDs, six DUSDs, 15 ASDs, GC DoD, CIO DoD, IG DoD, DCAPE, DOT&E, three DDR&Es, two Deputy Comptrollers, DCFO, three DDIs, 12 PDASDs, and 46 DASDs of the 48 authorized DASDs and 250 senior executive service personnel. The defense agencies and DoD field activities (DAFAs) directors report to a senior official in OSD as illustrated in Chapter 19, Figure 2. The under secretaries of defense as principal staff assistants (PSAs) listed below and in bold report to the secretary of defense and deputy secretary of defense. Those listed directly under the USDs report directly to the USDs themselves. The following includes the changes from the FY21 NDAA that were enacted at the close of the Trump administration. The FY21 NDAA eliminated the Chief Management Officer and the CMO organization and created two new Assistant Secretaries of Defense in statute. One was added and one was required to be one of the existing ASDs.

Reporting to USD (Policy):

1. DUSD for Policy
2. ASD for Indo-Pacific Security Affairs
3. ASD for International Security Affairs
4. ASD for Strategy, Plans, and Capabilities
5. ASD for Special Operations and Low-Intensity Conflict

6. ASD for Homeland Defense and Global Security

7. ASD for Space Policy

Reporting to the USD (Research & Engineering):

8. DUSD for Research and Engineering

9. DDR&E for Research and Technology

10. DDR&E for Modernization

11. DDR&E for Advanced Capabilities

Reporting to the USD (Acquisition & Sustainment):

12. DUSD for Acquisition & Sustainment

13. ASD for Acquisition

14. ASD for Nuclear, Chemical, and Biological Defense Programs

15. ASD for Sustainment

16. ASD for Industrial Policy

17. ASD for Energy, Installations, and Environment

Reporting to the USD (Personnel & Readiness):

18. DUSD for Personnel & Readiness

19. ASD for Health Affairs

20. ASD for Readiness

21. ASD for Manpower and Reserve Affairs

Reporting to the USD (Intelligence and Security):

22. DUSD for Intelligence and Security

23. DDI for Warfighter Support

24. DDI for Counterintelligence, Law Enforcement, and Security

25. DDI for Collection and Special Programs

26. DDI for Intelligence and Security Programs and Resources

27. Director of National Reconnaissance Office (a PAS)

28. Director of National Security Agency (a military dual-hat with CYBERCOM)

29. Director of Defense Intelligence Agency

30. Director of the National Geospatial Agency

31. Director of the Defense Counterintelligence and Security Agency

Reporting to the USD (Comptroller)/Chief Financial Officer (CFO), DoD:

32. DUSD (Comptroller)

33. Deputy Comptroller for Program and Budget

34. Deputy Comptroller for Budget and Appropriations Affairs

35. Deputy CFO

Reporting to the Secretary and Deputy Secretary as PSAs:

36. Chief Information Officer, DoD

37. ASD for Legislative Affairs

38. General Counsel, DoD

39. Director of CAPE

40. Director of OT&E

41. Inspector General, DoD

42. ATSD for Public Affairs

43. Director of Net Assessment

Each senior official oversees a staff, mainly civil servants as well as military officers detailed from their service. Authority is exercised through the PSAs (in some cases, through their subordinates). This is also true for the ASDs under the PSA USD(P). It should be clear that a non-PAS official is not equivalent to a PAS official. A review of Figure 2, "OSD Personnel by Office," reveals the staffing supporting the executive leadership. Figure 3 illustrates the OSD's makeup in further detail.

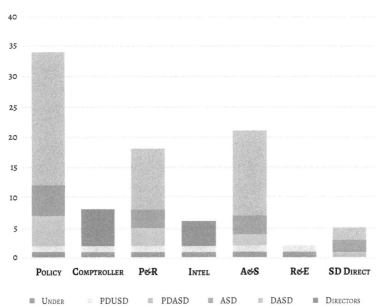

FIGURE 2: OSD SENIOR MANAGEMENT PERSONNEL BY OFFICE - 2020

FIGURE 2 ILLUSTRATES THE ORGANIZATIONAL MAKEUP OF THE DoD OFFICES.

FIGURE 3: OSD PERMANENT AND TEMPORARY MANPOWER SEPTEMBER 2020
(MILITARY AND CIVILIAN)

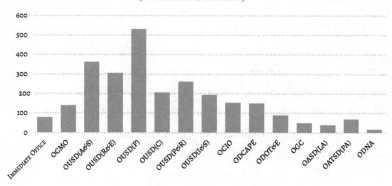

FIGURE 3 SHOWS THE STAFF LEVELS FOR BOTH THE MILITARY AND CIVILIAN OFFICES IN OSD.

Figure 3 shows a total of 2,655 people supporting the existing structure. Of note, these figures do *not* include the Joint Staff, the DAFAs' headquarters staffs, COCOM staffs, or the staffs from the military departments. The 450 detailees are not counted on the chart in Figure 3. Contract support is also not counted on the chart. It is more useful, then, to look at the costs. OSD spends about $350 million per year on civilian pay, the military departments spend about $90 million a year on pay, and OSD spends about $850 million on outside support and studies.

In 2018, Congress, believing the DCMO had not been successful as a Level III position, further enhanced the role by changing the designation to "CMO" and elevating it to a Level II, the same as the deputy secretary and secretaries of the military departments. They also provided the role with some specific additional statutory authorities in the management area over and above those when the DCMO was established in 2008.

However, by 2020, Congress's disappointment in the office was clear; the FY19 NDAA mandated an independent review of the position. This review, conducted by the Defense Business Board, recommended the disestablishment of the CMO while enhancing the role of the Deputy Secretary as the Chief Operating Officer

(COO). In 2020, the SASC and HASC both included provisions in their versions of the FY21 NDAA to abolish the CMO. Now law, the CMO position was abolished and emphasis was placed on enhancing the Deputy Secretary of Defense's role as the Chief Operating Officer of the DoD.

Conclusion

Dozens of studies and reviews over the years have included numerous recommendations for streamlining OSD to make its output timelier and more relevant and to stress its oversight role versus one of direct management and running programs. Further, numerous studies have recommended instituting tight controls on OSD and headquarter head counts. As evidenced by the ever-increasing size, scope, and complexity of OSD, few of these controls have either been fully implemented or survived over time when they were.

In summary, OSD is a constantly evolving entity, which is appropriate, as threats and priorities change. In terms of PAS officials, the number of OSD officials has grown from four in 1949 to 34 today, including the secretary, deputy secretary, six under secretaries, six deputy under secretaries, 15 assistant secretaries, and five other PAS officials (such as DoD general counsel). Moreover, this leadership and agency growth has been accompanied by substantial growth in lower-level positions, such as deputy assistant secretaries which total 46 today, as well as more than 240 senior executive service (SES) and nine general officers and flag officers. These numbers have been matched with considerable growth in staff support at all levels as well, which is one of the reasons Congress directed cuts. As a result, there are a number of OSD core functions that are understaffed while others are overstaffed.

Throughout this process, OSD must be intentionally cautious of not falling victim to Flournoy's "tyranny of consensus," and instead champion dialogue, debate, and even disagreement to produce the most effective solutions. OSD cannot afford to simply remain in line with the bureaucratic norms if it truly desires to successfully adjust its focus and governance structures toward great power competition, especially with China.

Chapter 5: Roles and Responsibilities of the Secretary and Deputy

This chapter originated under President George W. Bush as a memorandum to the Secretary and Deputy Secretary of Defense at the time. Understanding the roles of and relationship between the two highest-ranking officials in the Pentagon is critical to successful decision-making and to assembling a leadership team. As such, this memorandum has been provided to every secretary and deputy since its 2001 inception, including the incoming Trump administration in 2016 and the incoming Biden administration in 2020.

In a machine as large as the U.S. government, there are many moving parts that must operate in sync to work successfully. As with any machine, manuals abound—not only for how it should function as a whole, but also for the relationships between the parts. For the DoD, much has been written about its warfighting and interagency missions, its relationship with the private sector, and the roles of senior civilian and military officials. There is, however, a less scrutinized—but no less important—set of relationships between the Pentagon's senior civilians themselves. These relationships are less grounded in statute or regulation and more based on precedent, often stemming from past experiences and the personal relationships of their predecessors. Some come to the Pentagon with considerable prior exposure to DoD and a solid grasp of its practices. Others arrive with little to no DoD experience and instead rely on their prior experiences in the private sector. The difficulty of adjusting depends on the job and one's ability to work in a team and split responsibilities. There is no more serious and sensitive a division of labor than the one that exists between the secretary and the deputy secretary of defense.

This chapter offers thoughts on what a useful relationship and functional distinction might be between the SecDef and the deputy (also referred to as the DepSecDef or DSD). Of course, it has to be understood that one size does not fit all, and that except in the rarest of occasions, the SecDef is unlikely to pick their own deputy, though they can certainly provide a highly influential recommendation. Hopefully, these two senior leaders will have known each other, and their backgrounds and skills will be complementary rather than duplicative or fully distinct. But whether prior experience provides a useful balance or not, it is worth considering what roles these two officials might fill and how their functions might best be synced to work successfully.

This discussion examines the various relationship models used by the secretary of defense and deputy secretary over the last 40 years. Based on their preferences, strengths, and backgrounds, different secretaries have asked that their number two serve as an alter ego, or a management-oriented Chief Operating Officer (COO). A division of labor that should prove more durable leans toward the latter, using the private sector model as the best relationship to guide the department.

In most general terms, the secretary should function as "Mr./Ms. Outside," leading matters primarily related to the department's interaction with the world beyond the department, including all military and intelligence operations, engagements with the White House, Congress, foreign governments and foreign policy, the media, and the public. The DSD should be "Mr./Ms. Inside," with a focus on management, budgets and programs, personnel, equipment and acquisition, training and readiness, installations and real estate, and the overall functioning of the military services and the numerous defense agencies.

The scope of responsibilities and the frequently brutal time frames required for decisions in the world of national security inevitably means that the secretary leads and the deputy manages. The secretary sets the vision and the deputy executes it. This relationship reflects the division of labor in some major corporations in the roles played by Chief Executive Officer (CEO) and COO. As the CEO of one major corporation once commented, "My job is to focus on where we're going; the [COO's] job is to watch how we're doing." The size of the department and the relevant statutes governing it make a similar division of responsibilities essential for DoD.

Every SecDef faces the challenge of ensuring their deputy is maximizing their strengths and experiences while creating a high degree of managerial complementarity. It is essential that the secretary and the deputy are in lockstep on the mission of the department. As simple as this sounds, its importance cannot be overstated. Clarity and simplicity are hard to achieve, and if lacking, their absence leads to complexity that fuels greater bureaucracy, internal lag, and increased costs. In the view of most, the department's mission is warfighting—protecting, defending, preempting, and, when necessary, engaging the enemy directly. Over time, the numerous demands placed on the Pentagon have caused it to lose some of its focus on this core function and allowed other priorities to supersede it.

When contemplating how to employ the deputy in the model of a COO, the secretary must consider the sheer size of the Department of Defense. The Pentagon's operating budget is larger than the annual revenue generated by any Fortune 500 Company. At $634 billion, the 2020 DoD base budget is 21% larger than the annual revenue of Walmart ($524 billion), the top-ranked company on the Fortune 500 listing, and more than six times larger than Boeing ($93.4 billion), one of the top-ranked aerospace and defense firms (although two-thirds of its revenue is in commercial aircraft). The sheer size of the DoD dwarfs any corporation, even those with the largest product lines and widest international presence. The demands of even the most active board of directors, shareholder community, and senior corporate management team pale in comparison to the demands placed on the DoD by the Congress, the president, other administration leaders, the media, and the voting public. Even if the deputy secretary's chief management functions were not mandated by statute, having someone serve as the DoD COO is a managerial necessity, and the deputy's seniority makes the position a natural fit.

Congress has underscored this approach by disestablishing the Chief Management Officer position it created in 2018. The FY21 National Defense Authorization Act (NDAA) provides support to enhance the deputy's role as COO of the DoD.

Maj. Gen. Arnold Punaro, USMC, Ret. discusses the organization of the Office of the Secretary of Defense and the new National Defense Strategy with Secretary of Defense Jim Mattis. Mattis served in the position from 2017-2019.

QUALIFICATIONS FOR THE DEPUTY POSITION

Since the appointment of Steven T. Early as the first deputy secretary of defense in May 1949, over 30 individuals from various backgrounds and formative experiences have held the position. Early, for instance, was a professional newspaper reporter covering the Navy Department who had been an essential political advance man for Franklin D. Roosevelt during his vice presidential campaign of 1920. Later, Early helped Roosevelt with media relations and briefly served as President Truman's press secretary. Following Early, deputies came mostly from the legal and investment banking professions and, like Early, tended to have strong political and media connections. Deputy Secretaries Robert A. Lovett, Robert B. Anderson, Thomas S. Gates, and Roswell Gilpatric all represent this early trend.

Over the past 30 years, by contrast, defense deputies have tended to come with backgrounds dominated by senior government service, congressional staff experience, and notable national security expertise in the academic community.

Of the 11 individuals who have served during this time frame, only three have had significant business backgrounds (Shanahan, England, and Atwood), with most others having served as congressional staff or academics (White, Hamre, de Leon, Wolfowitz, Lynn, Carter, Work, Norquist, and Hicks). Most had previous service in the Pentagon or elsewhere in government in senior positions, usually at the under secretary level (Taft, Perry, Deutch, White, Hamre, de Leon, Wolfowitz, England, Lynn, Carter, Work, Norquist, and Hicks). This previous Pentagon and government experience has been the key credential equipping the more recent deputies to manage the Pentagon and its numerous complex processes and organizations. This experience has also been helpful to the deputies overseeing efforts to convert the president's and secretary's strategic vision and directions into programmatic and budgetary reality. Accordingly, the deputy does not have to be a "titan of industry," such as David Packard, co-founder of Hewlett-Packard (HP). Assigning a role for the deputy is less about where the deputy came from than about a division of labor and commander's intent.

Options for the Secretary-Deputy Relationship

Since the 1947 National Security Act created the DoD, defense secretaries and their deputies have primarily had one of three relationships, listed in further detail below.

1. Alter Egos

Some secretaries and deputy secretaries have functioned rather symbiotically as alter egos. They do not clearly distinguish their roles; they prioritize and assign issues on an ad hoc basis instead. Occasionally both the secretary and deputy secretary will weigh in on the same issue, using their unique perspectives to provide guidance. A successful alter ego relationship existed between Secretary Robert McNamara and his first Deputy Roswell Gilpatric. In that famous instance, Gilpatric was among the first opposing an airstrike and advocating a blockade, a position McNamara ultimately embraced.

One may argue that this arrangement gives the department two secretaries for the price of one; in reality, it may confuse a bureaucracy that desperately needs routine management, clarity, and structure to function properly.

The alter ego relationship has usually arisen in the past because a deputy secretary either has not had the background or does not have the willingness to operate as a true deputy. In the corporate world, this is often the case for the COO, who is seen as the heir apparent and is groomed to be the future CEO; however, this is not the expectation for the deputy, whose position requires a different skill set than the secretary. Since the establishment of the Department of Defense, only six deputies have become the defense secretary (Lovett, Thomas, Gates, Carlucci, Perry, and Carter), with Carlucci and Carter only assuming the secretary role after leaving the department and returning years later. Accordingly, the deputy position has not been historically used for succession planning. Since the alter ego model requires the two personalities to be a natural fit—a rare occurrence that cannot be relied upon to happen regularly—it too often leaves major challenges unaddressed by either the secretary or deputy. Because of this, the alter ego model has mostly proven unsuccessful. However, lightning does occasionally strike twice, and recent administrations have seen the deputy spend a larger percentage of time in the alter ego role, most notably with Ash Carter.

Arnold Punaro, as Chairman of the Secretary of Defense's Reserve Forces Policy Board, confers with Deputy Secretary of Defense David Norquist, the Chief Operating Officer of the department, in a session on key issues impacting the Guard and the Reserve. As Deputy Secretary of Defense, Norquist's role is mostly internal management, including the budget, acquisitions, personnel and readiness, and chairing the Deputy's Defense in Management Group (DMAG), one of most senior governing bodies in DoD.

2. POLICY-ORIENTED

Some deputy secretaries have functioned primarily in a policy role. Paul Wolfowitz and Ash Carter are probably the clearest examples. These deputies played a prominent role in the policy development and operational oversight processes of the department, and they tended to work closely with the Under Secretaries of Defense for Policy and Intelligence, the Chairman of the Joint Chiefs and the Joint Staff, the combatant commands (COCOMs), and defense agencies and DoD field activities (DAFAs) involved in intelligence collection and analysis. This can lead to a significant role with both the National Security Council and the Department of State. In the past, this was a relatively common role played by Deputy Secretaries Lovett, Gilpatric, Vance, Nitze, and Rush.

Although on the surface this relationship seems equivalent to the management-oriented deputy secretary, in practice it is not. In the modern era with the 24-hour news cycle, a Congress somewhat more inclined to insert itself into immediate issues of foreign and military policy, and the more visible role required of the secretary as the face of the Pentagon, the secretary simply cannot delegate many matters of policy to a deputy. Furthermore, because of these demands, the secretary simply does not have the time to accept a larger role in regular management.

The president and cabinet, the Congress, and foreign leaders will not accept the deputy standing in for the secretary in policy discussions just because the secretary has decided to attend to matters of management. The secretary retains national command authority, which also cannot be delegated to the deputy. Accordingly, using a policy-oriented deputy secretary increases the workload of a secretary who must then both externally lead and internally manage the department. Issues where the secretary does not have sufficient time to manage inevitably end up being either poorly managed or fester as unmanaged distractions. Thus, having a policy-oriented deputy is inadvisable.

3. MANAGEMENT-ORIENTED

Some deputies have a strong orientation toward management. This has typically been the case for deputies with successful business backgrounds. Robert Anderson, Charles Duncan, David Packard, Don Atwood, Gordon England, and most recently Patrick Shanahan exemplify this type of deputy secretary. Although he did not have a business background, Frank Carlucci earned a reputation as a "tamer of federal bureaucracies" for his highly active and successful role in department management while serving as deputy secretary. Management-oriented deputies have focused on the business processes of the Pentagon to make sure that those processes deliver the required military capabilities. To provide this management expertise, these deputies work closely with and oversee Cost Assessment Program Evaluation (CAPE), the Chief Information Officer (CIO), Director of Administration & Management, the Under Secretaries for Acquisition & Sustainment, Research & Engineering, Procurement & Readiness, and Comptroller, nearly all of the DAFAs, the military departments, and the National Guard Bureau.

Over the past three decades, deputies with strong national security credentials, based in either the academic world or congressional staffing, have also provided significant managerial oversight to the department (such as Hamre, White, de Leon, Lynn, Carter, Work, Norquist, and Hicks). Although many of these deputies have also brought considerable policy experience to the job, they have focused their attention on management while occupying the deputy's chair, ensuring the various functions and organizations of the department translated the vision and guidance of the president and secretary into strategies, programs, and budgets.

The deputies with business and national security credentials most closely align with the statutory and directed responsibilities of the position itself. Deputies with these backgrounds can substantially reduce the burden placed on the secretary. With a management-oriented deputy, the secretary can focus almost exclusively on their national security responsibilities and the directives from the president and Congress. Although the secretary will certainly remain the defense official with ultimate responsibility for the efficient functioning of the department, a deputy who keeps a keen eye on the Pentagon's institutional processes will lift a significant daily burden from the secretary's shoulders.

Deputy Secretary of Defense Patrick Shanahan and Maj. Gen. Arnold Punaro, USMC, Ret. discuss the role of the Deputy Secretary of Defense as the day-to-day senior management official of the department. Shanahan served as Deputy from 2017-2019 and as acting Secretary of Defense in 2019. Shanahan once referred to DoD as the Department of "Getting Stuff Done."

INTERACTIONS WITH THE UNIFORMED MILITARY

As part of their focus on national strategy, defense policy, and ongoing operations, the secretary must maintain a very direct relationship with the Chairman of the Joint Chiefs of Staff, who serves as the principal military advisor to the president and secretary. While not in the chain of command, the chairman supervises the planning and execution of all military operations and is the "military face" of the department.

Within the Joint Staff, the secretary inevitably interacts directly with the Intelligence Directorate (J-2), Operations Directorate (J-3), and the Strategic Plans and Policy Directorate (J-5). The secretary also deals directly with the combatant commanders on operational matters as the only civilian member of the chain of command below the president. The secretary's relationship with their uniformed commanders and staff are of great importance both in their role of establishing a forward-looking vision and in an advisory capacity to the president.

The deputy needs to focus on daily, routine management of the department, and should relate through the chairman and vice chairman to the J-1 (Personnel), J-4 (Logistics and Supply), J-6 (Command, Control and Communications), J-7 (Training and Doctrine), and particularly the J-8 (Force Structure, Resources and Assessments). The DSD exercises these responsibilities through the Deputy's Management Action Group (DMAG), the Joint Requirements Oversight Council (JROC), and other decision bodies that focus on the manning, training, and equipping of military forces.

Given the secretary's responsibilities in representing the department to the president and other important outside groups, having a close and functional relationship with the senior military leadership is important. Within the Pentagon, this means a solid relationship with the chairman and the service chiefs, the other members of the Joint Chiefs. The OSD staff can provide the secretary with the civilian perspective from those areas where they have supervisory responsibilities, but in those places where the chairman has a staff element without an OSD counterpart, such as J-3, the secretary will need to receive advice and insight from the chairman. Since the vice chairman generally focuses on the institutional processes of DoD, the relationship between the vice chairman and the deputy secretary should be similarly close in areas involving departmental management.

THE BOTTOM LINE

The deputy secretary should, by and large, remain "bolted to the desk" and ensure the Pentagon's day-to-day functions are being completed and should make as many necessary decisions on behalf of the secretary as the secretary has clearly delegated to him or her. The USD for Policy should represent the department in the myriad meetings outside the building, and the deputy should only travel outside Washington on those occasions where his or her personal presence at a facility or location will serve to enhance understanding of the functions being performed, or to get a firsthand feel for the implementation of management decisions that have been made. He or she should also employ the time-tested "management by walking around" technique in the Pentagon and be totally accessible on the SecDef's schedule. The secretary and deputy should never be gone from the building at the same time on travel outside Washington. Unfortunately, unless actively managed, this can become an all-too-frequent occurrence. Figure 1 provides a breakdown of the different duties allocated toward the SecDef and DepSecDef positions.

Figure 1: Notional Division of Labor: SecDef & DepSecDef

SecDef (SD)	Both	DepSecDef (DSD)
	SD Lead	
National Strategy	Sr. Military Personnel	Budget&Programs Preparation
Military Strategy	Sr. Civilian Personnel	Financial Management
Strategic Vision	Public Affairs	Business Management
Global Posture	Missile Defense	CAPE
Operational Planning	Interagency Coordiantion	
Senior Level Reviews	Major Cmte Presentations	Acquisition Working Group
	WMD	Acquisition
	Wounded Warrior	Acquisition Reform
POTUS Briefings	Legislative Issues	Requirements Generation
NSC Briefings		Requirements Validation
Deployment Orders		
Operations		Civilian Personnel Policy
Special Operations	DSD Lead	
Military Personnel Policy	DoD Reorganization	Medical Programs and Policy
Intelligence Programs	Budget Presentation	Information Networks
Intelligence Community		Network Security
SRO Process	Homeland Defense	System Integration
	Defense Science Board	Installation Management
Strategic Forces	Quality of Life Programs	Readiness
Active/Reserve Balance	Detainee Policy	Foreign Weapons Sales
		Infrastructure
Defense Policy Board		Defense Industrial Base
Major Media Events		Defense Business Board
		Reserve Forces Policy Board

FIGURE 1 ILLUSTRATES THE DIVISION OF TASKS BETWEEN THE SECDEF AND DEPSECDEF.

Even when the backgrounds of the secretary and the deputy have a high degree of similarity, their roles—as defined by the secretary—need to be complementary, not duplicative. As many past secretaries have discovered, managing the largest enterprise in the world is a daunting task. This will be the case even when the strategic environment is reasonably peaceful and quiet; it will be a much greater challenge when it is not, as has been the case for several decades now. Typically, the most successful SecDef-DepSecDef relationships occur when the secretary focuses their efforts externally while the deputy focuses internally. No statute or regulation directs this distinction, but the record of the past six decades strongly suggests it is the most successful.

Chapter 6: Creating and Monitoring the Secretary's "Battle Rhythm"

Like the previous chapter, this material also dates back to the administration of President George W. Bush. Since then, it has been provided to every chief of staff—not only the secretaries of defense, but also the deputies—as well as to many of the officials who work in their orbit. It is designed to help them organize and operate one of the most demanding and critical functions in the Pentagon, where the "tyranny of the daily inbox" can suffocate needed focus on mid- and long-term problems.

Every secretary of defense enters office with a set of goals to be accomplished in concert with administration priorities. Some secretaries have made their goals institutional in nature, like Secretary Rumsfeld's National Security Personnel System. Others' goals have centered on core national security interests, such as Secretary Gates's top three priorities upon entering office: "Iraq, Iraq, and Iraq." Secretary Mattis had three main priorities, and Secretary Esper kept these and added one more. But the wise secretary of defense will recognize that no matter their dedication to accomplishing their defined goals, "the enemy has a vote," meaning inevitable unforeseen challenges will arise during their tenure. Moreover, the secretary must recognize that much of their time will inevitably be spent dealing with the international security environment, domestic political issues, internal management firefights, and the daily problems that flow from leading the administration of the world's largest, busiest, and most complex organization: The Department of Defense. Therefore, the secretary's immediate office staff should help them to:

- Identify goals and set top-level priorities, then assign the planning, implementation, and accomplishment to a clear lead office and individual. Then they must track progress with regularly scheduled meetings with the secretary and by employing dashboard metrics.

- Pivot the secretary to crisis management as emergencies arise, recognizing that the secretary of defense must keep the country safe, protect our core interests, and look after the troops.

- Recognize when an emergency has supplanted all other goals and must receive the secretary's nearly undivided attention.

- Set and communicate the expectations of the secretary for decision making, correspondence, staff meeting attendance, and other senior-level engagements.

HEADACHES

Every secretary of defense enters office with the expectation that he or she will be able to "tame the beast," certainly to a degree previously unseen. As the inevitable challenges and distractions surface, there will be a tendency to believe they are unique to the current time. However, in actuality, the sources and varieties of headaches a SecDef faces are usually timeless, often predictable, and have likely occurred with similar amplitude and frequency during past administrations. Because of this, front office staff should be able to get ahead of them. With certainty, many major headaches will arise in areas including:

- Continuation of, and changes to, budget issues and a continually revised Future Years Defense Program (FYDP).

- Serious cultural problems, including sexual assault and general officer misconduct.

- Long-term leadership vacancies and overall staffing issues.

- Management challenges, including growth in overhead and compensation coupled with reductions in force structure and readiness.

- The unsustainability and unaffordability of the fully burdened and life-cycle costs of the all-volunteer force (AVF), including health care, retirement, pay and benefits, antiquated personnel management policies, and support costs for the total force, both active and reserve.

- The Congress, White House, and National Security Council (NSC), each with its own agendas, priorities, expectations, and demands.

- Maintaining message discipline and message direction to both internal and external audiences.

In addition to these potential major issues, the secretary should also be prepared to address and solve potential operational headaches, including matters such as:

- Bringing the various conflicts across the Middle East to a responsible end.

- Until then, triaging the cuts from the major global thorns, including Iran, Syria, Iraq, Yemen, Libya, North Korea, Turkey, and inevitably others.

- Maintaining friendships with NATO and other close partners as they deal with their own challenges and internal debates.

- Managing renewed great power competition with a rising China and a revisionist Russia.

- Averting sudden shocks from major terrorist acts or cyberattacks.

Looking at the secretary's list of policy and operational headaches, a few perennial sources of trouble seem to be their fundamental causes. If these areas are properly monitored, front office staff may be able to stop a crisis before it gets started in earnest.

SecDef's Key Areas of Focus

1. Looking after the Troops

The DoD hosts the world's largest bureaucracy. Like most bureaucracies, the system functions properly until it faces some element of stress. The front office can predict personnel crises based upon which parts of the personnel system will soon face an unusual level of stress. For example:

"You go to war with the Army you have, not the Army you might wish you have." The military and civilian leadership seriously underestimated the duration and nature of the wars in Iraq and Afghanistan. This has usually been the case in post-World War II conflicts and contingencies. In addition, for the first time since the Korean War, post-surge stabilization and counterinsurgency operations in Iraq and Afghanistan have required a significant mobilization of Guard and Reserve units. Adjusting to new circumstances is not one of the strengths of a bureaucracy, and the personnel, acquisition, and logistical systems were quickly out of sync with the battlefield. This led to Secretary Gates's famous statement that "the troops are at war, but the Pentagon is not." Bureaucratic processes and procedures, as well as the pace under which they proceed, are likely unsuited for the stress and dynamic conditions of a major conflict.

a) Managing the Defense Health Care Establishment: Iraq and Afghanistan produced the most significant number of combat casualties since Vietnam, although not on the scale of Vietnam. While the peacetime military health care system could deal with civilian medical issues and routine training casualties, the large influx of combat casualties created by the wars caught the U.S.-based military treatment facilities flat-footed. Counterintuitively, this was the result of improved medical technology; since the immediate battlefield care was superb, lives were saved that would have been lost in previous conflicts, leading to more patients in the facilities.

This was compounded by the fact that the system was significantly reduced at the end of the Cold War. For example, the conditions some wounded warriors faced at Walter Reed were deplorable, and because no one in a leadership position had appreciated that the military medical system would be incapable of receiving and treating a large influx of newly-wounded troops, no one appreciated the problem until the press broke the story. This was all the more distressing because, while the medical treatment in the field was both revolutionary and spectacular, the major military treatment facilities (MTFs) were simply unprepared and seemingly unaware that they were not facing business as usual.

As has been seen over the past decade, the cost of defense health care is the fastest-growing segment of the defense budget, having increased from $30 billion in 2006 to nearly $50 billion in 2019. In the early 1990s, it was believed that the Pentagon, unlike the experience of the country as a whole, had been successful in restraining health care costs. However, the savings were largely masked by the post-Cold War drawdown and the closure of numerous MTFs. This area promises to be a major challenge going forward, and as the defense budget comes under more pressure and receives more scrutiny, it will have to receive considerable senior-level attention.

b) *Military Families:* It remains important that military family programs are maintained and adequately funded. Secretary Esper specifically emphasized the need to improve programs on spousal employment and childcare. If the DoD falls short in any of these areas, the inevitable political storm will ensnare any secretary and dominate their agenda for weeks, if not months.

c) *Disability Health Evaluation System:* Although jointly held with the Department of Veterans Affairs (VA), this remains one of the critical points of failure for both departments that garners a large amount of political attention. Despite recent pronouncements that the backlog has been diminished, concerns linger that problems will persist. In addition, there remains much to be done regarding the compatibility of the DoD and VA health record systems. Many veterans report delays with processing their cases because these two systems remain quite distinct, despite assurances that they will be better integrated.

d) *Sexual Assault and Harassment:* Despite the department's focus on preventing sexual assault, sexual harassment, and retaliation against those who report, the statistics have not improved, and in some cases, have gotten worse. As many senior leaders have said, this is a readiness issue, as well as a major problem for the ability to recruit and retain the best people. Congress remains hyper-focused on this issue and has repeatedly put forward the proposal to take commanders out of the chain of command on sexual assault cases. The front office needs to recognize that they have not been winning this fight and that it needs to do much more to address this unacceptable problem.

e) *Military Suicides:* Iraq and Afghanistan produced more and faster rotational deployments than our troops have ever experienced in the nation's history. The stress of those deployments had a psychological impact on our troops, leading to increased rates of suicide. While this crisis is not so neatly preventable as some of the others, it, too, could have been foreseen or at least identified and addressed earlier. After a decade of veteran suicides exceeding 6,000 per year, the daily suicide rate of 20 former service members has now become a nationally publicized issue.

It is clear that Post-Traumatic Stress Disorder (PTSD) and Traumatic Brain Injury (TBI) will stress the system external to DoD for decades, even though most of those who suffer will have long left active duty. The basic trend in each of these cases—and what makes future cases predictable—is that a new phenomenon impacting the troops led to a surge in the use of a support system that was not accustomed to, or designed for, surge operations. If the front office can identify in advance what parts of the personnel support system will face new stress, it can predict where crises will occur and avert them ahead of time.

Given fluctuations in force structure, the recruiting, separation, and retirement processing systems will face stress, as will programs for transition to civilian life. Despite significant efforts, the transition programs are still not optimized for the anticipated battle rhythm outside DoD. The secretary is likely to face calls in the future for a greater focus on helping veterans transition and find employment, and depending on the seriousness of the crisis, the clamor could build to a level that distracts from other priorities.

2. PROTECTING U.S. INTERESTS

The secretary will always be held responsible for assisting in the identification and understanding of, as well as the securing of, our vital interests. The Pentagon will routinely play a major role in preparing the National Security Strategy and will itself craft a National Defense Strategy and a National Military Strategy. All of these documents need to be clear in identifying threats and establishing priorities for funding.

Across the government, and outside the government, there are many voices stating numerous views on what the interests of the nation are and what they should be. It serves the interests of the DoD and the nation well when the department engages in these discussions and shapes these views. Accordingly, the secretary's staff can protect their leader from an ambush by staying attuned to emerging issues and threats to U.S. interests before they become an item of widespread concern.

3. WINNING WARS

The secretary's staff needs to help win any ongoing war. (In this case, a "war" is any U.S. troop deployment involving combat.) If the war cannot be won, the secretary's staff needs to help them recognize the likely outcomes and develop options for responsibly extricating the United States from the conflict. For wars that have not yet begun, the secretary's staff should help the secretary figure out if they can be won, and how. If they cannot be won, the staff should advise how to avoid them without weakening U.S. prestige.

Besides the obvious and negative moral implications, any war the U.S. enters but does not win will become an albatross for the secretary, exemplified in the way the Vietnam War haunted Secretary McNamara throughout the remainder of his life. General Andrew Goodpaster, a close aide to President Eisenhower and former Supreme Allied Commander, developed the fundamental question that should always be asked: "Does the commitment of American troops contribute to the well-being of the American people?" As General Goodpaster put it: "If the answer is 'no,' then solve the issue through other means. If the answer is 'yes,' then start developing deployment plans and options. If the answer is 'we aren't sure,' then come back and brief me when you are."

4. HUMANITARIAN CRISES

Serious humanitarian crises, whether foreign (such as the Ebola outbreak in West Africa) or domestic (such as Hurricane Katrina in the Gulf Coast region and now more recently, the COVID-19 pandemic), require a response of some kind, and the secretary's staff should anticipate the demand for military resources and action. Regardless of the national response plan and any Department of Homeland Security (DHS) articulated role, major disasters incapacitating governments at any level across multiple states can only be handled by DoD.

This is not a statement of policy but a simple fact. In almost any emergency action, only the DoD has the full capability to stage and sustain a deployment and to provide assets for such specialized assistance as security, supply distribution, and medical care. No other agency of government can provide such comprehensive response on such short notice.

It is worth noting that as of November 2020, there are still over 40,000 members of the National Guard and Reserves activated to support various COVID-19 efforts. Moreover, the Chief Operating Officer of Operation Warp

Speed is a four-star Army general, further demonstrating the military's support during domestic crises.

5. Major International Developments

Americans' appetite for overseas deployments has diminished following conflicts in Afghanistan and Iraq. The secretary's staff must help decide when and where to intervene and to be ready to explain any decision to the public when it is inevitably questioned. Actions in Syria, Yemen, and Iran are recent examples of this.

6. Strengthening Alliances and Expanding Partnerships

The secretary must nurture American friendships, both with our older European allies and with newer Asian partners. Their staff must recognize and avert the weakening of friendships and provide advance warning of public breakups whenever possible. During the Obama administration, it was consistently stated that "building partner capacity" was a major objective, but the efforts to do so proved to be more meager than hoped and largely unsustainable. Clearly, more work needs to be done in this area. During his tenure, Secretary Mattis emphasized the importance of strengthening alliances and expanding partnerships, even designating it as a top priority. This is also a clear goal of the Biden administration. Additionally, the Pentagon can further develop these relationships through training missions, combined operations, and foreign military sales. The Pentagon needs to be constantly looking for new opportunities and monitoring difficulties with ongoing efforts.

7. Displaying Strength to Potential Adversaries

Americans don't like their country to appear weak. Therefore, the secretary's staff must help develop options when near peers, adversaries, or provocateurs take unexpected action. The U.S. response to Chinese expansion of its Air Defense Identification Zone (ADIZ) is an example of a well-executed response, but the responses, or lack thereof, to North Korea's recent missile advancements and the latest Russian cyberattacks have drawn criticism from many corners.

8. THE BODY POLITIC

External forces will always be a ready source of ambushes, since the Congress and media both have incentives to harshly criticize the executive branch. The secretary's staff must help predict and even avoid an ambush by cultivating good sources in the following communities:

a) Congress: Members of Congress personally benefit from investigating controversies, and the hearing calendar is an excellent indicator of what big stories might break in the coming weeks. Having a few staff sources in leadership, on key committees, and with senior members can also provide critical advance leads and tips. Thus, the Office of the Secretary of Defense for Legislative Affairs team must constantly be on a proactive footing to search for this intelligence, and the front office must work closely with the Assistant Secretary of Defense for Legislative Affairs (ASD(LA)), meeting regularly outside of normally scheduled staff meetings to better understand what is happening in Congress vice waiting for the incident or information to come to them and then react. Establishing a program that routinely brings important members of Congress to the Pentagon for meetings and briefings can be enormously valuable in providing important information while gauging the congressional mood.

b) The Media: A political crisis doesn't really become a crisis until the media gets involved. Usually, media sources are better for alerting the front office to "second stage" ambushes—after the secretary has already faced an initial ambush when a story breaks. Like the legislative affairs office, the front office staff must take a proactive approach with the Assistant to the Secretary for Public Affairs to better understand what is happening so they can better inform and advise the secretary. And it must be noted that there are significant events happening in the nation and the world that are not captured by today's version of the *Early Bird Brief* (the day's major news feed). A routine and frequent interaction with the media outside of the formal press conference can pay major dividends. Gen. Colin Powell demonstrated this during his tenure as Chairman of the Joint Chiefs and was most successful in using the media as both a sounding board and an "early warning" mechanism. In contrast, Secretary Mattis's Pentagon was often criticized for its infrequent interactions with the media; Secretary Esper directed a return to traditional practices, which has not been universally accepted by the press. There will be emphasis on the new Secretary of Defense Lloyd Austin to significantly increase interaction with the press.

c) GAO and Private Watchdogs: While they produce many more reports and studies than there are actual crises, many reports are certain to grab the public's attention. Good watchdog contacts provide a ready sense of what issues are likely to come up in their investigations, and how that information can occasionally flag a crisis before it becomes an ambush.

MANAGING THE PENTAGON

Although the routine management of the Pentagon should be delegated to the deputy secretary of defense (DSD), the secretary has to maintain a relatively detailed general knowledge of how their goals and priorities are being translated into policies, programs, and budgets. Policies of great importance to the secretary would include:

1. PROMOTION POLICIES AND SELECTING SENIOR MILITARY LEADERS

In an era where units are becoming smaller and more modular, each one can get significant visibility in the 24-hour news cycle. The secretary needs to consider how far down he or she wants visibility of significant command selections: certainly, at the four-star level, probably for certain three-star positions, and likely for some two-star positions. This is one of the most important processes and functions the secretary has. Picking the right military leaders should not be left to just the services or the JCS. Only a civilian—i.e., the president—can nominate and subsequently appoint military leaders, subject to advice and consent of the Senate.

2. SEPARATION POLICIES DURING DRAWDOWNS AND FORCE-STRUCTURE CHANGES

With the wars across the Middle East having wound down, and major budget pressures certain to continue during this period of rising deficits and increasing national debt, what force reduction approaches will be used? Will it be simple discharge (determined how and by whom?), early retirements (for how many and at what level?), and/or separation incentives? A good roadmap exists from policies implemented during the Cold War drawdown, which involved much larger numbers. This should be a useful benchmark for any similar reductions in the future.

3. BUDGET PRIORITIES AND GUIDANCE

There is always the need to establish priorities that the various budget and resource allocation communities can grasp and act on. In too many instances, the program and budget guidance provided in the upper-level policy documents, such as the Strategic Planning Guidance (SPG) and the Defense Planning Guidance (DPG), are simply too vague for the program and budget communities to translate into priorities and budget lines. The secretary needs to clearly articulate where more or less resource risk is to be taken between readiness, force structure, infrastructure and bases, quality of life programs, science and technology, or procurement and modernization.

The Pentagon resource community, led by the comptroller and the Cost Assessment and Program Evaluation (CAPE) director, is entering a period where tradeoffs will be necessary due to a budget-constrained environment. This requires an entirely new set of procedures and skills radically different from ones associated with those for adding resources—the environment that the current generation of resource officials have experienced. Difficult decisions will have to be made across services, operational areas, and functional areas. The winners will be ungrateful, and the losers will be livid. Numerous appeals will be made to the secretary. In order to make these tough decisions, the secretary must understand the context in which they were originally introduced and the degree to which they reflect current priorities. Decisions often have to be made and then reinforced against the considerable resistance of bureaucratic inertia. As one former Pentagon resource official noted, "what appears to be a decision is actually an invitation to further discussion."

ORDER OF BATTLE

In order to help the secretary accomplish his or her goals and work through emergencies, the front office must have a battle rhythm to organize the workflow of the office. The front office is a gladiator arena of screaming needs, continual crises, and taskers issued with responses due yesterday to the White House or Congress. The office must categorize and prioritize its tasks if it is to accomplish anything meaningful during a secretary's tenure. Failing to do so leaves the secretary exposed to spending the majority of his or her time simply hoping to stave off failure. The issues that need the secretary's attention need to be placed into three broad areas depending on their immediacy:

1. THE CLOSE-IN BATTLE

The wild dogs are already inside the fence every day in the front office, but sometimes their bark is worse than their bite. The front office must determine which tasks and crises demand the secretary's immediate attention.

2. THE NEAR BATTLE

Besides the baying hounds of the close-in battle, the secretary also has barbarians at the gates—the near battle. These are the future crises that are almost upon us but have some degree of maneuver room attached to them, allowing the secretary's staff to put them off or head them off. The decision to put off the near battle until it becomes the close-in battle reflects a judgment that the crisis is unlikely to grow worse with the passage of time. The decision to head off a near battle—to engage immediately—reflects a judgment that the crisis will certainly worsen with time and resolving it early will take less of the secretary's effort. Any battle that can be put off without harming the secretary's strategic efforts or making more demands on the secretary in the near term should be delayed. There are too many other crises that cannot be delayed or deferred, and putting off a crisis whenever possible will give the secretary a chance to pursue other goals.

3. The Far Battle

These are the crises that haven't yet materialized. The secretary's staff can identify these under the broad rubrics designated in the "Headaches" section. Although the temptation is always to ignore the far battles until they come near or even close-in, depending on their magnitude, the secretary's staff can save many headaches—and the secretary's legacy—by wisely counseling to get ahead of certain far battles before they become all-consuming, in terms of time and energy.

4. Goals

Last, yet most important, are those proactive items the secretary chooses that are not foisted upon him or her by outside sources or antagonistic events. The secretary's staff must help develop these goals, keep an eye on them, and work them to completion if possible. The secretary's staff must also help realize when their goals are overcome by external events and must be set aside, or significantly modified for the good of both their legacy and the country's security needs.

During a speech to a national security audience, Maj. Gen. Arnold Punaro, USMC, outlines what he describes as the "close-in battle," the "near battle," and the "far battle" for those engaged in national security decision-making. Punaro taught a popular graduate-level course on national security decision-making at Georgetown University for 10 years.

Anatomy of a Fiasco

A fiasco occurs when an emergency is allowed to proceed from far battle, to near battle, to close-in battle without meaningful action taken by the secretary until the crisis becomes an all-consuming issue. Near the end of Secretary Rumsfeld's tenure, the Iraq War assumed this character. Even if a secretary survives a fiasco, the experience exacts great costs in time, energy, and political capital that could have been dedicated toward other goals or priorities.

Fiascos almost always begin as looming, difficult far battles. The secretary and their staff need to size up such battles to gauge the probability that they become fiascos. Not all far battles can grab the nation's attention to the degree that qualifies as a true fiasco, so the secretary's staff must help separate potential disasters from simple annoyances that won't last in the breakneck pace of the modern news cycle.

As a fiasco is proceeding from a far battle to a near battle to a close-in battle, the sooner the secretary's staff can identify and zero in on it, the better the secretary will be able to address the issue itself, and the sooner it will depart the news cycle. A secretary who continues to reserve their time and effort for other issues while a fiasco is unfolding will find themself pilloried and their other efforts largely ineffectual. Therefore, it is vitally important for staff to help recognize when a fiasco will dominate all other aspects of the secretary's agenda and reserve time and energy for overcoming that challenge before turning to other items.

RECOMMENDATIONS

The secretary's front office must be organized to manage the flow of work up and down the chain of command from the secretary. It must alert the secretary to the headaches and battles described above and help pivot whenever necessary. It must keep close track of the secretary's proactive goals to ensure they are not lost in the oncoming waves of crises that greet the office each day. And it must continually—perhaps twice daily—take stock of what issues confront the secretary as close-in, near, and far battles to determine where the hours of their day can be most productively invested.

The only way the staff can do this is by being as inclusive as possible. They, too, need to be proactive rather than reactive with their time. They need to be able to reach into the Pentagon's massive depths and pull out the right information in a timely fashion. In order to do all of this, they need to construct their day around the basics: knowing what is happening on the Hill, in the media, the services, and the agencies. This requires a ruthless use of the "0730 meeting" and not just reading the *Early Bird Brief* – but being one too.

It also requires meeting with the key USDs and ASDs on a regular basis to understand the latest and greatest issues that they are dealing with and to see those coming from across the horizon. More importantly, it requires that the staff not be consumed with being the SecDef's shadow, i.e., following them around to endless meetings. Rarely should all staff be in a meeting together with the secretary. Thus, this requires a strong division of labor to ensure the store is being watched and minded for information. Someone needs to be reviewing the packages, and someone needs to be managing the issues. Regarding those assigned as military staff, their role needs to be somewhat restricted, the general rule being that anything political is not to be placed in their inboxes. Figure 1 provides guidance to assessing and managing the three battle rhythms.

FIGURE 1: CONCEPTUAL SUMMARY

Close-in Battle	Near Battle	Far Battle
SOURCES	SOURCES	GOALS
- Crises - Orders - Decisions and guidance - Correspondence	- The Congress - The Media - The Watchdogs - The Administration - Internal Management Demands	- What are they? - Who is tasked? - Progress? ISSUES - Looking after troops - Protecting interests - Politics
QUESTIONS	QUESTIONS	QUESTIONS
- Order of priority among other close-in battles? - Is this really a close-in battle, or a near battle? (Or is this not really a priority, but someone is pretending it is?) - Does the secretary have to do this? - Is this a fiasco that is going to devour the secretary until it is given undivided attention?	- Will this problem get worse or stay the same if we leave it alone? - If we head this battle off, can we address it with less time and effort? - What are the chances this becomes a fiasco if left unaddressed? - Can the secretary delegate this battle?	- What parts of the troop support system are going to be stressed in ways they haven't been before? - What future operations or foreign developments are going to create risks and opportunities for the secretary and the country? - What will be the hot-button political issue?

FIGURE 1 DEFINES IMPORTANT QUESTIONS AND PRIORITIES FOR EACH "BATTLE RHYTHM."

ORGANIZATIONAL THOUGHTS

The secretary must establish an immediate office that serves their unique needs, fits their specific background, and complements their individual expertise. Current corporate approaches are for small immediate offices, but the focus assigned to those in the office is more significant than their numbers. While building their office, the secretary should consider the following steps:

1. **Select a capable, versatile, and experienced chief of staff (C/S) and senior military assistant (SMA).** Defense secretaries generally have a civilian chief of staff and a senior military assistant. Each fills an important role in assisting the secretary to manage both the department and its key external stakeholders.

   In general, the civilian C/S communicates the secretary's wishes and coordinates the actions of the senior Pentagon civilians, particularly the Senate-approved political appointees. In addition, the C/S serves as an important conduit to Congress and other major agencies of the executive branch, such as the National Security Council (NSC) staff and the Office of Management and Budget (OMB). This suggests that an effective C/S arrives with experience in those organizations, particularly Congress. Former holders of the office include Jeremy Bash (who had previously served as Secretary Leon Panetta's C/S at the CIA), Eric Fanning (who went on to be the Secretary of the Army), and Robert Rangel (who would become Senior Vice President for Government Relations at Lockheed Martin).

   The SMA, by contrast, should be a senior military officer with credentials and experience dealing with the service chiefs, the Joint Staff, and the combatant commanders, since a military officer more comfortably connects with these key internal constituencies.

   A three-star military officer has filled the SMA position since Secretary Cohen started the norm in the late 1990s, but both one- and two-star officers have held it in the past, including Brig. Gen. Colin Powell, the SMA for Sec. Casper Weinberger. In general, an officer selected for this key role is one widely seen as destined for a fourth star, such as General Powell, Gen. James Jones, Adm. William Owens, Gen. Brantz Craddock, and Gen. Peter Chiarelli.

The SMA cannot be asked to partake in political situations or issues. They are best to work the orders book and military-specific issues, be the primary conduit with the JCS, and ensure that the secretary's travel is properly planned and executed. One must be careful not to go beyond these areas.

2. **Select a small number of civilian assistants to the SecDef, reporting to the SecDef through the C/S. The assistants can each be assigned a focus on the following functional and operational areas:**

    a. Personnel and Readiness

    b. Congressional Relations and Public Affairs

    c. Budgets, Programs, and Acquisition

    d. Operations and Intelligence

    e. The Executive Branch and Interagency Process

    f. Personnel Recruitment (in coordination with White House Liaison Office)

These assistants should coordinate with the major staff elements and senior leadership within DoD, and their major function is to keep the secretary informed of activities in their areas, and to clarify the secretary's preferences and policies to the senior leaders in the department with whom they routinely interact. This takes individuals with great functional knowledge, experience, and significant diplomatic skills. Additionally, the individuals should understand that they are staff and not decision-makers.

These assistants will be engaged in the close-in battles, coordinate as needed the near battles, and ensure appropriate thought is given to the far battles. In any battle, however, their full allegiance is to the secretary.

3. **In the old days, the special assistants worked for both the secretary and the deputy secretary.** It would be advisable to return to that practice. This is better than a deputy with his or her own separate staff. The titles would be "Special Assistants to the Secretary" and "Deputy Secretary of Defense." I should note that this has been one of my longstanding recommendations that has garnered very little support over the years, despite having been the norm for many decades in the past.

Chapter 7: The Service Secretary – Service Chief Relationship

In a hierarchical organization like DoD, the tone that leadership strikes often influences the culture of those below them. Therefore, a close professional relationship between the service secretaries and the uniformed service chiefs is critical to similarly close relations between the civilian-dominated service secretariat and the military staff. This chapter is derived from a memorandum written at the beginning of the Obama administration for the incoming service secretaries and chiefs. It has been delivered, with updated information relevant to the issues of the day, to every subsequent service secretary and chief upon selection for the posts over the last 12 years.

Dr. Lewis Sorley, in his biography of Gen. Creighton Abrams, wrote that upon becoming the chief of staff of the Army (CSA), Abrams observed, "The secretariat and the Army staff have never been a team. There is petty jealousy, there is bickering, and I want to smooth out the relationship and get a joint effort going between the secretariat and the Army staff, and I want it [to be] one team." Abrams had considerable experience in the field as a troop commander, but he had also spent extensive time at the upper levels of the Department of the Army, most notably a decade earlier as the Army's vice chief of staff. His comment illustrates how deciding the working arrangements and the division of labor between the secretary and the service chief has been an enduring challenge.

Even before the formal creation of the DoD in 1949, there was a tension—sometimes creative and sometimes less so—between civilian service secretaries and their uniformed counterparts. The civilian secretary is, by statute and tradition, the senior official in the military department, but within the department itself, the service chief tends to be better known. Due to a service chief's lengthy career of service, this person has deep knowledge about the history, recent actions, and issues impacting the department as a whole.

The Goldwater-Nichols Act (GNA) of 1986 had several objectives, and one of the more significant ones was to clearly define the roles and responsibilities of the service secretary and the service chief. It did so in a manner that moved the service secretary from being the perceived senior of the two to being designated the de jure senior and was quite contentious. Indeed, the GNA not only gave the service secretary direct responsibility for all of the major functions performed by the service department, but it also essentially reduced the service chief's role to three functions: serving as a member of the Joint Chiefs of Staff (JCS), presiding over the service military staff, and assisting the secretary in ways designated by the civilian head of the department. This did not quite mean that a service chief's job became "other duties as described," but it was certainly viewed by some as close.

It is, therefore, worth addressing the nature of the relationship between a service secretary and the service chief, such as the Chief of Staff, Army (CSA); the Chief of Staff, Air Force (CSAF); the Chief of Space Operations (CSO); the Chief of Naval Operations (CNO); and the Commandant of the Marine Corps (CMC). Establishing a close, functional relationship between the service secretary and the service chief must be a major objective of the individuals occupying these positions, as it is essential to creating a similarly close relationship between the civilian-dominated service secretariat and the uniformed military staff.

General Abrams recognized the problem of competition and conflict during his tenure as the Army vice chief from 1964 to 1967. During this time, Abrams served two secretaries of the Army, Stephen Ailes and Stanley R. Resor and, according to Dr. Sorley, had good relationships with both. Obviously, he did not feel these positive personal relationships were reflected between the Army's civilian and military staffs, suggesting how difficult personal relationships are to translate across a large institution.

Achieving the desire of General Abrams to create "one team" is a worthy objective for any of the service departments, but one that takes constant attention by the services' secretaries and chiefs. When service headquarters staff suspect distance or friction between the top two leaders, the possibilities of dysfunction grow rapidly. This can impact and seriously handicap the service efforts across the Pentagon and even with Congress.

If this were an easily addressable problem, it would have been resolved in past decades, but its endurance suggests the scale of the challenge. So, the issue becomes, what are some steps that can be taken to minimize, if not fully eliminate, this tension that is seemingly chronic within the service departments?

Much of this discussion will focus on the tenure of John O. Marsh Jr., the longest-serving Army secretary in American history. Although he was largely underappreciated during his tenure by the Army at large, he was well respected and appreciated by the senior leaders who served under him in the Pentagon during his near decade in office. All who worked with Marsh, both civilian and military, from both the Army secretariat and the Army staff, felt he set an example for service secretaries worthy of emulation.

Secretary Marsh was a former Virginia congressman who had served on the House Appropriations Committee and became close to then-House Minority Leader Gerald R. Ford, even though Marsh was a Democrat—a little-known fact that he preferred to receive little mention once he left politics. Marsh's relationship with Ford assumed greater significance when Ford became president in 1974. Shortly afterwards, Marsh became counselor to the president with cabinet rank. He departed government when President Carter was elected but was appointed Secretary of the Army by President Reagan and became the only political appointee to serve throughout the entire Reagan administration.

For many at the time, Marsh compared unfavorably to the younger and more visible Navy Secretary John F. Lehman. But structurally, Marsh labored under a significant limitation compared to Lehman, one encapsulated by Marsh's second chief of staff, Gen. John Wickham, who once commented, "Three Marine divisions are in the law. Six hundred ships are in the Republican platform. Eighteen Army divisions ain't in nothing."

Wickham's comment reflected the Reagan administration's focus on nuclear weapons (the SALT and START agreements), strategic strikes (restarting the B-1 bomber program), and a 600-ship Navy for extending presence and deterrence in a domain where the U.S. was dominant. Understandably, the capital-intensive budgets of the Air Force and Navy grew more than the Army's during the first years of the Reagan buildup, but the Army did not do badly either. By the end of Secretary Marsh's tenure, which lasted as long as three CSAs, the Army had regained its footing through the fielding of the famous "Big Five"—the M1 tank, the Bradley Fighting Vehicle, the Apache and Blackhawk helicopters, and the Patriot air defense missile. This was quite an achievement, made possible by a secretary who loved the Army and three chiefs of staff who worked closely with him. When Navy Secretary Lehman left office in 1987, some admirals boycotted the ceremony. When Secretary Marsh left office in 1989, his ceremony was attended by nearly all who had served with him in the Department of the Army.

BACKGROUND

The position of Secretary of the Army is a descendent of the Secretary of War, one of the original cabinet offices in President Washington's administration. The first Secretary of War was retired Gen. Henry Knox, who had been a key subordinate to General Washington during the Revolutionary War. Accordingly, the Army secretary is, by executive order, the third most senior official in terms of succession in the modern DoD, behind only the secretary and deputy secretary of defense. The War Department originally oversaw naval affairs as well. However, within a few years Congress split the Navy off into its own cabinet-level department with its own secretary. Over time, the Navy Department contained both the U.S. Navy and the U.S. Marine Corps. In 1947, the Army Air Corps was separated from the Army and became the U.S. Air Force, with its own military department containing a secretariat and military staff. These separate organizations were all reconnected and subsumed by the DoD after World War II.

For four decades after the consolidation into DoD, the secretaries and chiefs occasionally clashed over who had priority in which area of responsibility. Finally, the legal scope and authority of the service secretaries was clarified and greatly expanded by the 1986 Goldwater-Nichols Act (GNA). In essence, this key legislation made clear that secretaries are the senior officials in the service departments with direct responsibility for numerous functions as outlined in Title 10 Section 7013 of the U.S. Code: recruiting; organizing; supplying; equipping, including research and development (R&D); training; servicing; mobilizing; demobilizing; administering, including the morale and welfare of personnel; maintaining; construction, outfitting, and repair of military equipment; construction, maintenance, and repair of buildings; and procurement of property.

In addition, the secretaries under the provisions of the GNA have "sole responsibility within their departments" for the following: acquisition; auditing; comptroller's office (including financial management); information management; inspector general's office; legislative affairs; and public affairs.

When GNA became law, this magnification of the secretaries' position was a surprise to many, as there had been occasional talk of eliminating the service secretary positions. It is generally thought that the service chiefs were expecting such an outcome. But the GNA changes were consistent with a major objective of Senator Goldwater, Senator Nunn, and Representative Nichols to "strengthen civilian authority." Many in the armed forces are still surprised to learn that the service secretaries actually have such broad, specifically prescribed, statutory authority, whereas the chiefs do not. Under the provisions of the GNA and Title 10 of the U.S. Code, the chiefs' role within the service departments is essentially to "preside" over the military staffs and basically "perform such other military duties, not otherwise assigned by law, as are assigned to him by the president, the secretary of defense," or the service secretary.

This relative narrowing of the role of the chiefs was driven by another major objective of the GNA: to improve military advice to the president. The GNA sought to do this in many ways, including the placement of greater weight on the role performed by the service chiefs as members of the JCS. Indeed, the law provides more detail on the joint responsibility of the service chiefs than it does on the actual management of their services.

Because of the desire to expand civilian control and to reduce the size of the service headquarters, several functions that had previously been the primary responsibility of the chiefs moved from the military staffs to the secretariats. The most significant changes were in the areas of financial management (FM), where the service comptrollers and budget offices within the military staffs were converted to deputy positions within the office of the assistant secretaries for FM, and the elimination of the deputy chiefs for research, development, and acquisition, with that position also being relegated to a military deputyship in the office of the civilian assistant secretaries for research, development, and acquisition.

Historically, the civilian secretariats had served what was essentially an oversight role, whereas the military staffs had provided the detailed expertise. The rough breakdown was that secretariats traditionally focused on the external, such as relationships with the Hill, the Office of the Secretary of Defense (OSD), and other government agencies, whereas the military staffs looked more at the internal relationships with their commands and the Joint Staff. Given that GNA gave the secretaries authority to assign staff responsibilities, the civilian leaders did so following the principle of placing responsibility where it could best be exercised.

As the GNA was being debated in Congress, it was generally opposed by the sitting service chiefs, including Gen. Wickham (although reforms along the lines of GNA had been supported by his predecessor, Gen. Edward C. "Shy" Meyer). Army Secretary Marsh kept his views to himself, although he did privately support language in the GNA requiring the CSA to keep the secretary fully informed of planned military operations, a reflection of Marsh's displeasure at being out of the loop on the Grenada operation in October 1983. The fact that Marsh and Wickham joined together and embraced the changes after the law passed was an important factor in their relatively smooth implementation within the Army. There was a similar smoothness in the other service departments, including the Navy—which had historically opposed any efforts to lessen the perceived autonomy of the service chief.

The bottom line from this period was that although the reforms brought with them the very real possibility of bureaucratic turmoil, they were enacted across the Pentagon with only minor disruption. The major issues to be worked out involved those offices where former deputy chiefs—the comptroller and R&D positions—became deputies to assistant secretaries. This was particularly true in the dispute over how to categorize the preparation of the service program objective memoranda (POM). Were they an exercise in financial management or strategic planning? The secretariats generally argued the former and the military staffs the latter. This disagreement notwithstanding, the new military deputies learned quickly to be "responsible to the secretary and responsive to the chief," and this became common practice.

SOME LESS-HAPPY HISTORY

Some Army secretaries worked well with their CSAs. Some did not. The relationship Secretary Marsh had with his chiefs was based fundamentally on familiarity and respect. General Wickham had worked with Marsh years earlier as the executive officer for Secretary James Schlesinger when Marsh was the

Assistant Secretary of Defense for Legislative Affairs (ASD(LA)). The ASD(LA) experience had also schooled Marsh in understanding the different levels of expertise and ability that existed between civilian and military officials, insights unquestionably magnified by Marsh's service as a Lieutenant Colonel in the Virginia National Guard.

Marsh gave his service chiefs great latitude, but he did insert himself into a divisive area: general officer (GO) selections and assignments. Marsh wanted to be *informed* of GO assignments for the Brigadier and Major Generals, but he wanted to be *involved* in the selection of division commanders, a group which generally formed the pool from which the future senior leaders would emerge, such as Maj. Gen. Gordon Sullivan who was commanding the First Infantry Division in 1987. Marsh was more involved with the appointments of the three- and four-star generals; however, in nearly every case, Marsh backed the recommendations of his chiefs of staff, recognizing that their insights were likely more familiar than his, although the disparity diminished as Marsh's tenure continued through the 1980s.

This had an enormous effect, not only on the shape of Army leadership but also on the trajectories of individuals. Take, for example, Gen. Colin Powell, whose career would have likely been curtailed within the Army following a less than complimentary officer evaluation report he received while serving as an assistant division commander. Despite this, Powell's superiors, including Gen. Carl Vuono and Secretary Marsh, selected Powell for other key assignments in the Pentagon working for Defense Secretaries Weinberger and Carlucci—assignments that paved the way for Powell to be the National Security Advisor for President Reagan and Chairman of the Joint Chiefs for President George H.W. Bush.

The relationships Secretary Marsh had with his chiefs, however, were very different from those of his predecessor, Clifford Alexander. Alexander was more interested in the implementation of the all-volunteer force (AVF) concept and the advancement of social and equal opportunity programs. Both issues were certainly of great importance as the Army, along with the other services, was struggling with recruiting when Alexander assumed office.

At the same time, the services were wrestling with strained race relations, reflecting those in broader society. However, Alexander did not seem to be concerned with the general condition of the Army itself, which was once famously described in testimony by his second Chief of Staff, General Meyer, as a "hollow army." Accordingly, the personal relationship that evolved between Alexander and his first Chief of Staff, Gen. Bernard W. Rogers, started poorly and steadily degenerated, while the relationship with his second Chief of Staff, General Meyer, never advanced beyond cordial.

Rogers, who himself had advanced numerous innovative changes to the Army's personnel system and culture while a division commander and later as the Deputy Chief of Staff for Personnel, felt that Alexander's proposals were too ambitious in both content and timing. It was rumored that their relationship had become so contentious that the door connecting their offices had been locked, although it was unclear from which side.

The fissure between the two culminated in a public split over the pending reassignment of Gen. Sam Walker, the commanding general of NATO's Allied Land Forces Southeast, headquartered in Turkey. This NATO position was being eliminated, and Walker needed to move to another four-star position, with the obvious assignment being commanding general of Army Forces Command in Atlanta. Alexander, however, opposed the appointment and instead insisted the post go to another officer, Lt. Gen. Robert M. Shoemaker. Walker was close to Rogers, having succeeded him as the West Point Commandant of Cadets, and he came from a distinguished Army family. Walker's father, Gen. Walton Walker, had commanded the Eighth Army in Korea during the early phases of the Korean War before dying in a jeep accident. This made the Walkers only the second father-son team to achieve four-star rank. Moreover, the younger Walker was highly regarded throughout the Army. But, because of Alexander's opposition,

Shoemaker got the job and the promotion, leaving Walker to accept either an early retirement or a demotion. He opted for the former.

The discord did not go unnoticed by those around them. It is generally thought that President Carter's decision in 1979 to appoint General Rogers as the Supreme Allied Commander, Europe (SACEUR) was motivated to some degree by a desire to move him out of the Pentagon and end his feud with Secretary Alexander.

Although he was never known to publicly comment on the Walker episode, Secretary Marsh was, no doubt, fully aware of it; after retirement, General Walker became the superintendent of the Virginia Military Institute, where Marsh served on the board of trustees. Alexander's last and Marsh's first chief, General Meyer, who assumed his position largely because of the Walker incident, no doubt played a significant role of informing Marsh of the importance of the chief's role in selecting and matriculating GOs.

When the Clinton administration took office in 1993, it was nearly a year before senior civilians were appointed for the military departments. During this period, the service chiefs all spent several months as acting service secretaries. Inevitably, the civilians in the service secretariats, with no senior civilian leadership, were reluctant to express positions on matters such as programming and budgeting—a reluctance that resulted in the military staffs dominating routine processes and making many necessary decisions that could not be deferred. This created an awkward situation when the newly-confirmed service secretaries began to arrive in mid-1993, followed in most instances by the arrival of the newly-confirmed assistant secretaries months later. In the Army, the new assistant secretaries (ASAs) arrived with the belief they needed to reestablish the civilian control they felt had badly eroded during the H.W. Bush administration. Two problems quickly emerged.

First, the services' POMs were nearly finished and close to submission to OSD. Given that developing these POMs had been uncommonly difficult, due in no small measure to the very late release of Secretary Aspin's Bottom-Up Review

(BUR), which had required the revisitation of many previous decisions—most significantly the BUR's reduction of the Army to 10 divisions, whereas the draft POM had been developed assuming 12 divisions. Numerous other changes and revisions had also been made hurriedly, and new priorities were established, basically by the Army staff.

The new ASAs wanted to review and reconsider all of these decisions. Army staff took this as not just a challenge but an outright rejection of months of work that was scheduled for submission to OSD in a matter of days. The ASAs, for their part, were unwilling to "rubber stamp" a POM that, in their view, locked in for five years (the time frame of a POM) decisions they had minimal input on, especially since the POMs would likely last beyond their tenure in office. This resulted in immediate friction between the civilian secretariat and the military staff.

Second, the Clinton ASAs, particularly the ASA for Manpower and Reserve Affairs, took office with a two-item agenda: to expand military service to all people no matter their sexual orientation and to expand military occupational specialties (MOS) and units to all genders. However, despite the correct vision these goals embodied, the way in which they were implemented ruffled a number of feathers. For example, the "Don't Ask, Don't Tell" policy that emerged was largely crafted outside the services, and many in uniform believed it had been forced on them. Combined with the friction over the POM submission, these actions created considerable disharmony across the military departments.

This led to a cold and distant relationship between the Army secretary and chief that never warmed. However, at the staff level, conditions improved considerably, mainly driven by the efforts of the Assistant Secretaries for Research and Development and for Installations and Logistics. One of these officials, Assistant Secretary Michael Walker, would eventually become the Under Secretary of the Army, an appointment that further calmed some previously troubled waters.

Nonetheless, the poor start of the relationship between the Army secretary and chief, and the poor initiation of a collaborative partnership between the secretariat and Army staff created unhelpful conditions that took years to heal.

LESSONS TO BE LEARNED

A strong, close partnership between the service secretary and the service chief is essential. If a close partnership cannot be established, then a cordial and professional one is the minimum relationship necessary to avoid harmful friction and dysfunction.

A good relationship should be built on several elements:

1. Recognition of the Hierarchy

From the beginning, the service chief must recognize the secretary's seniority as leader of the department. Moreover, the service chief must understand that their position serves an advisory role to the secretary and they possess little direct authority. In order to ensure successful cooperation, the chief needs to initiate the development of a positive relationship with their secretary. Surprisingly, this can prove difficult depending on the background, expectations, and agenda of the secretary.

2. Visible Teamwork

In the 1980s, Secretary Marsh and General Wickham made it a point to occasionally walk the halls together and drop in on various staff sections within both the secretariat and the Army staff. This would most often occur when recognition and appreciation were merited for a particular staff action that had furthered the Army agenda, particularly during program and budget deliberations. Fulfilling General Abrams's "one team" aspiration will only happen if the team leaders are themselves seen as one team.

3. Collaboration on Many Fronts

It is essential that the department establishes priorities that are emphasized both internally and externally. The secretary and chief can have their own unique goals, but their overall purpose must be in sync. For example, Secretary Marsh designated annual "Army themes," which included a variety of important issues and topics within the Army community. Themes ranged from morale (i.e., Yorktown: Spirit of Victory) to the Constitution (e.g., in 1987 to celebrate the bicentennial signing) and included other matters such as Army families, Army values, and physical fitness. While General Marsh spearheaded these ideas, Chief Wickham endorsed and echoed them wholeheartedly as well. In a hierarchical organization like the military, joint efforts are much more likely to be well received and fully implemented.

In another example of successful secretary–chief collaboration, Secretary Marsh and Chief Wickham coordinated to foster dialogue with lawmakers. Secretary Marsh hosted a weekly breakfast with members of Congress to discuss key issues. During these meetings, Chief Wickham would often join the conversation by entering through a connecting door, seemingly by accident. This allowed Secretary Marsh and Chief Wickham to raise key issues with important congressional personalities in a less formal setting while working as a team.

DEFINE INDIVIDUAL ROLES

While the chief's responsibilities within the service are largely "as assigned" by the secretary, there should be agreement on what these will be. In general, the chief should focus on internal service issues and ask for support from the secretary where needed. Meanwhile, the secretary should focus on external issues and ask for support from the chief as required.

The chief will always have greater understanding of the service's current conditions, ongoing operations, recent history, and senior personalities, as well as the strategic and joint environment because of his or her position on the JCS. The chief needs to ensure that the secretary is appropriately aware of the strategic environment and the operational response to it. The military staff has intelligence and operations sections that do not exist in the service secretariat, making this provision of information a necessity.

Conversely, the secretary needs to work to ensure the chief is aware of major external dynamics, particularly those occurring in OSD, the broader executive branch, Congress, and the public at large. The secretariat contains the Assistant Secretaries for Financial Management and Acquisition and Logistics, the Chief of Legislative Liaison, and the Chief of Public Affairs (legislative liaison and public affairs being led by active duty general officers), offices that do not have a corresponding reflection in the military staff. The secretary needs to be comfortable involving the service chief in all of these functions whenever and wherever needed.

As a former Congressman, member of the House Appropriations Committee, cabinet official, and senior OSD official, Secretary Marsh was fully acquainted with and well-known in numerous key offices outside the Army. He knew Defense Secretaries Weinberger and Carlucci in previous roles in earlier administrations, a familiarity allowing easy access to them. Moreover, he had been involved with the reorganization of the intelligence community for President Ford. General Wickham had wider exposure than usual for a service chief, having been director of the Joint Staff, senior military assistant to the SecDef (for Schlesinger and briefly for Rumsfeld), and commander of U.S. Forces Korea (USFK), a sub-unified command. Both had wide experiences that they synchronized remarkably well, with Marsh primarily working external relations and Wickham more internally focused.

To that end, General Wickham usually worked out at the Pentagon Officers Athletic Club during the lunch hour, while Secretary Marsh worked out several times per week at the House gym—each clearly working his assigned "constituencies." Though Marsh and Wickham's relationship and personal histories made them somewhat unique in these roles, their example should remain a paradigm of what is possible if the right people are put in place and work together to accomplish the common goals.

Coordinate the Secretariat and the Service Staff

Under Title 10, the secretary is to ensure there are no duplicative offices and activities in the military department. There are certainly offices in the secretariat with no military staff counterpart, and vice versa. However, there are offices in the secretariat and military staff where there is clear functional overlap, such as the Assistant Secretary for Manpower and Reserve Affairs and the Deputy Chief of Personnel. A particular challenge is presented by the secretariat's Financial Management Office and the military staff's Resources and Force Structure Office. The secretary and chief need to be constantly cognizant of this overlap and ensure functional lanes are well marked and understood.

The secretariats are best equipped by structure, history, and often personality, to provide oversight and an external focus. Military staff is best equipped to develop policy and direction having an internal focus. In most cases, these two separate focuses are apparent and work themselves out, with two notable exceptions: priorities and programming. Both of these focus areas need to be military functions led by the military staffs' operations and resources sections.

These two military staff offices are best equipped to establish suggested priorities for each service as a whole while remaining independent of institutional biases. The secretariat, by contrast, being more functionally constructed, will inevitably be less objective—human resources will want higher priority on personnel programs, acquisition and logistics more on procurement and sustainment, and so forth. Priorities should be developed by the military staff, reviewed and approved by the chief and vice chief, then taken for final approval to the service secretary.

Programming is not budgeting, a fact that is often not recognized by assistant secretaries for financial management (FM). The GNA was quite clear that the budgeting function is to reside in the secretariat, where it is under the FM. Budgeting consists of formulating the budget for the year due for submission, articulation and defense of the budget on the Hill, and execution of the budget when appropriated. Programming is the development of a five-year plan, integrated by program elements, of which the first year becomes the budget the department will submit to Congress for the upcoming fiscal year. The military staff offices are much better positioned, under the guidance of the service chief and vice chief, to understand service needs and priorities; the secretariat, with its external focus, is better positioned, under the guidance of the secretary and under secretary, to understand administration priorities and what is supportable within Office of Management and Budget (OMB) and on the Hill.

Then there is the somewhat unique case of the acquisition program, which needs serious attention from both the secretary and the chief. For the most part, the secretary and the secretariat are responsible for the management of the acquisition process. However, many of the worrisome acquisition failures over the past two decades originated in failures of the requirements process—a military staff function—to develop achievable objectives that are informed on the state of contemporary technologies and cognizant of costs and risks. In other words, they were asking for things that simply weren't feasible from either a capabilities or cost standpoint, and sometimes both.

Defense Secretary Mark Esper was aware of this issue. In his previous role as Secretary of the Army, Esper and then-Army Chief of Staff, Gen. Mark Milley, set up a process for reviewing the large majority of Army programs using an approach the media dubbed "Night Court." Program managers and organizational leaders had to appear before a committee chaired by Esper to detail how their efforts conformed to the newly-announced defense strategy, one that shifted the future focus from counterinsurgency to big power competition. This effort redirected some $25-$30 billion across various modernization efforts. As Defense Secretary, Esper used the same approach for program reviews at the DoD level, with a degree of emphasis on the defense agencies and DoD field activities (DAFAs). General Milley, as Chairman of the Joint Chiefs of Staff, joined Esper in this effort and led reforms of the Joint Requirements Oversight Committee (JROC) and other elements of the Joint Staff.

The Army has also established the Army Futures Command (AFC) by bringing together components of the existing Training and Doctrine Command and the Army Materiel Command. This is an explicit effort to more closely tie requirements to acquisitions. In achieving this, the AFC is utilizing a series of cross-functional teams (CFTs) aligned to its major priorities. Each CFT is led by a two-star officer and overseen in its efforts by a four-star general. The assigned objective of each CFT is to strike a balance between often competing constraints: requirements, acquisition, science and technology, testing, resourcing, costing, and sustainment. Army Secretary Ryan McCarthy announced that he was open to accepting risk and program failure; however, he wanted to "fail early and fail cheaply."

This is clearly an example worthy of emulation, and other services are reported to be considering a similar concept, although its rather secretive procedural approach has left some in Congress unhappy.

Maj. Gen. Arnold Punaro, USMC, Ret. and Secretary of the Army Ryan McCarthy exchange greetings before their meeting to discuss major military department issues and the role of the service secretaries and service chiefs under Title 10.

CONCLUSION

The secretary and chief can be a powerful team if they understand their distinct roles and functions, and if they maximize the merits and backgrounds each brings to the job. In general, the secretary needs to provide the external perspective and focus, while the chief should provide the internal perspective and focus. The secretary must represent the service to key external audiences, starting with the president and descending through the other offices of the executive branch and Congress, while the service chief must articulate the needs of the service to remain trained and ready.

Together, they must develop a clear partnership and develop the "one team" approach sought by General Abrams so many decades ago. If establishing this partnership and working as a team were an easy task, it would not have required so much effort by myriad highly capable men and women, sometimes without success. When the relationship between the secretary and chief becomes distant or uneasy, the relationship between the service secretariat and the military staff will mirror it. When that happens, the department as a whole suffers.

Chapter 8: The Assistant Secretary of Defense for Legislative Affairs

In 2015, Defense Secretary Ash Carter requested this white paper concerning the relationship between the DoD and Congress – a main responsibility of the Assistant Secretary of Defense for Legislative Affairs (ASD(LA)). This memorandum outlines the best ways to organize and operate the ASD(LA) office to ensure the priorities of the secretary and administration are understood and supported on the Hill. This material has been continuously updated and provided to DoD's senior leadership since 2015, and now reflects the situation in 2020 and the issues the new DoD leadership will face in 2021.

Given the current political makeup and hyperpartisanship in the Congress—an aggravated condition unlikely to abate in the 117th Congress in 2021—significant attention needs to be given to the organization and role of legislative activities in DoD. The ASD(LA) office serves as the Pentagon's lead organization in coordinating activities with Congress. This paper focuses on specific interest areas, including the current decision-making environment and the challenges it presents; the fundamental missions of ASD(LA); the overall DoD LA structure and approach; the background, tenure, and qualifications of the ASD(LA); and other stakeholders on the effectiveness of the Office of the ASD(LA) as it now exists. It also includes suggestions on needed improvements to the DoD-congressional relationship.

THE CURRENT CONGRESSIONAL ENVIRONMENT

By any measure, the current environment on Capitol Hill is highly contentious. Assigning even the most generous assessment, it is certainly different from the traditional relationship the department enjoyed with Congress and its major committees through the challenges of the Cold War and into the early years of the 21st century.

Dr. Tom Mann of the Brookings Institution and Dr. Norm Ornstein of the American Enterprise Institute (AEI) have coauthored two books addressing the contemporary changes in the personality of Congress: *The Broken Branch: How Congress is Failing America and How to Get It Back on Track* (Oxford Press, 2006), and *It's Even Worse Than It Looks: How the American Constitutional System Collided With the New Politics of Extremism* (Basic Books, 2012).

In *Broken Branch*, Mann and Ornstein – who occupy very different positions on the political spectrum – argue that the problems with Congress escalated with the "collapse of the center in Congress, the growing polarization of the parties, and the decline in accountability… [that] contributed to a climate on Capitol Hill that we found unsettling and destructive." While Mann and Ornstein noted contentiousness in Congress is nothing new, they observe how "to grizzled veterans like us, with more than thirty-five years of Congress-watching, the differences are palpable and painful. Taken together, they have made for a broken branch, one that needs major change if it is to recapture its proper role in the constitutional system."

In *It's Even Worse Than It Looks*, which was published six years after *Broken Branch*, Mann and Ornstein argue that both political parties have become quite extreme in their views and adversarial in their approach to politics and governing.

The hyperpartisan environment described by these scholars has paradoxically combined with increased internal party fractiousness. The latter has been only increased by weakened senior congressional leadership, a trend that traces its roots back to the post-Watergate period. Because of this, congressional power today is widely dispersed, unevenly applied, and heavily influenced by internal caucuses and outside groups. Consequently, party leaders – especially those in the House of Representatives – are constantly struggling to control their own conferences. Examples include former Speakers John Boehner (R-OH) and Paul Ryan (R-WI) and their struggles with the Tea Party wing of their party. Additionally, Speaker Pelosi is now facing tensions between moderate Democrats and progressives within her caucus. Aware of the highly contentious environment, Senate Leader McConnell orchestrated the Senate legislative agenda to ensure his members facing reelection didn't take any "tough" votes.

Weakened congressional leadership, hyperpartisanship, and internal party fractions further complicate the work of the ASD(LA) and similar offices throughout government. Issues that once could be handled in Congress at the senior leadership level now must be adjudicated with numerous members and staffs, some of whom are not even on the appropriate committees of jurisdiction.

While the Senate Armed Services Committee (SASC), the House Armed Services Committee (HASC), the Senate Defense Appropriations Subcommittee (SAC-D), and House Defense Appropriations Subcommittee (HAC-D) have managed to remain fairly bipartisan in their approach, the three basic processes of Congress as a whole—budget, authorization, and appropriation—are badly broken. Each of these processes is fundamental to DoD's priorities, plans, and programs.

While the authorization committees continue to pass the National Defense Authorization Act (NDAA) on an annual basis, the process is rarely ever conducted on the correct timeline. Because of this, the NDAA is rarely able to guide the appropriations process or be finalized before the beginning of the fiscal year. Since its establishment by Senator Richard Russell in 1959, the NDAA has been vetoed six times over its 61-year history. On several recent occasions, no Senate version cleared the full chamber, forcing the conference report effort to rely on only the SASC-approved version. The number and types of amendments that are permitted are significantly more limited than in recent decades. Additionally, the document has become more complex and convoluted over the years. In its early years, the authorization bill consisted of five pages of bill language and four pages of report language. This compares to the FY20's final bill and report, which totaled 1,794 pages of congressional guidance direction, statutory provisions, and detailed funding tables.

When executed correctly, the budget process is supposed to set overall spending and revenue totals using guidance from an annual concurrent budget resolution. In reality, the budget resolution process has failed six times over the last 10 years. Because of these failures, there has been no agreed-upon budget framework to guide the spending process, a major frustration for both leaders and practitioners. These frustrations are nothing new; previous recommendations from 1974 sought to fix the need for an overall framework that set spending, revenue, and deficit targets.

Twelve appropriations bills have not been passed by their October 1 deadline since 1996 (FY97). With few exceptions over the last 20 years, nearly every fiscal year has started with a continuing resolution (CR).

There has been an average of five to six CRs each of these fiscal years for an average duration of 137 days. There have even been three full-year CRs, while the shortest was 21 days in 1999. CRs are always detrimental to DoD's execution of well-programmed budgets. CRs are set at the previous year's level, and do not permit program increases or adjustments or new starts. For an organization as large and complex as the DoD, this is a major dysfunction and creates waste and inefficiencies. Despite several recent bipartisan efforts to fix the budget process, nothing has changed. For defense especially, this is an important process as the budget resolution sets the level of defense spending that authorizations and appropriations follow. Even then, it's not always approved at the Pentagon-requested level.

Following the passage of the Budget Control Act (BCA) in fall 2011, the super committee failed to find the required savings. This triggered a sequester of FY13 funds, and DoD resources were constrained during the majority of years in the decade-long sequester. During this same time, DoD absorbed 96% of the mandated cuts from planned spending levels. This is from a "ceiling" established in the BCA that was $500 billion lower than what DoD planned in the president's budget for 2012. The sequester caps were another $500 billion lower than the BCA ceiling. This had a negative impact on wartime readiness, capabilities, and preparedness.

Omnibus appropriations have been a significant feature in Congress's power of the purse. Between FY86-FY16, 43% of the 390 appropriation acts were omnibus appropriations with 29 (7%) resulting in full-year CRs. An omnibus rolls all government spending into one massive bill.

Authorization and appropriation bills require 60 votes in the Senate to pass. There is no "nuclear option" or reconciliation procedure to bypass this requirement. As a result, the party in the minority has greater leverage over budget proceedings in the Senate. Democrats, for example, are unlikely to go along with increases in defense spending absent some deal on domestic spending. This pattern played out for four years during the Trump administration, and with an evenly split Senate in 2021, the same playbook will apply.

The outside lobby groups, from veterans groups (such as the American Legion, VFW, Iraq & Afghanistan Vets) and service-based groups (such as AUSA, Navy League, AFA, Marine Corps League, NGAUS) to industry (NDIA, AIA, PSC) and benefits-based groups (MOAA, military associations), have demonstrated a far greater ability to shape legislation that runs contrary to the Pentagon's wishes than in previous eras. Some associations have shifted their approach from pushing for a strong national defense to advocating for more benefits for their members, whether it is a policy shift, a higher benefit, or blocking DoD's requested reforms. A former deputy secretary of defense has summed up this shift, saying "the slogan has changed from 'praise the Lord and pass the ammunition' to 'praise the Lord and pass the benefits.'" The individual defense companies' lobbying expenditures (and political contributions) are also at an all-time high, further demonstrating competing influences on DoD.

In this negative framework, Congress retains its constitutional power and eventually has the final word on funding, oversight, confirmation, and declaring war. It is also a historical fact that divided government is the norm, not the exception, as further detailed in Chapter 3. It is within this difficult reality that DoD legislative efforts and organizations must improve their approach. It is worth noting that congressionally-driven major organizational reforms such as the Goldwater-Nichols Act (GNA) in 1986 and the 2016 breakup of the Under Secretary of Defense for Acquisition, Technology and Logistics have passed over the strong objections of the department under both Republican and Democratic administrations.

The Missions and Functions of ASD(LA)

DoD Directive 5142.01, dated September 13, 2006, states the ASD(LA) is the principal staff assistant (PSA) to the secretary of defense and is responsible for the *overall supervision* (emphasis added) of DoD legislative affairs. In this role, the ASD(LA) performs the following functions (all emphasis added):

- Developing a legislative strategy *supporting* the administration's policies and agenda.

- Developing policies and plans *supporting* the legislative strategy.

- Issuing policy and procedural guidance to other OSD PSAs and "DoD components" on *conducting* legislative liaison.

- *Overseeing and coordinating* legislative liaison functions.

- Developing policies for *coordination* between OSD PSAs and other DoD components.

- Providing *"advice and assistance"* to the secretary of defense and other senior officials in the presentation of the DoD legislative program.

- *"Manage and direct"* DoD participation in congressional hearings and investigations.

- *Coordinating and overseeing* responses to congressional inquiries and reports.

- *Coordinating support* requirements for requested congressional travel.

- Providing for *processing* personal security clearances for members and staff.

- Performing other duties as assigned by the secretary of defense.

Looking at all of these duties, it is clear that the ASD(LA) oversees a wide variety of missions. Unquestionably, these are all necessary functions that are important to the work of DoD. However, nowhere in the official delineation of the responsibilities and functions of the ASD(LA) does it state that the ASD, or assigned subordinates, have the responsibility of "advocating" for the department.

Some former ASD(LA)s believed that advocating for the Defense Department was "statutorily forbidden." Under this view, the primary function of the LA office was to answer questions from Congress, transmit other relevant information that might be germane to legislative responsibilities, provide administrative support as needed, and clarify the positions of the department and its leadership.

This perspective is a narrow and likely incorrect interpretation of the role and function of the ASD(LA) office and is opposite from the approach taken during the Cold War, an era where the office was seen as highly successful. Most former ASD(LA)s concur with this assessment, as do LA leaders within the service branches. From the latter's perspective, they were routinely required to take advocacy positions regarding an administration's programs, budgets, nominations, and inquiries that the ASD(LA) was unwilling to express.

Historically, the ASD(LA) has embodied the successful advocacy approach. As long as the office supported the president's budget and policies, this did not violate lobbying prohibitions. While the LA office cannot call a defense company and coordinate their support for specific programs in the budget, there are no similar restrictions on the legislative branch, as they are allowed to organize traditional grassroots support. Advocacy denotes a proactive approach rather than a reactive one. Many officials in the military departments have stated that over time, they had greatly reduced attending scheduled coordinating meetings with the ASD(LA) as the only things discussed were "schedules and the status of questions for the record (QFR) and information for the record (IFR)."

In this increasingly partisan and confrontational era described by Mann and Ornstein, the routine representatives of the department who work Capitol Hill need to be more involved in advocacy and recreating the "two-way street" relationship of yesteryear. If Congress is to be in on the "landing," they also have to be in on the "takeoff." Congress understands the difference between consultation and coordination and being "informed" of things at the last minute. Moreover, after-the-fact notification has been a staple of the Trump administration, a practice that has invited bipartisan criticism.

For the civilians assigned to ASD(LA), particularly those who are political appointees, strongly representing the views of the administration would seem to be an expected role. If it is not treated as such, even while the service LAs simultaneously feel that is their role, then a commonality of purpose will be difficult to establish.

There needs to be DoD guidance on advocacy, detailing how it "supports the administration's policies and agenda" as described in DoD Directive 5142.01. According to a review of relevant literature, advocacy is a natural function to be performed by any executive branch office performing legislative liaison duties, particularly one with the broad scope of responsibility represented by the DoD budget. This interpretation is consistent with Office of Management and Budget (OMB) directives and Government Accountability Office (GAO) rulings on the subject.

The ASD(LA) office must meet several demands, a reality illustrated in greater detail by the following figures. Although these charts reflect what is unquestionably a massive workload in terms of tracking, managing, and oversight, the workload has been quantitatively declining in almost all cases recently, with the exception of legislative reports being tracked. In some cases, such as nominations, this can be a natural development as an administration enters its final years, which we saw at the ends of both President Obama's second term and President Trump's first term. Nonetheless, this still represents a major workload for a relatively small staff of 45—only marginally larger than the pre-9/11 staff of 32. Over time, the LA staff has fluctuated from a high of 51 to the current level of 45, a reduction due in part to headquarters cuts. In the fall of 2020, over 40% of the Pentagon's 60 presidentially appointed and Senate-confirmed (PAS) positions had no Senate-confirmed individual filling the position. The following five figures provide greater insight into legislative affairs matters.

FIGURE 1: HEARINGS BY CALENDAR YEAR

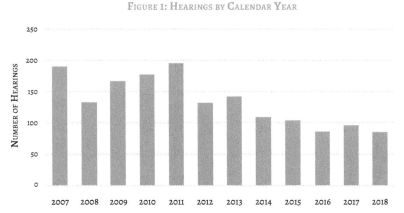

FIGURE 1 DEPICTS THE NUMBER OF HEARINGS PER CALENDAR YEAR, WHICH REQUIRE COORDINATION FROM THE LEGISLATIVE AFFAIRS OFFICE.

FIGURE 2: QUESTIONS AND INFORMATION FOR THE RECORD BY CALENDAR YEAR

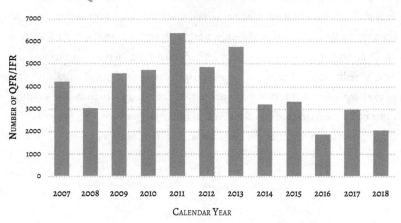

FIGURE 2 ILLUSTRATES THE QFR AND IFR PER YEAR.

FIGURE 3: NDAA APPEALS BY FISCAL YEAR

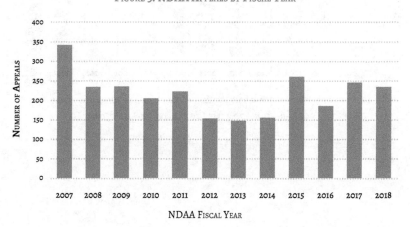

FIGURE 3 SHOWS THE NUMBER OF NDAA APPEALS BY YEAR.

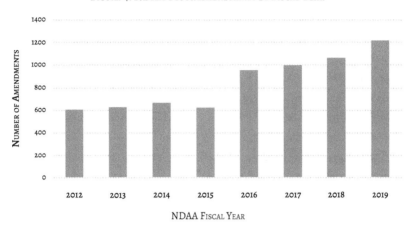

FIGURE 4: NDAA FLOOR AMENDMENTS BY FISCAL YEAR

FIGURE 4 DEPICTS THE NUMBER OF NDAA FLOOR AMENDMENTS PER YEAR.

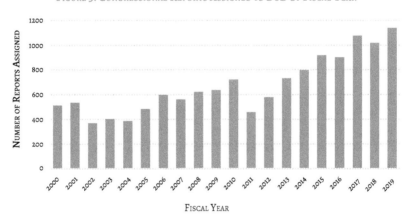

FIGURE 5: CONGRESSIONAL REPORTS ASSIGNED TO DoD BY FISCAL YEAR

FIGURE 5 ILLUSTRATES THE NUMBER OF CONGRESSIONAL REPORTS ASSIGNED TO THE DEFENSE DEPARTMENT BY YEAR.

One of the most important roles of the ASD(LA) is guiding DoD nominees through the Senate confirmation process. As of December 2021, DoD has 61 positions requiring Senate confirmation (PAS positions). Guiding this many individuals through the confirmation process is a constant workload that requires a specialized set of skills. This is especially acute at the beginning of an administration. Recent trends show that the confirmation process has significantly slowed, both in terms of nominating individuals and in terms of time they spend on the Senate executive calendar.

The Trump administration, for example, took a significantly longer time than the Obama administration to confirm the first slate of positions below the secretary of defense, such as the deputy, under secretaries, assistant secretaries, service secretaries, and service assistant secretaries. The Trump administration took, on average, over seven months to nominate top PAS officials, and the Senate took over three months to confirm them—for a total of about 11 months from nomination to confirmation.

The Obama administration, by comparison, took an average of five months to nominate and two months to confirm, for a total of seven months. Though the Senate Democratic leader can take some blame for this slowdown during the Trump administration by objecting to the traditional routine use of unanimous consent to approve non-controversial nominations, the Senate can't confirm someone who hasn't been nominated. Incoming administrations need to vet and nominate their officials as soon as possible to prevent similar delays.

STAFFING AND ORGANIZATION OF THE OFFICE OF THE ASD(LA)

Legislative affairs offices in large public and private sector organizations are generally structured in one of two ways: organized to reflect the major external "customer," or organized to reflect the internal organization itself.

In contemporary Washington, under the first model, the office would likely have teams for the executive branch (or the primary agencies of relevance within it), the Senate, House, state governments, and local governments. These teams would then represent or coordinate all external interactions with their assigned "customers."

The second model groups the teams by internal business units—the product, service, or interest that they are promoting (i.e., ships, electronics, or aircraft)—which they represent to all interested customers (i.e., Congress, the states, etc.). Figure 6 illustrates these two models in greater detail.

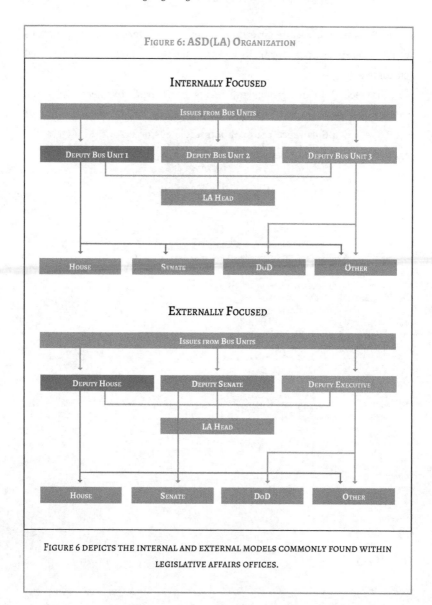

FIGURE 6: ASD(LA) ORGANIZATION

INTERNALLY FOCUSED

FIGURE 6 DEPICTS THE INTERNAL AND EXTERNAL MODELS COMMONLY FOUND WITHIN LEGISLATIVE AFFAIRS OFFICES.

In other words, under the first model, the LA team would know the particular customer but have less expertise on the product, whereas under the second model, the teams would be experts on the internal products and line of business but have less expertise about the customer.

Most companies have experimented with both organizations, and many have found a hybrid structure to be effective. This is the case for both the broader Defense Department and the ASD(LA) office in particular. There are legislative teams for the House and Senate, another for the intra-government efforts, and still others aligned with the major internal OSD organizations of the under secretaries. In addition, the existence of the service legislative liaison (LL) offices provides a further alignment by "business unit." Given DoD's complexity, sheer size, large number of customers, and the historical basis of the services, this hybrid model is arguably the best approach. Figure 7 depicts this hybrid structure in greater detail.

FIGURE 7: OFFICE OF THE ASD(LA)

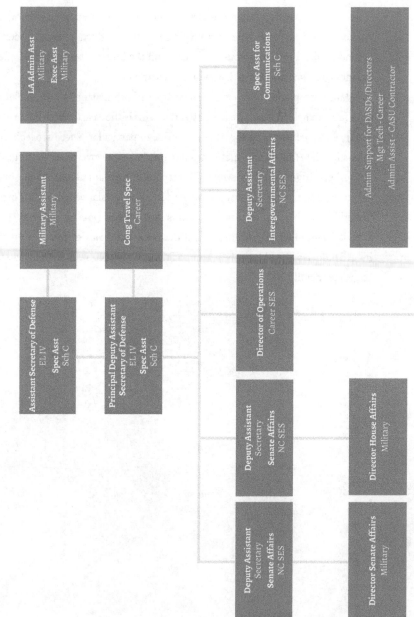

Policy Division
Team Chief
Sch C
Spec Asst-Legal Affairs/Detainees/NATO/Eur
Military
Spec Asst-GSA/Cyber
Sch C
Spec Asst-ISA
Sch C
Spec Asst-SO/LIC Spec Ops
Policy
Military
Spec Asst-Asia Pacific
Sch C

Ops/Intel Division
Team Chief & Opa
Military
Spec Asst-Imel/Space
Military
Spec Asst-Nll
Sch C

Leg Operations Division
Supv Leg Analyst
Leg Analyst
Career
Leg Analyst
Career
Leg Res Spec
Career
Leg Asst
Career
CHAARS
Program Support
IT Contractor (shared)

Human Resources
Admin & Mgmt Spec
Career
Mgmt Serv Spec/Personnel
Career

AT&L Division
Team Chief
Sch C
Spec Asst Acquisition/Logistics
Military
Spec Asst Weapons Systems
Military
Spec Asst -Installations & Envir
Sch C

P&R Division
Team Chief
Sch C
Spec Asst-Mil/Civ Personal
Policy
Military
Spec Asst-Health Affairs/Reserve Affairs
Military

Legislative Research Division
Team Chief
Sch C
Leg Res Spec Sonc
Career
CASU Contractor
CASU Contractor

Admin
Mgmt Serv Spec/Admin
Career
Mgt Tech Career
Cong Assistants
CASU Contractor
CASU Contractor

IT Support Contractor
Contractor

FIGURE 7 ILLUSTRATES THE DIFFERENT OFFICES AND STRUCTURES WITHIN THE ASD(LA) OFFICE.

Additional consideration should be given to the proper role of separate legislative personnel within the under secretariats. A former ASD(LA) commented that a major difficulty was maintaining message discipline within OSD, specifically within the offices of the under secretaries—a challenge because many of the senior leaders in these offices had significant Hill experience themselves, with their own connections and networks. Eliminating LA personnel within the offices of the under secretaries and moving them to ASD(LA) was an effort to instill greater operational and message discipline, thus creating the hybrid structure. Some contend it would be preferable to leave these staff members in the offices of the under secretaries (excluding the office of the comptroller for reasons associated with mandated appropriations and budget liaisons). The demands from Congress on USD Policy, USD P&R, USD R&E, and USD A&S are such that having the right legislative liaison person in these under secretary offices can be valuable.

A good example of how this worked involved Bethany Bassett, who served as the LA official in USD P&R at the beginning of the Obama administration. She was the duty expert on all the complex, emotionally, and politically charged issues. She coordinated closely with Elizabeth King, the ASD(LA)—the key to making this model work.

As demonstrated by Bassett and King, coordination is vital. Having legislative leads in the offices of the under secretaries can work for the enterprise. That person could also keep the secretary of defense's front office assistant who covers important issues current and up to speed. Several former ASD(LA)s do not agree with such an approach, but if you have highly capable experts in key areas who recognize ASD(LA) as the final word, it can work under either model.

Given the scope of the responsibilities assigned to ASD(LA) and the increasingly chaotic environment in Washington where more players are present on the playing field than in the past, recent reductions in ASD(LA) staffing, driven by budget realities and efforts to reduce "backroom" overhead, have likely gone too far. During a period where many demands are increasing, ASD(LA) manpower has been decreasing, as shown in Figure 8. The staffing requirement should be revisited.

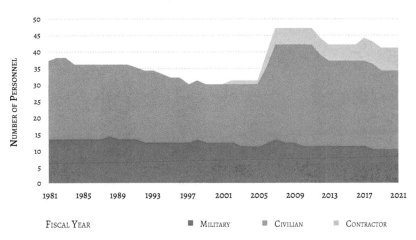

FIGURE 8: ASD(LA) MANPOWER BY FISCAL YEAR

FIGURE 8 ILLUSTRATES THE MAKEUP OF ASD(LA) PERSONNEL OVER FOUR DECADES.

On the other hand, staffing constraints on ASD(LA) might be feasible if closer relationships were established with the service LL offices. Even with recent reductions in staffing, the service LL offices have nearly twice the assigned personnel strength of ASD(LA) itself, as depicted in Figure 9. The service liaison teams could be used as "force multipliers," but historically have fought hard to maintain their independence. The same applies to the CJCS legislative office, which typically works closely with the OSD policy shop.

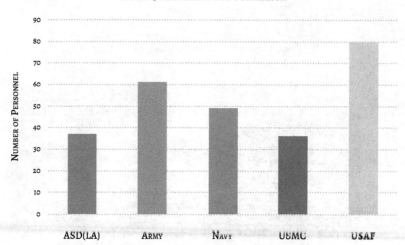

FIGURE 9: LA MANPOWER COMPARISON

FIGURE 9 DEPICTS THE NUMBER OF PERSONNEL PERFORMING LA FUNCTIONS IN THE DoD.

In the case of the Army Office of the Chief of Legislative Liaison (OCLL), a large effort is dedicated to answering correspondence, reported as over 50,000 items per year (or nearly 200 per day). This effort clearly dwarfs the correspondence burden of ASD(LA) in dealing with correspondence directed to the secretary and deputy secretary, as seen in Figure 10.

FIGURE 10: CORRESPONDENCE DIRECTED TO SD OR DSD

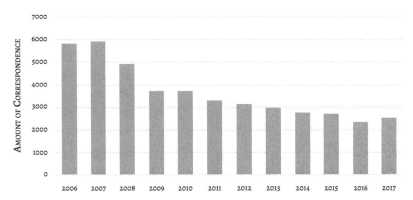

FIGURE 10 ILLUSTRATES THE DECREASING AMOUNT OF CORRESPONDENCE DIRECTED TO THE SECRETARY OF DEFENSE OR THE DEPUTY SECRETARY OF DEFENSE.

In the area of correspondence and travel support, closer coordination with the service LL offices would result in greater efficiency. Additionally, this could also encourage closer relations between the services and the ASD(LA) overall.

Nonetheless, the ASD(LA) should seek to operate at the policy level, leaving as much as possible of the tactical level operation to the services. Clearly, written inquiries coming to, or directed at the secretary, deputy secretary, and the under secretaries of defense need to be handled in a timely manner by the ASD(LA). During the tenures of several past secretaries, inefficiency has grown; the number of inquiries has decreased while reply times have increased. In order to maximize efficiency, the department should conduct an analysis to determine its current processing time and subsequently work to improve it. Inquiries not directly addressed to top officials should be passed down to lower-level legislative liaison offices.

The combatant commands (COCOMs)' LA offices are another area where closer coordination, and perhaps organizational change and consolidation, should be considered. Similar changes have been enacted in the defense agencies, where once-large congressional-relations offices have been consolidated into smaller congressional support offices (CSO). However, the COCOMs' LA offices have continued to grow, illustrating the need for expedient change.

Given the existing political environment and the increased visibility and stature of the COCOMs following the 1986 GNA, there are numerous inquiries that go from Congress directly to COCOMs requesting information, assessment, and office calls. A former ASD(LA) indicated that it has become quite difficult to manage and even be aware of these efforts, as the COCOMs seem to be exercising their implied authority to reply directly to congressional inquiries. This also seems to be happening with little coordination and control being exercised by the CJCS's small LA office.

It may be appropriate to approach this in one of two ways: Direct the CJCS to exercise control over this situation by requiring all replies and actions with Congress be coordinated with the JCS LA office (which would then inform and coordinate with ASD(LA)); or, as with the defense agencies, restrict the COCOMs to very small LA offices, and take other steps to discourage COCOMs from working directly with Capitol Hill. Congress will push back hard if they believe the uniformed military—Joint Staff, services, and COCOMs—are being "restricted" in their dealings with Congress, but such a confrontation is likely required to achieve a consistent, uniform, and informed message.

Additionally, the LA office needs to better coordinate between congressional authorizers and appropriators. ASD(LA) primarily deals with the SASC and HASC—the authorizers—while the comptroller's Budget and Appropriations Affairs (BAA) Office primarily deals with the appropriators—the House and Senate Defense Appropriations Subcommittees. There has historically been a certain level of tension between the two separate committees in Congress as their priorities do not always align, but their jurisdictions do.

The SASC and HASC are also among the only committees to insist on passing an annual authorization bill for DoD. The BAA is required by law to be separate and distinct from the ASD(LA), and it manages all communication between OSD and the appropriators on all topics. By statute, the ASD(LA) is the senior legislative assistant in the Pentagon. As such, the two organizations should find a way to work more closely together and coordinate their activities better to ensure the DoD is speaking with one voice on matters of appropriation and authorization.

THE BACKGROUND AND TENURE OF THE ASD(LA)

Quite clearly, the ASD(LA) should be an individual with considerable experience on Capitol Hill. It is difficult to develop strategies for dealing with a body of 535 divergent members if one has never actually worked there. It is most desirable to have someone with experience in drafting, marking up, conferencing, and planning legislation. Since DoD's establishment, 21 individuals have served in the ASD(LA) role. Three of those individuals were military officers, but having experience on the Hill has been the most universal denominator.

On four occasions, the office has switched from being an assistant secretary of defense to an assistant *to* the secretary. This change in designation, and a de facto downgrading of the position, was often driven by the need to create another ASD position elsewhere in OSD. The last such downgrading occurred in the first year of the Clinton administration, but the position was then restored to the ASD level in September 1994 and has remained there ever since. This ensures the office has the clout needed in the Pentagon—and with State and the National Security Council (NSC)—to gain the support required for any given issue. In a rank- and protocol-intensive organization such as DoD, clout matters. As the staff director of the SASC in this timeframe, I drove an effort to codify this position as an assistant secretary, which proved successful.

Past ASD(LA)s have included John O. Marsh Jr., a former member of the House Appropriations Committee (who would go on to be the Secretary of the Army for President Reagan), and Powell A. Moore, a former chief of staff to Senator Richard Russell and a former Assistant Secretary of State for Congressional Affairs. Dave Gribben, ASD(LA) to Secretary Cheney, worked on

Cheney's congressional staff. Others, such as Elizabeth King, have come from personal staff on the Hill. The ideal candidate would be someone who has served as a senior staffer for a senior member on one of the major defense committees, or better yet, a defense committee staff director. However, such individuals are often hard to recruit. An individual who has served as the head of Washington operations for a major corporation and who has also served on the Hill, or had previous time in the Pentagon, would also bring the necessary skills to the job. Additionally, the secretary of defense should meet with the ASD(LA), the DoD general counsel, and the top public affairs official at least once a day.

Whoever fills the role, a major consideration has to be a close relationship with the secretary and deputy secretary. Within the immediate office (or inner circle) of the secretary, there must be a continual and comfortable presence by the senior public affairs official, the general counsel, and the ASD(LA). These three officials need to be fully aware of the secretary's views, actions, preferences, and immediate needs. An ASD(LA) who does not have this close relationship will find it difficult to be active and proactive on the secretary's behalf and will find his or her role reduced to the more administrative duties. Should this become known to others, the ASD(LA)'s ability to coordinate and direct actions will be significantly diminished.

Without a close relationship and constant access to the secretary, the ASD(LA) will become just another official in OSD, finding it difficult to manage the legislative activities of the under secretaries, the services, and the COCOMs. A final desirable trait would be an excellent working relationship with the White House's legislative office and chief of staff's operation, which ensures closer coordination and message unity across the executive branch. Steve Hedger, the ASD(LA) under Secretary Carter, benefited greatly from this connection.

Ideally, the tenure of an ASD(LA) would match that of the secretary, but given the scope, complexity, and sensitivity of the position, it should run at least four years. Under no circumstances, however, should it be expected that the functions of the position can be effectively performed by an individual who does not have the clear support and confidence of the secretary.

Even if the ASD(LA) has all three of these key qualifications, they will not be effective if the secretary is unwilling to work with Congress. A good example of this was Powell Moore. Moore had his start on the SASC under legendary Chairman Richard Russell, possessed extensive experience in White House legislative affairs, served as an Assistant Secretary of State for Legislative Affairs, and worked in the Washington office of the largest defense contractor, making him an ideal candidate by any measure. However, Secretary Rumsfeld, with his disdain for Congress, was unwilling to implement many of the traditional activities as Powell recommended. Rumsfeld was able to survive his poor relationship with Congress because of the wars in Afghanistan and Iraq that it felt pressured to fund, but ultimately, he was replaced with Robert Gates.

CURRENT TRENDS IN THE ASD(LA) FUNCTION

As suggested previously, interviews with several individuals with knowledge of and interactions with the trends in the Office of the ASD(LA) over a number of administrations have been less than complimentary. It is common in any organization that many feel the operations in their areas being conducted by a higher organizational entity are less than ideal, so this may not be surprising; nonetheless, some observations are noteworthy.

Several noted that some ASD(LA)s did not have a close relationship with the secretary. This may have been an unavoidable circumstance given that President Obama's first defense secretary, Robert Gates, a holdover from the previous administration, did not inject himself into senior staffing positions, except to exercise a veto. Moreover, President Obama's subsequent defense secretaries, especially Chuck Hagel, did not have long tenures. As highlighted in Professor Hugh Heclo's 1977 book, *A Government of Strangers*, administrations are largely populated with individuals who have never worked together, often have little personal knowledge or connection to one another, and have often moved on by the time familiarity and trust have developed. Certain positions, such as ASD(LA), however, require immediate familiarity, comfort, and trust as necessary conditions for success.

The general feeling expressed in the military departments has been that ASD(LA) has been "little value added" in providing insights or support to other LA activities throughout the department. The office has come to be seen as more administrative than insightful, and reluctant to take firm positions in advocating positions and programs seen as important to the services, agencies, and commands. Former senior LA officials from activities outside OSD stated that they rarely attended routine coordinating meetings with the ASD(LA) because they were neither "useful nor informative, with much more information being requested than provided." If this situation still exists – or ever existed – it should be rectified immediately.

RECOMMENDATIONS

1. Selection of an ASD(LA)

The ASD(LA) should (ideally) be someone with whom the secretary is close and comfortable. This position is truly among the handful where such a close relationship is more than just desirable.

The ASD(LA) needs solid experience and an intimate awareness of the congressional process, the culture of Congress, and practical demands of the experience. The most desirable background for the ASD(LA) would be significant Hill experience, preferably developed on a Senate committee staff. This is because of the importance of intense management of the confirmation process, a functional jurisdiction of the SASC. If the ASD(LA) does not have this background, comes from personal staff, or comes from the House side, then either the principal deputy or the deputy for Senate affairs needs to be well versed in the confirmation process.

Recent history has shown that there is considerable turnover in the presidentially appointed and Senate-confirmed (PAS) positions. Contemporary studies have shown that confirmation can take as long as 18 months, with subsequent service being less than two years. This means that in the absence of a well-managed confirmation process run by a skilled confirmation team, several senior-level policy positions can go unfilled for much of an administration. This was certainly pronounced in the Trump administration, but primarily due to the slowness of the White House in sending nominations to the Senate, which is beyond the control of the Pentagon and ASD(LA).

Staffing of the ASD(LA) office should reflect the majorities in Congress in at least some key positions, even if the president is of a different party.

2. Organization of the Office

The existing hybrid structure of the office is likely the best that can be achieved. The complexity of the Defense Department, the histories of the military departments, and the unsettled political environment probably suggest no viable alternative approach.

Some areas of the office need additional focus, such as the management of the nomination process. The office has a major requirement regarding nominations and confirmations that it may not be well structured to accomplish, especially in a period of hyperpartisanship. The confirmation process is more art than science and benefits from the support of outside experts with considerable experience in this area.

3. Relationship with Other LA Offices

Without question, the Office of the ASD(LA) needs to focus on legislative strategy and operations rather than administration, and it needs to lead rather than merely provide oversight and coordination to other legislative liaison offices.

Steps must be taken to reduce the sense in other LA offices that the office of the ASD(LA) adds little to their efforts. Elements of this belief will naturally evaporate with the appointment of an ASD(LA) matching the requirements as prescribed above, but in an era of constant pressures to reduce staff, increasing department-wide coordination of legislative affairs and initiatives is the surest way to solve this issue.

4. Control of the COCOMs' LA Office

Because of their enhanced visibility and influence since the Goldwater-Nichols Act, Congress seems increasingly inclined to go directly to COCOMs with questions and requests. Unsurprisingly, the COCOMs seem to be increasingly inclined to respond, directly providing answers and observations. Regrettably, on balance, this is ultimately unhelpful and most likely contrary to Title 10.

The COCOMs need to direct inquiries to the Office of the Chairman of the Joint Chiefs of Staff (OCJCS) LA with copies provided to the ASD(LA) and the service LLs where appropriate. The OCJCS LA should coordinate responses and ensure the COCOMs are not running independent operations and providing responses to Congress that might reflect their narrow, regional perspectives while perhaps being somewhat inconsistent with a more global perspective. This would be more consistent with the command structure established by the GNA.

However, Pentagon leadership must emphasize that the ASD(LA) is the primary office for controlling and coordinating all matters relating to legislative affairs. This needs to be fully understood by service secretaries, the CJCS, and the service LL offices. Routine matters such as regular correspondence should be handled at the lowest level possible; however, all communications with Congress with a policy dimension, as defined by the secretary of defense, needs to be coordinated by and flow through the ASD(LA). In this regard, the CJCS needs to make this absolutely clear to the combatant commanders, and the under secretaries need to make it similarly clear to the defense agencies they supervise.

Conclusion

The environment in which any LA office must operate is enormously more complex than 20—perhaps even 10—years ago. Required staff reductions, often based upon percentage reductions uncorrelated to mission responsibilities, should be avoided. Such an approach is essentially applying the sequestration methodology, which has been widely denounced, to office structure.

It is likely, however, that some additional efficiencies can be realized in the areas of clearances, correspondence, and travel. Managing correspondence is a major challenge, and an IT system should be evaluated to replace the existing Congressional Hearings and Reporting Requirements Tracking System.

Lastly, in some form, either written or verbally expressed, the ASD(LA) and their office need to recognize the need to be advocates for the Defense Department in all its dimensions—personnel, budgets, policy, acquisition, operations, structures, strategies, and missions. Should this present an issue regarding assigned military personnel, then they may have to pass this function to civilians and perform other functions; but the lack of an advocacy orientation makes it difficult for any ASD(LA) to adequately meet the needs of the secretary and other senior DoD officials. When it comes to advocating the defense program to an organization as large and distributed as Congress, this cannot be something left in the personal inboxes of the secretary and the deputy secretary. Without an effective legislative operator, the administration and the secretary's priorities, programs, and strategy will not be fully supported nor fully implemented.

CHAPTER 9: THE JOINT CHIEFS OF STAFF, SERVICE CHIEFS, AND THE GOLDWATER-NICHOLS ACT

This chapter, drafted during the 2015-2016 Senate efforts to update the 1986 Goldwater-Nichols Act (GNA), was written to provide those debating the reforms a sense of the history of GNA: how it came about, what it tried to address, and what it specifically did not cover. As the staff director of the SASC when the legislation was drafted and approved—over the objections of DoD—I have a keen understanding of its history and intent.

The history of the Joint Chiefs of Staff (JCS) goes back to their informal establishment during World War II. The service chiefs – uniformed heads of the nation's military services – simultaneously serve as head of their service and as JCS members. Their role has evolved over the years, particularly after the reforms of the 1986 GNA. The Act was named after Senate Armed Services Committee (SASC) Chairman Barry Goldwater and Alabama Representative Bill Nichols. Sen. Sam Nunn, Goldwater's partner in SASC leadership, provided much of the intellectual capital for the Act.

Since the GNA, there have been several adjustments on the roles played by the military service chiefs and the responsibilities they have within their services, though none have been nearly as drastic. While the WWII chiefs were largely autonomous rulers of their respective domains and served as direct advisors to the president, the GNA statutorily transferred many of their traditional roles to the civilian secretaries. The chiefs found their joint roles clarified and expanded, while their service roles were largely concentrated on presiding over their department's military staff.

Recent legislation, particularly in the area of acquisition, has returned some of these original responsibilities to the service chiefs, leaving their joint responsibilities largely unchanged. However, we need to assess whether this is a useful adjustment – analysis that requires understanding how we arrived at the current situation in the first place.

The Service Chiefs as JCS members

The JCS originally came into existence during World War II and were used by President Franklin Roosevelt to develop strategic direction, organize the industrial effort, and coordinate the activities of the armed forces. President Roosevelt, having himself served as the assistant secretary of the Navy during the Wilson administration, recognized the historical independence of the military services. Knowing that the services were administered by strong personalities, he felt it was important to have an officer serve as the chairman of the assembled group. Perhaps predictably, the service chiefs resisted this suggestion until General George Marshall, the Army chief of staff, suggested that Admiral William D. Leahy would be a choice acceptable to all the service leaders.

As with most ideas originating with Marshall, this was a helpful and insightful suggestion. Leahy had served as the Chief of Naval Operations from 1937-1939. After retiring from this position, he was appointed by President Roosevelt as the U.S. ambassador to France. After accepting the offer from Roosevelt, Leahy assumed the title "Chief of Staff to the Commander-in-Chief," and although considered by many the first Chairman of the Joint Chiefs of Staff (CJCS), he never officially held this title. However, when the five-star rank was created in December 1944, Leahy was the first officer promoted to the new rank, followed in succession by General Marshall, Admiral King, General MacArthur, Admiral Nimitz, General Eisenhower, and General Arnold.

As the JCS, the group met with President Roosevelt frequently to discuss items such as budget concerns and industrial priorities. Famously, at one such meeting, General Marshall, recognizing Leahy's military heritage and the president's own service in the Department of the Navy, commented, "Mr. President, as you are Commander in Chief of all the armed forces, I feel I must insist that you stop referring to the Navy as 'us' and the Army as 'them' during these deliberations."

During WWII, the JCS (in this configuration) was heavily involved in strategic planning and theater-level operations. They attended nearly all of the major strategic conferences of the war – Casablanca, January 1943 (codenamed SYMBOL); Washington, May 1943 (TRIDENT); Quebec, August 1943 (QUADRANT); Cairo, December 1943 (SEXTANT); Tehran, December 1943 (EUREKA); and Yalta, February 1945 (ARGONAUT). In these conferences, the JCS usually met with their allied counterparts to form the Combined Chiefs of Staff, as shown in the following photo.

The Combined Chiefs of Staff deliberate during the QUADRANT Conference on August 23, 1943, in the midst of WWII.

After the war, the National Security Act of 1947 and its 1949 amendment codified the JCS, with the latter legislation formally establishing the role of CJCS. However, from 1949 until the GNA's passage in 1986, the chairman was characterized in this manner by one observer:

> The CJCS is, in essence, the ambassador between the JCS and the secretary of defense. He has the great advantage, alone among the chiefs, of knowing the mind of the secretary of defense, derived from the continual contact with him. Consequently, one of his most important functions is in presenting JCS advice in the best possible form for the secretary of defense.

Prior to the GNA, the Navy was usually the most vocally opposed to any suggested unification of the services, the establishment of a powerful CJCS, or oversight by the Joint Staff (JS). As Fleet Admiral William Halsey Jr. testified to Congress in late 1945, he was:

... unwilling to have the chief of the Army Air Force pass on the question of whether or not the Navy should have funds for building and maintaining a balanced fleet. One might just as well ask a committee composed of a Protestant, a Catholic, and a Jew to save our national souls by recommending a national church or creed.

Nonetheless, the move toward greater unification, which slowly became known as "jointness," edged forward, and regional commands were established in the late 1940s. Under the original idea, each of the unified commands operated with one of the service chiefs serving as an "executive agent" representing the JCS. This arrangement was formalized on April 21, 1948, within a policy paper titled the "Functions of the Armed Forces and the Joint Chiefs of Staff." This paper is also informally known as The Key West Agreement.

The goal of The Key West Agreement was to better unify the services by pairing the Air Force and Navy to collaborate on nuclear warfare and the Army and Marine Corps on amphibious operations. Unfortunately, the agreement was not able to address the often-contentious interservice rivalry still plaguing the department today and the added redundancies between the services created by new ambiguities in service roles. The responsibilities of the unified commands were further expanded on September 7, 1948, when the regional commanders' authority was extended to include the coordination of the administrative and logistical functions in addition to their combat responsibilities.

Eisenhower made defense reorganization and greater unity between the services a top priority during his presidency. These efforts resulted in the Defense Reorganization Act of 1958, legislation which strengthened the secretary of defense's authority over the military departments, elevated the Chairman of the JCS, and doubled the size of the JS. It also strengthened the role of the unified commanders and removed the military departments from the operational chain of command—though the services never really adjusted to this modification and continued to dominate the decision processes until GNA.

Maj. Gen. Arnold Punaro, USMC, Ret. signs a copy of his memoir, On War and
Politics: The Battle Inside Washington's Beltway. *As illustrated in the memoir,
Punaro played an active role during the creation of the Goldwater-Nichols Act and all
major legislation, including intelligence, for over 24 years, including the 14 he served as
Senator Nunn's staff director on the SASC.*

LACK OF UNITY

The system created in the late 1940s sustained itself for another 40 years. But
in these decades leading up to the GNA, the services were anything but unified.

During the Vietnam War, each service felt like it was fighting its own war
with no unified effort, to the point where the evacuation of Saigon was split into
two separate commands: one at sea and one on land, each operating individually.
The 1961 Bay of Pigs invasion and the botched handling of the USS *Pueblo* and SS
Mayaguez seizures further exemplified the services' lack of communication and
unity. President Carter's Secretary of Defense, Harold Brown, once commented
that:

U.S. Army and Air Force units in Europe have difficulty communicating because their systems were developed separately and are not interoperable. Because the Navy and Air Force use different refueling equipment, tanker aircraft of one cannot refuel fighters of the other without an equipment change.

The framers of the GNA also referenced another operational problem further complicated by disunity: the 1980 Desert One debacle. Here, in an attempt to rescue 53 American hostages in Iran, eight service members died after a Marine helicopter collided with an Air Force transport plane in the middle of the Iranian desert. The tragedy was likely avoidable, but the individual units of the rescue mission had never trained together, and Marine helicopters, designed for use at sea, were not well equipped to operate in sandstorms – circumstances that unnecessarily endangered and cost the lives of service members.

Additionally, the invasion of Grenada three years later, although successful, lacked a joint operation conducted by an established and understood unified command. The Army and Marine Corps, unable to conduct a joint operation or even communicate reliably, basically divided the island in half. Marine helicopters refused to carry Army soldiers. Army units ashore were unable to call for naval gunfire support.

The disjointedness at Grenada was the straw that broke the camel's back; lawmakers became convinced that something needed to be done. Specifically, the various operational problems demonstrated a need for greater joint roles in planning, deploying troops, and command and control of operations. The shortcomings and insufficiencies of these operations set the stage for the GNA, which strengthened civilian control of the military and the role of the chairman, increased and expanded the authority of the JS, strengthened and clarified the function and reporting chain of the unified and (then) specified commanders, and generally reduced the authorities of the service chiefs. Subsequent operations gave more authority to joint commanders in operations and doctrine. Additionally, joint warfare doctrine was emphasized over service-centric doctrine.

CJCS General David Jones was one of the first military officials to articulate the problem before Congress when he told the House Armed Services Committee in 1982:

> It is not sufficient to have just resources, dollars, and weapon systems; we must also have an organization which will allow us to develop the proper strategy, necessary planning, and the full warfighting capability. We do not have an adequate organization structure today.

The service chiefs, on the other hand, strongly opposed the direction of the legislation in their testimony before Congress, especially the fact that it greatly enhanced the roles of the joint community at the expense of the detailed functions of the service chiefs themselves. Overall, the legislation made the service chiefs' positions clearly subordinate to service secretaries who would assign and define their duties. The key words of the civilian GNA indicated everything in DoD is subject to "the authority, direction, and control" of the civilian secretary of defense. In the military departments, the service chiefs were subject to the "authority, direction, and control" of the civilian service secretaries.

This was an enormous change to how the service departments had always been organized and how they operated. Adjustments to this culture are still underway some three decades later.

THE JOINT STAFF SYSTEM

Former Under Secretary of Defense for Policy Michèle Flournoy testified to Congress about what she described as the "tyranny of consensus." As Flournoy stated when describing DoD management trends:

> Perhaps the most pernicious of these is what I like to call "the tyranny of consensus" that has come to dominate the Pentagon. Getting the concurrence of a broad range of stakeholders on a given course of action too often takes precedence over framing and assessing a set of compelling options or alternatives to present to senior leaders for decision.

This "tyranny of consensus" remains an enduring problem within the Pentagon, but if it is bad now, it was worse then, never was it more prevalent and institutionalized than in the JS prior to the GNA. Since the JS worked for the JCS as a collective group, any issue being worked on could only be approved and forwarded by the CJCS if it represented the consensus view of all JCS members.

To create consensus, the JCS established what was known as the "Flimsy-Buff-Green" system (the names drawn from the color of the paper used addressing the issue at each step). The flimsy was the first JS cut at an assigned issue written by a JS action officer (AO). The JS AO would then convene a team from the services, with each service having a dedicated team to address such actions, that would review the flimsy, make suggestions, and move it on to the "buff" phase. If a consensus view emerged on the issues, and the services agreed with the product, then the paper would go "green" and be presented for final approval to the JCS. Several observers during the pre-GNA period described the system in critical terms (emphasis added):

- The system used to process JCS actions and decisions reflects the nature and intent of the JCS structure. It is a system that is based not only on coordination with the services but on their concurrence.

- It is a mechanism that maximizes the opportunities for compromise and resolution of disagreement at every step from the inception of the paper to consideration of the Joint Chiefs. It is a process of negotiation and unabashedly so.

- It is at the same time open to criticism for being *ponderous, slow, and productive of a tepid compromised product*, which represents service views far more than any Joint Staff view. In fact, it is difficult to establish even the existence of a "Joint Staff view" in many cases.

- It has been pointed out that the very nature of the flimsy-buff-green process, itself a reflection of the basic structure of the JCS, leads participants to *seek the lowest common denominator*, the loosest language, on which all can agree.

This system ended, for all practical purposes, on January 20, 1989—President George H. W. Bush's inauguration—when the CJCS, Admiral William Crowe, as the first chairman under GNA, informed the JS that it was now to function as his staff. Therefore, it was to seek input from the services in establishing positions, but it need not seek concurrence. Further, Crowe emphasized that there would be clear JS positions established on issues that he would present to the secretary of defense and, where requested, the president, in his role as primary military advisor to both. From that day forward, the CJCS arrived at JCS meetings in "the tank" after the other chiefs were present, and they all stood when he entered the room. It is worth noting that prior to the creation of the position of vice chairman as the number two military officer, the service chiefs took turns being "chairman" when the CJCS was out of town or on leave. Not surprisingly, the service chiefs also strongly opposed the creation of the vice chairman position at the time.

Accompanying this change was the enormously increased size of the JS. The GNA requirement for "joint duty experience" for consideration to promotion to flag rank had two near-term consequences: First, the number of joint positions as defined on the joint duty list (JDL) expanded; and second, higher quality officers began to seek assignments on the JS and the staffs of the regional commanders. Prior to this change, a joint duty billet was generally viewed as a dead-end assignment.

Part of this expansion of joint duty positions was made feasible by the GNA-directed expansion of the responsibilities of the CJCS. This included expanding the role in the preparation of programs and budgets by tasking him or her to provide "program and budget recommendations," make "alternative" program and budget priorities, and to play a role in the review and development of requirements. This squarely placed the CJCS into an area that had been the exclusive domain of the services prior to the GNA.

However, given that the tenure of Admiral Crowe's successor, Gen. Colin Powell, was largely focused on dealing with real-world conflicts like Operations *Just Cause* (Panama) in 1989 and *Desert Storm* (Iraq) in 1991, neither the CJCS nor the JS significantly inserted themselves into the program and budget debates early on. Consequently, during this timeframe, the chairman's program recommendations and the chairman's program review became very routine documents that did not reflect serious analysis or deliberation.

While serving as vice chairman, Adm. William A. Owens led an effort to energize the Joint Requirements Oversight Committee (JROC). While he was successful in the short term, this effort slowly evolved into another bureaucratic activity that produced more heat than fire and proved to be one more group requiring consensus. Nonetheless, to support these authorities, the JS grew in size with the J-8 (force structure, resources, and assessment) becoming a major staff section led by a three-star officer.

THE RISE OF THE CINCs

The GNA also resulted in expanded powers and visibility for the regional commanders, then known as commanders-in-chief (CINCs). Several articles began to appear in the media referring to the CINCs as equivalent to the Roman proconsuls of the past, a sentiment helped by the operations during the 1990s that greatly raised the visibility of these leaders. They included: General Maxwell

Thurman (Panama), Gen. Norman Schwarzkopf (Iraq), Gen. Wesley Clark (the Balkans), and Gen. Anthony Zinni (Iraq and the wider Middle East). CINCs were included in JROC deliberations and given a senior role by the VCJCS and the JS. They also saw their own staffs expand, driven by the need for more detailed plans and partly due to the effects of the JDL.

Over time, all of these factors slowly combined to methodically compress the role of the service chiefs. The service chiefs lost some of their control over programs and budgets, their formal role (as restricted by the GNA) made them subordinate to their service secretary, and they were gradually distanced from operational planning with the rise of CINCs.

In 2002, a service chief commented how, as a group, the JCS had not been consulted before the decision to invade Iraq was made "on the third floor." Later, when asked his view of the 2003 invasion plan for Iraq prepared by CENTCOM Commander Gen. Tommy Franks, another service chief stated that he had not seen it. This was a major departure from the period where services served as "executive agents" for regional and specified commanders and an even further departure from the WWII experiences of Leahy, Marshall, King, and Arnold.

In summary, when examining the service chiefs' role in operational matters, the pendulum has swung gradually from one extreme to the other. Like many things in management, there is a constant quest for the mean whenever structures or processes are seen as "out of balance." To correct this currently perceived imbalance, leadership might:

1. Include all the Joint Chiefs in operational planning.

2. Allow the JS to support, in select areas, the other Joint Chiefs regarding topics where JS expertise is pronounced.

3. Ensure all members of the Joint Chiefs have a pathway for routinely expressing their views to the secretary of defense and the president.

4. Rethink the requirement for all forces to be aligned in some manner to a combatant commander; unassigned forces should be under the services, not the JS.

Note: In the early 2000s, Secretary Rumsfeld changed the title of CINCs to combatant commanders (CCDRs) to avoid confusion with the president's constitutional role as commander in chief of the armed forces.

THE CHIEFS' ROLE IN ACQUISITION

In 1986, President Ronald Reagan created the "President's Blue Ribbon Commission on Defense Management" by Executive Order 12526. Commonly known as the Packard Commission, President Reagan instituted the commission over the objections of Secretary of Defense Caspar Weinberger. Former Hewlett-Packard Chairman David Packard, who had served as deputy secretary of defense under Secretary Melvin Laird during the Nixon administration, chaired the commission and chose Rhett Dawson as his staff director. Additionally, Ken Krieg served as a key staff member.

The fundamental intent of the Packard Commission was to study and suggest ways to simplify the acquisition system by consolidating policy and oversight, reducing reporting chains, eliminating duplicative functions and excessive regulations, and establishing an environment in which program managers and their staffs could operate as centers of excellence. It was thought that this effort would allow for a substantial reduction in the total number of personnel in the defense acquisition system, reducing them to levels that were comparable with commercial acquisition practices.

The major result of the commission suggested the acquisition chain of command be organized under a civilian "acquisition czar," and that the structure beneath this official report to him. Although many believe the acquisition structural change originated in the GNA, it actually came from the Packard Commission. Packard was the basis for the service acquisition executive (SAE), program executive officer (PEO), and program manager (PM) structure that now exists. It also was the basis for the establishment of the Under Secretary of Defense for Acquisition, whose domain and responsibilities had been steadily expanding until recently. The Packard Commission also placed a premium on recruiting highly qualified civilian personnel for the senior jobs, a goal that has produced mixed results over the last 30 years.

The 1987 National Defense Authorization Act (NDAA), reacting to the Packard Commission, directed that the service chief's organization responsible for research, development, and acquisition (RDA) be eliminated and merged into the new offices in the civilian service secretariat. Accordingly, in the Army, the Deputy Chief of Staff for RDA (DCSRDA) was eliminated and subsumed by the Office of the Assistant Secretary of the Army for RDA (then ASARDA, now ASALT), with the three-star DCSRDA himself becoming the "military deputy" to the assistant secretary.

At the time, the deputy chiefs in the military staffs served something of a line (operational) function regarding R&D and acquisition. The officers in these organizations, in general, had engineering, program management, and acquisition backgrounds in various disciplines such as aviation, munitions, vehicles, ships, and electronics. They were close to and familiar with the current state of technology.

The officials in the secretariat, by contrast, served more of an oversight role and tended to have backgrounds in the external activities of their departments, primarily in dealings with Congress. When the offices were merged, they tended to adopt the service secretaries' oversight perspective as opposed to the military staffs' operational perspective. In addition, although the three-star officers – now known as "military deputies" – were charged with "reporting to the secretary while being responsive to the chief," their connection to the military staffs became more distant.

During the 1980s, and especially during the Reagan buildup, the service chiefs played a major role in reviewing requirements (through their operations, force structure, and platform organizations), and translating them into programs, budgets, and, ultimately, acquisitions. In the Navy, this charted the path to the 600-ship Navy; in the Army, to the acquisition of its "Big Five;" and in the Air Force, to the restart of the B-1 and the simultaneous pursuit of the B-2, along with other stealth aircraft such as the F-117A. The chiefs also played a significant role in program reviews, evidenced by the presence of Gen. John Wickham in the decision briefing where he recommended the cancellation of the Division Air Defense system (DIVAD, also known as the Sergeant York). Chiefs also served as connective tissue between the requirements community (generally called the "force developers") and the acquisition community (generally called the "materiel developers").

With the establishment of the SAE/PEO structure and the elimination of the three-star RDA officers and their offices from the military staffs, the chiefs became more distant from the acquisition process. Unsurprisingly, the connections between the requirements communities and the acquisition communities also became more distant. Whereas there had once been routine dialogue between these two communities and the operators, such discussions have become less routine, with the requirements function growing more confused and—perhaps inevitably—less disciplined. This needed to be corrected.

With its 2016 NDAA, Congress indicated a concern that the service chiefs were now too distant from the acquisition process and sought a way to reengage them. This is consistent with comments made by Secretary Ash Carter to return a "customer focus" to the acquisition process. The items below offer a suggested approach to reengaging the service chiefs in the acquisition process:

1. Service chiefs should be designated the chief requirements officers of their service and should approve requirements documents for Major Defense Acquisition Programs (MDAP, also referred to as ACAT 1) and lesser programs at their discretion. The service chief should establish processes by which requirements are reviewed and approved and required timelines under which they should be finalized with the intention of reducing the time required for the release of requests for proposals (RFPs).

2. To fulfill the role of chief requirements officer, service chiefs should seek the reestablishment of their own RDA position within their service's military staff and have it reportable to them as they downsize their staffs overall. The chief should task this office to provide relevant and contemporary advice about existing technologies and facilitate routine conversations with industry about technological risks and expected costs.

3. The service chiefs should be the key players in "linking and streamlining" the requirements, acquisition, and budget processes as required by the FY16 NDAA and recommended by a Defense Business Board study I chaired in 2012.

4. The full intent of the letter and spirit of the FY16 NDAA regarding increasing the role and authority of the service chiefs should be fully implemented. The chiefs should reply to the law's requirement to ask for any additional authorities they need, and Congress should approve them.

In addition to the JS, the number of offices and activities involved in the acquisition process needs to be reduced. An internal Army report made two key observations, as summarized by *Defense-Aerospace*: First, "the number of personnel overseeing the acquisition process is rising, while the number of qualified, accountable professionals charged to develop and produce the product" is decreasing; and second, the acquisition process has developed a noncollaborative nature with "multiple opportunities for oversight staffs to question and challenge requirements."

In both the legislative and executive branches, too many oversight offices have been established over time. The number of such offices needs to be greatly reduced and those providing additional oversight, as opposed to additional insight, eliminated. This will require a major review but is essential to giving the service chief the authority and responsibility needed to improve and accelerate acquisition.

CONCLUSION

Over the past three decades, in both operational matters and acquisition programs, the roles of the service chiefs have been significantly reduced. For various reasons, service chiefs' key insights have become underutilized. The overall defense process would benefit from a rebalancing of these trends.

In today's complex world, collective wisdom is better than individual wisdom. Because of this, the chiefs should be more involved in the preparation and review of operational plans, and they should reengage in acquisition, particularly by playing a role in adding discipline to the requirements process and ensuring its connection with the acquisition process. Having done that, the chiefs will be much better positioned to ensure that their service programs and budgets better reflect immediate and future operational needs.

With such changes, the service chiefs of today will still not be the service chiefs of the early 1980s. The objective should not be to minimize opportunities to use their substantial experience, but to maximize its application in the joint arena. The architects of the GNA did not seek to reduce service expertise; they sought to maximize the joint perspective. The Grenada operation did not suffer because the services did not know what to do, but because the services did not know how to work together. Combining service capability with joint operations and planning is the "secret sauce," and the steps suggested above should help to enrich the recipe.

CHAPTER 10: THE CHAIRMAN AND THE COMMANDERS

This chapter was written in 2016 for incoming Defense Secretary James Mattis to give senior leaders a historical perspective of how the Goldwater-Nichols Act (GNA) fundamentally changed the relationships and powers of the secretary of defense, the Chairman of the Joint Chiefs (CJCS), and the operational combatant commanders (CCDRs).

Since the 1986 passage of the GNA, an increase in joint awareness among the military services, complemented by the rise in influence of the regional combatant commanders (CCDRs)[1], has proven to be an enduring challenge for the defense establishment. This evolution, directly attributable to the GNA, has been quite positive. While the law has been judged to be an overall success, with any endeavor undertaken over three decades ago, review and reflection are always useful.

The solidification of interservice cooperation can be subdivided into three components: enshrining the concept of "jointness" in law, enhancing the role of the regional commanders, and defining the role of the CJCS as the CCDRs' voice and connecting link to the secretary and the president.

---

[1] The acronyms CCDRs and CINC will be used interchangeably depending on historical relevancy.

JOINTNESS

In the pre-GNA period, the concept of jointness received very little emphasis in both officers' professional development and assignments. Officers were not evaluated nor rewarded for possessing joint qualifications or experience. Rather, joint experiences were often seen as a negative. For example, during their military education, some officers attended the staff or war colleges of another service. Rather than viewing the diversification and breadth of their cross-service education as a benefit, personnel assignment officers often viewed this negatively, believing that the young officers had forgone opportunities for additional (and presumably valuable) socialization with others in their service year groups.

Within the regional commands, officer assignments were greatly influenced by the service most traditionally associated with that command, whether by history or habit. For example, during the Cold War, U.S. European Command (EUCOM) was dominated by Army officers and supported by Air Force when necessary. Accordingly, 10 of the 11 EUCOM heads were Army Officers. Army's 50-year EUCOM dominance ended in 2000. Since then, the position has been evenly divided between two Army generals, three Air Force generals, a Marine general, and a Navy admiral.

This has also been the similar case in the U.S. Pacific Command (originally PACOM, updated to INDOPACOM in 2018), though INDOPACOM has proven to be more resilient against accepting more joint-focused changes. This trend is most evident in leadership, where every commander since 1947 has been a Navy admiral. In 2004, there was a moment of brief possibility for change with the nomination of Air Force General Gregory Martin as CINCPAC, but Martin withdrew his nomination after his SASC confirmation hearing. Although Martin primarily withdrew due to his answer about an Air Force acquisition scandal involving the proposed leasing of KC-767 tankers, many also believed that the Navy and its allies on the Hill, particularly Senator John McCain, were opposed to anyone but an admiral leading the Pacific theater. Accordingly, INDOPACOM has remained firmly in Navy hands.

This was also the case with the former Atlantic Command (LANTCOM), which may be largely responsible for directing Congress's attention to the issue of jointness. Of the 19 LANTCOM commanders, all but one have been Navy admirals – Marine Gen. John Sheehan, who held the post from 1994-1997, was the sole exception. However, LANTCOM's performance during the October 1983 operation in Grenada illustrated the limitations and dangers of having a single service dominate regional commands.

Since the end of WWII, LANTCOM had been tasked with patrolling and protecting the sea lines of communication between the U.S. and Europe. This duty was of the utmost strategic importance, as it provided the U.S. with the capabilities to reinforce its European allies in case of Soviet invasion. To emphasize LANTCOM's importance to NATO and European allies, the CINC of LANTCOM also held the title of Supreme Allied Commander Atlantic (SACLANT). Grenada, a small Caribbean island, was within LANTCOM's area of responsibility (AOR), though it was on the fringe of its mission; most of the focus was on Europe.

However, as communist adventurism around the Caribbean – especially around Cuba – raised fears of hostiles on our doorstep, focus began to move away from the traditional deep-water priority associated with the North Atlantic sea lanes and recenter on the Caribbean. When the decision to invade Grenada was made, SACLANT Adm. Wesley McDonald was given the operational task of executing the mission. Although McDonald had a sub-unified command within LANTCOM – the U.S. Forces Caribbean, which was headquartered in Key West, Florida – he elected to assign the operation to Vice Adm. Joseph Metcalf, the commander of the U.S. Second Fleet, headquartered with LANTCOM in Norfolk, Virginia.

McDonald's decision to assign the operation to Metcalf simplified communications, but it also meant that the headquarters controlling a ground operation had no assigned Army officers. Since the operational plan required

Army Rangers and at least one brigade of the 82nd Airborne Division, this was a serious shortcoming. In order to provide some ground expertise to the effort, the Joint Chiefs temporarily assigned Maj. Gen. H. Norman Schwarzkopf, the commanding general of the Army's 24th Infantry Division at Ft. Stewart, Georgia, to Metcalf's staff. Maj. Gen. Colin Powell, the chief military assistant to Defense Secretary Casper Weinberger at the time, selected Schwarzkopf for the mission because they needed "someone senior on board who understood ground combat." This was reflective of a glaring problem: There were no Army officers on either McDonald's or Metcalf's staff. Later, Schwarzkopf recalled how when he arrived at LANTCOM, McDonald simply told him to "try and be helpful," since "we don't need the Army giving us a hard time." Accordingly, numerous problems and mishaps plagued the operation, leading Powell to later characterize Grenada as a "sloppy success" that highlighted the need for jointness within the services.

Consequently, the GNA focused on reversing the missing jointness by making it a qualification for promotions. This specifically applied to those selected for promotion to general and flag officer and required candidates to participate in a two-year tour in a designated joint position. Given that all the services had their own requirements for professional military education (PME) plus specialty training and, of course, field time, finding time in an officer's career to fit in joint experience proved to be something of a challenge.

The Pentagon sought to address this issue by expanding the number of billets on its newly-created joint duty list, adding flexibility in managing officers' careers. Furthermore, the department became more judicious in selecting the officers sent to senior joint PME courses, such as those at National Defense University, since the GNA required that over half of those officers be assigned to joint billets upon graduation. Balancing all of these requirements still proves to be something of a work in progress. The Army, for instance, recently announced a program where joint duty qualifications can be achieved through either accumulated service time, joint duty points, or a combination of both. The Pentagon is also addressing the bureaucratic challenges of measuring joint experience with formal directions laid out in DoD Instructions 1300.19, the Joint Officer Management Program.

Although joint officer management has continued to be a challenge, the resulting increase in joint awareness and cooperation has been almost universally praised. Successful missions including *Operation Just Cause* in 1989, *Operation Desert Storm* in 1991, *Operation Uphold Democracy* in Haiti in 1994, and the operational and tactical performances seen in *Operation Enduring Freedom* in Afghanistan and *Operation Iraqi Freedom* in Iraq have shown that the "sloppy success" of Grenada in 1983 is clearly in the rearview mirror.

The attempt at jointness, however, tends to be contrasted with what has been named a "General Staff System," such as the one used by Germany in the 19th and 20th centuries. It is always useful to be reminded of the distinctions between the two. Under the General Staff concept, as practiced by Gen. Helmuth von Moltke the Elder, the chief of the Prussian General Staff from 1857 to 1888, a small cadre of promising young officers were selected early in their military career and intensely trained for general staff duties.

Once selected and trained, they became General Staff officers and were distinct from others within their service—mainly the Prussian army. The General Staff was small, usually about 350 officers and never more than twice that number. Although such officers had a regimental affiliation and would leave for field commands on a determined schedule, they always returned to the General Staff. Although this resulted in an efficient system where von Moltke and other senior leaders knew their subordinates well, it also came to be identified with the rise and solidification of German militarism.

The jointness doctrine advanced by the GNA is essentially the inverse. The officers chosen for joint duty by their services are ones considered to have great potential, which is why they are placed on a track for promotion to flag rank. However, none of these officers ever actually leave their service. Unlike the General Staff system, where officers occasionally went to a service and then returned to the General Staff, the post-GNA system is one where service officers are occasionally assigned joint duty positions and then return to their service. The quality of the Joint Staff improved after the passage of the GNA, and such duty was defined and designed to be career enhancing. Importantly, it has only a faint resemblance to the German General Staff concept.

USAF Combatant Commander of the U.S. Northern Command and NORAD General Lori Robinson and Maj. Gen. Arnold Punaro, USMC, Ret. discuss NORTHCOM's major role in civil support of the homeland and the increased use of the Guard and Reserve components.

THE RISE OF THE COMBATANT COMMANDERS

In 2001, *Washington Post* reporter Dana Priest wrote a series of articles about the expanded role regional CINCs were playing. She later won a Pulitzer Prize for the series and crafted the articles into a book, *The Mission: Waging War and Keeping Peace with America's Military*. Priest stated that the GNA effectively made the CINCs "proconsuls," a reference to a delegated position of authority in the Roman Empire. A Roman proconsul was normally a military soldier carrying on a campaign in the name of the appointed civilian consul. John Hamre, the former deputy secretary of defense and now the CEO of the Center for Strategic and International Studies, has testified that combatant commanders (CCDRs) have taken on numerous roles that are more appropriately led by other civilian officials.

In American history, a number of officials, both civilian and military, have been delegated enormous power to run distant holdings or administrative areas. These include William Howard Taft as governor of the Philippines in the early 1900s, Gen. Douglas MacArthur as the leader in post-World War II Japan, Gen. Lucius Clay who performed a similar function in occupied Germany, and even diplomat Paul Bremer in Iraq following the 2003 American invasion.

But as Priest accurately described, with the enhancement of their position after the GNA, the CINCs had become a power unto themselves. The chain of command was clarified as leading from the president through the secretary of defense, making the CINCs functionally disconnected from the military departments and technically disconnected from the CJCS. As Priest would later describe, their role "evolved without a grand strategy or a centralized look and without much of a systematic lash-up between other obvious parts of the U.S. Government, namely State, Commerce, and Justice." In other words, in its efforts to create a military officer who could unify, coordinate, direct, and in times of conflict, command forces, the GNA had created a very prominent "chief among equals."

Much of this enhanced responsibility flowed from two simple facts: scope and funding. In the domain of scope, the CCDRs were the most senior, visible American officials having a wide view of the social forces and trends within a region. In writing her *Washington Post* series, Priest noted that she had traveled to 24 countries with four regional CCDRs. In terms of protocol, the ambassador in a country outranks the CCDR, but in practical terms this was not the case. The CCDRs arrived on their own plane, accompanied by a large staff, and were generally greeted with full military honors followed by a large motorcade into the capital. By contrast, even assistant secretaries of state, who technically oversaw the ambassadors in their areas, flew commercial and carried their own bags.

There were further complications in how Defense and State define AORs. The AORs for CCDRs not only do not correspond to the geographical areas of the assistant secretaries of state, they do not even divide the world into the same number of regions. Whereas there are six regional assistant secretaries of state (not counting the Assistant Secretary of International Organization Affairs), there are only five regional commanders (not counting the U.S. Northern Command). This creates some sizable headaches for those responsible for interagency coordination on the ground. One CCDR once complained that his AOR fell within the zones of four different assistant secretaries at Foggy Bottom.

Back in Washington, the confusion is not lessened. For example, the U.S. Central Command's (CENTCOM) AOR includes one country in Africa (Egypt) and now includes Israel, which was previously in the AOR of EUCOM. At State, the Bureau of Near Eastern Affairs (NEA) does include Israel, along with all the countries across North Africa from Egypt to Morocco. All African countries except Egypt are in the AOR of the DoD's Africa Command (AFRICOM). Thus, NEA has to rope in AFRICOM and CENTCOM on any matter that involves, for example, Israel, Egypt, and Libya.

The factors listed give the CCDRs exalted status and give the commanders significant resources they may use to promote their missions.

Starting in the early 1990s, the CCDRs were tasked by the CJCS to prepare and present a theater engagement plan (TEP) to the JCS. The TEP was intended to have the CCDRs identify major efforts that they had underway to enhance training and facilitate coordination with regional partners. A major component of the TEPs focused on what were then called CINC Exercises. These tended to be rather large-scale endeavors, some involving troops and others restricted to command post exercises, designed to solidify relations in the military-to-military sphere. But given the longevity of Clausewitz's famous dictum on the connectivity between war and politics, these efforts inevitably had a degree of

State Department interest. However, since the annual defense budget measures over 18 times larger than that of State and USAID combined, the majority of the funding for these events came from defense coffers.

Because of this, these exercises were not originally embraced by the DoD and military services that crafted the annual budgets. In general, the exercises were placed on a lower priority than more traditional service training, especially in an environment where there was a degree of resentment attached to the elevated status of the CCDRs. In one instance, during budget formulation, one service zeroed the requested CINC exercises planned by the commander of EUCOM as part of his TEP. In that case, the service chief, recognizing the visibility such exercises had gained, stepped in to restore the funding.

In relative terms, the costs of the exercises were quite modest—as is true for the individual cost of any specific item when viewed as part of a $700 billion budget. However, when resources are constrained, such as during the sequestration regime attached to the 2011 Budget Control Act, the marginal dollar becomes more important and, therefore, more hotly debated.

The net result was that the CCDRs were able to offer and then execute programs exceeding anything the State Department could provide. Matched with the other advantages the CCDRs inherently brought to the table, their emerging role as the major American players on the regional landscape solidified.

But of even greater significance was the warfighting result. Starting with the effectiveness of SOUTHCOM, commanded by Army Gen. Maxwell Thurman during *Operation Just Cause* in 1989, which quickly and relatively cleanly achieved the mission of taking down the corrupt regime of Panamanian strongman General Manuel Noriega, it was clear that the new focus on jointness and the cleaner command structure had great merit. This was seen on a much larger scale the following year during *Operations Desert Shield* and *Desert Storm* conducted by CENTCOM under the command of Army Gen. H. Norman Schwarzkopf. Notably, Schwarzkopf's plan for ejecting Iraqi forces from Kuwait started with a 37-day air campaign, followed by a major ground campaign, supported by naval forces that led the Iraqis to fear an amphibious landing in their rear. Every operation since that time has had the clear stamp of jointness and CCDR command, and from the tactical perspective, all have been successful. The translation of such military success into the political domain, however, remains a quest that is only partially satisfied.

Nonetheless, this increase in the scope of responsibility, visibility, and activity of the CCDRs has come with a largely unexpected cost: additional staffing. In order to be more visible, more widely traveled, and to craft things such as the TEPs and integrated priority lists (IPLs), the command staffs grew to meet demand. Although it is difficult to determine exactly how large this increase has been, it has been significant enough to be noticeable.

Whereas CCDR staffs were once largely restricted to the intelligence (J-2), operations and plans (J-3), and logistics (J-4) functions, the additional responsibilities brought the need to add staff elements for personnel (J-1), policy (J-5), cyber and communications (J-6), training and doctrine (J-7), resources (J-8), and assessments and evaluations (J-9). In total, military and civilian staffing of the joint regional and functional commands now measures over 41,000 people. In addition, because of Congress's desire for more information from the regional commanders themselves, many commands have had to establish their own legislative liaison offices to bolster their public affairs operations. Some of this additional staffing on the military side has also likely been stimulated by the services' need to get as many officers as possible joint certified.

General Norman Schwarzkopf, USA, Commander of the U.S. Central Command during Operation Desert Shield-Desert Storm, prepares to testify before the Senate Armed Services Committee (SASC) in 1991. The SASC required the combatant commanders to testify annually on their responsibilities. From the left: SASC Staff Director Arnold Punaro, Chairman Senator Sam Nunn, General Schwarzkopf, and Committee Counsel Rick DeBobes.

THE CJCS/CCDR RELATIONSHIP

The GNA empowered the CJCS by making it the senior officer in the American military, stating that the role would be the principal advisor to the secretary of defense and the president. The GNA also provided a formal vice chairman, making the JS its staff, and improving the quality of the staff itself. However, it also removed any confusion over the CJCS's place in the operational chain of command: the position sits firmly outside of it. For some, this diminished the CJCS's authority in favor of increasing civilian control of the military. But in actuality, the chairman works closely with the CCDRs.

The relationship between CJCS Colin Powell and his CCDRs, Generals Thurman and Schwarzkopf, was established during major joint operations. Here, the CJCS provided support to the CCDRs at the policy level by explaining their plans to the commander-in-chief and giving them top-level cover when necessary with the President and Congress. This assistance has proven invaluable over time.

There have been times when CJCS relations with a CCDR have been somewhat testy, such as between CJCS General Powell and SOUTHCOM commander General Thurman (who had once been senior to Powell in the Army), and the one that existed between CJCS Gen. Hugh Shelton and EUCOM's Gen. Wesley Clark during the Kosovo operation in 1999. Shelton and Secretary Cohen were concerned that Clark's frequent appearances on the national news ran the risk of him getting ahead of formal policy, perhaps leading to the development of a situation similar to the one that resulted in General MacArthur's relief by President Truman in 1951.

However, the CJCS has generally proven to be an effective transmitter of CCDR issues, concerns, and plans to the secretary and president. Moreover, as the senior military officer on active duty, the CJCS—even out of the formal chain of command—exerts no small amount of influence over its implicitly subordinate regional commanders. There is one area, however, where the authority granted to the CJCS by the GNA and his requests for input from the CCDRs have not met expectations: resourcing.

The GNA expanded the responsibilities of the CJCS beyond strategic direction and war planning into such areas as readiness, logistics planning, force capabilities, and advice on requirements, programs, and budgets. These were all areas that had previously been the purview of the military departments and service chiefs. Significantly, the GNA even required the CJCS to offer to the secretary of defense "alternative program recommendations and budget proposals within projected resource levels and guidance provided by the secretary, in order to achieve greater conformance with the priorities [established by the secretary]."

These expansions inserted a joint officer into top-level management. Although it should have been seen as inevitable, the GNA authors evidently never envisioned the JS growth that would be needed for the CJCS to address these newly-assigned responsibilities.

In order to address the resourcing duty, the chairmen making this transition, Adm. William Crowe and Gen. John Shalikashvili, took two steps. First, they assigned the vice chairman the job of energizing and overseeing the Joint Requirements Oversight Council (JROC), which reviewed and validated joint requirements. Second, they tasked the CCDRs with developing and submitting integrated priority lists (IPLs) of their resource needs. Over time, neither effort has fully addressed the CJCS's resource responsibility.

The JROC, despite good intentions from several vice chairmen beginning in 1994 with Adm. William Owens, has never been totally successful in either originating or coordinating priorities across the services. Being unable to address the major issues of requirements and force structure, the JROC retreated into smaller issues existing in areas agreed to be narrowly joint, sometimes called the "operational commons." Over time, the JROC itself developed a large supporting staff administering an increasingly complex process known as the Joint Capabilities Integration and Development System (JCIDS).

As for the IPLs, their limited utility stemmed from the fact that they offered ideas on things to be added to the defense program but failed to identify items that might be eliminated. In other words, they were not useful for balancing a budget. As one CCDR once commented when confronted on this topic, "I can tell you what I want, but I'm not prepared to tell you what I don't want."

There is nothing easy or uncontroversial about formulating and presenting programs and budgets. The process the Pentagon uses for this purpose, while very likely the best in government, has clear limitations. However, the GNA, with its goal to include the CJCS in this effort, has resulted in more staff, with little more to show for it. If the CJCS and the CCDRs do not intend to usefully participate in this arena, then they should ask for statutory relief from the responsibility and reduce the staffing that has developed to support it.

The GNA was successful in its mission to improve jointness in the services. Military operations undertaken since the 1986 passage of the GNA have been much better planned, organized, integrated, and executed. Still, there has been significant growth in the staffs that support these senior officers, with much of the increases driven by the greater demands placed on an official with greater authority. However, a review should be conducted in areas where increased staff size has not created additional impact. In the absence of such an effort, the size of the defense overhead is likely to continue increasing unchecked.

Chapter 11: Roles of the Chairman and Vice Chairman of the Joint Chiefs of Staff

This chapter originated in 2015 when a sitting secretary of defense asked me to help with his upcoming decisions in selecting the new chairman of the Joint Chiefs of Staff (CJCS) and the new vice chairman of the Joint Chiefs of Staff (VCJCS), the military's two most senior positions. My input was not focused on specific individuals but rather on the requirements of the positions, the experiences necessary to succeed, and the expectations of the Goldwater-Nichols Act (GNA) for those two essential positions. In short, this chapter lays out methods for finding the right officers with the needed experience and qualifications. These recommendations are based on years of prior observation and my firsthand knowledge of what the framers of the GNA intended. Since its inception, this memorandum has been updated and redistributed to senior OSD officials whenever a new chairman or vice chairman has been selected.

When the CJCS and VCJCS positions become vacant, careful consideration should be given to the two positions and their differing requirements and responsibilities. When determining which officers would best fill these roles, the decision makers would benefit from revisiting the GNA's eight goals, which have a direct statutory bearing on these positions.

History

The position of CJCS was established with the 1949 amendment to the National Security Act of 1947. The concept intended to have the CJCS provide military advice to the president that reflected a consensus of the Joint Chiefs, rather than having the president himself sort through the differing views of the service chiefs. The CJCS had no direct command authority. This holds true to today.

In August 1949, President Truman appointed Gen. Omar N. Bradley, then Army chief of staff who had established himself as a major military figure during World War II, as the first CJCS. The following year, Bradley was promoted to five-star rank so he would not be outranked by his supposed subordinate, Gen. Douglas MacArthur, who received his five-star rank in WWII. Bradley would be the last military officer promoted to five-star rank and also the only CJCS with five stars.

With the exception of Adm. Arthur Radford (President Eisenhower's second CJCS), the first nine chairmen were selected from among the service chiefs, or a former service chief in the case of Gen. Maxwell Taylor, appointed by President John F. Kennedy. This was quite understandable as these were the senior officers with whom the president would be most familiar. Given they all had significant combat experience from WWII, they were well-known, national figures. (The unified and specified combatant command structure in the field was still in its formative stage).

Beginning with Gen. John Vessey in 1982, none of the next seven chairmen were former service chiefs, suggesting the emerging perception that the CJCS should have recent field experience in the strategic and operational demands most encountered by the unified and specified commanders-in-chief (CINCs), as combatant commanders were then known. This trend was unbroken until 2007 when President George W. Bush appointed Adm. Michael Mullen, then the Chief of Naval Operations (CNO).

However, Mullen's appointment was largely driven by the decision not to reappoint Gen. Peter Pace as CJCS for a second two-year term. While Pace had previously served as vice chairman and commander of U.S. Southern Command, he was expected to face a difficult Senate reconfirmation battle if appointed to a second two-year term. Additionally, Secretary Rumsfeld changed the title of officers running the unified commands from CINCs to combatant commanders (CCDRs) to avoid confusion with the president's constitutional role as commander in chief of the armed forces.

The first VCJCS, Air Force Gen. Robert Herres, was appointed in 1987. The GNA made the VCJCS the second-highest-ranking military officer (above the service chiefs) and assigned duties to the position "as may be prescribed by the chairman with the approval of the secretary of defense." Other specified responsibilities for the VCJCS were largely associated with succession or substituting for the CJCS. The GNA also mandated that the CJCS and VCJCS be chosen from different military services, but it was further recommended in hearings and other discussions that they be chosen from different service pairs (the pairs being the historically linked Army-Air Force and Navy-Marine Corps). Evidently, the GNA authors did not expect the VCJCS to "fleet up" to chairman but, because the position passed by only one vote in the Senate Armed Services Committee (SASC), the authors left open this option. Heading to conference, the Senate bill included the vice chairman position, while the House bill included provisions for prior joint experience of general officers. Consequently, both positions were added in compromise.

In 1986, the GNA elaborated on the criteria for the CJCS, stating a candidate should only be appointed after having served as either the vice chairman, a service chief, or a CCDR. However, the GNA provided ample latitude for the president to make other choices if it was determined to be "necessary in the national interest." The GNA also stressed that a service chief should have first served either as a CCDR or in a senior operational joint role, underscoring the fact that the GNA authors wanted service chiefs to bring a joint orientation to their role as a JCS member.

The framers of the GNA, including myself as the staff director of the SASC, felt previous joint experience to be a necessary credential for service at the senior military level. This prerequisite—sometimes formal, sometimes not—applied to the CJCS, the VCJCS, the other Joint Chiefs, and the CCDRs. This was a serious concern for several reasons, most stemming from disasters that precipitated the GNA.

The investigation into the 1983 bombing of the Marine Barracks in Beirut, Lebanon determined that the chain of command was convoluted, contradictory, and so extensive that it prevented quick decision-making, leaving the commander of the European Command (EUCOM) with many responsibilities but insufficient authority. The study, conducted by retired Adm. Robert Long – himself a former head of Pacific Command (PACOM) – argued there was too much interference in the mission from both Washington and the Marine Corps bureaucracy, a conclusion greatly resented by then-Marine Corps Commandant Gen. P.X. Kelley. From this study, it became evident that the services' parochialism – something that was supposed to be rooted out by their sublimation into the DoD – had not only persisted but was also causing deadly consequences.

Within days of the Beirut bombing, the U.S. invaded Grenada. Although the mission was eventually a success (a fact frequently cited by Defense Secretary Weinberger during his GNA testimony to argue against the need for defense organizational reform), the mission was still too costly in terms of time and casualties.

With these two events fresh in their minds, the GNA advocates set out to greatly increase joint experience in leadership by making it a prerequisite for command of the unified commands as well as for service on the JCS. They were immediately impressed when President Reagan nominated a rare kind of officer – Adm. William Crowe – to replace General Vessey as chairman.

Adm. Crowe, the former commander of PACOM, had gone out of his way to carve out a career far from the Navy's normal progression. Crowe had been a diesel submariner and had taken time from traditional naval duties to earn a Ph.D. in international relations at Princeton. As the *New York Times* noted: "Admiral Crowe has an unusual amount of experience in joint positions where his Navy loyalties were subordinated to responsibility to all the services." This was the ideal that GNA sought to normalize, making him a worthy fit.

While Crowe was in favor of reform – a fact known by Senator Goldwater, Senator Nunn, and their senior SASC staff, including myself – he kept quiet on this position from the other senior military leaders. Despite this, Crowe's appointment alone was a major advancement for reform; in open testimony, General Vessey had been rather subtle about reform.

After the GNA passed, Crowe was initially cautious in exerting control over the Joint Staff (JS), as the law mandated. However, on January 20, 1989 – the day President George H. W. Bush was inaugurated – Crowe summoned all JS officers down to the division chief level and announced that he was implementing "Phase 2" of the GNA, meaning the JS would no longer use the old consensus process regarding the services. Their input would be sought and considered, but they would not have veto power over either JS decisions or his own.

Although not a point of major discussion at the time, the GNA appreciably expanded the CJCS's management responsibilities beyond strategic direction and war planning into such areas as readiness, logistics planning, force capabilities, and, most significantly, providing advice on requirements, programs, and budgets. The GNA even required the CJCS to offer to the secretary of defense "alternative program recommendations and budget proposals within projected resource levels and guidance provided by the secretary, in order to achieve greater conformance with the priorities [established by the secretary]."

This was a major insertion of the CJCS into top-level management areas. Although somewhat predictable, the GNA authors never envisioned the huge staffs that would grow to support these newly-assigned responsibilities. As the JS grew, certain SASC members questioned the utility of the change.

Although the directorate for force structure, resources, and assessment (J-8) on the JS intended to draft alternative recommendations, the position has grown considerably. However, this growth has not always translated into the CJCS providing such alternatives with any degree of consistency. In the past, the CJCS has simply provided a brief memo to the secretary that the service budgets and program objective memorandums (POMs) were satisfactory. This is well short of the intent of the GNA and a major insertion of the CJCS into top-level management areas.

Similarly, the CCDRs have not provided the intended level of detail when articulating their own resource needs through means including integrated priority lists (IPLs). Additionally, some CCDRs have indicated that they lack the sufficient staffing to even develop IPLs and complete other resource inputs. Talking about the IPLs, one resourcing authority noted: "As the Holy Roman Empire was neither 'Holy,' nor 'Roman,' nor an 'Empire,' so the IPLs are neither 'integrated', nor 'prioritized' – but they are a 'list.'" However, if the CJCS is to play a serious role in resource allocation, CCDRs' inputs must become more detailed, timelier, and seriously considered.

For their part, the service chiefs maintain a covetous attitude toward POM preparation, taking advantage of a small loophole in the GNA regarding financial management. Though the legislation clearly states that the service secretaries are responsible for budgets and financial management, the POMs have been kept under the purview of the service chiefs.

Shortly after the passage of the GNA, the CJCS assigned oversight of these expanded budget and requirement duties to the newly-created vice chairman. Implicitly, while the CJCS would focus on developing events on the world scene, the VCJCS would focus on the internal planning and management of the Pentagon, offering alternative views to those of the services. Accordingly, those who have served as the VCJCS tend to have a background weighted more toward defense management than military operations. None of the 11 officers who have thus far served as the VCJCS have been former service chiefs, although all but three had previously served as CCDRs. During his time as VCJCS, Adm. William Owens was given the assignment by the chairman to attempt to control the requirements process through his chairmanship of the Joint Requirements Oversight Council (JROC). Owens made a credible attempt in this regard, but that effort has now expanded into the Joint Capabilities Integration and Development System (JCIDS) process, which has further added to Joint Staff size.

The division of labor that has evolved between the CJCS and the VCJCS—the former focused on operational issues with the latter focused on managerial issues—is consistent with the intent of GNA. This also confirms the judgment of the GNA authors that the vice should not be a "training position" for becoming chairman. The authors did not believe the VCJCS, if the person met the expectations of the duties of the position, would have the background and experience to be CJCS. The recent amendments to GNA in 2017 state this intent more explicitly.

ORIGINAL OBJECTIVES OF THE GNA

In assessing how the roles of the CJCS and VCJCS have evolved, it is useful to reflect back on the original objectives of the GNA:

1. Civilian Primacy

The GNA addressed both administrative and operational dimensions but significantly prioritized operational matters. The overall push of the GNA was to balance joint and service interests and enhance civilian control of the military. The chief purpose was to strengthen civilian authority and control of the military. The authors were very clear in this goal as the language in Title 10 makes nearly every action in DoD subject to "the authority, direction, and control of the secretary of defense."

2. Consolidated Management

The GNA sought to improve military advice by clarifying and expanding the responsibilities of the CJCS in several ways. First, the chairman was made the principal military advisor to the president, secretary of defense, and the National Security Council (NSC). Second, the chairman was handed the duties previously performed by the corporate JCS, in addition to the new duties assigned. Third, he was given a vice chairman to assist him. Lastly, he was given full control over the JS, whereas previously the collective Joint Chiefs controlled it.

3. Direct Chain of Command

The GNA sought to place clear responsibility for the accomplishment of assigned missions on the CCDRs and ensure that their authority is commensurate with their responsibility. The act eliminated all confusion on the operational chain of command by mandating that it run from the president to the secretary to the unified commander. The legislation gave the CCDRs the ability to streamline the chain beneath them to promote accountability and avoid recurrence of the tragedies that led to the new law.

4. Articulated Plans

The GNA sought to increase attention to strategy formulation and contingency planning by requiring the president to submit an annual report on national security strategy. The CJCS was required to submit fiscally constrained strategic plans, and the secretary was instructed to prepare policy guidance for the preparation and review of contingency plans. It required civilian assistance for the secretary in his or her review of contingency plans, ultimately vesting this role for the Office of the Under Secretary of Defense for Policy.

5. Budget Efficiency

The GNA sought to provide for a more efficient use of resources by assigning additional duties to the CJCS, such as advising the secretary on the resource priorities of the unified commanders and assessing whether program and budget submissions of defense components conformed to strategic plans and unified command priorities. However, as noted previously, the GNA authors did not envision the immense staff growth that has occurred in both the CCDRs and the JCS for fulfilling this role. Given the current environment and the way in which these responsibilities have been addressed, perhaps the scope of these activities should be reconsidered and likely reduced.

6. Continuity and Jointness

The GNA sought to enhance the effectiveness of military operations by granting authority in peacetime and wartime. The CJCS was given responsibility for developing joint doctrine and joint training policies.

7. Reduce Redundancy

The GNA sought to improve DoD management by addressing deficiencies such as excessive supervisory spans of control, unnecessary staff layers and duplication of effort, growth in headquarters staffs, poor supervision of defense agencies, and an unclear division of work among defense components. In this specific regard, the act has clearly not created the desired improvements.

Although assessments of GNA are overwhelmingly positive, not every objective was fully achieved; any law that has been on the books for over 30 years should be reviewed. The GNA is certainly no exception. Operational reforms have achieved much of what was desired and expected, yet some criticism continues on the question of whether there has been too much emphasis on jointness and OSD oversight. In the view of some, the current arrangement—built to fix past imbalances—has itself become unbalanced. The focus of the GNA was clearly on the operational side, with aspirations regarding defense management remaining a secondary concern. Arguably, as a result, key efforts on the management side have been disappointments.

Any "GNA II" should review operational practices but focus primarily on defense management where numerous duplications have emerged, certain authorities granted have not been exercised, and other spans of control have been exercised too broadly.

A key point in the GNA is that it did not set the appointments of the CJCS and VCJCS on the same schedule. The authors wanted to give a new president the flexibility to select a CJCS and concluded that the four-year tours of the service chiefs would prove too restrictive. Yet they also saw that it would be virtually impossible to "fire" a sitting chairman. Consequently, the law provided for two-year terms and the chance at reappointment for a second term. The authors, being members of Congress and their staff, also wanted the Senate to be able to reconfirm these senior leaders, ensuring that a full four-year tour would only be possible for leaders that conferred appropriately with the legislature. In the case of Gen. Colin Powell, a never-publicized issue was addressed in a closed session during his reconfirmation.

However, as General Powell's example illustrates, a pair of two-year terms fulfilled at irregular intervals does not lend itself to stability. Furthermore, the Senate having the de facto ability to cut a chairman's tenure in half put unnecessary pressure on the apolitical nature of these military leaders. In the FY17 NDAA, the CJCS and VCJCS positions were converted to singular four-year terms. I am proud to have been a proponent of this, as the new setup means that those leaders do not have to weigh political popularity in their recommendations, advice, or decisions, many of which are difficult enough as it is.

To avoid the further disruption caused by having both the chairman and his vice rotate in and out at the same time, the tours have been staggered by two years so that the JS and the national command authority have some continuity, even during transitions. The verdict was to short-tour one (limiting him to just a two-year term) instead of extending the other. Vice Chair Gen. John Hyten started his two-year term in November 2019, while Gen. Mark Milley started his four-year term as chairman in October 2019. In fall 2021, a new vice chairman will be confirmed and begin a four-year term, achieving the two-year stagger.

Once they take up their respective offices, it's important to note the role the CJCS and VCJCS play in the NSC process. The VCJCS is a participant in the deputies' meetings, which frame the basic issues or options for the principals. When the principals meet, the chairman usually accompanies the secretary. The VCJCS should initially articulate the DoD position as the military official with the deepest programmatic and resource knowledge. As the deputies tee up options, having that resource-informed perspective is helpful and having someone with a track record representing the secretary's enterprise-wide view is important.

There is a good pre-GNA example of the desirable backgrounds of the CJCS and VCJCS. In the mid-1980s, the Army chief was Gen. John Wickham, a former commander of U.S. Forces in Korea (USFK), vice chief of staff, director of the JS, commander of the 101st Air Assault Division, and senior military assistant to the secretary of defense. In other words, he had CCDR, internal Army management, joint, and civilian office experience—the proverbial whole package. His vice chief was Gen. Maxwell Thurman, who in previous posts was director of Army Program, Analysis and Evaluation (PA&E); head of Army recruiting command; and deputy chief of personnel.

These two officers were a highly effective team because their skills and backgrounds complemented each other tremendously. During this period, the Army restructured itself to 18 divisions, learned how to recruit effectively, fielded the Pershing II missile in Europe as well as each of its "Big Five" modernization programs, established the Army's aviation and special operations branches, and revolutionized its training processes. General Wickham focused on the strategic, while General Thurman focused on the institutional – perspectives reflected in their respective congressional testimonies where Wickham described strategic direction and Thurman provided programmatic detail.

In the same vein, Chairman Admiral Crowe and Gen. Robert Herres, a former commander of U.S. Space Command, complemented each other well. The same is said for CJCS Gen. John Shalikashvili, a former Supreme Allied Commander Europe (SACEUR), and Adm. William Owens, who had served as the

Navy N-8 and whose tenure as the VCJCS saw the JROC become a major player in requirements, program, and budget issues.

Despite reforms instituted by Adm. James A. "Sandy" Winnefeld during his tenure as vice chairman, the JROC and JCIDS have grown far too bureaucratic and time-consuming. There is clearly enormous merit in having a CJCS highly experienced in strategic and operational issues thinking about "what we're doing and where we're going" and a VCJCS focused on "how we're doing and how we get there." Hopefully, by following this approach, there will be opportunities to streamline both the JROC and JCIDS.

The last four CJCSs – Admiral Mullen, Gen. Martin Dempsey, Gen. Joseph Dunford, and Gen. Mark Milley⌐ broke the pattern that had existed since 1982; these men were appointed while serving as a service chief. Mullen came to office during a difficult period when there were alleged confirmation concerns for his predecessor, Gen. Peter Pace, and Dempsey had only served as the Army chief for three months. Nonetheless, Mullen, Dempsey (who had also served briefly as the commander of CENTCOM), and Dunford (who had been the commander in Afghanistan) all had solid credentials on strategic issues and were well complemented by their vice chairmen, all of whom also had experience as CCDRs (Gen. James Cartwright at STRATCOM, Admiral Winnefeld at NORTHCOM, and General Selva at TRANSCOM) and as senior program staffers (Cartwright as J-8 and Winnefeld in senior warfare and transformation programs for the Navy and JFCOM). General John Hyten, the current VCJCS, came from commanding STRATCOM. But, as with all previous VCJCSs, neither Cartwright nor Winnefeld nor Selva nor Hyten had been a service chief. General Milley and General Hyten also mirror this previous approach.

Past experience suggests that it is difficult for a CJCS to perform the duties of evaluating requirements, devising alternative programs and budgets, and developing department-wide capability trade-offs if his or her past senior military experience comes from having been either a service chief or service vice chief. This is one of the reasons the GNA authors wanted service chiefs to have key joint operational roles first. Senior service officers have a major responsibility for advocating for their service and campaigning for its needs and requirements. It is understandably difficult for an officer to move from that role, particularly during an era of constrained resources and on-again, off-again sequestration, to one requiring the recommendation of reductions that will inevitably be seen as one service being reduced to benefit another. The zero-sum politics would only create more friction between the services.

Similarly, the evolution of the VCJCS toward a more technical and programmatic background with some recent distance from his commissioning service also has great merit. It is, therefore, of note that no VCJCS has come from the Army, where the focus has always been more on labor than capital. In a period where some major challenges are addressing reduced manpower, controlling the fully burdened cost of personnel, and finding the technologies that best preserve capability at lower manning levels, the ground forces are the least likely to produce an officer with this past background or future perspective.

General Mark Milley, USA, Chairman of the Joint Chiefs of Staff and Maj. Gen. Arnold
Punaro, USMC, Ret. hold the 4th Marine Division Commanding General's guidon.
Punaro, former commanding general of the 4th Marine Division, also holds a small vial
of black sand from Iwo Jima that Milley keeps close by to honor his father who served as a
Navy corpsman with the 4th Marine Division during the battle of Iwo Jima 75 years ago.

THE PRESIDENT'S RELATIONS WITH THE MILITARY

As clearly stated by the GNA, which provided a needed clarification, the
CJCS is the principal military advisor to the president in his role as commander in
chief. The CJCS should be constantly mindful of this responsibility and authority,
and the president should be respectful of it always and the burdens it places on
the CJCS.

The CJCS has to synthesize the inputs of many military officials—the service
chiefs, the CCDRs, the senior staff of the JCS, and even to some degree the senior
OSD staff—into coherent observations and recommendations for the president.
This synthesis will span many areas, including strategic direction, operational
decisions, operational planning, budget allocations, and can even reach down

to issues where the strategic and tactical intersect, such as they did with the Bin Laden raid. The CJCS has to exercise his or her authority in this regard and spare the president from wrestling with too many conflicting opinions regarding complex issues. However, the CJCS needs to also recognize that there will be times when the president will need to hear other, sometimes opposing, views. In this regard, the judgment of the CJCS becomes vital in exercising his or her role as principal advisor, not sole advisor.

The president must rely on the CJCS for this, yet not be shy about soliciting other views directly from the service chiefs or the CCDRs whenever desired or needed. The president may also solicit views on military matters directly from other members of the NSC or the OSD staff. However, when it comes to military matters, the president should resist suggestions to go outside the formal chain of command regarding major issues.

For instance, in deciding strategic direction in Iraq, President George W. Bush solicited the advice of an outside group that included academics and retired military officers who met with him without the presence of the CJCS. In addition, one of the retired military officers was using a back channel to the commander in Iraq, resulting in information and recommendations flowing to the president without any input from either the CJCS or the responsible CCDR. The president, as one member of this ad hoc group commented, has the right to "consult with anyone he wants." This is certainly true, but consulting with such a group on a major strategic decision without the presence or input of the CJCS will be perceived as a vote of no confidence in the military leadership and will damage, if not destroy, an important relationship.

The president should make an effort to become personally familiar with other senior members of the military. Dinners in the White House with the service chiefs, as President George H. W. Bush used to do and Presidents Obama and Trump continued, help develop an important relationship and provide the president with additional insights to the differing positions within the services. The president should also take advantage of certain routine opportunities that, on the surface, appear mundane but serve an important purpose, such as reflecting a familiarity with and respect for military culture. Attending certain military ceremonies—commemorations, retirements, and promotions, for example—can be useful and provide an informal opportunity for evaluating senior leaders for consideration as future CJCS, VCJCS, or service chiefs.

Famed Duke military historian Russell Weigley once noted that President Abraham Lincoln went through several commanders of the Army of the Potomac—the principal element of the Union army and the one opposing Confederate Gen. Robert E. Lee—until he found the one he was confident would aggressively press the war: Gen. Ulysses Grant. Weigley speculated that had the war occurred a decade earlier during the presidency of Zachary Taylor, this search for the right Union commander might not have taken so long as Taylor, being a former general himself, already knew the senior military leaders rather well. Accordingly, becoming familiar and comfortable with contemporary military leaders can serve a significant purpose.

Other recommendations the CJCS should encourage and the president should seriously consider include:

1. See and Be Seen in the Pentagon:

The president usually comes to the Pentagon for a formal briefing by the secretary and CJCS once or twice a year. This might be expanded to a quarterly event and include visits to the service secretaries and service chiefs. When it comes to budget formulation, allocation, and execution, the vast majority of this is done at the service level, as funds are primarily appropriated to service accounts. However, services can feel their key role is not understood beyond the Pentagon and that they are very junior partners to OSD and the Joint Staff. A presidential visit with them would enhance their morale and signal understanding of how the building actually functions.

2. Visits to the CCDRs:

The president should visit with the CCDRs in their headquarters once a year. Three of these headquarters—CENTCOM, SOCOM, and SOUTHCOM—are in Florida, making access easy. The same is true of a visit with NORTHCOM and SPACECOM in Colorado, STRATCOM in Nebraska, or TRANSCOM in Illinois. COCOM headquarters in foreign locations should be visited routinely during visits abroad.

3. Service Birthday Appearances:

Over the past two decades, all of the military services, taking after the Marine Corps, have begun recognizing and celebrating the service's birthday. These are: Army – June 14 (also "Flag Day"); Marine Corps – November 10; Navy – October 13; Air Force – September 18; Coast Guard – August 4 (although an organization within the Department of Homeland Security since 2003, the USCG's role as a military service should be recognized) and as of December 2019, Space Force on December 20. The president should consider participating in these ceremonies and, perhaps, hosting a "cake cutting" in the White House.

4. Appearances at the Service Academies:

The president, vice president, and secretary of defense should continue the practice of giving commencement speeches at the three major service academies. The president should not follow a fixed rotation but give the commencement speech at the academy celebrating a specific milestone. For instance, the West Point class of 2019 graduated just days before the 75th anniversary of the Normandy landing (the class of 1944, including Cadet John Eisenhower, actually graduated on June 6), and the Air Force Academy class of 2019 was its 60th class. Going forward, these are the types of events at which the president might consider giving the commencement address. In addition, the service academies provide a superior venue for major presidential addresses regarding security policy, as President Obama and President Trump have both done. However, the occasion must be chosen carefully; commencement addresses should not be used for major policy addresses. Historically, these fall flat with both the graduates and their families, such as Vice President Gore's commencement speech at West Point in 2000. If a president would like to give a policy address at a service academy, he or she should choose a visit other than a commencement to do so.

5. Meeting Returning Units:

On occasion, when a major unit or headquarters returns from a deployment, the president should welcome the unit home. This will provide the president a chance to congratulate the leadership and the troops and mingle with family members before and after the arrival.

6. Participate In Command Post Exercises (CPX) and Simulations:

There are several senior military educational institutions in close proximity to Washington that routinely conduct simulations of various contingencies, from nuclear confrontation to other stressful scenarios. The institutions include the National Defense University at Ft. McNair, the Army War College in Carlisle, PA, and the Marine Corps Combat Development Command at Quantico. In addition, there are public policy organizations that also conduct simulations of conflict scenarios and even budget allocation assessments. These are in addition to those that are conducted within the Pentagon and at several COCOMs, including STRATCOM and NORTHCOM. In many of these scenarios, an individual with senior-level experience is selected to play the role of the actual president. Participation by a notable civilian trains the military staff, but simulating with the actual president has greater value, both for him and the troops. The president should, therefore, personally ask to participate in one simulation and one major CPX per year. Such an effort will familiarize the president with military procedures, military language and jargon, the thought process of senior leaders, as well as the time intervals in which decisions must be made and in which action must be taken.

SUMMARY

As they have evolved over the past four decades, the roles of the CJCS and VCJCS require officers with backgrounds and experiences that are distinct yet complementary. The CJCS should have experience in the strategic and operational community, be fully immersed in the perspectives of regional commanders and the CCDRs, and ideally possess recent senior-level combat experience. The VCJCS should have experience with the institutional and managerial side of the defense establishment, be aware of the demands of the CCDRs, and stay immersed in the institutional processes of the defense establishment while understanding emerging technologies. These are quite distinct skill sets, and while it may be overly simplistic to view these two roles as being those of "the operator" (the CJCS), and "the manager" (the VCJCS), using this general paradigm as a reference while selecting new occupants for these key positions is worth considering.

The CJCS and VCJCS should be continuously mindful of their role in representing the military to the president and representing the president to the military. This is a responsibility that exceeds serving as the principal military advisor to the president, especially as recent decades show a decrease in military and combat experience among presidents. Of the past eight presidents, extending back 40 years, only two – Presidents Carter and George H. W. Bush – possessed any significant military experience. The others—Reagan, Clinton, George W. Bush, Obama, Trump, and Biden—either possessed little or no operational military experience. Accordingly, contemporary CJCSs must fill this experience gap and provide the president with insight into the world of military operations, society, and culture.

As always, there is room for improvement, and some changes to the existing GNA structure are worth serious consideration in the coming years:

- Include all the Joint Chiefs in operational planning.

- Delegate "resource allocation" authority to the CJCS in terms of balancing combatant commanders' needs, but not authority to deploy forces.

- Reemphasize the chain of command, specifically that the SecDef and CCDRs should go through the chairman, while making it clear the chairman is not in the chain of command.

- Lessen the duplication between the OSD and Joint Staffs in the personnel, legal, policy, logistics, requirements, and administrative areas.

- Significantly reduce the scope, size, complexity, and staffs associated with JROC and JCIDS, if not eliminate them altogether.

- For service chiefs, recreate an increased role in linking and streamlining requirements, acquisition, and budgets by creating the Army equivalent of the research, development, and acquisition position. This direct support to the service chief should be restored only as part of a serious reduction in the overall size of the other staffs of the military departments.

- The service chiefs should be designated as the chief requirements officers of their service.

Arnold Punaro visits with the Chairman of the Joint Chiefs of Staff General Colin Powell, USA, as Powell was completing his second two-year tour as chairman in September 1993. Punaro served as staff director of the SASC during Powell's Senate confirmation and two tours as chairman.

CHAPTER 12: DEFENSE REFORM: UPDATING THE GOLDWATER-NICHOLS ACT

This chapter also has its origins in the 2015 Goldwater-Nichols Act (GNA) reform deliberations. Dubbed "GNA II," it was spearheaded by the chairmen of the Senate Armed Services Committee (SASC) and House Armed Services Committee (HASC) at the time, John McCain and Mac Thornberry. It outlines what has changed since 1986, what has worked well and what has not, and contains numerous recommendations for updating the GNA. This information was provided to the incoming administration in 2016 to give them a sense of what reforms were still needed. As one of the staff directors of the SASC when the GNA was drafted and passed, I also oversaw the implementation and first decade of the legislation firsthand. I have continued to track it over its tenure.

In 1986, after several years of study, Congress passed two major pieces of reform: the GNA and the Packard Commission recommendations. The GNA focused on reforming the "operational" side of the chain of command while the Packard Commission focused on the "management" side. Because both were passed the same year, many think they were the same piece of legislation, but they were mostly separate bills. When former SASC Chairman John McCain and others talked in 2016 about updating Goldwater-Nichols, they were referring to both.

In general, the GNA shifted operational power from the military departments
and the service chiefs to the joint arena. Packard shifted management power
from the service chiefs to a centralized acquisition system led by civilians who
reported to a newly-created senior civilian official at the Office of the Secretary
of Defense (OSD). In the minds of many (including myself as one of the staff
architects of both in '86), there is a continuing need to update the GNA-Packard
system for current threats and realities, as long as it does not erode civilian
control of the military, undermine the independence of the chairman of the Joint
Chiefs of Staff (CJCS), complicate the operational chain of command (i.e., the
Beirut fiasco in 1983), or undermine a clear acquisition chain of command.

It is important to note that these efforts are not underway to fix a broken
system, as was the case in the 1980s, but rather to tweak issues that have arisen
from 30-year-old legislation. Today's military is not nearly as fragmented as
it was 30 years ago, but new reform efforts are important to ensure that DoD
is appropriately adapting to today's threats and realities and to ensure the
balance among the service, joint, combatant command, and OSD interests
are appropriately distributed. While there have been lots of improvements
in acquisition, particularly with Secretary of Defense Ash Carter and his USD
for Acquisition, Technology, and Logistics Frank Kendall—and then the latter
succeeded by the two offices of USD (Research and Engineering) Mike Griffin
and USD (Acquisition and Sustainment) Ellen Lord—here, the measure is not
how far we've come, but rather how far we have to go.

In October of 2015, Chairman McCain kicked off a series of hearings on
possible defense reforms, with noted experts testifying about the need for
modifications. The SASC heard extensive testimony from think tanks, former
senior civilian and military DoD officials, former SASC staffers like myself,
and prominent specialists on operations and management. McCain's then-
counterpart on the HASC, Rep. Mac Thornberry, led his committee in its own
set of hearings. The resulting hearing record is comprehensive and indicates the

extent of the adjustments that are needed. Significant discussion has followed in the years since, and some changes in the statutes have occurred.

The pro-reform testimony, advocacy, and work by OSD and relevant think tanks since 2015 cover a large swath of subjects, but generally fall into three categories.

The first group is an amalgamation of things I have been most vocal about in the decades since I left the Senate staff in 1997. It's primarily a concern about the size, cost, and redundancy in management layers of OSD, the JCS, the defense agencies, the combatant commands (COCOMs), and the military departments. Basically, there's so much bloat that it's hard to single out any one place for reprimand. However, the duplication between the Joint Staff (JS) and OSD—particularly in the areas of policy, personnel, logistics, communications, and resources—seems the obvious place to start. Congress should carefully examine this and understand there will be strong opposition to eliminating duplication, as both JCS and OSD want to retain their current capabilities.

There has been a fair amount of smoke (though not yet the fire needed to enact change) about the growth in size and responsibility of the COCOMs and whether they are losing their warfighting focus and engaging in activities like budgets and programs that the framers of the GNA wanted them to avoid— the Special Operations Command being an exception. To address this, Congress would need to spell out what activities are beyond the scope of the COCOMs. Congress did look at refocusing them on warfighting, but nothing was decided in legislation.

Similar smoke (and an emerging fire) surrounds the size, cost, and complexity of the defense agencies and DoD field activities (DAFAs), particularly those whose functions are not core to DoD or are mostly commercial in their operations. Congress could consider a different management structure, recognizing the complexities in this area. The last several National Defense Authorization Acts (NDAAs) took steps to address these concerns with the creation of the chief management officer (CMO) as the top defense official with a laser focus on internal management. They also required a major review of all the DAFAs and that the CMO review their budgets. Secretary Esper initiated a department-wide review in his own office soon after his confirmation. However, Congress concluded in the FY21 NDAA that the CMO construct was not working and directed the office be disestablished.

Nevertheless, a popular suggestion is to simply restrict the size of all the activities, either by mandating caps, cuts, or both. Some argue for across-the-board cuts, others argue for targeted reductions. Reforms must include reducing layers of management, including very senior positions. While some minor adjustments have been made in these areas, there is still much to be done. Congress has balked at many of the needed reforms and pushed back on much of the savings Secretary Esper found in his fourth estate review. As indicated in Chapter 19 on DAFAs, significant changes are long overdue.

The National Security Council (NSC) is another target for reform. In fact, the size and activities of the NSC have produced smoke for years, and recently the fire was identified. The NSC has continued to grow in staff size with ever-increasing micro-management of the national security departments. Despite controversy and objections from the White House, the 2017 NDAA placed a 150-person cap on the size of the NSC staff. A positive assessment of its effectiveness could theoretically lead to caps in other organizations.

The second category purely focuses on military issues. Most directly, there is concern about the current line-up of COCOMs, the standing up of separate cyber and space commands, and the possibility of shifting from a regional focus to a global focus. Congress also considered possible consolidations or eliminations. The SASC leaders publicly supported the Cyber Command, which President Trump later elevated from a subsection of STRATCOM to its own unified COCOM in 2018 and the stand-up of the U.S. Space Command in 2019. To offset the addition of a new COCOM, Congress could also consider a cap on their total number as well as their size and regulations that would require DoD to undergo some consolidation. In shifting the COCOMs and JCS to more of a global focus, this consolidation could fall to the CJCS.

The combatant commanders (CCDRS) and the Pentagon undoubtedly will resist any eliminations or consolidations, but they should be open to reviewing the commands – especially when it comes to changing from a regional to global focus. The SASC signaled a major revamp of the military strategy requirements under the chairman's statutory duties. The FY17 NDAA also significantly restructured DoD's approach to developing the important strategy documents, which had previously been criticized as a waste of time and energy because their unclassified nature meant that Congress gleaned little new insight from them. The National Security Strategy (NSS) became a classified document with an unclassified summary. The Quadrennial Defense Review (QDR) was replaced with a classified National Defense Strategy (NDS). Lastly, the National Military Strategy (NMS) was streamlined to focus on the military's role in executing the NDS.

In a chaotic and fluctuating world, there is a perennial need to improve the quality of professional military advice. Congress has heard strong testimony that the Joint Chiefs should have more of a voice on operational and contingency matters and that the Joint Staff should provide support to the other chiefs in the areas of JS's unique expertise. This would be a change from current practice. While the CJCS is the principal military advisor, there is a belief that the other members of the Joint Chiefs – now a total of eight – should be given a greater voice in the chairman's deliberations. No change has occurred here, as a consensus has not been found, but there is also definite grumbling about the independence of the CJCS. Some believe the chairman's position had become too much of a supporter of administration policies in recent years, particularly in administrations known for insisting on no dissenting opinions. To deal with this, Congress replaced the chairman and vice chairman's two two-year tours with automatic four-year tours. 2019 was chosen as a transition period for the vice chairman with just a two-year tour, while the chairman switched directly to a four-year term in September of

2019. This approach put them on a staggered interval and is in line with other leadership reforms of the past few years.

The SASC also built on Secretary Carter's proposal to eliminate four-star positions as part of thinning out management layers and "brass" creep. The FY17 NDAA mandated 25% reductions in both flag officers and senior executive service (SES) civilians. Furthermore, it instituted an increase limit of 15% on the national emergency exemption that OSD and the services had been using to circumvent the regular statutory personnel caps, as well as a cap on the amount that the Pentagon can spend on contractors—set at 25% below the FY16 baseline.

The joint duty provisions that originated in the GNA in 1986 have become too restrictive and too burdensome in an era when more flexible personnel management is needed. The NDAA provided some relaxation of the joint duty provisions, but it needs constant review to ensure the flexibilities are sufficient to compete with the private sector.

And finally, the category that experts from industry and government most vehemently agree on: the broken acquisition system. There has been concern for years that the requirements, acquisition, and budget processes are too complicated, too big, and too slow. The Joint Requirements Oversight Council (JROC), for example, started as a well-intentioned idea, but has turned into a bureaucratic monster and should either be eliminated or significantly reduced in terms of scope and process. Congress should look to streamline it, which would reduce the role of the vice chairman and the J-8 in these areas where the services and OSD are already prominent. Again, the opposition to any reforms here has been consistently strong, so the streamlining and reductions in bureaucracy are still needed.

One proposition that many seem to be in favor of is to get the service chiefs even more involved in the acquisition role and to provide them the authorities to do so. The SASC could build on the changes they have made in past years. Those changes were coupled with a serious reform of the USD for Acquisition, Technology, and Logistics (AT&L), whose reach substantially exceeded what the Packard Commission envisioned when it conceived of the position in 1986. The FY17 NDAA broke up the large, complex, and cumbersome office into two positions. First, it created a new USD for Research and Engineering (R&E) to focus on ensuring the U.S. maintains the technological advantages found under the previous defense research and engineering office. The other duties of AT&L will continue via the office of the USD for Acquisition and Sustainment (A&S), a critical position of leadership. There is a constant need to review and recalibrate technology and acquisition processes to best serve the national security, defense, and military strategies.

The GNA-Packard reforms of 1986 moved the DoD light-years ahead of where it had been in almost every way. The years preceding the reforms brought to the forefront evidence of catastrophic failures that had to be addressed. The imperative today is to focus the Pentagon's output and reforms on staying ahead of China and ensuring we have a military, economic, and technological lead. While we are ahead, we need to preserve our advantages. Where we are behind or losing ground, we need to focus on closing the gap and then forge ahead.

CHAPTER 13: THE UNSUSTAINABLE PERSONNEL COSTS

This chapter is based on testimony originally delivered in May 2017 before the Senate Armed Services (SASC) Subcommittee on Personnel during a hearing on modernizing the defense personnel system. The original testimony was the result of serving on a Bipartisan Policy Center task force that drew together previous, individual analyses of the problems in the personnel system and laid them out in a cohesive and compelling manner, along with needed corrections. My contribution to that task force included detailed work and analysis I had been conducting for over 20 years on the fully burdened life-cycle costs of the all-volunteer force (AVF), costs which are unsustainable.

As a member of the Bipartisan Policy Center's Task Force on Defense Personnel, I was involved in producing its 2017 report entitled *Building a F.A.S.T. Force: A Flexible Personnel System for a Modern Military*. I was honored to work with the innovative minds and steadfast patriots looking to drive change in the way DoD recruits, trains, retains, manages, and retires its people, concepts I've been interested in since Sen. Sam Nunn served as chair of the SASC Manpower and Personnel Subcommittee in the 1970s when I was providing staff support.

The report presents the need to improve DoD's defense personnel systems to better meet ever-changing future national security needs and our country's evolving service-age population. It offers a comprehensive package of 39 bipartisan proposals to improve the effectiveness of military personnel policy. As a whole, these recommendations aim to prepare the military to confront the threats of the future while also keeping promises made to today's service members.

Many of DoD's challenges will take years to address. Despite the urgent need for reform and the strategic challenges that exist throughout the world, the U.S. military continues to serve as the bedrock of national security, protecting our citizens and interests, preserving regional stability, rendering humanitarian assistance, and imparting stability to the world. The demands on our U.S. military personnel have never been greater, yet an outdated personnel system, rising personnel costs, and the growing divide between our military members and the nation they serve pose significant challenges to recruiting and retaining the talented people necessary to meet our country's ever-changing security needs.

THE PERSONNEL SYSTEM – TIME FOR A CHANGE

The combination of regulation, culture, and tradition that forms the DoD's personnel system is long overdue for reform. Its statutes, policies, and information systems have not kept pace with demographic or technological changes. While core U.S. national security interests have largely remained constant in the quarter century since the end of the Cold War, the threats arrayed against those interests have changed dramatically. Today's global security environment is faster paced, more mercurial, and increasingly daunting (especially China) than ever before. This environment should be the primary factor for policymakers to consider when deciding how to reform the personnel system.

Personnel management reform should include a strategy for a modern military workforce that is diverse, technologically skilled, and provides flexible career opportunities. This new system must be viewed by potential entrants as a desirable and competitive career option, as attracting high-quality applicants is of utmost importance. The new system must develop professionals, promote institutional values, embrace diversity, and maintain key elements of service culture. It must produce a force that both represents and is connected to the population it protects. The system must be fair with transparent policies, practices, and processes. It should be cost-effective, produce ready service members, and be seamlessly integrated across components. It must be much more flexible and incorporate world-class business practices in terms of assignments, advanced schooling and training, family considerations, and nontraditional opportunities. Ultimately, our armed forces must remain capable of deploying rapidly and sustaining military power in response to a variety of threats at home and abroad to alter or win the nation's wars, support our allies, and defend our interests.

The Defense Officer Personnel Management Act of 1980 (DOPMA) and its follow-on reserve component counterpart, the Reserve Officer Personnel Management Act of 1994 (ROPMA), updated the original 1947 personnel policies in place for much of the Cold War. Through DOPMA, Congress hoped to accomplish three main goals: provide a predictable and uniform promotion system, standardize career lengths across the services, and ensure proper proportionality of senior officers through the force. Seeing as DOPMA and ROPMA were passed decades ago, the key essential first step to modernizing the personnel system requires making bold statutory reforms to these pieces of legislation.

I had the opportunity to work on DOPMA with my boss, Sen. Sam Nunn, as a relatively new Senate staffer in the 1970s. Senator Nunn chaired the Manpower and Personnel Subcommittee when DOPMA was revised over a four-year period in the late 1970s. By then, the post-WWII system had been in place almost 25 years and had become outdated with the institution of the all-volunteer force (AVF). Similarly, the legislation updated in the 1970s is now painfully outdated. Our current personnel policy is complex and burdensome, not only to the individual military member and his or her family, but also to the organization as a whole.

Like most pieces of massive legislation, DOPMA/ROPMA resulted in some unintended consequences, one of which is the "up-or-out" promotion system. Currently, officers generally have two opportunities for promotion at each grade. If an officer fails twice, he or she is required to separate from the service, retire if eligible, or continue to serve until retirement in their current grade with no chance of being promoted.

Subsequent legislation, such as the Goldwater-Nichols Act (GNA) in 1986, created requirements for officers to accomplish specific items primarily related to joint service at certain times throughout their careers to remain competitive. While well-intended, forcing service members to tick the same types of boxes regardless of military occupational specialties heavily discourages them from pursuing alternative career paths and often penalizes innovative career choices. The resulting product has created a professionally homogenized officer corps that lacks the broad array of experiences seen in upper management of large, private-sector organizations. Worse, instead of harnessing the knowledge of these seasoned officers, the "up-or-out" system pushes service members out of the force when they are most experienced.

Suggested Personnel System Reforms

A competency-based career management system organized around the mastery of knowledge, skills, and abilities would encourage more flexible career paths, thereby permitting longer assignments, greater opportunity for graduate education, time-outs for family responsibilities, the lateral entry of skilled professionals, and longer overall careers. Such changes better reflect the new career patterns in the private sector and offer a more competent and seasoned force with less turnover and attrition.

From 2005 to 2008, I was fortunate to chair the congressionally mandated independent Commission on the National Guard and Reserve where we addressed these very issues. The commission recommended that Congress implement a more flexible promotion system based on the achievement of competencies.

Under this new system, the timing of and opportunities for promotion should vary by competitive category (career field), depending on service requirements. The report also makes the correct point that both the up-or-out nature of the 20-year career and the limited ability for the military to quickly meet manpower needs creates inefficiencies, resulting in higher costs. As RAND economist Richard Cooper testified to Congress, the only way to truly control costs for the professional military is to change the up-or-out promotion system to selectively reduce personnel turnover and to change accession requirements.

Furthermore, merging DOPMA and ROPMA into a single system would create a personnel system best suited for today's concept of the "Total Force." The Total Force includes all organizations, units, and individuals that provide the capabilities to support the DoD in implementing the National Defense Strategy (NDS). It encompasses the regular active component members, the reserve components (which includes the National Guard), civilians, members of the Individual Ready Reserve, and contractors. In implementing policy reforms for the Total Force, the reserve components must certainly be included. They have transformed from a seldom-used Cold War strategic reserve in the 1970s and 80s to an indispensable operational force that is frequently and routinely employed to meet the nation's defense needs. Over one million members of the Guard and Reserve have been mobilized since 9/11. As this book goes to press, over 40,000 members of the Guard and Reserve are deploying in the U.S., supporting COVID-19 efforts, weather disasters, and wildfire response, while others are involved in overseas operations.

Moreover, the department's culture needs to embrace active and reserve members, as well as civilian employees as members of the same team—not separate competing teams. To that end, the department should encourage and incentivize continued service in the Reserves to preserve talent from the active component that would be otherwise lost through reductions or routine transitions from the active force.

The department should encourage and facilitate a seamless transition between the active and reserve components. As the military strives to become more adaptable to an unpredictable security environment, it should remove barriers impeding access to the talent in its Reserves. Reserve component service should be an option throughout a military career as a means of preserving costly investments in training and experience.

Achieving this level of active-reserve permeability requires congressional action. Federal law demands officers who desire to transition between the active and reserve component gain a separate reserve-officer commission through a process known as "scrolling." This process takes up to six months and likely discourages many highly-qualified personnel from continuing to serve in the Reserves. To facilitate the transition, Congress should amend current statutes to create a single type of commission, a "universal appointment," in lieu of the current regular and reserve commissions. Only after creating this culture of permeability and support for a continuum-of-service paradigm will we be able to recruit and retain the best talent for our military.

Creating an integrated Total Force pay, travel, and personnel management system is one particular reform that will facilitate the others. This system, if modernized (i.e., enabling access via mobile phone or apps), will increase permeability by enabling streamlined transitions between components. Additionally, it will improve the ability of reserve component members to manage their careers by enabling seamless movement of all administrative and other records between components and services.

Early attempts to field a DoD-wide system— Defense Integrated Military Human Resources System (DIMHRS) —failed after significant costs. Having learned from this experience, both the Army and the Air Force are currently working to institute Integrated Pay and Personnel Systems—Army (IPPS-A) and Air Force Integrated Pay and Personnel System (AF-IPPS)—which could serve as models for the other services.

Some other personnel reforms may include adopting best hiring practices from the private sector to advertise, apply for, review, and select the best-qualified candidates for positions across the Total Force. In order to provide access to the deepest talent pool possible, it is also important to ensure all members have opportunities to compete for special assignments or educational opportunities without fear of their careers being negatively impacted.

The services are experimenting, on a very small scale, with sabbatical programs to allow service members on active duty to take time off for educational or other personal reasons. The Army's Career Intermission Pilot Program is already seeing the first return of soldiers to the force who participated. The next step is to broaden the program and allow those in uniform to consider it as simply another option on the way to a more fulfilling military career. These opportunities should be available to all service members in order for them to meet the changing demands in their personal lives, to benefit from full-time educational opportunities, or to respond to family and employment obligations.

Members should have the ability to pause promotion clocks during periods where they would be less available for military service. During periods where personal needs or civilian professional requirements make military service difficult, pausing promotion clocks would prevent members from being forced out due to lack of competitiveness for promotion, and allow them to continue service once these demands subside. Not to mention, they would return with more robust and diverse experiences.

Further, the reserve component has great potential to contribute to specialties that are more immediately transferable from civilian occupations, such as health care, public affairs, and cybersecurity. Unfortunately, current policy doesn't maximize this potential, and the military is missing an opportunity when only a small percentage of members with these valuable skills choose to remain in the reserves following completion of initial active service. When considering the substantial resources spent on training service members, the magnitude of this loss is only magnified. This is perhaps most acute for the cyber mission.

As the DoD builds the cyber force, use of these valuable skills developed by civilian industry, at little to no cost to the government, can provide immense benefits to the department. The Reserve Forces Policy Board (RFPB) formed a Cyber Task Group in 2013 to study the best use of the reserve component in this area. Following careful review, the RFPB recommended reserve component personnel be included in the development of Cyber Mission Force requirements to reduce long-term costs while also leveraging civilian-acquired skills, service-invested training and experience, and continuity and longevity.

The RFPB also recommended the secretary of defense direct a Total Force approach toward manning the Cyber Mission Force. The study also recommended CYBERCOM and the services review niche cyber needs outside the cyber mission force construct to take advantage of the full range of civilian-acquired skills within the reserve component.

The FY17 National Defense Authorization Act (NDAA) authorized the secretaries of the military departments to conduct pilot programs to recruit and confer original appointments to qualified individuals as commissioned officers in a cyber specialty. This was certainly a step in the right direction, but it did not include members of the reserve component. I encourage Congress to expand this authorization. If the reserve component is utilized effectively, it can be a valuable source of uniformed talent, with the added benefit of valuable private-sector experience, often at lower cost. This concept benefits the nation just the same if military members leave the active component to pursue career goals in the private sector yet remain in reserve service.

Military service often runs through families. Maj. Gen. Arnold Punaro stands with his two sons, 2nd Lt. Dan Punaro, newly commissioned in the Army, and Maj. Joe Punaro, USMC, at Fort Benning following Dan's graduation from Officer Candidate School in 2013. Personnel reforms are important to ensure military service remains an attractive career choice for future generations.

RISING PERSONNEL COSTS

Our domestic fiscal environment is just as challenging as our complex and unstable security environment. Budget impacts created by the 2011 Budget Control Act (BCA) and sequestration resulted in deep annual cuts to U.S. military readiness and capabilities until 2017. Since the passage of the BCA, security conditions have changed and are dramatically less stable than they were in 2011, when strategic competition with state actors was on the back burner. Military personnel systems must be financially sustainable for both the DoD and taxpayers. Furthermore, these systems must complement—not displace—other national security needs.

A high quality, professional force must be competitively compensated, but inefficient compensation costs cannot be allowed to force out other military necessities. Honoring the commitments made to current service members, military retirees, and their families is both a military necessity and a moral obligation for policymakers. However, it is also imperative to ensure that future generations of service members are competitively compensated while also receiving the best training and equipment available.

By many accounts, the AVF has been a great success. It has provided the military with high-quality personnel and has proven effective in both peace and wartime. Military leaders, politicians, and the American people all prefer it to the alternative. Accordingly, the AVF is here to stay. It is expensive, however, and the cost growth trends are unsustainable on their current path for both current and deferred compensation.

Former Secretary of Defense Thomas Gates, chairman of the 1970 commission that recommended the AVF, warned three fundamental changes were needed to ensure sustainability of the system. First, he recommended reforming the up-or-out promotion system. Second, he recommended eliminating the cliff retirement system, which only benefits those who stay 20 years and then incentivizes them to leave right away. And third, he recommended changing the pay and compensation system from one based on tenure and longevity to one that rewards skills and performance. In the 47 years since the AVF was introduced in 1973, the department and Congress have only touched a few of these items. As the costs continue to rise, it should not surprise us that more recent former secretaries of defense, such as Gates, Panetta, Hagel, Carter, Mattis, Esper, and many former senior military leaders, like Gen. Ron Fogleman and Adm. Gary Roughead, have all emphasized the unsustainable nature of AVF costs.

The independent Congressional Budget Office (CBO) and Government Accountability Office (GAO) both released a number of analytical reports documenting this reality, as have many members of the think tank community. One such analysis is the interim report by the Military Retirement and Modernization Commission. Highly overlooked, this 300-page report was published in June 2014 and documents the full costs related to running the AVF both inside and outside DoD. Concerning AVF costs, the report concluded that the all-in costs measure well over $410 billion per year; this amount is well in excess of the 30% of the DoD budget benefits-based lobby groups are fond of quoting. Moreover, this number does not include the staggering $1 trillion in unfunded liabilities for military retirees; today, we have approximately 2 million retirees receiving compensation compared to over 1.3 million on active duty and another 800,000 in the Guard and Reserves. With astronomical costs of this magnitude, there is consensus from defense experts across the board that these adverse trends must be addressed.

Funding levels for military personnel have more than doubled over the past two decades. Since 2000, funding has grown over 121% in current dollars and over 32% in constant dollars. Within this time frame, military pay per service member has increased at a greater rate than comparable pay for civilians. Enlisted service member compensation levels are now equal to the 90th percentile of civilians with comparable education and experience (83rd percentile for officers). Other personnel-related costs not funded in the military personnel account, such as health care, commissaries, dependent education, housing, and family programs, are expected to exceed $48 billion in 2020.

DoD has adapted to these higher costs by relying more on the Guard and Reserves, providing taxpayers with a true bargain in terms of cost. Before the Vietnam War, the Guard and Reserves comprised only 26% of the Total Force. However, with the end of the draft and the establishment of the Total Force policy in the early 1970s, that proportion began to rise. By the end of the Cold War, when the full cost of sustaining the AVF was becoming apparent, the Guard and Reserves comprised 36% of the Total Force. By FY15, the proportion grew to 38%. In some services, such as the Army, the reserve component, comprised of both the Guard and Reserves, exceeds the size of active component Army force, exceeding 50% of the Army's military capability.

As the department faces fiscal challenges from internal cost growth and external budget pressures, the question arises whether the fully burdened and life-cycle cost growth for the active component can be sustained long-term. That requires an assessment of relative costs and capabilities for active, Guard, and reserve personnel.

All analyses show that Guard and Reserves cost much less in peacetime. At the individual level, guardsmen or reservists cost 15% (according to GAO) or 17% (according to the National Commission on the Structure of the Air Force) of comparable active duty personnel. However, the relative cost increases when full-time support, equipment, and operations are added. For ground units, analyses found that Guard and Reserve forces cost the following proportion of active duty forces:

- Congressional Budget Office: 30%

- RAND: 23-25%

- DoD's Total Force Policy Report to Congress: 25-26%

- Commission on the National Guard and Reserve: 23%

- Reserve Forces Policy Board (RFPB): 22-32% (all functions, not just ground)

These standard comparisons capture pay, unit costs, and some benefits. However, they leave out benefits that significantly increase the active duty costs: permanent change of station moves, commissary facilities and operations, family housing, daycare, healthcare, dependent schools, and parts of retirement, as well as costs borne by the Departments of Labor, Education, Treasury, and Veterans Affairs.

The RFPB has shown that the entirety of these benefits adds tens of thousands of dollars to the annual costs of one full-time active duty soldier. Some have argued that these benefits should not be considered compensation and are incidental to military life. I disagree. These are services that civilians and reservists also use but must pay for themselves. Further, like compensation, these benefits exist to help recruiting and retention; if they do not actually benefit this purpose, they should be eliminated. At the very least, we should move forward with the RFPB's recommendation that DoD needs to assess and better understand these costs so future manpower analyses can be informed by accurate cost data.

Successful changes are possible, as illustrated by the Air Force's and Navy's successful integration of their reserve component forces as associate units and blended units through shared active component and reserve component platforms. This system successfully utilized the Total Force while also reducing costs and increasing efficiency. Additionally, this model of associate units and blended units with shared platforms has been successfully tested and proven, most namely by the Air Force and the Navy during *Operation Enduring Freedom* and *Operation Iraqi Freedom*. By combining active component and reserve component capabilities into multi-component units, there is potential for large cost savings and increased readiness within the reserve component operational force due to an increase of active personnel in the units. Alternatively, there should be enhanced opportunities for Guard and Reserve personnel to serve on active duty staffs and in key positions that are traditionally held by active personnel to help prepare them for senior assignments. This would also create a larger pool from which to select senior reserve component leaders.

The 1992 NDAA, which instituted the active component/reserve component Title 11 program, provides another avenue for active component military members to serve in reserve component units. However, history suggests that Title 11 programs have never been fully manned. Additionally, the Title 11 program was not regarded as career enhancing—particularly for O-6s competing for general officer/flag officer promotion. Therefore, in order to have better integration in the Total Force, measures should be taken to make these assignments more attractive. As an example, the USMC Reserve's Inspector Instructor Program could serve as a model for the other services to utilize as a Title 11 reserve component integration tool.

In this fiscally-constrained environment, it is also essential that we maintain an Operational Reserve. An Operational Reserve provides ready capabilities that are accessible, routinely utilized on a predictable basis, and fully integrated for military missions that are planned, programmed, and budgeted in coordination with the active component. This was one of the fundamental issues studied by the Commission on the Guard and Reserve. Serving as chairman of the Commission of the Guard and Reserve, I was skeptical of this task going into the study; I knew the difficulties associated with changing policies, budgets, and laws. However, following two and a half years of research, we concluded in support of the Operational Reserve as supported by DoD. I am even more convinced now that maintaining an Operational Reserve is essential. This does not mean the balance and mix of the Total Force should remain static and conform to the current plans or that every unit can always be at full combat readiness at all times, but an appropriate mix is essential.

The nation cannot afford to ignore the rich capabilities of the National Guard and Reserves nor the lessons learned and experience gained over the last 19 years of combat and other operations. Reserve component members bring unique capabilities and professional expertise to the Total Force gained through years of experience in the civilian sector. The department must learn to better harness this expertise going forward. Rich repositories of talent reside in the reserve component that are cost-prohibitive to develop in the active component (i.e., doctors, nurses, lawyers, computer analysts, cyber experts, engineers, etc.). After enduring a period of significant force structure reductions and budget cuts, continued investment in a strong National Guard and Reserve force provides numerous benefits to the Total Force and is essential in achieving U.S. national security objectives going forward. It is equally vital that senior leaders understand the importance of and define specific roles for Reserve forces in future strategic and operational plans.

BRIDGING THE GROWING CIVILIAN-MILITARY DIVIDE

The growing civilian-military divide cannot be ignored. The Abrams Doctrine, first articulated by the legendary Army leader Gen. Creighton Abrams, can serve as a key component in addressing this issue. This doctrine is just as relevant today as during the divisive Vietnam War, as it states: the Army should not go to war unless the nation goes to war, and the nation goes to war only if the Guard and Reserves are mobilized to join the fight.

As a Senate staffer in 1973 who had also recently completed a tour as an infantry platoon commander in Vietnam, I had a chance to meet General Abrams when he came to see my boss, Senator Nunn. During this meeting, General Abrams outlined his thoughts on maintaining a powerful Army in the climate of a shrinking active component, which had been decreasing since the U.S. combat drawdown in Vietnam. 1973 also marked the first year the AVF came into effect. In his new force structure, Abrams embedded a relationship between the active and reserve components. He intertwined the two groups so closely that it would be impossible to employ the active component in major conflicts without also relying on the Guard and Reserves. Additionally, he ensured that as the active force was drawn down, the Army's combat power was also increased. Secretary of Defense Melvin Laird used this philosophy to create the Total Force policy, which was then implemented by Secretary of Defense Jim Schlesinger. It has proven incredibly successful.

I offer my own career as proof. Before I met General Abrams, I had no intention of going into the Marine Corps Reserves, which were not viewed with the same prestige in the 1970s as they are today. However, his vision of their importance convinced me to join. The capabilities and the cultural barriers of the Guard and Reserves did not change overnight and only took place after the call-up of the Guard and Reserves in *Desert Shield* and *Desert Storm*, the increased use of the Guard and Reserves during the 1990s, and the over 1 million service members that have been mobilized since 9/11. Over this time, General Abrams' vision has now been proven correct many times over. The country requires a powerful ground force, and the Total Force Army is embedded in the fabric of our nation from its revolutionary roots, and this same doctrine applies to all of our reserve components.

At the changeover event between Chief of the National Guard Bureau General Joseph Lengyel and General Frank Grass in 2016, Secretary of Defense Ash Carter said,

> Today's Guard is battle-tested – an agile, flexible, deployable force with combat experience and a broad range of skills gained both on the battlefield and in civilian life. The National Guard is a critical component of our total force, bringing to bear the experience and skills of our citizen warriors wherever and whenever needed to confront the challenges of a complex world.

This was a powerful statement from the civilian leader of the world's largest and most complex organization, with almost 3 million employees in 2020 (comprised of over 1.3 million active duty personnel, 775,000 full-time civilians, and 800,000 Guard and Reserves), over 5,000 facilities on over 30 million acres of land worldwide, and an annual budget of over $730 billion.

Carter went on to say,

> The more deeply integrated the Guard becomes in all facets of planning and execution, the better prepared the nation becomes. The presence,

skill, and readiness of citizen warriors across the country give us the agility and flexibility to handle unexpected demands, both at home and abroad. It is an essential component of the total force and a lynchpin of our readiness.

Let me repeat that—the lynchpin of our readiness. And they live in communities throughout this great country.

In addition to members of the Guard and Reserves being an ever-present fixture in our communities, there are other opportunities to integrate military members back into society after their active service is complete. To partially address the issue, Syracuse University, in partnership with DoD, the Schultz Family Foundation, and the private sector, is participating in a job placement and training program called "Onward to Opportunity." Originating at Joint Base Lewis-McChord and Camp Pendleton, they have launched similar initiatives at 16 additional military installations over the course of the last few years. This program is a definite step forward. However, a more comprehensive program needs to be developed that will provide a "one-stop shop" for transition, ease military members and their families into civilian life, and help to retain hard-won combat experience and skills in the Total Force.

Military members are recruited and enter service from the communities in which they grew up and went to school. Members often return to these locations upon completing active service and many remain affiliated with the military by serving in a Guard or Reserve unit or by joining the Individual Ready Reserve. Others leave the military entirely and enter our veteran ranks.

The current transition process begins and ends at their last active duty location, which is very rarely in the community from where they came or where they intend to live and work. While transition programs have been improved, the programs do not thoroughly cover transitions beyond discharge and instead are primarily focused on pre-discharge preparations. As a result, separating service members end their service in one location and must abruptly begin new lives with little or no coordination between their separation points and their ultimate home communities.

In order to provide a more holistic, coordinated transition and promote the well-being of our members, families, and communities, DoD should integrate and facilitate collaboration of all government resources that are geared toward the transition process. This recommendation was outlined in the April 2012 Report by the RFPB, "Avoiding Past Drawdown Mistakes to Enhance Future Total Force Capabilities." In this report, the RFPB recommended the development of long-term "one-stop shop" reserve community transition centers, utilizing existing and well-established programs in community facilities throughout the country. This recommendation could be executed as Military Entrance Processing Stations (MEPS) in reverse, which would serve as transition facilities where service members would complete the separation process while experiencing a positive hand-off from the military to their civilian communities.

When service personnel first leave their communities to begin their military service, they enter service through MEPS. When they leave the military, they should transition out at a community-based location where all government agencies and community-based organizations are present. These stations would optimally be established in or collocated with existing Guard armories and Reserve centers throughout the United States, of which there are 4,189. In addition, the Guard and Reserves have more than 157,588 full-time people already supporting these centers. This "whole of government, whole of society" approach would provide direct links to employers, educational and technical training institutions, local medical resources, veterans service organizations, local chambers of commerce, and Departments of Labor and Education representatives. Embedding these facilities in Guard armories and Reserve centers would also offer immediate access to those service members who want to continue to wear the uniform by facilitating instant entry into one of the reserve components.

Recruiting for talent retention will become increasingly important as reserve component mobilizations and deployments continue to decrease and we continue to rebuild readiness after the damaging sequestration budgets. A key way to capture technical skills and proficiency as well as to save money would be to encourage more members who separate from the active component to serve in the Reserves. In data pulled for 2020 from the Reserve Component Personnel Data System, of those active component members who separated with less than 20 years of service, an estimated 61,757 will join the Guard and Reserve out of a total of 141,498. If the reserve component can capture even more valuable talent from the active force, this could save training dollars, achieve higher experience levels, and increase the overall readiness of the force.

Take, for example, an Air Force enlisted aerospace propulsion mechanic who completes their service at Joint Base Langley-Eustis, Virginia, and returns home to Atlanta, Georgia, to be officially discharged. After completing initial base out-processing functions at Langley, they would report to Dobbins Air Reserve Base (ARB) in Marietta, Georgia, to receive their discharge after linking into the "total force and total community" resources already established there. At Dobbins today, a Developmental Training Flight (DTF) unit prepares delayed enlistment airmen for basic training and enhances their understanding of the Air Force mission and military culture. Their mission could be expanded to serve those airmen transitioning back to civilian life.

Furthermore, Dobbins ARB is near the VA Atlanta Regional Office, Atlanta VA Medical Center, Decatur VA Clinic, multiple community-based outpatient clinics, Atlanta MEPS, and a significant number of large civilian employers. Private sector partnerships could be struck with companies like Delta Airlines, based out of Hartsfield-Jackson International Airport in Atlanta, to secure civilian employment for separating service members. With points of contact established by these community-based entities in the Dobbins Center, transitioning service personnel would be able to access all of them. The service member separating at Dobbins would become acquainted with Air Force Reserve, Air National Guard, and other reserve component opportunities in the local area and the benefits of reserve component service—things like TRICARE Reserve Select, tuition assistance, and others. Whether the individual leaves at one year, four years, 12 years, or 20 years, this community-based transition program underscores the lifelong and holistic commitment we make to the force.

Secretary of Defense Ash Carter welcomes Arnold Punaro to his personal office in the Pentagon. Punaro had the privilege of serving on Secretary Carter's transition team and helped him through his Senate confirmation process in early 2015. As staff director of the SASC in 1993, Punaro handled Carter's confirmation as Assistant Secretary of Defense during the Clinton administration.

CONCLUSION

The Pentagon's one-size-fits-all personnel policies are in need of major updates. From enlisting and commissioning to retiring and transitioning back to the civilian world, DoD needs to offer more flexible options for military members to manage their careers. The Bipartisan Policy Center's *F.A.S.T. Force* report offers the most comprehensive policy recommendations for bringing the department's personnel system into the 21st century. The recent modifications to up-or-out promotions are a first and long-anticipated step in this direction, and the momentum they offer should be used to enact further reforms.

The department needs to conduct a comprehensive review of the fully burdened and life-cycle costs of active military, Guard and Reserves, defense civilians, and defense contractors in direct support of the department. Their total costs run in excess of 60% of the entire DoD budget and have been growing considerably, thereby prompting the verdict by most recent secretaries of defense that they are unsustainable. In terms of benefits, those who are currently serving should be grandfathered under the current system. However, considerable savings can occur even in near term budgets – specifically in the Future Years Defense Program (FYDP) – if future benefits are modified for new military members. Rising personnel costs contribute directly to the ever-shrinking fighting force.

Chapter 14: The 1974 Budget and Impoundment Control Act

This chapter was written in 2016 for informational purposes and was provided to the incoming presidential administration and other defense leaders. It is intended to educate on the often-confusing process of budget impoundment. Impoundment is the refusal by the president to spend funds that have been appropriated by Congress. The issue of when the failure to obligate appropriated funds—specifically funds appropriated for military aid to Ukraine — counts as an "impoundment" was a key issue in the 2019-2020 impeachment deliberations.

Background

The president submits a budget to Congress for the federal government every fiscal year as Congress, under Article 1, retains "the power of the purse." No funds may be spent by our government in the absence of an appropriation. Congress must pass appropriations bills to provide money to carry out government programs for that year. An enacted appropriations bill signed by the president provides the specific amount of funds that can be spent on authorized activities. Congress has recognized the need to give agencies some budget flexibility by providing them with limited authority to make spending adjustments. For example, Congress may give agencies the ability to reallocate funds from one appropriations account to another, called transfers, or from one purpose to another within an appropriations account, which is called reprogramming. The nature of these flexibilities varies from agency to agency, depending on their relevant appropriation or authorization bill.

The current budget process was established by the Congressional Budget and Impoundment Control Act of 1974, also commonly referred to as the Congressional Budget Act (CBA). This act curtailed the power of the president to withhold federal funds once they'd been appropriated by Congress. Until 1974, the president could unilaterally decide not to spend some of these funds. Historically, every president since Thomas Jefferson has used the power of impoundment, but none utilized this power more than President Nixon, who withheld funding for programs he disapproved, such as federal dollars for water pollution programs. As a result of concerns regarding the expanded use of presidential control – worries only exacerbated by Watergate – Congress restricted presidential power through passage of the CBA.

Under Title V, which is also known as Impoundment Control Act (ICA) of 1974, the president can only withhold appropriated funds temporarily – called deferrals – or propose to Congress permanent cancellations of budget authority – called rescissions. For rescissions to take hold permanently, Congress must approve. In January 2020, the Government Accountability Office (GAO) ruled that the Trump administration violated the ICA by withholding congressionally-appropriated security assistance to Ukraine for several months in the summer of 2019.

KEY PLAYERS IN THE BUDGETING PROCESS

In order to better understand the appropriations timeline, function, and allocation, let's first examine the roles of the Office of Management and Budget (OMB) and executive agencies in this matter:

Once an appropriation bill has been signed by the president, OMB has the responsibility to apportion funds to the relevant departments or agencies. Usually, these apportionments are requested by the agencies and then signed by the OMB deputy associate directors after review to ensure that apportioned amounts correspond to the actual appropriated figures in statute.

When Congress has not passed new appropriations bills, an agency must operate under a continuing resolution (CR). Under a CR, agencies operate at a minimal level until their regular fiscal year appropriations are enacted.

OMB's apportionment for the period of the CR must ensure that agencies spend at a formulaic rate identified in the CR. The formula, which may change from one CR to another, is the product of negotiations among various factions in Congress and the administration. Agencies may not obligate funds under a CR that impinge on final funding decisions of the Congress.

Normally, a CR makes the amounts available subject to the same terms and conditions specified in the enacted appropriations acts from the prior fiscal year. The CR may also establish additional terms and conditions. Typically, agencies are not permitted to start new projects or activities during the period of the CR. This is a major impediment to keeping agencies current, given the country's increasing reliance on these CRs over the past several decades.

After OMB apportions funds, agencies allocate the money towards specific functions within each specific apportionment. While agencies possess the legal autonomy to best decide the specific allocations for their appropriated funds, they must follow the overarching guidelines set by OMB. In reality, agencies and appropriations committees and subcommittees may reach informal arrangements with one another to make sure the funds are allocated as intended. While these agreements are not formal or legally binding, agencies typically adhere to them.

Further oversight is outlined by the Antideficiency Act, which charges agencies with keeping their spending within permissible limits throughout the fiscal year. If tenets of the Antideficiency Act are violated, agency leaders are responsible for reporting violations to the president via the OMB director, Congress, and the comptroller general. Moreover, if an agency requires more funds than initially appropriated by Congress, additional funding is requested through the OMB to Congress.

THE ICA IN ACTION

According to the OMB, an impoundment is defined as "any executive action or inaction that temporarily or permanently withholds, delays, or precludes the obligation or expenditure of budgetary resources." Impoundments are actions or inactions committed by the president or a federal agency. There are two categories of impoundments: recissions and deferrals. To better understand impoundment, let's look at an example. For instance, if OMB did not apportion funds to an agency for reasons of reducing federal expenditures or because of a policy stance opposed to the programs for which the programs were enacted, then this would constitute an impoundment. Following the ICA, if the president wants to allocate less to an agency or program than the amount apportioned by Congress, he or she must submit a request and obtain approval from both chambers within 45 days. If enacted, this is called rescission. Unless Congress explicitly approves the rescission, funds must be released from the Treasury. In the request, the president must identify the targeted agency, affected programs, amount of funds to be rescinded, and reasons for rescission. Mandatory spending related to entitlement programs is not subject to rescissions.

The ICA also allows the president to defer appropriated funds on a short-term basis. A deferral is any executive action or inaction that temporarily withholds or effectively precludes the obligation or expenditure of budgetary resources with the intent of using the funds before they expire. Prior to the ICA, the president could defer funds for any reason and did not require explicit approval from Congress, although each chamber retained the right to disapprove a deferral. However, the ICA allows the president to defer funds for three reasons: to accommodate special and/or unexpected contingencies, to bolster savings by implementing more efficient practices, and to exercise deferrals specifically provided for by law. Now, a proposed deferral is automatically considered approved unless the House or the Senate passes legislation specifically disapproving it.

To defer funds, the president submits a message to Congress setting forth the amount, the affected account and program, the reasons for the deferral, the estimated fiscal and program effects, and the period of time during which the funds are to be deferred. The president may not propose a deferral for a period of time beyond the end of the fiscal year, nor may the president propose a deferral that would cause the funds to lapse or otherwise prevent an agency from spending appropriated funds. Additionally, the president may not defer funds for policy reasons (e.g., to curtail overall federal spending or in opposition to a particular program).

In the Ukraine security assistance case, the GAO ruled that OMB did not propose a rescission of the funds as required by law and, therefore, did not meet the limited circumstances to allow a deferral of the funds. In this case, under the Impoundment Control Act, the decision by the administration to withhold these funds was ruled by the GAO to be illegal.

The comptroller general (who is also the head of the GAO) oversees and reviews all proposed rescissions and deferrals. The comptroller general also guides and counsels Congress on the proposals' legality and impact on budgets and programs, notifies Congress of any rescission or deferral not reported by the president, and also retains the ability to recategorize an incorrectly classified impoundment. Further adding to their oversight powers, a notification by the comptroller general to Congress possesses the same legal effect as an impoundment message from the president.

As a general practice, only deliberate curtailments of expenditures are considered impoundments; actions with other purposes that incidentally affect the rate of spending do not fall under this category. For example, if an agency wishes to postpone a contract award as a result of a vendor disagreement, this suspension would not be classified as an impoundment. Or, if for some reason, an agency has legitimate difficulty finding appropriate contractors to carry out a particular program or project, the delay in the expenditure would not be considered an impoundment. However, if the delay is for the explicit purpose of reducing an expenditure, then it is categorized as impoundment. Not surprisingly, the distinction between reasonable administrative actions and undeclared impoundments can often cause debate over whether a particular action falls into the latter category.

CONCLUSION

If our government is to function as intended by the Founding Fathers, Congress has to exercise its power of the purse, providing appropriation for all government operations. Once a bill is signed into law, the president should obligate those funds on a timely basis. If the president objects to some of the funding, he can veto the bill, which then provides Congress the opportunity to either override the veto or remove the offending provision. However, the president cannot impound funds unilaterally as was done by President Trump with Ukrainian-designated funds. Congress also needs to return to passing all appropriations bills by the beginning of the fiscal year, October 1. Not only is this approach "regular order" – it's also just good government.

Chapter 15: The Planning, Programming, Budgeting, and Execution (PPBE) Process: The Road Back to "First Principles"

The Planning, Programming, Budgeting, and Execution (PPBE) is the DoD process for allocating resources; it is the heart and soul of DoD's decision-making process on all money matters. This chapter originated in November 2014 as a series of observations and reviews on DoD's process for planning and executing a budget. At that time, senior leaders in DoD were also looking at reforming the PPBE process and requested my input. I provided this white paper to incoming SASC Chairman John McCain and subsequent leaders in this arena. In 2020, after further requests from Congress and OSD, this paper was updated again, this time focusing on how the PPBE could be changed to reflect the new National Defense Strategy.

Then-Secretary of Defense Robert McNamara created the Planning, Programming, and Budgeting System (PPBS) in 1961 to establish a framework for connecting strategic objectives with resources. The department renamed the system to PPBE in 2003 to underscore the importance of better managing the *execution* of budget authority provided by Congress. The fact that this system has endured for over a half-century is testament to the utility it provides. Its importance has been recognized by nearly all senior defense officials who have served in the Pentagon subsequent to McNamara.

Over the years, other government agencies have been directed through executive order to install something similar to the DoD PPBE system, and most agencies have complied. Nonetheless, over time, the 60-year-old DoD system has suffered from four continuing challenges: the lack of detailed planning guidance establishing clear objectives and priorities, the generally unsatisfactory synchronization of the phases of the process, an under-focus on metric-based outcomes related to established mission areas, and an over-focus on the budget phase. Over the decades, Pentagon leaders have attempted to address the first two issues but have demonstrated little interest in the last two. It is overdue for DoD and Congress to address all four.

Maj. Gen. Arnold Punaro, USMC, Ret. and Deputy Assistant Secretary of Defense for Strategy and Force Development Elbridge Colby discuss strategy formulation. During his time at OSD, Secretary Colby was instrumental in developing the new National Defense Strategy focused on great power competition and played a key role in developing the defense guidance for the PPBE process.

The Need for Planning and Guidance

Throughout the years, the need for a more detailed guidance document has become more apparent. Over time, the Defense Planning Guidance (DPG) document has become increasingly generalized, a trend that needs to be reversed. As described by an Obama-era PPBE working group, the DPG needs to "clearly articulate high (must-do) and low (take-risk) priorities." The fact that this objective was even cited as a necessity illustrates how such clarity has not been a common contribution of the planning guidance in the recent past.

Over the years, the DPG and other feeder documents, including the chairman's Strategic Planning Guidance (SPG), have evolved into highly brokered articles lacking in precise direction and clear priorities. In most instances, this ambiguity was preferred by the services, as it allowed them more leeway to argue that their Program Objective Memorandums (POMs) and their budget submissions were in compliance with the guidance. Additionally, the lack of detail meant there were few benchmarks to measure service and component compliance, further giving the services key advantages in arguing for additional funds. In other words, without a clear roadmap to follow, the services were free to chart their own course—and they did.

Another major issue with the planning guidance centered around its typically untimely release. As designed, the PPBE is a rather heel-to-toe system, one beginning with a series of planning documents that sequentially increase in detail. The administration in power should offer a strategic concept that guides the subsequent development of a more detailed defense strategy leading to the articulation of a still more specific planning document, complete with identified tasks and priorities. Such a system would look roughly like Figure 1.

FIGURE 1: PPBE PROCESS

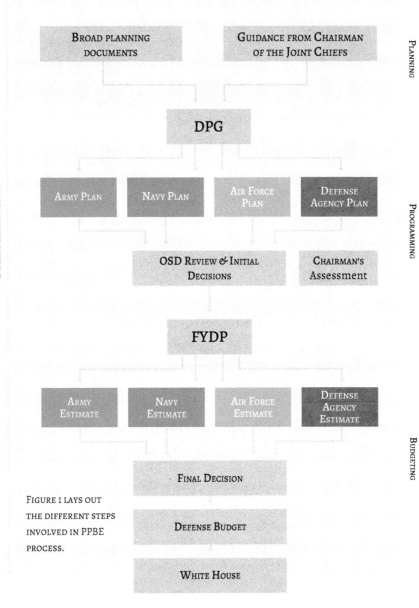

FIGURE 1 LAYS OUT
THE DIFFERENT STEPS
INVOLVED IN PPBE
PROCESS.

However, recent practice has permitted the planning documents to pile up on each other, making them more duplicative than iterative. Additionally, the documents tend to remain vague, rather than moving from strategic to tactical. An extreme but instructive example of the problem occurred in September 1993. Here, Defense Secretary Les Aspin developed his major guidance document – a Bottom-Up Review (BUR). This document was finalized and released on September 28, 1993, the same day that service POMs were due for submission to the Office of the Secretary of Defense (OSD). The two documents contained conflicting priorities.

Here, the Army, having been informed the BUR would establish a force structure of 12 active duty divisions, submitted a POM reflecting this same number along with its supporting infrastructure and long-term investments. But surprisingly, the BUR directed an Army of only 10 divisions. This meant that the budget review period was largely spent redoing Army force structure—along with all the second- and third-order changes required—rather than addressing budget line items.

REVIVING THE MAJOR FORCE PROGRAMS

On several occasions, there have been efforts to fix the timeliness of the Defense Planning Guidance (DPG). However, less effort has been focused on an equally serious shortcoming—enhancing its content. Without question, the timeliness issue is real and should certainly be addressed, but the more difficult issue is in crafting a DPG that establishes clear programmatic direction and priorities. What would such a DPG actually look like? How would it be constructed?

An obvious approach, one harkening back to the original principles of the McNamara PPBS concept, would involve crafting a DPG that lays out detailed guidance by "mission area" (output ordering, as detailed in Figure 2) rather than by military service. The original PPBS approach actually provided a guide for doing this, namely prioritizing the Major Force Programs (MFPs) of the Future

Years Defense Program (FYDP) rather than the service stovepipes, as shown in Figure 2.

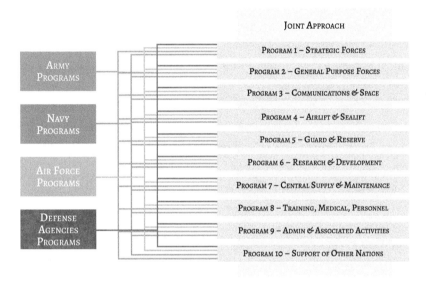

FIGURE 2 ILLUSTRATES THE FYDP STRUCTURE BROKEN DOWN BY MAJOR FORCE PROGRAMS.

The services oppose such a move, as it would make it harder for them to defend their programs and budgets. Meanwhile, OSD staff has opposed the change because it would require greater effort in reviewing and updating the entire FYDP and its underlying program elements, which number in the thousands. This reluctance to utilize the MFPs – despite this being the original intention by McNamara and his comptroller, Charles Hitch – is best demonstrated by the fact the original MFPs have hardly been changed since they were created in 1961, despite the numerous reforms and reshufflings of the department and the dramatic changes in the external threats.

For example, in the Pentagon's annually produced "Green Book," the MFP categories have changed little since first established. One exception occurred in 1987 when Congress, disappointed with the failed response of the DoD in the 1980 operation to rescue American hostages being held by Iran, directed the creation of the position of Assistant Secretary of Defense for Low Intensity Conflict (SO/LIC) and the establishment of the U.S. Special Operations Command (USSOCOM). To give the funding for this command greater visibility, Congress also directed the creation of MFP 11—Special Operations Forces. In essence, this made USSOCOM the only combatant command with its own politically-appointed assistant secretary and its own MFP.

The other major change to MFPs was the 2017 addition of "Space," which presumably occurred because of President Trump's desire to create a separate Space Force. However, other than these two examples, the original MFPs have not changed. As noted in a 1999 study conducted by the Business Executives for National Security (BENS) on PPBS, Secretary McNamara emphasized that these mission areas were never meant to be permanent and that the outputs desired of the DoD today are certainly different than those he faced 40 years before. This remains true currently, and the original MFPs are now roughly six decades old.

As the MFPs were initially designed to highlight the missions most important to DoD leadership, their static nature is unintentional but significant. At their creation, the MFPs were central to an effort by the Kennedy administration to craft a defense strategy, five-year program, and budget built around expected outcomes. Since the DoD faced a broad spectrum of challenges, it was necessary to attempt a categorization in general form as to what missions existed requiring specific outcomes. Of course, when Kennedy was elected president, the major programmatic challenge was the so-called "missile gap" between the U.S. and the Soviet Union in terms of strategic nuclear capabilities. It was, therefore, unsurprising that "Strategic Forces" became MFP 1.

What McNamara discovered upon taking office, however, was that no missile gap actually existed. The intelligence community (IC) projected that based upon investment and procurement trends, the missile gap would likely become a reality within five to six years. Meanwhile, McNamara also discovered that the separate military services were each pursuing their own individual response to this challenge. Further, the branches were doing so in an uncoordinated way with no established objectives. Here, the three services had significantly different ideas on what the Soviet nuclear target base was—in other words, what should be attacked in the event of nuclear war—and little agreement upon criteria for the types of targets. Accordingly, each was pursuing its own programs, designed to attack the targets each felt appropriate, with no common understanding of how much damage to the Soviet Union would deter it from risking a nuclear war.

After considerable work by the Joint Chiefs of Staff (JCS) in 1960-61, President Kennedy was briefed on Single Integrated Operational Plan (SIOP) 62. In essence, this plan called for a massive nuclear strike, either preemptively or in retaliation, under the Eisenhower concept of massive retaliation. Kennedy and McNamara, mindful of the actual numbers of nuclear weapons possessed by both the Americans and Soviets, wanted a more flexible SIOP, resulting in SIOP-63. In order to provide guidance on the desired levels of destruction, McNamara and Hitch established metrics for MFP 1 and forced the services to craft programs that played complementary roles in achieving their criteria of what would create nuclear deterrence. This was initially to hold at risk 25-30% of the Soviet population and 67% of its industrial base, although these numbers were later lowered to 20-25% and 50%, respectively.

Whether such metrics were reasonable or unreasonable—and there were differing views across the services and the commands—these statistics provided benchmarks to measure success and inform future planning. They also provided a way for the services to compete against one another. For example, the Air Force Atlas missile was relatively more accurate than the Navy's submarine-launched Polaris missile, but it was less secure and survivable. Moreover, Atlas carried a warhead up to six times more powerful than Polaris. In strategic terms, Atlas was much more suited as a first-strike weapon, while Polaris was more suited as a retaliatory weapon. And because of the accuracy differentials, Atlas was more suitable for a counter-force strategy, while Polaris was more counter-value—best used for area targets such as cities.

With the establishment of the MFPs, best illustrated by MFP 1, the McNamara team (known as the "whiz kids") was trying to define the outputs the DoD wanted to achieve and establish benchmarks against which to measure progress. Conceptually, the focus on outputs was the major change, one applauded by Rand Analyst (and future Defense Secretary) James Schlesinger. In 1968, while writing about the McNamara approach, Schlesinger said:

> There is no question that most of the program-budgeting structure will survive, as it should. It is not only another way of structuring budgets; it is an improved way. I myself doubt whether the same attention will be paid to the long-range program and the accompanying documentation requirements, as at present. Nonetheless, the output ordering of expenditures represents an enormous structural improvement.

In other words, Schlesinger recognized the merits of the MFP approach but also foresaw the difficulty of using the MFPs as an enduring management device. Moreover, as the Vietnam War increasingly dominated the defense debate of the 1960s, there was little energy devoted toward developing metrics for the other MFPs. As a result, this structure slowly fell into disuse. Currently, it is only used as a very crude method of tracking expenditures over time, but it is not used as the "output ordering" for which it was once designed—though it could be.

The first step in solving this would be in reconsidering and redefining the MFPs themselves. As McNamara himself noted during a 1999 interview, the MFPs should reflect both a strategic and managerial environment. Both dimensions have changed significantly over the past 60 years, and the MFPs should follow suit.

For instance, when McNamara became defense secretary, the nation still used conscription to fill out the ranks. The draft ended in 1973, and since that time, the nation's military manpower has been met by the all-volunteer force (AVF). Yet, the AVF comes with additional burdens in terms of direct costs (for salaries), professional development (as volunteers tend to stay longer), benefits (such as medical care), and housing (because the majority of the current force is now married). In addition, there have been other societal changes with major impacts, such as junior service members no longer being amenable to living in the large open platoon and squad bays of the past.

So, a new set of MFPs, when included in the FYDP, might best be constructed into two major categories – warfighting and support. A suggested construct might look like the one shown in Figure 3.

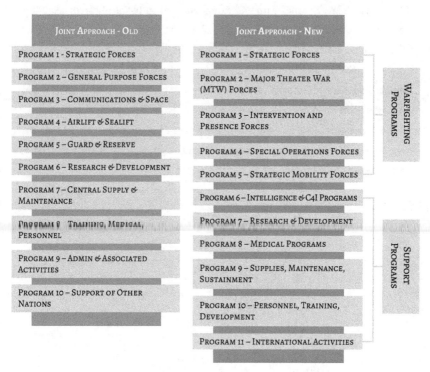

FIGURE 3: A NEW FYDP STRUCTURE (REORGANIZED BY PROGRAM CATEGORY)

FIGURE 3 DEPICTS THE OLD AND NEW FYDP STRUCTURES.

The FYDP structure suggested in Figure 3 recognizes the reality of certain strategic changes that have happened since 1961. Strategic forces remains an area of significant focus, particularly in an era where such systems are much more accurate, and, as we approach a period when all legs of the long-standing strategic triad are in need of modernization or recapitalization, expensive. This means that choices have to be made.

Over the last two decades, the nation has been involved in low intensity but deadly conflict. This has resulted in increased use of not only Special Operations Forces (SOF) but "specialized forces." However, the recent National Defense

Strategy (NDS) documents mandate a return to great power competition, also known as near-peer competition. While forces optimized for one type of conflict can be used and be useful in another, they are not a one-for-one substitute. Therefore, this structure shows the creation of MFPs for major theater war (MTW) forces (MFP 2) and intervention and presence forces (MFP 3). In addition, since a much smaller global basing structure has occurred since the end of the Cold War era, the need for strategic mobility has increased, hence a more detailed "strategic mobility" (MFP 5) component.

Clearly, in the current strategic environment there is a premium on enhanced intelligence and a global communications system for its distribution and fusion. As a noted authority once stated: "Precision weapons require precision intelligence." This would inevitably lead to the focus shown by MFP 6. Additionally, in order to address the concern surrounding America's eroding technological superiority, an MFP 7 focused on research and development is required. And of note—the simple fact that health care has been the fastest-growing portion of the defense budget for several years strongly argues that medical programs (MFP 8) receive particular attention.

A major reason the MFPs fell into disuse over the years is that no one "owned" them. If there are to be specific metrics established for each (identifying and describing the output expectations), then someone—or some staff element—has to "own" the MFP. In some cases, the owner is relatively clear. The Assistant Secretary of Defense (ASD) for Health Affairs would be an obvious owner of MFP 8; however, given that each service has its own research and development (R&D) structure, the owner of MFP 7 would require some degree of consideration. The recent creation of an Under Secretary of Defense for Research and Engineering might make that identification much easier.

The fundamental need, therefore, is twofold: create new MFPs appropriate for the current strategic environment, and designate an individual to be the MFP owner, who is responsible for establishing output metrics.

FIGURE 4: JROC/JWCA ANALYSIS CONSTRUCTS

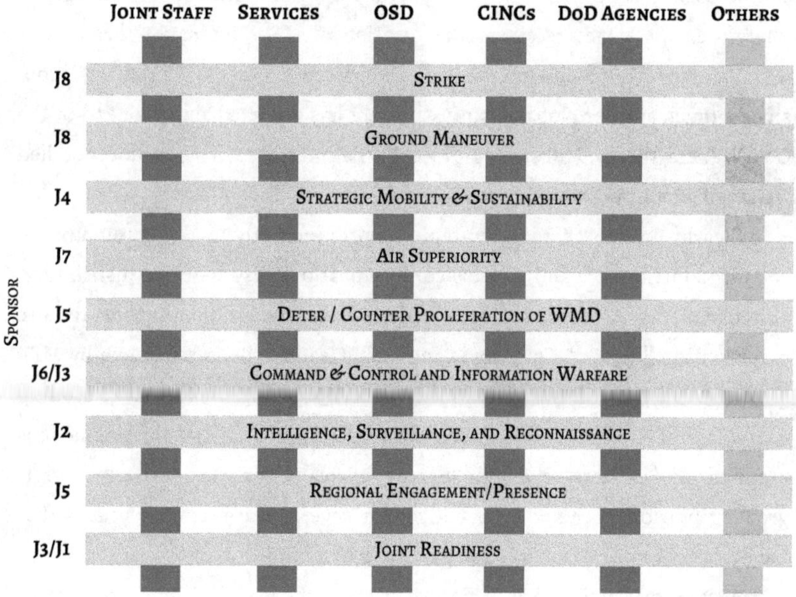

	JOINT STAFF	SERVICES	OSD	CINCs	DoD AGENCIES	OTHERS
J8			STRIKE			
J8			GROUND MANEUVER			
J4			STRATEGIC MOBILITY & SUSTAINABILITY			
J7			AIR SUPERIORITY			
J5			DETER / COUNTER PROLIFERATION OF WMD			
J6/J3			COMMAND & CONTROL AND INFORMATION WARFARE			
J2			INTELLIGENCE, SURVEILLANCE, AND RECONNAISSANCE			
J5			REGIONAL ENGAGEMENT/PRESENCE			
J3/J1			JOINT READINESS			

(SPONSOR — left axis label)

FIGURE 4 DEPICTS THE STRUCTURE TO IDENTIFY REQUIREMENTS, DEVELOP METRICS, AND SUGGEST TRADE-OFFS.

The similarity of Owens' concept with the original PPBS structure advocated by McNamara and Hitch is rather striking. It is also impressive that this structure placed an emphasis on regional engagement/presence forces seven years before the 9/11 attacks and the U.S. interventions in Afghanistan and Iraq. At the time, regional engagement/presence was utilized in the U.S. mission in the Balkans ordered by President Bill Clinton, as well as the U.S. intervention in Haiti. Neither mission rose to the level of commitment seen with the 2003 invasion of Iraq and the subsequent challenges it created, but these operations illustrated the distinctions between these more limited missions and major conventional conflict.

Owens attempted to establish mission areas across all of the traditional Defense Department stovepipes, but, unlike the original McNamara construct, he added OSD, the Joint Staff, and the Commander in Chiefs (CINCs) of the regional and specified commands. This made for a broadly inclusive effort but also added a larger number of voices to any resulting discussion.

Owens's JROC effort was useful and served to highlight several areas where there were certainly operational shortfalls, but it suffered from three critical shortcomings. First, the endeavor had no mechanism to identify trade-offs in areas determined to be deficient. Although the effort, for example, emphasized the need for greater air capabilities, it made no effort to suggest what area or program would be the "bill payer" to fund it.

Second, and related to the first item, unlike McNamara in his initial efforts, neither Admiral Owens nor his boss, Gen. John Shalikashvili, the JCS chairman, had any authority to order changes to the existing service programs. Moreover, the other formal JROC members, the service vice chiefs, were fully disinclined to suggest something from their service that might be sacrificed. This should have been self-evident, as the vice chiefs spend the majority of their time prioritizing their own services' programs, meaning they had already rejected a host of claims from their own internal constituents.

Third, although the idea of the JROC was to give voice to the needs of the CINCs, the field commanders never seriously contributed to the effort. For some, it was a matter of staffing, feeling their headquarters had neither the time nor the expertise to comment on the broader resource issues of the DoD. Meanwhile, others saw the effort as beyond their relatively nearer-term focus. One CINC, for instance, preferred that the Army upgrade its fleet of OH-58D helicopters rather than pursue the advanced Comanche helicopter, which would never be operational during his tenure. If nothing else, the initial JROC effort showed that the services had longer-term planning horizons than did the regional commands.

In the years since the Owens effort, the JROC process has become more complicated and seemingly less relevant. It is hard to find many champions of the current process, now known as the Joint Capabilities Integration and Development System (JCIDS), anywhere in the defense enterprise—including the defense industry. In many ways, like the original PPBS itself, the JROC process was an effort with good intentions that somehow never reached its potential.

WHAT NOW?

As previously stated, the PPBE process would greatly benefit from returning to first principles, which means redefining the MFPs to make them relevant to contemporary circumstances and modern missions. The structure described in Figure 3 would be a good start. However, in order to be fully beneficial, there has to be a division of labor between OSD and the Joint Staff so that their POM review efforts, as depicted in Figure 1, are not programmatically duplicative at best and operationally redundant at worst.

The MFPs shown in Figure 3 as the Warfighting Programs should primarily be the domain of the Joint Staff under the authorities assigned to the chairman by the GNA. As stated, the CJCS was inserted into the program-budget business by the GNA and tasked to recommend "alternative" programs and budgets. Accordingly, it would be advisable for the CJCS, as the top military officer and the senior representative of the COCOMs, to establish the warfighting metrics and outputs desired. By extension, the CJCS should then be the primary evaluator of the programs submitted by the services to measure their compliance with the guidance and metrics. In this effort, overseeing the warfighting MFPs, the OSD staff would perform a supporting role.

For the support programs, the roles would be reversed. The OSD staff would take the lead in establishing objective outcomes and the metrics that measure them, while the JS would provide support and additional perspective.

For both program sets, however, any alternatives that filled existing gaps, eliminated duplications, or adjusted programs in the direction of greater efficiency and synergy would have to be approved by the secretary of defense. Regardless of the structure used or the process established, this inevitably requires the presence of a secretary who has the courage and willingness to make major decisions.

To no small degree, Secretary McNamara was unpopular in the Pentagon because he displayed such determination in establishing the foundations of today's PPBE. While more recent secretaries have stated they wanted major changes and advocated for new budget and programmatic outcomes, they did not actually pursue them. Secretary Donald Rumsfeld during his second tenure comes to mind. Although Rumsfeld advocated an adoption of the "revolution in military affairs" and military transformation, consistent with the campaign positions and statements of President George W. Bush, as one of his senior staff commented, Rumsfeld was never in a position to make the tough decisions. And like McNamara and Vietnam, much of Rumsfeld's time in office was consumed by his efforts to deal with an unpopular and now considered largely unsuccessful war, which limited his ability to focus on defense transformation.

THE CONGRESSIONAL DIMENSION

Outside of the DoD, Congress is an important external dimension in the PPBE process. After all is said and done, the ultimate result of PPBE is a defense budget, and the ultimate recipient of the budget is Congress. Unquestionably, it would be useful if Congress played a role in the development of the budget rather than just evaluating and adjusting it upon receipt.

If DoD were to rethink and then redesign its MFPs to reflect contemporary missions, it would be equally useful if Congress would reconsider its committee structure, especially within the two authorizations committees—the House Armed Services Committee (HASC), and the Senate Armed Services Committee (SASC). With their subcommittee structure, these committees are already organized along lines similar to a mission orientation.

In an ideal world, the subcommittees could be adjusted to match the new MFPs and could hold hearings where mission outputs and metrics were discussed and debated. For example, SASC's current seven subcommittees

(Strategic Forces, Personnel, Cybersecurity, Emerging Threats and Capabilities, Airland, Seapower, and Readiness and Management Support) and the HASC's seven (Strategic Forces, Military Personnel, Readiness, Tactical Air and Land Forces, Seapower and Projection Forces, Intelligence and Special Operations, and Cyber, Innovative Technologies and Information Systems) would perfectly match each other and the MFPs.

In the real world, however, any sweeping redesign of congressional committees to match the DoD MFPs would likely be so ambitious an undertaking that the effort might outweigh the benefit. Plus, it might insert a degree of impermanence should DoD change the MFPs again at some point. It should be possible, though, to achieve much the same result by simply assigning the MFPs to existing subcommittees having similar jurisdiction.

For example, under the existing MFP 1, strategic forces, the match to the HASC and SASC subcommittees of the same name would be easy. In other cases, either the existing MFPs of Figure 2 or the proposed ones shown in Figure 3 would merit some consideration. For example, where to best vest strategic mobility would require deliberation.

While a less ambitious approach, this change would still be beneficial, as it would be useful to have DoD articulate its desired goals for allocated resources. It would also be beneficial if congressional committees and subcommittees coordinated with the department on its planning assumptions and metrics before it focused on the subsequent budget submission.

From the left: Dr. John Hamre, CSIS President and CEO; General Jim Jones, former Commandant of the Marine Corps, Supreme Allied Commander Europe, and National Security Advisor; former SASC Chairman Senator Sam Nunn; former SASC Chairman Senator John Warner; and Maj. Gen. Arnold Punaro, USMC, Ret. discuss the importance of collaboration between Congress and the DoD and the need for a bipartisan approach to national security. This photo was taken at the Center for Strategic and International Studies in October 2016 during the book launch for General Punaro's memoir, On War and Politics: The Battlefield Inside Washington's Beltway.

CONCLUSION

Overall, the PPBE has served the nation well. While it is an imperfect process, its contributions have been significant, especially when considering the expanse of the problems it seeks to address. Still, the PPBE has wandered far from its original idea and has become a system focused on inputs rather than outputs and on complexity rather than unity of effort. The PPBE has suffered from a lack of managerial discipline, with its phases being described in the report of the 1994 Commission on Roles and Missions (CORM) as "operating semiautonomously," thereby creating "unnecessary turbulence" while failing to generate "thoughtful debate on issues."

Returning PPBE back to its original intent will likely require considerable effort and commitment to breaking from norms and institutional preferences. However, the leadership must be willing and capable to institute reforms such as this, even when it undoubtedly proves difficult. The external strategic environment and the internal trade-offs are such that if the status quo continues, the unfortunate outcome will be "the ever-shrinking fighting force."

CHAPTER 16: THE OFFICE OF MANAGEMENT AND BUDGET AND THE NATIONAL SECURITY BUDGET PROCESS

This chapter originated from a white paper written for the incoming Trump administration and transition team in 2016. The material was designed to provide an overview of the Office of Management and Budget's (OMB) culture, process, and role in national security. It has been updated to reflect 2020 numbers unless otherwise stated.

From its humble creation in the Budget and Accounting Act of 1921, the Bureau of the Budget (BOB) has evolved into a major staff arm of the presidency with control over executive branch budgeting. Since 1970, when BOB was reincarnated as the OMB, its functions have grown from budget development and execution to management oversight, regulatory review, and legislative clearance for federal agencies. In this role, OMB occupies a place of enormous importance in the funding of the DoD and the overall functions of American national security.

While OMB has acquired new functions over time, the OMB has always worked to achieve the president's policy goals, especially when the goals involve cross-cutting issues that impact more than one department or agency. No other organization in the executive branch has such wide oversight responsibilities.

It is unsurprising, therefore, that each of the last four presidents has asked an OMB director to serve as White House chief of staff, and that five of their OMB directors have also served as cabinet secretaries – all of which underscores the salience of the institution and its service as an effective central nervous system for the federal government.

Resolving policy and budget conflict is inherent to OMB's mission, whether the conflict is between two agencies, or between an agency and OMB or other White House offices. Once a decision has been made and becomes official and public – be it a budget, authorizing legislation, a regulation impacting the private sector, or some other policy directive – OMB and the departments should, and normally do, function as allies in their public support or advocacy for the president's proposals or decisions.

OMB STAFF

OMB is a fairly small organization whose size has decreased over time. The institutional staff of OMB peaked in 1975 at 686, but then shrank to 453 by 2018. Most of the staff are civil servants. The exact number of political appointees varies, but usually, 80% are nonpolitical. Of the political staff, seven are Senate-confirmed. Often, they hire a number of support staff who are also political appointees to help them in their roles.

The professional culture of OMB's career civil servants emphasizes nonpartisan analysis and neutral competence. At the same time, employees have to be responsive to the political leadership once policy decisions are made, and then together they devise a budget that reflects the administration's political and policy priorities. As adjustments are being made, they are known to keep relevant information within a tight circle. OMB staff have a strong sense of professional discretion.

OMB works closely with other White House staff as well as with the relevant programmatic or operational experts in federal agencies. They interact with their counterparts across the executive branch on budgetary, regulatory, and management matters and can identify the relevant agency experts to pull in to advise or assist the White House on a particular matter. These working relationships are particularly critical in the beginning of an administration when the agencies have very few political appointees in place. Of the roughly 1,200 positions requiring Senate confirmation, over 200 nominees had been confirmed six months into both the George W. Bush and Obama administrations, and only 50 at the same point in the Trump administration.

Three OMB policy appointees – the director, the deputy director, and the national security program associate director (PAD) – can address issues concerning the DoD budget, although their roles will vary from administration to administration and even among different individuals within the same administration. Sometimes the OMB deputy director is intimately involved; sometimes, less so. The deputy may provide the president and the director with a capable "relief pitcher" for times when there are multiple demands on the director. At other times, the deputy serves the director by working with cabinet secretaries and in managing the many facets of OMB. In other cases, the deputy spends much of his time representing the president on Capitol Hill.

Likewise, the PADs operate differently depending on the administration, their personal relationships within the DoD, the depth of their national security background, and their personal operating style. Generally, most DoD political appointees initially discuss budget issues with the PAD and, if not resolved, then go to the deputy director or director for resolution.

The Trump administration moved the former National Security PAD Robert Blair to the White House, where he worked as an assistant to the president and an advisor to OMB Director Mick Mulvaney when he served as acting chief of staff. In a further break from tradition, the Trump administration also appointed a new national security OMB PAD, Michael Duffey, who came from the Pentagon. However, this was not an entirely new pattern, as former administrations have also moved OMB political appointees to the White House, where they continued to work, to various degrees, in the budget policy arena.

OMB AND OTHER WHITE HOUSE ENTITIES

The National Security Council (NSC) is the principal White House institution that advises on and coordinates national security strategy, working through the interagency process, and responding as needed to national security crises. In 2019, the NSC and the companion Homeland Security Council directly employed only 58 people. However, this number is misleading; the NSC also houses several nonpermanent personnel who are "on loan" from DoD, the Department of State (DoS), the Department of Homeland Security (DHS), and the intelligence community (IC). These temporary members usually occupy policy or program-focused positions.

Historically, the NSC was a small office that worked in concert with many departments to ensure cohesive security policy. It has since swollen from an agile staff of 40 in the early 1990s to a bureaucracy of 400 in less than a span of 30 years. In response to criticism, mostly from DoD, about the operational intrusiveness of the oversized NSC during the Obama administration, Congress capped the statutory number of professional staff at 200 (support staff not counted). Hopefully, this has precipitated a decline in NSC micromanaging, but more cuts should follow if it is clear the NSC continues to usurp the traditional roles of the national security cabinet agencies.

The NSC does not have a formal role in the OMB budget process, nor does it typically have expertise in resource planning. Nevertheless, most decisions made in the NSC framework have resource implications, making regular OMB-NSC interaction necessary. NSC views and NSC-coordinated interagency discussions can cause important implications for the president's budget. In return, budget decisions made in the OMB process can facilitate or limit NSC and interagency policy options.

The OMB-NSC relationship is critical to successfully planning the president's policy priorities and brokering conflict among agencies. NSC views on policy priorities can sometimes differ from those espoused by national security agencies and departments. OMB, working with both the departments and NSC staff, tries to help resolve these competing priorities. In recent years, OMB has been represented at NSC-coordinated interagency meetings on a wide variety of security issues. OMB is normally at the table when key security policy decisions are discussed and decided, especially when such deliberations involve financial consequences. OMB ensures that agency budgets reflect resource implications of these decisions.

In order to manage tensions that arise from a competitive and sometimes chaotic budget process, the DoD's senior-level leaders must coordinate with OMB and the NSC. Sometimes, conflicts arise that require the involvement of the president. This should not be surprising given the significance of the issues debated.

Aside from the NSC, OMB also interacts with other White House offices routinely. For example, the Office of the Vice President may be engaged when the vice president's defense concerns and equities are at stake. For example, then-Vice President Biden had a significant interest in nuclear nonproliferation, while his successor Vice President Pence took the lead on the new Space Force at DoD. Other White House offices can also weigh in occasionally on selected defense policy and budget issues. For example, the Obama administration's Offices of the First and Second Ladies exercised considerable influence on a variety of military family and veterans' issues that ultimately impacted budget levels and, thus, required coordination both with the NSC and OMB.

OMB vs. Congressional Players

On the Hill, the defense authorizers and defense appropriators both serve as key legislative actors who generally pass closely-aligned bills. Annually, the administration submits a defense authorization bill to Congress. Here, the president proposes changes and policies regarding the implementation of defense and intelligence programs. Given the influence of the legislation, it must be cleared by OMB, who also pulses agency views on the content. In contrast to the stalled authorization bills of many domestic agencies, both the Senate and House Armed Services Committees (SASC and HASC respectively) have successfully passed their annual authorization bills for 60 consecutive years. While the federal agencies typically lead their own budget and authorization processes, the OMB and White House will often be involved, especially if there are high-ticket items included in proposed legislation.

THE NATIONAL SECURITY BUDGET

Unsurprisingly, the size of the defense budget is a major budget policy issue. This matter possesses implications not only for national security, but often influences the amount of funding allocated toward domestic priorities and the administration's overall fiscal plan.

In the first stage of budget development, the OMB provides DoD with budgetary guidance on the base amount of funding the department will receive. The base amount is decided after significant consultation with the national security advisor, the head of the National Economic Council (NEC), the president's chief of staff, and the president. Often, the NEC takes the lead in developing broad economic policy goals, as the council is interested in the impact strategic issues have on the national economy. During this process, OMB works to balance the competing demands on the federal purse while simultaneously promoting deficit reduction. Typically, DoD argues for additional funding each year, citing the need to address gaps in military readiness or bolster technological capabilities relative to the perceived national security threat.

Throughout this process, OMB uses a taxonomy called "Function / Subfunction" to track federal government funding. There are 19 functions within this structure, with national defense categorized under the "050" classification. Within the 050 category, there are three subfunctions: 051 (the DoD), 053 (atomic activities within the Department of Energy), and 054 (defense-related activities). When discussing national security spending, it is always important to specify the exact function and subfunction.

As the subfunction categories illustrate, a considerable amount of national security funding is actually allocated outside of the DoD itself. Because of this, the president and Congress must provide sufficient funding to all defense-related agencies, not just the DoD, in order to fund and foster a strong national security apparatus. Other important departments include: Department of Veterans Affairs; Department of State (which also includes foreign assistance agencies like the U.S. Agency for International Development and the Millennium Challenge Corporation); DHS (which also includes the Coast Guard); Department of Energy (DoE); and various other intelligence and counterterrorism programs. Additionally, the Department of the Treasury funds defense-related tax expenditures and the amortization of unfunded military retirement liabilities. When totaled, the spending of these non-DoD programs currently amounts to almost as much as the entire Pentagon budget.

Case studies from different administrations over the past four decades underscore how the security budget process can play out. Let's take a look through the last six presidencies for a better understanding.

1. President Reagan's administration:

President Reagan called for a major buildup in defense spending – an annual increase of 7% adjusted for inflation for five consecutive years, or $1.6 trillion – during his campaign. This spending increase was set to occur during a period of declining government revenue, largely due to tax cuts also initiated by President Reagan. During his campaign, he also called for balancing the budget, though this goal proved unachievable.

President Reagan advocated for increased military spending to counter what he termed "the greatest military buildup in human history" on the part of the Soviet Union. While Reagan had already cut back sharply on domestic spending, OMB Director Stockman warned of the need to make additional cuts in social programs, highways, and other kinds of nondefense spending to achieve the president's goal with defense. Such cuts, identified as "drastic," were seen as politically unpopular.

Although the OMB Director was tasked by President Reagan with finding additional savings, Stockman wanted DoD to absorb some of these reductions in order to lighten the burden on politically-sensitive domestic programs. Stockman was also concerned about reducing the deficit and attempted to persuade Reagan and his advisers to accept some cuts in defense spending by publishing an article in *The Atlantic*. Here, Stockman argued that $10-30 billion of efficiency or waste-related savings could be found within the defense budget. The final pitch between Defense Secretary Weinberger, himself a former OMB Director, and Stockman occurred in front of President Reagan. In this debate, Secretary Weinberger illustrated that an "OMB soldier" constrained by OMB-desired levels for DoD spending was a weaker version of the "DoD soldier." Weinberger emerged victorious; while DoD's request was watered down somewhat, President Reagan approved a significant defense increase.

2. President George H.W. Bush's administration:

Gorbachev's determination to reform the Soviet economy, crippled in part by runaway defense spending, spurred his accommodation with the West and ushered in the end of the Cold War. Although few expected the fall of the Berlin Wall in November 1989, and even fewer anticipated the collapse of the Soviet Union itself two years later, these events ushered in calls to reduce American defense spending. Plans to draw down defense spending were in action but were disrupted and tabled in mid-1990 when Iraq invaded Kuwait. The subsequent *Operation Desert Storm* momentarily suspended the defense reduction initiative, but the efforts resumed after the successful conclusion of the mission.

The Pentagon, led by General Colin Powell and the Joint Staff, developed a plan for the new, post-Cold War "Base Force." Powell, anticipating the major defense cuts, believed it was better for DoD to guide the process than resist and eventually have undesirable goals given to them anyway. Powell's plan called for the termination or reduction of several major acquisition programs, including the Navy's Seawolf submarine and the Air Force's B-2 bomber. After discussions with President Bush, Secretary Cheney agreed to most of the reductions that had been advocated by the Joint Staff and OMB. Nonetheless, many were concerned that even with DoD's force structure and acquisition cuts, the allocated defense still did not match the needs of the Base Force. This tension was still present when President Bush lost his bid for reelection to then-Arkansas Governor Bill Clinton.

3. President Clinton's administration:

Clinton's first defense secretary, former HASC Chairman Les Aspin, arrived at the Pentagon with a firm vision of a new, smaller defense program crafted from a study conducted by the HASC under his tutelage. Consequently, Aspin immediately directed the FY94 budget left on his desk by outgoing Secretary Cheney be reduced by a further $11 billion. Aspin simultaneously launched his own review of the overall defense program, one that brought the force structure to even lower levels than the proposed Base Force. For example, whereas the Base Force envisioned an Army of 12 active duty divisions (down from the existing 18), Aspin's Bottom-Up Review (BUR) shrank it to 10. The other services saw similar reductions. But as with the Base Force, the new OMB allocation for defense did not adequately fund the smaller BUR force.

By the end of 1994, Aspin's successor, Secretary William Perry, had to appeal to OMB and President Clinton for additional defense spending. This was granted in late 1994 under a program named the "Presidential Defense Initiative (PDI)." The naming of the PDI left the impression that the additional funding for defense, nearly $3 billion, was for new capabilities and systems; in actuality, it was much more a continuation of the effort to match the emerging defense program with emerging budget toplines. As it turned out, the defense program – particularly the acquisition program – underwent significant reductions until 1998 when a personal appeal from JCS Chairman General John Shalikashvili ended the long decline. From that point forward, the DoD began to recover much of its lost budget authority.

4. President George W. Bush's administration:

At the start of the second Bush administration, the question of defense spending amounts flared up again, but this time with considerably less public airing of differences – either within the White House or between it and DoD – than during the Reagan-Stockman era. President Bush had run for office arguing that a new military was needed for a new technological era, and he decried the use of American military might for nation-building. As he said at one point, "Great powers don't wash windows." Early on in the Bush administration, key officials discussed the size of the defense increase. From there, they communicated by OMB to DoD to help the department frame their base budget request. Interestingly, the topline that emerged in FY02 was essentially identical to the one that likely would have been proposed by Vice President Gore had he won the election.

At the same time, Defense Secretary Donald Rumsfeld, much like Secretary Aspin, launched a complex review of the defense program with the idea of quickly moving into a new era often called the "Revolution in Military Affairs" (RMA), a euphemism that described a more technologically-advanced force. Unsurprisingly, after the attacks of September 11th, 2001, the entire defense landscape was significantly altered, and the RMA was largely abandoned. In the aftermath of 9/11, the White House, NSC, OMB, and Congress agreed to authorize increases in defense spending, funds that were largely requested as an emergency supplemental for what would become the Global War on Terrorism (GWOT). While defense budgets increased and the military force structure expanded during this time, there was little new technology introduced to the forces. Instead, President Bush's military embarked on missions incredibly similar to the nation-building efforts he had criticized on the campaign trail.

5. President Obama's administration:

At the beginning of his first term, President Obama assumed office with two main national security goals: first, to devise a plan to slowly withdraw from the conflicts he had inherited in Iraq and Afghanistan, and second, to pursue new technological capabilities, particularly in the areas of networking, intelligence and surveillance, and unmanned systems. These efforts alone are expensive and complicated to pursue concurrently, but Obama also had the added challenge of providing the necessary economic stimulus to bring the U.S. out of the Great Recession.

These efforts – both domestic and international in nature – resulted in expanding deficits and increasing national debt. In response to these rising costs, the Obama administration and Congress passed the 2011 Budget Control Act (BCA), which set caps on both defense and domestic discretionary spending. Despite this, President Obama's inflation-adjusted base defense budget still totaled higher than under Presidents Ronald Reagan and George W. Bush. Here, Congress provided some flexibility on the limits and used the Overseas Contingency Operations (OCO) funding, as it was not subject to the caps. Throughout the entire cap relief process, the Obama administration sought to provide equal treatment for both domestic and defense categories of discretionary spending.

Yet even within defense, major budget issues arose. For example, there was significant debate over what share of 050 funding capped by the BCA would be apportioned to the DoE to use for nuclear facilities and weapons modernization. In this scenario, more funding for the DoE meant less funding for DoD, and the Defense Department was acutely aware of this zero-sum game. In order to resolve this issue, both the DoE and DoD conducted a joint study and participated in numerous meetings with the NSC and OMB.

6. President Trump's administration:

Through his presidential campaign, President Trump made higher defense spending a central promise. In the President's FY20 request, OMB

Director Mulvaney sought to adhere to the BCA while still increasing the funds available for defense-related purposes. Consequently, he decided to maintain the defense budget request at the statutory caps but added considerable resources to the OCO request. Within OCO, there were two categories of funding: $66 billion in traditional OCO dollars for warfighting needs and $98 billion in OCO-for-base funds. The latter is essentially money set aside for regular base activities but classified under the OCO label in order to avoid the BCA's statutory budget caps. While controversial, this practice had precedent; previous administrations' budget requests had done this as well, although not to such a significant extent. Congress, too, had begun explicitly funding some of DoD's base-budget activities with OCO appropriations in 2016.

Linking Strategy, Planned Efficiencies, and Budget

New administrations often bring new policy priorities and strategies. In 2017, the Trump administration identified military readiness as a priority and immediately requested an increase in defense spending. The administration communicated its new national security policies in the National Security Strategy (NSS), which was released in December 2017. That document provided the starting point for DoD to develop its defense strategy in support of the president's NSS. The subsequent National Defense Strategy (NDS) was released in January 2018. The NDS identified changes in military objectives and priorities that guided the allocation of resources.

Since the start of the Trump administration, DoD's total spending has grown from $649 billion in 2017 to a request for $718 billion in 2020, an average annual growth rate of 3.5% in real (inflation-adjusted) terms. The often-referenced total of $750 billion reflects the entire 050 budget function, though DoD does represent about 95% of all 050 spending. This growth reflects the administration's efforts to align spending with its strategy. DoD justified the rapid increase in spending for 2017 and 2018 as a short-term effort to focus on replenishing depleted stocks of munitions and addressing concerns about readiness that DoD's leadership contended were the result of constraints placed on discretionary spending by the 2011 BCA. DoD's leadership indicated that the 2020 budget request was the first request to align budget and strategy, meaning that funding in the 2020 Future Years Defense Program (FYDP) was sufficient to support the NDS.

After the large increases in spending from 2017 to 2020, the 2020 FYDP shows a 4% overall decrease from 2020 to 2024, or a 1% average annual decline. To achieve the FYDP's five-year funding reduction period, DoD is undertaking a series of business processes, systems, and policies performance improvement initiatives, which it expects to increase effectiveness and performance. Additionally, DoD plans to apply savings from these efforts to support high-priority activities articulated by the NDS. Under this approach, DoD says it achieved about $5 billion in programmed savings for 2017 and has set a target of $46 billion for the years from 2018 to 2022. The question remains as to whether it is able to achieve such savings.

For FY21, OMB's guidance is in line with the new 2019 budget agreement and is flat compared to FY20; the president submitted a budget at that number, which has been generally supported in Congress.

OCO SPENDING OUTSIDE BCA CAPS

Starting in 2001, the defense budget contained two significant components: the base defense budget and the OCO budget. Other agencies, including DoS, DHS, and those within the IC have also utilized OCO budgets throughout the years, though all on a much smaller scale than DoD.

Originally, DoD's OCO request sought to cover "temporary and extraordinary" incremental costs associated with military operations in Iraq and Afghanistan. However, as OCO funding is not subject to the BCA's discretionary funding caps, the OCO budget can and has served as a relief valve to reduce pressure for base budget tradeoffs. While the OMB and DoD reached agreement on criteria for deciding what could be funded in the OCO budget versus base budget, major exceptions have been subsequently granted by the OMB.

Since 2001, reaching an annual agreement on both the size and contents of the OCO request has required considerable interaction between OMB and DoD. Over the years, OCO has become an indefinite, flexible funding source for ongoing and emerging global military operations. As it has been in continuous use since 2001, OCO has clearly proven it is in no way a temporary or a one-time emergency expense fund.

DoD's 2020 FYDP went much further than earlier budget requests in shifting base-budget funding into OCO. Total funding in the 2020 budget request would have exceeded the BCA's caps in 2020 and 2021 by $173 billion and $153 billion, respectively. In its request for 2020, the Trump administration divided DoD's total budget into four categories: base budget ($545 billion), emergency ($9 billion), OCO for base ($98 billion), and OCO ($66 billion). DoD structured its request for total funding in FY20 and FY21 so that the base budget would remain below the BCA's caps, requesting that the remainder be designated as either emergency funding or OCO funding. However, in all four major defense bills, Congress removed the base-related OCO spending and moved it into the traditional base budget.

The Trump administration's FY21 request reverted base force funding that was carried in OCO back to its traditional position, which now includes it in the base force funding levels. Between the increase in caps as well as the specific number included for OCO in the 2019 Bipartisan Budget Act (BBA) for FY21, budgeting has returned to traditional methods in FY21.

CHANGES TO FY20 AND FY21 DISCRETIONARY SPENDING CAPS

The 2011 BCA created annual statutory discretionary spending caps for defense and nondefense spending. These caps remain in effect through FY21. Throughout this decade-long period, across-the-board reductions (i.e., sequestration) were triggered to eliminate the excess spending if appropriations exceeded their limit for a fiscal year. Previously-enacted legislation increased these discretionary spending caps for each year from FY14 through FY19.

The most recent BBA was enacted on August 2, 2019. It raised the 2011 BCA's discretionary spending caps for FY20 and FY21, made other BCA-related changes, including an extension of the mandatory spending sequester through FY29, and suspended the statutory debt limit until August 1, 2021.

Section 101(a) of the 2019 BBA increased the caps on defense and nondefense budget authority for FY20 and FY21, the final two years of the BCA's spending caps. For FY20, the 2019 BBA raised the defense discretionary cap to $666.5 billion (a $90.3 billion increase) and the nondefense cap to $621.5 billion (a $78.3 billion increase). For FY21, the BBA raised the discretionary defense cap to $671.5 billion (an $81.3 billion increase) and the nondefense cap to $626.5 billion (a $71.6 billion increase).

For the first time, the BBA also allocated an amount for OCO in addition to base resources ($71.5 billion in 2020 and $69.0 billion in 2021), further normalizing OCO's "emergency but not emergency" type of spending.

Figure 1: The Bipartisan Budget Act of 2019 (P.L. 116-37) Discretionary Budget Authority (Billions of $)				
	2020	Change From Prior Cap	2021	Change From Prior Cap
NON-DEF*	621.5	+78.3	626.5	+71.6
DEF**	666.5	+90.3	671.5	+81.3
OCO***	71.5		69.0	
TOTAL	738.0		740.5	

*NON DEF INCLUDES ALL NON-DEFENSE DISCRETIONARY SPENDING. IT EXCLUDES ANY EMERGENCY APPROPRIATIONS.

**DEF ROW INCLUDES FUNDING FOR BUDGET FUNCTION 050 -- THE MILITARY ACTIVITIES OF THE DEPARTMENT OF DEFENSE (DoD), THE NUCLEAR-WEAPONS RELATED ACTIVITIES OF THE DEPARTMENT OF ENERGY (DoE) AND THE NATIONAL NUCLEAR SECURITY ADMINISTRATION, THE NATIONAL SECURITY ACTIVITIES OF SEVERAL OTHER AGENCIES SUCH AS THE SELECTIVE SERVICE SYSTEM, AND PORTIONS OF THE ACTIVITIES OF THE COAST GUARD AND THE FEDERAL BUREAU OF INVESTIGATION.

***BBA 2019 ALSO SPECIFIES THE FUNDING LEVELS FOR THE OVERSEAS CONTINGENCY OPERATIONS (OCO) ACCOUNT FOR FY 2020 AND FY 2021.

FIGURE 1 ILLUSTRATES THE BUDGET CAPS SET FOR FY20 AND FY21.

The 2019 BBA's combined increases ($322 billion) to the FY20 and FY21 discretionary caps are marginally larger than the combined FY18 and FY19 cap increases ($296 billion) and much larger than the two-year cap increases agreed to for FY16 and FY17 ($80 billion combined) and FY14 and FY15 ($63 billion combined).

DoD Budget: Classified Section

The National Intelligence Program's (NIP) budget funds the 17 agencies and organizations that make up the IC. Most of the IC budget is requested and appropriated within DoD's budget and is classified. As in the case of DoD, the development of this interagency budget involves a joint review process whereby OMB examiners participate in the internal discussions of the various intelligence agencies in the beginning of the annual budgeting process. Since 2001, as with the DoD budget, the IC has placed both annual base budget and OCO requests. This is not surprising given the IC's significant role in Iraq, Afghanistan, and other anti-terrorism activities.

Traditionally, OMB sends guidance in the early fall to both the DoD and the Office of the Director of National Intelligence (ODNI), prescribing their proportional funding shares within the DoD budget, as the majority of IC funding must fit within the overall 050 funding level. While OMB's guidance helps reduce (although not always completely) conflict later on between DoD and the ODNI as they develop their respective budgets, most of OMB's role in the IC budget process is not public. The Director of National Intelligence releases unclassified budget totals for the National Intelligence Program (NIP) and Military Intelligence Program (MIP), but does not provide unclassified budget details for other agencies.

FIGURE 2: INTELLIGENCE PROGRAM FUNDING PROFILE

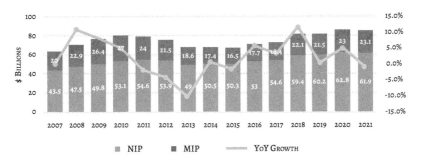

FIGURE 2 ILLUSTRATES TRENDS IN INTELLIGENCE FUNDING FROM 2007-2020.

DoE's National Nuclear Security Administration (NNSA) National Security (050) Spending Outside of DoD

The NNSA is a quasi-independent entity within the DoE with close ties to DoD and its nuclear missions. It is primarily responsible for the safety, security, and reliability of the nation's nuclear deterrent capabilities. DoE also undertakes a variety of important national security missions, including preventing nuclear proliferation, designing and developing nuclear propulsion plants for the U.S. Navy, and securing the nation against nuclear terrorism and responding to radiological and nuclear emergencies. Because NNSA funding falls within the 050 function, it also had to adhere to the defense budget's BCA spending caps, forcing trade-offs between DoD and NNSA budget requests. As noted in earlier discussion, one of the more contentious issues during the Obama administration was finding resources within the DoD budget to modernize NNSA's nuclear weapons enterprise. Even with expanded national security resources, this issue will likely reappear in the future given NNSA's nuclear modernization needs and other competing national security priorities.

National Security Spending Outside Budget Function 050

The DoS, DHS, and Department of Veterans Affairs (VA) are the three agencies tasked with national security capabilities that receive funding outside the 050 budget function. In addition to these three departments, foreign assistance agencies including USAID and the Millennium Challenge Corporation and a variety of smaller agencies such as the American Battle Monuments Commission, Armed Forces Retirement Home, and Selective Service System also fall outside of the 050 categorization.

In 2020, the State Department requested $40 billion for both diplomatic and foreign assistance missions. This funding is included under the 150 budget function.

VA administers a health care system and benefits for military veterans, including disability payments, education assistance, housing loan guarantees, health services, and support (jointly with the Department of Housing and Urban Development) for homeless veterans. Funding for these programs falls under budget function 700 (titled "Veterans Benefits and Services") and has increased significantly.

The Trump administration's 2020 VA request totaled $220.2 billion with $123.2 billion (56%) allocated toward mandatory programs, which have grown over 11% from the previous year. Since any eligible veteran is legally entitled to receive VA benefits, the mandatory programs are not subject to congressional appropriations. Examples of mandatory programs include veterans' disability compensation and educational assistance.

DHS is responsible for American border security, immigration enforcement, cybersecurity, and disaster relief. In 2020, the Trump administration requested $51.7 billion (this is a net budget authority figure), which represented a 24% increase from the previous year.

DHS spending has its own complexities, as the department does not have responsibility for all homeland security-related funding. Other agencies, such as DoD and the Department of Health and Human Services, carry out a number of homeland security programs and activities. At the same time, nearly a quarter of the DHS budget is committed to programs that are not wholly homeland security activities, such as Coast Guard's rescue-at-sea responsibilities. As the only coordination organization within the executive branch, the OMB plays a key role in integrating homeland security budgets.

CONCLUSION

Historically, both domestic and defense spending have been relieved from BCA caps, as proven recently in the 2019 BBA. Usually, defense fares better than domestic spending. Defense spending has also benefited from OCO, both in funding true emergency needs and for financing typical defense base activities. As of 2019, Congress and various administrations have provided $400 billion in relief through four statutory cap adjustments and the use of OCO for base budget activities. The fifth statutory adjustment in the 2019 BBA added another $170 billion for defense in 2020 and 2021. Moreover, the 2019 BBA's OCO funding adds additional funds allocated for base activities.

Looking to FY22 and beyond, there are currently no caps on defense and nondefense discretionary spending. This is positive, as legislated budget caps, such as those in the 2011 BCA, have generally failed to serve as effective ceilings and mechanisms for deficit control. However, given the continued dramatic increases in deficits, it is likely that some lawmakers will reintroduce the idea of budget caps in the near future.

According to CBO, the United States is expected to spend more on debt interest than defense by 2024. Even more concerning, the CBO projects that the budget deficit is expected to exceed GDP by 2029. In this environment, Treasury will need to borrow more money – money that will likely come from China. As of May 2019, China is the largest foreign holder of Treasury securities. This is an untenable situation for the U.S. While the so-called deficit hawks experienced amnesia throughout President Trump's tenure, they'll likely be cured once the Biden administration takes office, especially as the debt ceiling has to be increased in 2021. The ill-advised sequester was the result of the debt ceiling debate and compromise in 2011. We can expect national security funding to be under considerable pressure, from deficits and increasing mandatory spending, just like the Gramm-Rudman-Hollings and sequester eras.

CHAPTER 17: DEFENSE BUDGETS DURING PRESIDENTIAL TRANSITIONS

Administration transitions can be disruptive to DoD operations, and working to ensure a smooth and seamless transfer of leadership is key to maintaining a strong national defense and operational continuity. The first section of this chapter originated as a white paper written at the request of transition officials in 2016 who wanted to better understand how the budget process worked during previous transitions. It examines the budget dynamics for both the Clinton-Bush and Bush-Obama transitions and has been updated to include an in-depth analysis of the Obama-Trump transition.

The term "defense budget" most often refers to the total combined amount of discretionary budget authority appropriated for the Department of Defense, atomic energy defense activities, and other defense-related activities. When reports discuss the defense appropriation bill, the portion of DoD's budget for military construction and family housing activities are excluded since those items are funded in the appropriations bill for Veterans Affairs. The term "defense spending" most often refers to the total outlays actually spent or projected to be spent in a given fiscal year by DoD (including military construction and family housing but excluding atomic and other activities funded by other agencies). Defense spending can also refer to the National Defense Authorization Act (NDAA), which authorizes funding for DoD activities. It Is important to verify the type and source of funding for defense to give context to the data and to make sure any comparisons between sources and trends over time are as accurate as possible.

PART 1: HISTORICAL CONTEXT – THE CLINTON-BUSH AND BUSH-OBAMA TRANSITIONS

In order to best understand the current budget climate, it is necessary to first look at the budgeting dynamics for both the Clinton-Bush and Bush-Obama transitions.

2001: PRESIDENT BUSH, SECRETARY OF DEFENSE RUMSFELD

Under the leadership of Secretary Rumsfeld, President Bush's first defense budget, often called the "Blueprint Budget," was released by OMB a month after Bush's inauguration on January 20, 2001. The 207-page document formally titled "A Blueprint for New Beginnings" included budget totals and highlights, discussions of major policy initiatives, and agency summaries. That April, OMB released the details supporting the FY02 budget, a current services baseline.

Since the FY01 Appropriations Act was enacted before the inauguration, the incoming Bush defense leadership team had already identified serious shortfalls in the appropriated amounts. The major deficits centered on the defense health program, military pay, and readiness. The Rumsfeld team was adamant about seeking a FY01 supplemental to cover these and other perceived shortfalls.

However, the incoming OMB did not want to seek a supplemental; its focus was instead on producing the FY02 budget. Rumsfeld eventually decided to focus only on FY02 and defer discussion of FY03 and beyond until after the Quadrennial Defense Review (QDR) and preparation of the annual Defense Policy Guidance (DPG).

There is no evidence that Rumsfeld had any substantive leadership meetings involving the services over modifications to the FY02 budget request proposed by the outgoing Clinton administration. Instead, there were a series of memoranda addressing budget issues from the acting comptroller to the budget lead on the transition team. Service participation consisted of memoranda/briefing slides that sketched out lists of funding needs. These inputs were submitted to the USD Comptroller from the service budget officers.

The acting comptroller then prepared a memorandum to Secretary Rumsfeld that reflected analysis done by the comptroller and the Program Assessment & Evaluation (PA&E) staff, which later became Cost Assessment and Program Evaluation (CAPE). The memorandum listed service requests and OSD's recommendations on specific issues. In early March, the services briefed Rumsfeld on their shortfalls, which he reviewed and used to prioritize their requests. This process led to a request for a major budget increase. The Clinton administration had proposed FY02 topline of $310 billion; the Rumsfeld team sought an additional $30-$40 billion.

The remainder of March-April 2001 was consumed by review and negotiations between OMB and the department. In the end, OMB eventually agreed to a FY01 supplemental of $6.1 billion and a FY02 budget request of $328 billion ($18 billion more than the Clinton budget). Service inputs on the FY02 budget came in early June 2001. Program budget decisions on the FY02 request were published in mid to late June 2001, and both the FY01 supplemental and the FY02 budget were submitted to Congress in June 2001.

Maj. Gen. Arnold Punaro, USMC, serving as the Director of the Marine Corps Reserve (far left), meets with President Bush, Secretary of Defense Donald Rumsfeld, and the other Reserve chiefs to discuss the mobilization of the Guard and Reserve six days after 9/11. Over one million members of the Guard and Reserve have been mobilized since 9/11.

2009: President Obama, Secretary of Defense Gates

Because Secretary Gates continued to serve as secretary of defense in the Obama administration, the transition from Bush to Obama had a very different internal bureaucratic dynamic than the prior transition. In the January/February 2009 edition of *Foreign Affairs*, Gates authored an article titled "A Balanced Strategy." The ideas outlined in this article served as strategic guidance during the defense transition. At the time of Obama's inauguration, the FY09 Appropriations Act had been passed along with $65 billion for the Global War on Terrorism (GWOT), known as the "GWOT bridge." The incoming administration needed to prepare and request a GWOT supplemental to fund remaining projected FY09 GWOT costs. The GWOT funds would ultimately be carried in an account named Overseas Contingency Operations (OCO).

While discretionary, OCO-designated funding does not count toward the BCA caps, which makes it an attractive funding mechanism. Some observers see OCO as a necessary vehicle to address complex demands emanating from our country's ambitious national security strategy. Critics have described OCO as a loophole or "gimmick"— morphing from an account originally intended for replacing combat losses of equipment, resupplying expended munitions, and transporting troops through war zones to a financing source for DoD's "peacetime" base activities. As the discussion below shows, recent presidents and Congresses have expanded the use of OCO for base activities over time.

A FY10 defense budget had been prepared by the outgoing Bush administration. The Bush OMB had originally provided a topline of $524 billion for DoD, but by the inauguration, their FY10 defense budget request had jumped to $581 billion. Historically, outgoing administrations will increase their previously-adopted five-year FYDP above the actual amount submitted to Congress. This creates a higher baseline for the incoming administration and has been done by both Republican and Democratic administrations.

The Obama OMB soon provided a pass back – when the White House literally passes revised drafts of proposed budgets back to the agencies that wrote them— which identified FY10 toplines for both "war" and "non-war" with "high" and "low" estimates for the Future Years Defense Program (FYDP) for FY10 through FY15. Additionally, the administration developed an appeals process and prepared analysis to focus on what could or could not be funded at various spending levels. By late February 2009, Secretary Gates agreed to a FY09 OCO supplemental of $78 billion, a FY10 base budget topline of $533 billion, and a FY10 OCO budget of $130 billion.

Like Rumsfeld, Gates decided to focus only on the FY10 budget and defer discussion of FY11 and beyond until after the QDR and issuance of the DPG. For Gates, the main challenge was reducing the outgoing Bush budget of $581 billion down to $533 billion.

With the FY10 topline set, a review process was launched. The administration formed issue teams to review 12 specific issues. Over a six-week period in February and March, the department held a series of large and small group meetings to discuss the findings and recommendations of the issue teams. The large group met a total of seven times; membership was similar to the current Deputy's Management Action Group (DMAG). The small group met two to three times a week and was chaired by Secretary Gates. Its members included only the comptroller of PA&E (CAPE) and Joint Staff, with other participants on an as-needed basis. Gates was provided with issue-oriented books prepared mostly by PA&E (CAPE).

That February, the Defense Department asked the combatant commands (COCOMs) to identify their top five needs. The small group then made the final decisions on the FY10 budget, which were transmitted to the Defense Senior Leadership Council (now known only as the SLC) in late March.

The administration submitted the FY09 war supplemental, which totaled $78 billion, to Congress on April 9, 2009. On May 11, OMB issued the details supporting the FY10 president's budget. DoD submitted its FY10 budget to Congress in June. On August 13, the president submitted another FY09 budget amendment to grow Army end strength by 22,000, reallocating just over $1 billion from Army, Navy, and Air Force procurement accounts to support this increase.

President Clinton, Senator Nunn, Senator Thurmond, Les Brownlee (far right), and Arnold Punaro (far left) meet in the Oval Office as President Clinton signs the Defense Authorization Bill in 1996. This was Senator Nunn and Staff Director Arnold Punaro's 23rd consecutive defense bill signed into law.

PART 2: RECENT DEVELOPMENTS – THE BUDGET CONTROL ACT OF 2011 AND THE OBAMA-TRUMP TRANSITION

Understanding the BCA and larger budget context is key to framing defense resource issues in the modern day, and particularly during the Obama–Trump transition. The BCA caps created serious constraints within the Department of Defense as it pursued its National Defense Strategy (NDS) and engaged in combat in Iraq and Afghanistan.

THE SIGNIFICANCE OF THE 2011 BUDGET CONTROL ACT (BCA)

The 2011 BCA set spending caps on both defense (050) and nondefense (non-050) discretionary spending. The BCA sought to decrease the annual federal budget deficits by a minimum of $2.1 trillion from FY12 through FY21, with approximately half of the savings to come from reductions in planned defense spending. After dealing with these unwise and unsound caps for 10 years, they were finally eliminated for the FY22 budget submission. This is a welcome relief, as Congress had to provide adjustments throughout the last decade.

The caps, still in effect for FY21, are enforced through a mechanism called sequestration. If appropriations that exceed a limit for a fiscal year are enacted, across-the-board reductions (i.e., sequestration) are triggered to eliminate the excess spending within the relevant spending category (defense, nondefense, or both). However, some programs or accounts get a pass from sequestration. For example, certain programs within the VA are exempt, including areas such as disability compensation, pensions, education benefits, and healthcare benefits. In DoD, military pay and allowances, as well as retired military pay, are exempt.

All 050 spending covers more than just DoD and intelligence activities included in DoD's budget. While DoD budget resources (referred to as budget subfunction 051) represent about 95%-96% of 050 spending, other non-DoD programs or activities also fall under the 050 cap. Funding for the National Nuclear Security Administration's (NNSA) nuclear weapons programs (referred to as subfunction 053) belongs to the 050 category. Additionally, several other defense activities of the FBI, Department of Homeland Security, Coast Guard, and a smattering of others (referred to as subfunction 054) fall under the 050 cap.

Roughly 2% of DoD's and other 053 and 054 agencies' accounts are classified as mandatory funding (e.g., military retirement accounts for DoD). These accounts do not count toward the BCA caps. But the overall 050 funding is discretionary and controlled by appropriation acts, which means the funding is subject to the BCA spending caps.

The BCA does not establish limits on the subfunctions (051, 053, and 054). Decisions on allocating resources among the subfunctions have occasionally raised tensions across different agencies. For example, there has been serious contention over how much 050 spending should be allocated for nuclear modernization efforts. Given that most of NNSA's infrastructure was built in the 1950s, it has recapitalization needs in the billions. However, the more funds NNSA receives, the less there are for DoD's other 051 programs and activities. Even within DoD's 051 total, there is competition between DoD and the intelligence community (IC) that has to be negotiated each year, often with involvement from OMB.

In February 2009, the Obama administration released a document that changed GWOT's name to "Overseas Contingency Operations" (OCO). In the FY11 appropriations cycle, the Obama administration moved away from submitting supplemental appropriations requests for war-related activities, relying instead on the regular budget and appropriation process. This approach suggested that the funds, while war-related, largely supported predictable ongoing activities rather than unanticipated needs. Such funding on a much smaller scale also appeared later in the Department of State and Department of Homeland Security. Both the Obama and Trump administrations have been accused of using OCO as a "slush fund" for defense since OCO is not subject to any of the BCA caps.

According to a 2019 Congressional Research Service (CRS) report, the total OCO spending between FY01 and FY19 reached $2 trillion. While this paper focused on 050 spending, it is important to note the significant resources for veterans' benefits and services that fall outside the 050 budget function. The Trump administration budget request for the Department of Veterans Affairs (VA) in FY21 was $243.3 billion, a 10.2% increase over the enacted FY20 level. More than half of this ($134 billion) is mandatory spending. Adding VA to the other 050 programs produces a total security spending of around $1 trillion per year. Such spending really should be considered as part of the overall security spending debate since it captures the fully burdened and lifecycle cost of the all volunteer force (AVF), but rarely is.

2017: PRESIDENT TRUMP AND SECRETARY OF DEFENSE MATTIS

This section closely examines the issues framing the FY17 and FY18 transition budgets. In both of these budgets, the Trump administration added substantial funds for defense. On the campaign trail, then-candidate Trump underscored his intent to increase defense spending. After taking office, the Trump administration did not want to wait until the FY18 budget proposal and instead began modifying the FY17 budget started by Obama. His defense policy officials argued that significant spending increases were urgent because the 2011 BCA had reduced the Pentagon's necessary funding and had undermined force readiness.

The following points provide insight into the evolution of the FY17 budget:

- February 2016: The Obama administration submitted its original FY17 defense budget request to Congress, which included $523.9 billion for DoD's base budget and $58.8 billion for OCO, for a total of $582.7 billion (excluding mandatory funding).

- November 2016: The Obama administration submitted an amendment to the OCO request for 2017, seeking an additional $5.8 billion primarily to maintain about 8,400 troops in Afghanistan and to support other DoD activities in Iraq and Syria.

- January-February 2017: President Trump asked Secretary Mattis to conduct a 30-day Readiness Review. That review led, in part, to the Trump administration's March 2017 request for additional FY17 appropriations for DoD.

- March 2017: The Trump administration released two defense documents that laid out its budget plan. One was from the OMB, *America First: A Budget*

Blueprint to Make America Great Again for FY17, and the second came from the DoD comptroller, *Overview – Request for Additional FY17 Appropriations.*

- President Trump sent a letter to House Speaker Paul Ryan on March 16, 2017, requesting an additional $30 billion for DoD ($24.9 billion more for the base budget and $5.1 billion more for OCO). Of the $24.9 billion additional base funding requested for DoD in FY 2017, 54% was designated for procurement. The revised 2017 request of $549.6 billion for DoD's base represented an increase of 5.3% over the 2016 enacted level. With the revised OCO now at $69.7 billion, the total DoD discretionary budget request rose to $619.3 billion. This represented an increase of almost $36 billion above Obama's initial budget ($582.7 billion).

- At a March 2017 hearing of the Senate Defense Appropriations Subcommittee hearing, Defense Secretary James Mattis described the request as "the first step in a three-phase, multi-year effort to restore readiness." He said the money was to be used "to get our aircraft in the air, our ships back to sea, and our troops back in the field with refurbished or new equipment and proper training." General Joseph Dunford, Chairman of the Joint Chiefs of Staff (CJCS), argued that funding for new equipment, especially aircraft, had been constrained by budget pressure at the same time that the services were using their current equipment at a higher-than-anticipated rate for missions in Afghanistan and elsewhere.

Figure 1: DoD's FY17 Budget (051) (Current $ in Billions)	Obama Request	Trump Request	2017 Enacted
Base 051	524	549	523
OCO	59	70	83
Total	583	619	606
BCA Cap*	524	524	524

*FIGURES EXCLUDE DOD'S MANDATORY SPENDING.
ESTIMATED 051 CAP WITHIN 050 CAP OF $551 BILLION PER THE *BIPARTISAN BUDGET AMENDMENT* OF 2015.

- As Figure 1 shows, Congress did not provide Trump his full 2017 request for DoD ($619 billion versus $606 billion). Congress held the base appropriations at $523 billion to not exceed the revised BCA cap, while it increased the OCO component to $83 billion. The final enacted total for DoD was still considerably in excess of the BCA cap.

The FY18 budget, the Trump administration's first fully developed budget, added significantly to FY17 defense spending. The Pentagon's argument was still the same: In a world growing more dangerous, the BCA had a deleterious effect on its readiness. Secretary Mattis argued that the BCA and sequestration have "done more damage to our readiness than the enemies in the field."

In January of 2017, Senator McCain, then chairman of the Senate Armed Services Committee (SASC), released a white paper, *Restoring American Power*, with his recommendations for the defense budget. The report argued that the BCA had to be abolished and that defense strategy should not be constrained by the budget. It recommended $640 billion for all of 050 in FY18, an increase of $91 billion over the BCA cap of $549 billion. His estimate for OCO was an additional $60 billion in funding for a total of $700 billion.

Figure 2: DoD's FY18 Budget (051) (Current $ in Billions)			
	McCain 2018 Rec.	Trump 2018 Req.	Final 2018
Base 051	610	574	600
OCO	60	65	71
DoD Total (OCO + 051 Base)	670	639	671
Non-DoD 050	30	29	30
Total 050 (OCO + 050 Base)	700	668	701
BCA 050 Cap	549	549	549

FIGURES IN THE TABLE ABOVE EXCLUDE $24 BILLION IN MANDATORY DoD SPENDING. THE SOURCE FOR "TRUMP REQUEST" AND "FINAL 2018" COMES FROM DoD COMPTROLLER BUDGET MATERIALS AND DOD'S GREENBOOK. THE SOURCE FOR THE McCAIN RECOMMENDATIONS IS *RESTORING AMERICAN POWER*.

President Trump's FY18 request, the combined base and OCO request for 050 being $668 billion, was $32 billion less than McCain's recommendation, but still $54 billion over the cap. The administration proposed to offset the requested increase in defense spending with reductions in nondefense spending to achieve equivalent deficit reduction. Congress did not support the nondefense reductions; it was a major point of contention for Democrats. Ultimately, this contention led to the first Trump administration government shutdown at the beginning of FY18.

In terms of the DoD topline, Congress gave the Trump administration more than what it wanted and closer to what McCain had requested for 050: $701 billion in base and OCO funding with most of the OCO for supporting the base. The BCA caps were pretty much only window dressing.

The FY18 funding supported the military services' requests for increased manning levels. The funding was allocated for an array of weapon capabilities such as the F-35 Joint Strike Fighter, KC-46 tanker, B-21 bomber, nine new ships (including the Virginia-class submarine), Joint Light Tactical Vehicle, and other investments in science and technology.

An Assessment

While the budget caps have framed the budget debate over the last decade, they have not reduced overall spending as intended. They did not achieve their intended effect for two major reasons. First, they were adjusted up by Congress several times, and second, Congress used OCO to circumvent them.

Since the enactment of the original 2011 BCA, five bills have adjusted the BCA caps upward — the American Taxpayer Relief Act (ATRA) of 2012, the Bipartisan Budget Act of 2013 (BBA 2013), the Bipartisan Budget Act of 2015 (BBA 2015), the Bipartisan Budget Act of 2018 (BBA 2018), and the Bipartisan Budget Act of 2019 (BBA 2019). The most recent bill, BBA 2019, was a two-year agreement that increased the spending limits for both defense and non-defense.

Between FY12 and FY21, total base defense spending under the original BCA caps was supposed to be more than $1 trillion less than the FY12 budget request projections over the 10-year period. The subsequent laws referenced above, however, raised the defense caps by a total of $435 billion over 10 years. In fact, base national defense spending returned to levels close to those projected in the FY12 Obama request. In addition to rising caps, OCO's role has grown much larger than originally intended.

The Trump administration's FY20 and FY21 requests differentiate OCO for base activities from OCO for contingency operations. The administration structured its request for total funding in 2020 so that the base budget would remain below the BCA's caps and requested that the remainder be designated as emergency OCO funding. Two-thirds of the OCO request in FY20 supported base budget and other "enduring" activities.

Figure 3 highlights how budgeting under the BCA and BBA has become more complex.

Figure 3: Trump Administration's Request for FY20 and FY21 (Current $ in Billions)		
	FY20	FY21
DoD 051 Base	535	636
OCO for Base	98	16
Total 051 Base	633	652
"Regular" OCO	71	53
Emergency	8	--
DoD 051 Total	713	705
Non-DoD 050	33	35
Total 050	746	740
BCA 050 Cap	576	590

SOURCE: *NATIONAL DEFENSE BUDGET ESTIMATES*, OFFICE OF THE UNDER SECRETARY OF DEFENSE (COMPTROLLER). ABOVE FIGURES EXCLUDE MANDATORY SPENDING.

Figure 3 also shows a new DoD category in FY20 called "emergency," a section designated for funding border wall construction and providing hurricane relief and recovery. Like OCO, emergency funding does not count against the caps. Including this category with OCO, the Trump administration requested $173 billion in funding exempt from the caps. However, Congress did not adopt this approach. The FY20 stated OCO was in line with OCO targets established, for the first time, by Congress in the Bipartisan Budget Act (BBA) of 2019: $79.5 billion in FY20 and $77 billion in FY21.

The administration's FY21 budget was almost in sync with the new law. DoD's total FY21 request declined by $8 billion between these two years — $713 billion to $705 billion — because of the $11 billion drop in OCO (to $69 billion). But 051 base spending increased by $3 billion.

THOUGHTS FOR THE NEXT ADMINISTRATION

Since the start of the Trump administration, DoD's total spending (OCO and base) grew from $607 billion in 2017 to a peak of $713 billion in FY20. The budget for FY21 is $705 billion. This growth reflects the administration's efforts to align spending with a defense strategy focused on strategic competition with China and Russia while also maintaining alliances and military bases abroad. Such a strategy is expensive and is responsible for why the U.S. spends more money on defense than the next 10 or 11 countries combined. Wars of regime change have also been very costly and, depending on how one counts, have totaled nearly $2 trillion through 2019, though some estimates place that cost closer to $6 trillion.

DoD's leadership indicated that the 2020 budget request was the first request to align budget and strategy, meaning that funding in the 2020 FYDP was sufficient to support the NDS, completed in 2018. The administration's recent FY21 budget request is relatively flat and projects no real growth when compared to FY20's enacted appropriation (without emergency disaster relief). To live within this more constrained environment, DoD is undertaking a series of performance improvement initiatives in business processes, systems, and policies. The department's intent is to apply savings from such efforts to high-priority activities in support of the NDS. Under these initiatives, DoD says it achieved about $5 billion in programmed savings for FY17 and has set a target of $46 billion for the years FY18 to FY22.

At the same time, the services have many outstanding bills in some of their major weapons programs, so difficult trade-offs will continue to be necessary. Given previous history, it is dubious that the savings from reform and performance improvements will generate enough dollars to pay for the wide range of requirements generated by the NDS. Senior civilian and military defense leaders have consistently testified that the defense budgets need real growth (over inflation) of 3% to 5% per year to successfully implement the NDS. Unfortunately, this is not the baseline of the current FYDP.

Looking towards the future, it is important to note that the 2019 BBA contains no statutory caps on 050 and 051 discretionary spending for FY22 and beyond. And since the caps disappear, the question will be whether OCO will remain, as its very existence was driven by the statutory caps. The reduction in the contingency operations and the pending reductions in deployed troops will open the door to reconsidering the OCO budget. Certainly, OMB has assumed that the OCO budget would eventually go away.

Yet, it is important not to forget that the most fundamental spending issue is not OCO versus base funding. It is the defense strategy and its associated requirements and costs. Many in the defense arena argue that the execution of our nation's defense strategy cannot be budget constrained. Others argue that defense, like other components in the budget, has to live within reasonable fiscal boundaries. For the 2020 transition, the Trump administration's baseline for DoD in FY22 through FY26 is a relatively flat budget and only provided a small placeholder for future OCO requirements of $20 billion, decreasing to $10 billion. Meanwhile, senior defense officials have consistently testified that it will take 3%-5% real growth to implement the NDS. Clearly, under flat budgets there will be a strategy vs. force mismatch.

The next administration will either have to re-examine the National Defense Strategy and reduce its requirements or assume greater risk with that strategy unless there is a bipartisan consensus to increase the defense budget, something that is unlikely. At the same time, the pressure for obtaining more bang for the buck and dealing with the significant percentage of the DoD budget allocated to personnel costs, overhead costs, and procurement and modernization costs will intensify.

MANDATORY SPENDING

Most of the trade-off debates engendered by the BCA have been between domestic and defense discretionary pots. However, these debates may diminish in the absence of caps. It is important to note that domestic and defense discretionary spending is overshadowed by mandatory spending, amplified even more by recent federal COVID-19 crisis relief. As a percentage of total federal outlays, defense is declining as mandatory spending and net interest are forecast to consume 69% of the budget in FY21. Interest payments represent over 11% within the 69% of mandatory spending.

Figure 4: Percent of Total FY21 Estimated Federal Outlays (Current $ in Billions)	
Defense Discretionary	16%
Non-Defense Discretionary	15%
Mandatory	69%

SOURCE: OMB'S HISTORICAL TABLES

So far, however, there is no indication that Congress is willing to reduce or even slow the growth of mandatory spending in any serious way, which would be accomplished by increasing taxes or decreasing mandatory spending. In the 1960s and 1970s, discretionary spending made up almost 70% of total federal spending. This spending ratio, coupled with the ability of decision makers to adjust priorities to reflect current needs for both defense and domestic requirements, has significantly decreased over time. This is largely due to the way mandatory spending (entitlements) and interest on the debt have crowded out discretionary spending, which now makes up less than 30% of the over $4 trillion spent annually (prior to COVID-19).

DEFICIT: WHEN SHOULD WE WORRY?

Despite the substantial growth of the nation's indebtedness, the deficit was not raised as a major issue during the Trump administration. While the U.S. federal debt has more than doubled since 2001, it hasn't led to higher interest payments. Customarily, economists have recommended Congresses and presidents to seriously consider reducing the long-term deficit, even though these suggestions have often fallen on deaf ears. The economists' thinking has been that government borrowing crowds out investment in the private sector. When this happens, private investors compete over the smaller pool of savings and bid up interest rates. Or, foreign savers step in and add to the pool of savings – or some combination of both. The view was that Americans would be worse off because domestic investment would be lower or foreign debt higher. Some national security experts have warned repeatedly about the economic insecurity the U.S. faces due to our reliance on foreign countries buying our debt.

Given the sustained decline in interest rates since the 1980s, other economists have argued that the debt and deficit costs are likely smaller presently and will continue to be in the future. Additionally, as forecasts predict interest rates for the government debt to stay low, the nation will be able to pay decreased amounts of interest while sustaining higher debt levels. For economists taking the new view, this reality is a large problem that requires policymakers to address deficits found within the real economy and not the budget – such as tackling persistent infrastructure and education deficits, which they see as more damaging to our economic and fiscal outlooks than the risks posed today by higher debt. With the changing administrations, there could be a rollback in President Trump's tax cuts for corporations and wealthy individuals. However, if this were to occur, these receipts would likely pay for more domestic spending rather than be utilized to lower the deficit.

Most economists agree that in the long term, deficits do matter. As my father used to say- when your outflow exceeds your inflow, your upkeep will be your downfall. If we truly desire a vibrant and innovative economy – especially one that can compete with China, a country whose purchasing power currently exceeds that of the United States – then trillion-dollar deficits are not sustainable.

The COVID-19 crisis and ensuing economic decline have further ballooned the deficit, moving us further away from reductions. Moreover, there is always the risk that interest rates will increase, adding to the uncertainty and fragility of the current economic situation. Additionally, many are already predicting that interest on the debt will be larger than the defense budget in the near term.

It is well-understood that the only viable approach to dealing with the long-term deficits will require political will that is not yet evident. Here, discretionary spending – including defense – will need to be constrained, the rate of increase in entitlement programs (including the very popular safety net and medical programs) must be adjusted, and we need to increase revenues. Ideally, this would be done in the manner recommended by the Simpson-Bowles commission, which encourages this to be a long-term, joint effort concerning all elements of the body politic. This is necessary to restore a sound fiscal situation for the future.

CHAPTER 18: CONTROLLING COSTS AND INCREASING ACCOUNTABILITY IN ACQUISITION

This chapter is based on a white paper that culminated from several decades of analysis and advice to leaders in both industry and government. These papers were often products of the many boards, commissions, and government task forces I have served on over the years, including a 2012 Defense Business Board study I chaired on streamlining the requirements, acquisition, and budget processes. As chairman of the National Defense Industrial Association (NDIA), I commissioned further studies and recommendations to provide Congress and DoD with industry perspectives. This resulting white paper has been updated and was distributed to leaders in Congress, industry, and the executive branch. Though the challenges it discusses appear to be timeless, the chapter itself has been updated to reflect 2020 data unless otherwise noted.

Acquisition reform is an area where each attempted solution can create more issues of its own. Additionally, it is often difficult to identify the root causes of problems. Despite this, nearly every new administration and Congress have stressed the need for improvements. Throughout time, some enduring questions on reform have persisted, including those on how to improve cost controls on major weapons systems, how to accelerate fielding new technologies, and how to hold people accountable for mistakes and failures. Unfortunately, these issues still persist, as they are rarely, if ever, solved. However, both the chairs and ranking members of the House and Senate Armed Services Committees (HASC and SASC respectively), as well as the senior acquisition officers in the Obama and Trump administrations, demonstrated renewed interest in the topic of acquisition and pushed continued reforms. As the new administration comes into the Pentagon, issues of acquisition costs and accountability will feature prominently in confirmation hearings of the Biden administration's senior DoD appointments, just as they have in past decades.

CONTROLLING COSTS

Over 160 major studies have been conducted on improving the general acquisition process, with many focused especially on controlling cost growth. Given the amount of focus this issue has garnered, it is unlikely that there is anything new or innovative that has not already been suggested in these reports, reflecting the old Washington adage that no one ever says anything new, but everyone has to be given the chance to say it. The immediate objective of this discussion, however, will be to raise issues that are hopefully somewhat different and work to amplify those with merit. Novel or otherwise, my views are based on issue familiarity gained from decades of experience as a Senate staffer, military officer, a senior executive with a major corporation in the defense industrial base, and a participant in and leader of numerous acquisition reform studies. Essentially, controlling costs inevitably involves some combination of:

- Controlling requirements.

- Avoiding delays in production and fielding.

- Aiming to incorporate the next "reasonable" technological advance.

- Placing realistic limits on the operational testing community.

- Communicating and negotiating effectively with industry.

Increased accountability, discussed in considerable depth below, will result from a streamlined acquisition process that is managed by senior acquisition leaders with long tenures – some have even said terminal (permanent) positions – allowing them to fully understand what the military calls "commander's intent." In many ways, increased accountability will, in itself, lead to increased cost control.

1. Requirements

The defense industrial base (DIB) base views the service program executive officers (PEOs) and program contracting officers (PCOs) as their customers. In the current environment, the suppliers will make every effort to meet the needs and desires of their customer. Given the significant shrinkage of the DIB since the early 1990s, company program managers (PMs) have become increasingly incentivized to meet all requirements initially established for a program, as well as those that appear later as the program progresses and matures. If it pleases their customers and enhances their prospects for future work and contracts, companies are inevitably incentivized to promise more than they can deliver. This phenomenon only increases as the existence of fewer companies makes them increasingly more dependent on a smaller number of programs, as the companies become more desperate to maintain their established presence in the defense marketplace. Accordingly, in some instances, as Norm Augustine, the former CEO of Lockheed Martin and one of the nation's most esteemed national security leaders, regrettably noted, this condition often means, "Desperate companies do desperate things."

As the DIB has shrunk over the past three decades, the requirements process has become increasingly unstable. This situation is driven by several factors.

First, actual needs have become increasingly uncertain in an unstable and chaotic international environment. Second, the system mandates a lengthy process, which is incompatible with the speed at which technology currently develops and changes. Third, the defense requirements community is bloated – it is too large, and there are too many stakeholders, the latter of whom possess too much authority to secure too many changes in established requirements authority.

While the military services establish the requirements, there is often not a total understanding of the financial costs and technological feasibility associated with them. In the joint process review, the former Vice Chairman of the Joint Chiefs of Staff (VCJCS) Admiral Sandy Winnefeld implemented real improvements, which have continued to be championed by Winnefeld's successors, Air Force General Paul Selva and General John Hyten. However, the Joint Requirements Oversight Council (JROC) has not demonstrated a record of turning down or constraining requirements, and its current Joint Capabilities Integration and Development System (JCIDS) process has become far too complex and time-consuming, despite Winnefeld's and Selva's efforts aimed to improve agility and timeliness.

Lastly, there is a tendency to prematurely pursue programs before understanding, establishing, and articulating the fundamental requirements associated with the project. Before acting, it is imperative to allow industry to evaluate the actual risk component associated in pursuing various paths.

For an example, look to deliberations over the Ground Combat Vehicle (GCV) several years ago. When DoD began its initial development, a senior Army general with a "heavy force" background stated that if the vehicle needed to weigh 70 tons to meet desired survivability capabilities, such weight would be acceptable. Shortly afterward, another senior Army general with a "light force" background stated that since the GCV was replacing the Bradley Fighting Vehicle, it could not weigh more than the Bradley's 25 tons. Obviously, this reflected a substantial difference of opinion rather than a debate on the actual need for the GCV. Inevitably, these radically differing observations caused industry to feel uncertain about the customer's wants and needs. After several months and $2.5 billion spent vainly pursuing configurations and technologies, the Pentagon canceled the GCV program. Although senior Army officers argued the cancellation was caused by budget (sequestration) pressures, most believed the vehicle was a victim of an uncertain operational need, which led to conflicting requirements.

2. Fielding the Initial Operational Capability (IOC) System

Recently, the Pentagon has expressed a desire to achieve 80% solutions rather than the often perceived gold-plated and highly costly 100% capability. While it is often thought that the defense industry champions excessive requirements, the industrial base often feels that the Pentagon, seduced by the latest capabilities it believes is necessary, often pushes forward hugely expensive and infeasible requirements. Although there have definitely been instances where suppliers essentially are asking a service PM "do you want fries with that?" the push for 100% solutions largely comes from the requirements community, occasionally with the support of an acquisition community held captive by its formal schedules and milestones.

If controlling costs is their true objective, the best approach for service customers is to not develop entirely new program requirements for each new piece of technology. Instead, service customers should focus on modifying and enhancing the existing system through Pre-Planned Product Improvements (P^3I). The P^3I can become programs of record, and if they do not develop as expected, they can easily be abandoned at considerably less cost than terminating (or significantly adjusting) a major program itself.

This approach aligns well with the "block upgrade" method. This model seeks to field the initial capability first and then work on adding improvements over time. Under Secretary for Acquisition and Sustainment Ellen Lord strongly advocated for pushing authority for program management out of OSD and down to the services. By doing this, Lord hoped to simultaneously encourage and incentivize program managers to speed up the acquisition process. Additionally, this system better incorporates feedback from users in the field, making the outcome more effective and useful to those actually using the technologies.

For example, in the mid-1980s, a request reached the vice chief of staff of the Army (VCSA) to delay the fielding of the new AH-64 Apache Attack helicopter, one of the Army's famous "Big Five" programs. This request was made because a then-classified program was working on a "fire-and-forget" Hellfire missile with a highly-automated fire control radar – a system that would later be fielded as LONGBOW®. Since the AH-64 was entering production, pilots were being trained, units were established, and LONGBOW was not yet out of development, the VCSA directed to move forward with the planned AH-64 program and add LONGBOW as a P³I when – and if – it successfully completed development. Since *Desert Storm* occurred before the launch of the LONGBOW equipped AH-64D, and it was another six years after *Desert Storm* before production AH-64Ds began to arrive, delaying the AH-64A in the late 1980s while awaiting LONGBOW would have been a most unfortunate decision. Moreover, both AH-64 and LONGBOW were developed and deployed with costs well controlled.

3. The Operational Testing Community

Since the mid-1980s, the operational testing community has added considerable additional costs to systems acquisition. Although enhanced operational tests were established with good intentions, they have resulted in excessive tests that are only loosely related to operational needs. Additionally, some tests must be performed at designated facilities that cannot be conducted outside of certain strict circumstances, such as particular weather or topographical conditions. All of these factors further slow down the acquisition process.

This has played out in the development of a variety of products, including the original Joint Light Tactical Vehicle (JLTV) competition. Here, suppliers were given 12 months to develop and produce original test articles, but the testing community was given nearly twice that amount of time to conduct testing. A senior executive, commenting on the unnecessarily long testing period, asked the necessary question: "Why do they get twice as much time to blow the articles up as I get to build them?" The testing community could not provide any robust explanation. In order to quicken the total product development time, all components of the process – acquisition and testing – must be similarly pressured to operate on a more efficient and accelerated timeline.

There are two major types of testing within the acquisition community: developmental testing (DT) and operational testing (OT). DT should be conducted by suppliers and supervised by customers. In contrast, OT should be carefully controlled by the customer acquisition community to ensure the tests reflect reasonable outcome and operation needs. Over time, there have been numerous instances where approved testing plans were modified on short notice. In almost all instances, the systems then failed to perform in roles they were never designed to fill, resulting in poor results, more expenses, and an overall longer process.

The PMs, both in industry and government, are motivated to have systems produced and fielded. However, testers often appear motivated to find a scenario or circumstance where a system does not perform satisfactorily, resulting in redesign, extra costs, and schedule slippage. Obviously, the function of developmental and operational testing is vital, and clear flaws must be corrected. However, improper, overly strident, or even irrelevant testing regimes need to be avoided, especially in an environment of rapid technological change and urgent operational need. This will only become increasingly necessary in the future, and the Pentagon must be willing to accept some risk in technology development in order to remain on par with new innovations.

4. Communications with Industry

Over the past few decades, communication between customers and industry suppliers has become too distant and indirect. This is not a uniform condition across the DoD; in general, the Navy is far better at communicating with its suppliers than the Army, and the other two services fall in between Army's and Navy's levels. Building on similar initiatives started by their predecessors, the Trump administration has developed more of a "two-way street" with industry.

When asked about the lapse of industry-service communication, a senior service officer replied: "I never talk to industry because I'm concerned that at some moment, in some way, I'll violate some law, somehow." This behavior is often the result of overly cautious legal advice and is both a most unhealthy attitude and inconsistent with the fundamental intention of any legislation.

At the highest levels, communications between industry and its defense customers must be continuous, conversational, and clear. Both parties must engage in frequent trade-off discussions to avoid surprises at the Milestone C (production), where the customer has often learned that the system, when equipped with all original and added requirements, has become unaffordable. Former Secretary of the Air Force Debbie Lee James instituted a program, Cost-Capability Analysis, to make such an affordability evaluation. This effort should be monitored and expanded where feasible.

DoD needs to recognize that the vast majority of technological expertise now resides in industry. Since the Packard Commission's elimination of the Deputy Service Chiefs for Research Development and Acquisition (in the Army this was the "DCSRDA"), the military career paths that once provided internal technological expertise have seriously eroded. This fact was further corroborated in the 2010 Decker-Wagner report, which was chartered by Army Secretary McHugh.

5. Incentivizing Industry Cost Control

Since industry acts as the government's agent in developing, designing, and producing weapons systems, the government must carefully and cleverly incentivize cost reductions. To do this, the government customer must have a thorough understanding of what motivates industry—contract awards, profit, and volume—and judiciously make awards, offer justifiable margins, and purchase products in bulk quantity in exchange for reduced costs and better performance.

When it comes to incentivizing industry to reduce costs and improve performance, competition has proven the most effective tool available. The government can structure competition in multiple ways depending on product needs and specific industry characteristics. For example, the government can hold a one-time competition for the development or production contract prior to a single award. The government can also use prototyping or lot and block purchasing to sustain competition throughout the development and production cycle. In order to successfully do this, the government must solicit participation from multiple competitors and dedicate the necessary planning and investment to sustain successful multi-party competition. Regardless of how competition is structured, the government must consistently maintain the option of program competition to deter specific contractors from monopolistic behavior.

Another good practice for cost-control involves structuring contracts to increase industry's profit margin in exchange for per-unit cost reductions as long as contractors experience a steady or better yet, increasing total profit. To achieve this outcome, the government will need to reconsider the idea of "fair and reasonable profit margins." Here, the government must view profit for what it is—a tool to incentivize desirable industry behavior—not an undesirable cost that must be reduced or stripped away. At a recent "industry day" for a series of major service contracts, a government contracting officer told industry representatives, "I know you need to make a profit, but we don't intend to pay for it." This type of attitude discourages competition, and, while potentially suitable for the short term, it is certainly disastrous in the long run.

Congress and the Pentagon also continue to add overhead and reporting mandates without any concern for cost. However, every additional lawyer or accountant hired by a contractor or the government to fulfill a legal or regulatory mandate results in fewer scientists, engineers, or technicians working on next-generation military technologies. While some mandates are essential, excessive regulations only increase costs, deepen bureaucracy, and weaken mission focus. Before enacting new mandates, the government must fully understand their costs and benefits. While a common-sense proposition, this may help reduce costs across the entire portfolio of federal programs.

The government can also place itself in a more favorable position to negotiate per-unit costs with contractors by purchasing in bulk. This is the fundamental explanation for the success of businesses like Walmart and Costco. Economies of scale are better achieved on low-risk, predictable purchases, where the government can couple bulk purchases with regular rounds of multi-party competition.

ACCOUNTABILITY

There are two basic challenges to establishing accountability in defense acquisition programs: the convoluted system that distributes authority across too many offices and individuals, and the government's assignment policies that rotate senior program managers and officials too frequently. These issues are underscored by an alarming fact: in recent decades, DoD has canceled over $60 billion worth of ongoing programs and no one – yes, no one – has ever been held accountable for the lost funds. Specific programs include the XM2001 Crusader, RAH-66 Comanche, Future Combat Systems, Defense Integrated Military Human Resources (DIMHRS), Armed Aerial Scout, and many IT programs.

By any measure, the senior acquisition executive (SAE), program executive officer (PEO), program manager (PM) system that emerged in the late 1980s creates excessive dispersion of authority. This model also exists in parallel with a largely separate requirements community and another separate functional acquisition policymaking community that exerts a "veto power" through peer reviews, further complicating and duplicating matters.

Changing the SAE/PEO system as a whole would be difficult, as it would entail significant changes to statutes. However, improvements to the existing system are possible. One proposal involves extending—perhaps going so far as doubling—the time a senior civilian or military manager holds his or her position. The arrival of the SAE/PEO system and the near-simultaneous arrival of an expanded effort to oversee programs conducted by OSD-level offices have created a complex web of authorities where accountability is far too distributed. While it is easy to find individuals who describe themselves as accountable, it is hard to find those who feel they are to blame. President Kennedy famously noted, "Success has many fathers; failure is an orphan." The current system has created many potential "fathers," but ironically, even more potential "orphans."

The government and DoD especially must recognize the unique nature of the defense industry marketplace. Unlike Adam Smith's free market concept, the defense marketplace contains few of the market attributes like those described in Smith's *The Wealth of Nations*. For example, because the defense marketplace possesses one buyer and a handful of suppliers, it can be characterized as monopsonistic. In this environment, there are significant barriers to entry, information is highly fragmented (often the result of security classifications), the market is highly regulated, and most uniquely, the buyer is the regulator. Moreover, the buyer is a distinctly intrusive customer who demands information on costs, supply chains, testing, and evaluations. All of these factors are unseen in any commercial market.

These characteristics, combined with the steady growth of new regulations and reporting requirements established in the name of cost control and market efficiency, have combined to make the defense marketplace relatively unappealing. As a result, more companies have elected to exit the market than enter it, meaning the number of large (prime) integrators has steadily decreased. This has also caused the supplier pool to shift toward smaller, more fragile sub-contractors. Additionally, all of these factors are diametrically opposed to DoD's aspirations to utilize competition to foster greater cost control and innovation. True cost control and acquisition reform will require recognizing the defense marketplace's significant distortion and working to better normalize it.

RECOMMENDATIONS

1. Streamline and discipline the requirements community.

There are too many "oars in the water" that possess some form of implicit "veto power." Requirements need to remain relatively firm after a system enters the second destination transportation (SDT) phase, and efforts to revisit and modify requirements need to be strongly discouraged. It should be presumed that in the absence of some compelling rationale – driven by a significant strategic or technological change – major changes will not be permitted. Service chiefs are the likely key to this discipline and should be held firmly accountable for disciplining their requirements processes. The service chiefs should know both projected costs and technical feasibility prior to approval. But, to creditably perform this function, they will need to have staff to provide them with the necessary technical information. They will also have to become comfortable with routine interactions with industry.

2. Field the IOC system.

Don't wait for the "objective" (full-up) system. Rather, it is more important to accelerate the system in the field and into the hands of the warfighters than to delay it because of the latest technological innovation. Discourage requirements changes but encourage P^3I – the insertion of new capabilities into systems after fielding. The operational force can help with this effort by bringing to it hard-won expertise. As the operators are unquestionably the best test and evaluation community available, they will also naturally assume this task as the ultimate customer. Apple Corporation, largely credited with developing and popularizing the mobile phone, started with the iPhone 1; they did not delay the introduction of the product until they had available to them all the functions now seen in the latest version.

3. Closely supervise the testing community.

The live-fire testing of the Bradley Fighting Vehicle in the mid-1980s did result in useful changes to fuel configurations and weapons storage, but some of these tests were unnecessary. For example, some tests only demonstrated that the vehicle was vulnerable to certain anti-tank weapons, which the technology was never designed to withstand. This redundant and irrelevant type of testing also occurred with the Marine Corps Expeditionary Fighting Vehicle (EFV) in 2005. Here, the testing community determined the vehicles had very low reliability, despite the fact that the vehicles tested were prototypes never intended to meet the reliability levels of production vehicles. To maximize efficiency and avoid redundancy, testing needs to be conducted against requirements that actually exist, not the ones the test community feels should exist. While this type of discussion can occur between the requirements community and the testing community prior to the release of a request for proposals (RFP), it is not something that a provider should discover on the test range.

4. Improve the communication loop.

Strongly encourage continuous, conversational, and clear interactions between defense customers and suppliers. Make it clear to the legal community that the interest of the Defense Department (and the nation) is best served by more – as opposed to less – communication. Congress never intended there to be an impermeable wall between DoD customers and their providers. In this regard, the senior leadership should set an example by meeting frequently with senior industry representatives. The

Obama administration's senior defense leadership identified this issue and to date, has been the most responsive and aggressive in working to reverse this trend. The challenge has been that below the most senior levels, it is often "lawyers *über alles.*"

Additionally, the secretary and the USD Acquisition and Sustainment (A&S) need to explain to the acquisition staffs (perhaps frequently) that the pathway to an innovative, competitive, cost-conscious industry is linked to profits. Far too often, those in government view profit as a measure of exploitation rather than an indication of added value. The government needs to understand that profit is a motive that encourages the private sector to work with government, rather than a cost discouraging it. Allowing justifiable fees will encourage more entrants into the defense marketplace, which badly needs more players, something implicit in Defense Secretary Ashton Carter's 2014 outreach to Silicon Valley. More competitors in the defense marketplace will translate into more innovation and more cost control. Innovation will nearly always follow the money.

5. Structure contracts to give industry a good reason to control costs.

This involves working to ensure a more competitive environment, using profit as a tool rather than viewing it as a cost, enforcing appetite control to limit new compliance mandates, and leveraging bulk economies of scale whenever possible.

6. Focus on accountability.

Internally, the department should make all efforts to narrow the wide galaxy of acquisition stakeholders. This will be easier to accomplish with the major acquisition programs and more difficult with smaller programs, but it is necessary. Additionally, the DoD should extend the tours of major program PEOs and PMs, doubling them in duration in as many cases as possible. The department should also consider making these assignments terminal, specifically for the most senior civilian and military officials. Over time, the service academies have mostly shifted the office of superintendent from a "growth" to a "terminal" assignment. West Point has also made them five-year tours, allowing the superintendent adequate time to install innovative changes and implement accountability.

Perhaps PEOs and major PMs should be viewed in the same manner, with these assignments changed to become lengthier and potentially even terminal. The most successful PEO of all time was Admiral Hyman Rickover, who, despite certain unconventional (even undesirable) characteristics and an oft-contentious relationship with suppliers, produced a highly successful nuclear Navy. The merits of this model should be considered, and the demerits recognized and avoided.

Additionally, DoD should continue efforts to reinvolve the service chiefs in the acquisition process and involve them in efforts to streamline the requirements, acquisition, and budget process while holding them accountable. Service chiefs are much better positioned than service secretaries to oversee and discipline the requirements process. They are also better positioned in this regard than the CJCS, the VCJCS, the JROC, and the Joint Staff. If the JROC continues to be involved in the requirements and acquisition processes, then its composition should be reconsidered, as there is an institutional conflict of interest when the service vice chiefs serve on the JROC. Other members of the JROC should likely be designated representatives of the combatant commanders, as they better understand immediate warfighting needs.

Conclusion

Despite the strong efforts of the Obama and Trump administrations to improve the overall DoD acquisition systems – efforts that have fielded some notable successes – the measurement is not how far we have come, but rather how far we still have to go. DoD still spends over $400 billion a year on goods, services, supplies, and equipment. Unfortunately, the reality is that the DoD is still spending more, taking longer, and getting less. Again, unless we reverse this trend, the Pentagon will continue to experience the "ever-shrinking fighting force."

CHAPTER 19: THE RISE OF THE DEFENSE AGENCIES

This chapter originated as a white paper in 2016 to provide the incoming administration with observations regarding the department's long list of defense agencies and DoD field activities (DAFAs), epicenters for increasing costs and personnel growth, and the need for significant improvements in output from these major elements of DoD overhead. These are the organizations responsible for defense-wide management functions such as logistics, health care, research and development, human resources, finance and accounting, information systems, the commissaries, and schools. My focus on the DAFAs had its inception in 1997 when I chaired the Defense Reform Task Force for Secretary of Defense Bill Cohen. In 2010, I updated this analysis for Secretary Bill Gates. In 2020, I co-chaired a major analysis of the DAFAs in the Defense Business Board's assessment of DoD management. Over the years, I have testified before Congress on my analyses in this area, and I have briefed senior DoD leadership, including former Secretary Esper and former Deputy Secretary Norquist, both of whom have actively and aggressively tackled these issues.

Former Secretary of the Army John O. Marsh once said that the Pentagon has a "hot water" line and a "cold water" line. The hot water consists of deployments and combat forces sent to dangerous places for complex operations – it's under the control of the warfighting chain of command, extending from the commander of a combatant command (COCOM) to the secretary of defense to the president (the warfighter missions). The cold water, by contrast, is the infrastructure and procedures within and across the Pentagon that raise, resource, train, equip, and sustain forces in the field (referred to as the "organize, train, and equip" (OTE) missions). Essentially, these are the nuts and bolts of the Title 10 responsibilities that reside within the Pentagon and its various components.

As can be seen by a casual perusal of the textbooks assigned for any academic course on national security, the hot water line gets the majority of the attention. Nonetheless, as one noted authority on defense issues commented, "If there's no cold water, there's no hot water." The major presence in the cold water line are the numerous DAFAs that have grown up under the overall DoD umbrella over the past 70 years. Of the 28 DAFAs that exist today, only one can trace its existence to 1952. Although, the idea of DoD organizations outside of the military departments wasn't formalized as a categorical distinction until 1986 with Goldwater-Nichols and the enactment of Sections 191-193 of Title 10. In FY19, the defense-wide activities accounted for over $115 billion in spending, which does not include the four large intelligence agency budgets. The increase in the number of DAFAs and their ever-increasing budgets is one reason why defense-wide spending has also ballooned, growing from less than 5% of the total DoD budget to almost 20% today. Historically, the DAFAs rarely received much attention from senior defense leaders or Congress, but given their size and scope of operations, there has been a great deal of interest in them over the last few years.

HISTORY

Until the National Security Act of 1947, which created the modern DoD from the Department of War and the Department of the Navy, each service contained its own distinct managerial and support structures and organizations. By forming the Department of the Air Force and redesignating the Department of War as the Department of the Army, the 1947 Act created three separate cold water lines, each managing its own – and sometimes competing – establishments for providing the departments with intelligence, supplies, facilities management, health care, acquisition, repair parts, fuel, and so forth. Although the 1947 Act placed the three departments under one Secretary of Defense, it actually did little to consolidate all the various functions required to run a military department. However, that effort began to slowly gather momentum in the following decade.

A major impetus for greater centralization was the Soviet Union's launch of the *Sputnik* satellite in October 1957. At the time, the United States was working on a satellite launch of its own using a Navy-developed vehicle named *Vanguard*. Despite American efforts, the Soviet success, which was quickly duplicated the following month with the launch of *Sputnik II* carrying a dog, was a deep humiliation for the United States, and especially the defense establishment. This national embarrassment was compounded in December 1957 when a Navy-designed satellite and launch vehicle exploded on the launch pad at Cape Canaveral, Florida.

The Soviet Union's achievements raised two major organizational concerns for the United States. First, it revealed issues about internal collaboration and cooperation within the Defense Department. The Department of the Army would argue for many years that the U.S. could have been first in space had the Army been given approval to proceed with its *Juno I* rocket, which was a modification of the existing *Redstone* missile developed by the Army Ballistic Missile Agency (ABMA), and the *Explorer* payload developed by the Jet Propulsion Lab (JPL). Second, to better integrate scientific innovation and military application, President Dwight Eisenhower created the Advanced Research Projects Agency (ARPA) the month after the *Explorer* launch. Now known as the Defense Advanced Research Projects Agency (DARPA), this agency was charged, as one authority put it, to make the United States "the initiator and not the victim of technological strategic surprise."

At that time, there was one other defense agency, the National Security Agency (NSA), which had been established in the Truman administration. The NSA was the descendent of several earlier organizations that had concentrated on signals intelligence, which is the effort to deduce an enemy's plans and operations by monitoring and analyzing its communications. A cipher bureau had been created for this purpose by the Army during World War I but then was disbanded with the armistice in 1919. It was re-established in the early 1940s as the Signal Intelligence Service (SIS) with a focus on breaking enemy codes. The Navy ran a similar organization in the Pacific known as Station Hypo, which successfully broke the Japanese communications code and played a key role in the Battle of Midway victory in June 1942.

Following World War II, the SIS became the Army Security Agency (ASA), which was slowly consolidated into the NSA starting in 1952. However, as is common with such efforts, the full incorporation of the ASA into NSA did not occur until the ASA's formal inactivation in 1976.

The real push toward managerial consolidation was driven by both strategic concerns at the end of the Eisenhower administration and efficiency aspirations in the early Kennedy years. Understandably, the first defense agency to appear during this period was the Defense Atomic Support Agency (DASA), which opened its doors in 1959. In 1971, DASA became the Defense Nuclear Agency (DNA) and then was renamed again to the Defense Threat Reduction Agency (DTRA) in 1998.

In August 1960, the National Reconnaissance Office (NRO) was established by President Eisenhower three months after the downing of an American U-2 reconnaissance plane over the Soviet Union. It was believed that satellites could provide useful intelligence information without the overflight risks posed by the U-2; however, Air Force-led efforts to achieve such a capability were behind schedule. Accordingly, the decision was made to consolidate the endeavor directly under the Office of the Secretary of Defense (OSD). This move initiated a trend that would continue for years to come, namely that when a service-led program was not producing the desired results on time or on budget, the Pentagon would consolidate the effort into a defense-wide program directly managed by an OSD official.

Kennedy's defense secretary, former President of Ford Motor Company Robert S. McNamara, believed that many core functions common across the DoD could be managed more efficiently if centralized. This conviction launched three new agencies in four years: The Defense Logistics Agency (DLA) and the Defense Intelligence Agency (DIA) in 1961 and the Defense Contract Audit Agency (DCAA) in 1965.

The consolidation trend, which was largely resisted by the services, continued through the Johnson era and into the Nixon administration with the establishment of the Defense Security Assistance Agency (DSAA) in 1971. The DSAA was later renamed the Defense Security Cooperation Agency (DSCA) in 2009.

After assuming office, President Ronald Reagan quickly made national missile defense capability a high priority. Accordingly, the Strategic Defense Initiative (SDI) was initiated in 1983 and the SDI Organization (SDIO) was established within DoD in 1984. Following the end of the Cold War, the SDIO became the Ballistic Missile Defense Organization (BMDO) and then the Missile Defense Agency (MDA) in 2002.

The 1990s saw continued growth of defense-wide agencies with the creation of the Defense Commissary Agency (DeCA) in 1990, followed by the Defense Finance and Accounting Service (DFAS) in 1990, and finally the National Geospatial-Intelligence Agency (NGA) in 1996. Moreover, the Defense Contract Management Agency (DCMA) started operating in 2000, and the Defense Health Agency (DHA) was established in 2013.

Over the past 70 years, the Pentagon has created 28 DAFAs spanning a wide variety of activities and missions. Many, such as the Defense POW/MIA Accounting Agency (DPAA) and the Pentagon Force Protection Agency (PFPA) were developed to support very specific missions. Others were established to integrate and streamline semi-related groups of activities, such as the DoD Human Resources Activity and the Defense Media Activity. The current state of DAFA and their OSD oversight is shown in Figure 1.

FIGURE 1: GROWTH OF DEFENSE AGENCIES AND DoD FIELD ACTIVITIES

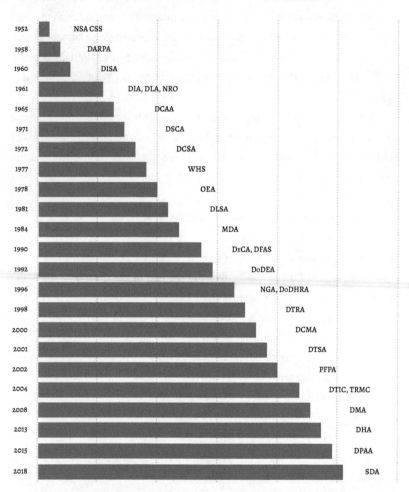

SECRETARY ESPER CORRECTLY FOCUSED THE DEPARTMENT ON IMPROVED MANAGEMENT AND REDUCED COSTS OF THE DAFAS.

IN FY19, DEFENSE AGENCIES AND DOD FIELD ACTIVITIES ACCOUNTED FOR $115.5 BILLION OF SPENDING BY YEAR-END.

From 1958 to 2018, the number of DAFAs grew from 2 to 28.

DARPA - Defense Advanced Research Projects Agency
DCAA - Defense Contract Audit Agency
DCMA - Defense Contract Management Agency
DCSA - Defense Counterintelligence and Security Agency
DeCA - Defense Commissary Agency
DFAS - Defense Finance and Accounting Service
DHA - Defense Health Agency
DIA - Defense Intelligence Agency
DISA - Defense Information Systems Agency
DLA - Defense Logistics Agency
DLSA - Defense Legal Services Agency
DMA - Defense Media Activity (FA)
DoDEA - DoD Education Activity (FA)
DoDHRA - DoD Human Resources Activity (FA)

DPAA - Defense POW/MIA Accounting Agency
DSCA - Defense Security Cooperation Agency
DTIC - Defense Technical Information Center (FA)
DTRA - Defense Threat Reduction Agency
DTSA - Defense Technology Security Administration
MDA - Missile Defense Agency
NGA - National Geospatial-Intelligence Agency
NRO - National Reconnaissance Office
NSA/CSS - National Security Agency/Central Security Service
OEA - Office of Economic Adjustment (FA)
PFPA - Pentagon Force Protection Agency (FA)
SDA - Space Development Agency
TRMC - DoD Test Resource Management Center (FA)
WHS - Washington Headquarters Services (FA)

FIGURE 1 ILLUSTRATES THE GROWTH OF DAFAs FROM 1952 TO 2018.

INTRODUCTION TO DAFAS

In general, DAFAs are large and often sprawling. Moreover, getting a precise picture of their scope and scale is always a challenge, especially given their participation in similar activities within the military services. Additionally, their official personnel headcount may not fully reflect their actual workforce costs; they often rely heavily on military manpower (paid for by the military departments) from the services and contractors (which are expressed as mission costs rather than workforce costs).

DAFAs are created by the secretary of defense to perform a supply or service activity common to more than one military service when such action is determined to be more effective, economical, or efficient. Moreover, the Defense Appropriations Act requires that the secretary certifies that the establishment of a DAFA represents a cost or workforce reduction. Additionally, the Goldwater-Nichols DoD Reorganization Act (GNA) of 1986 required that each DAFA be overseen by a senior OSD official or the Chairman of the Joint Chiefs of Staff (CJCS). While the CJCS is allowed, the department currently assigns this oversight role to one of the OSD Principal Staff Assistants (PSAs)—typically an Under Secretary of Defense (USD). The USDs are presidentially appointed, Senate-confirmed (PAS) positions, but not all PSAs with oversight responsibilities are PAS. (For example, the Assistant to the Secretary of Defense for Public Affairs is not a PAS position but provides oversight of the Defense Media Activity.) While a PSA may assign daily oversight to a subordinate ASD, the ASD is still with the undersecretary.

As mentioned previously, in FY19, defense-wide accounts (not just the DAFAs) spent over $115 billion—16% of DoD's total budget, including OCO and emergency funding. However, this number considerably understates the total expenditures of the DAFAs, as there are significant costs associated with military personnel assigned to these activities that are not reflected in the agency budgets and many of the DAFAs execute significant reimbursable support to the military departments.

Also, the budgets for the specific intelligence agencies are not released publicly. However, the unclassified totals are made available. For FY21, the National Intelligence Program (NIP) requested $62 billion, and the Military Intelligence Program (MIP) requested $24 billion. When comparing these totals to FY15 data, this is a net increase of 27%, showing how DAFA spending continues to rise. The military departments spend most of the NIP and the MIP. DIA holds the MIP for the COCOMs, but they are executed under control of the combatant commanders (CCDRs) and not the DIA.

Figure 2 highlights the final FY20 appropriations for DAFAs while breaking them down into functional categories and organizing them under their supervisory relationships. Many of these agencies are supported by the Defense Working Capital Fund (DWCF), some with non-appropriated funds and some using a mixture of both.

FIGURE 2: CURRENT DAFAs

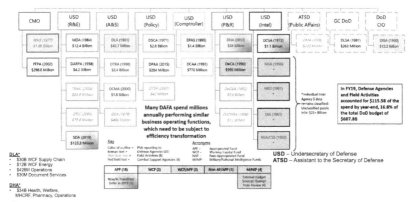

FIGURE 2 DEPICTS THE CURRENT DAFA BUDGETS FOR FY20, THEIR SUPERVISORY
ARRANGEMENTS, AND HOW THEY'RE FUNDED IN WHOLE OR PART.

Note: I have used some of these figures in my previous analyses over the years. I updated and included them in the recent Defense Business Board assessment of DoD management in a section on the DAFAs and DWCFs submitted to the secretary of defense in June 2020. This is a public document. I co-chaired the task force and served as primary author for the DAFA section. This most recent assessment benefitted from the other task force members and the staff, which is why the Defense Business Board logo appears on some of the figures.

AGENCY DETAILS

Within each of the 28 different agencies, there are unique structures, missions, and budgets. While metrics such as full-time equivalent (FTE) and employee totals are helpful in gaining a picture of each agency, they are not wholly indicative of the entire agency's size and scope. This section provides a breakdown of these details in order to provide a more accurate description of the different agencies.

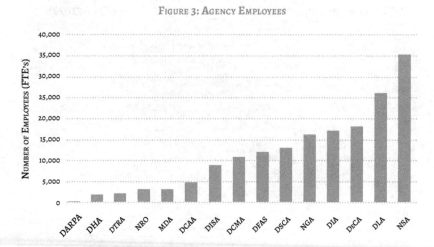

FIGURE 3 ILLUSTRATES THE NUMBER OF DA EMPLOYEES REFLECTED IN PUBLIC DOCUMENTS.

DARPA, the smallest agency with 220 direct employees, has long been considered one of DoD's top-performing agencies and is widely respected. However, DARPA maintains an outsized annual budget and leverages contractors to perform most of its work, making the total number of people involved in the agency's work much larger than appears on the chart.

The DHA is officially the second-smallest DA with only 1,700 employees. However, like DARPA, this small number is highly deceiving. DoD's overall health operations are arguably the largest in the world and may involve as many as 130,000 people DoD-wide when including the doctors, nurses, and medical staff that fall within its purview. Moreover, there are close to 10 million beneficiaries of the DoD health care system, including over five million retirees and their dependents. DHA can play games with their workforce reporting because they control the entire DHP and can mask the numbers "attributable" only to the agency versus what DHA is realistically using.

For the past several years, defense health care, mirroring American health care as a whole, has been one of DoD's fastest-growing budget expenses. Over time, it has grown from less than $10 billion a year to over $50 billion a year. Despite its unique function and size, it has been relatively immune from efforts to control costs associated with active duty personnel, reserve personnel, retirees, and their families. Trying to address the ballooning costs, the Pentagon established a medical oversight committee led by the late Admiral Donald Pilling. Pilling once commented that during the formulation of the five-year budget plan known as Future Years Defense Program (FYDP), his committee had allocated an additional $10 billion to the medical program, thinking that amount would meet the need. However, during the following budget review, they were then asked to add $6 billion more. "We paid a $10 billion bill so we could have a $6 billion bill," was how the Admiral described it.

In terms of personnel, the largest DA is the NSA, which totals some 35,000 military and civilian employees. Like the other agencies discussed, this number is likely not the total personnel that supports this key agency, as NSA is certainly supported by a large cadre of contractors, given the highly technical nature of its mission. Overall, the intelligence effort involves over 68,000 people directly employed by the NSA, DIA, and NGA. Adding the 3,000 employees of the NRO brings the intelligence effort itself to over 71,000 people. Moreover, there are additional personnel in the NRO from other agencies not included in the DoD totals. Clearly, the modern need for timely and precise intelligence has translated into a significant manpower investment. Three of the largest DAs in terms of manpower are engaged in intelligence and report to the Under Secretary of Defense for Intelligence and Security (USD(I&S)).

Overall, according to public data and only counting direct hires or FTEs, the DAs are manned by over 170,000 people, making them nearly as large as the Marine Corps. But another interesting perspective comes from reviewing their stated budgets, as shown in Figure 4.

FIGURE 4: DEFENSE AGENCY BUDGETS

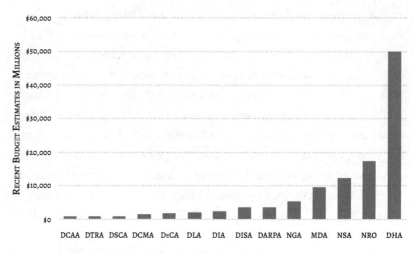

FIGURE 4 PROVIDES FY20 BUDGET ESTIMATES FOR A SELECTION OF THE LARGEST
DEFENSE AGENCIES.

DHA is the agency with the largest budget authority, totaling nearly $50 billion in its recent request. As illustrated by both Figures 1 and 4, the DHA is mainly a coordination agency; its relatively small staff size could not directly oversee, manage, and execute such a large budget alone. The department should insist on clarifying where all the health funds are spent, as they refuse to break them out in a clear fashion since most of the health funds are used in the military departments.

In contrast, the intelligence DAs maintain their heavy presence with three of the top five positions – the fourth taken by the technologically-intensive Missile Defense Agency (MDA). Similarly, DARPA appears small in manpower but large in budget allocation, reflecting its heavy reliance on contractor support to complete its intense technological work.

It is important to emphasize that actual budget levels may give an incomplete picture of the scope of agency activities. For example, DFAS, the world's largest finance and accounting organization, operates under a Defense Working Capital Fund (DWCF) concept. In other words, it charges a fee for handling the pay, contract, and accounting services it provides to its customers – mainly the military services. Colossal amounts of funding pass through DFAS, but the organization itself has a rather small budget.

In 2018, DFAS processed 136 million pay transactions, routed to both military and civilian personnel with funds drawn from numerous appropriations. Simultaneously, it processed over 13 million invoices, largely from defense contractors of various sizes, and paid an overall $558 billion in disbursements. In addition, DFAS handled approximately $542 billion in foreign military sales. In total, DFAS participated in transactions totaling over $1 trillion – an amount considerably larger than its $1.4 billion budget.

This is much the same with DLA. Although the DLA direct budget is merely $1.7 billion, it handles $37 billion in goods and services and manages a supply chain of some five million items spread across a global distribution network, all while supporting 2,400 weapons systems. Fuel is one of the vital products procured by the DLA, as the DoD is the largest single daily consumer of fuel on the planet. It consumes over 90% of the fuel used by the U.S. government, and the Air Force alone consumes 10% of the nation's aviation fuel on a daily basis. The DLA is likely the largest commodity provider in the world and is certainly the most impactful, though its budget may not indicate that at first glance.

Maj. Gen. Arnold Punaro, USMC, Ret. meets with Secretary of Defense Mark Esper to brief him on recommended reforms to the DAFAs, the DWCF, and DoD overhead.

DAFA CHALLENGES

As concluded in the recent Defense Business Board (DBB) study, the DoD does not have the integrated management structure, business systems, and financial controls to coherently manage and effectively oversee these 28 DAFAs. Consequently, the DoD cannot ensure that the priorities of any given administration are fully implemented in the most effective, efficient, and economical way as required by Title 10.

Additionally, there are issues of authority and ability. In the Defense Reform Task Force's 1997 review of the DAFAs, we concluded that the senior officials supervising DAFAs were traditionally more focused on their policy responsibilities than their management responsibilities – something that remains true today. In addition to a lack of management focus, there are layers of bureaucracy that further cloud visibility into DAFA operations. Moreover, there are also experience issues, demonstrated in the way the major business-oriented DAFAs are run by government personnel with limited experience in managing major business operations. These DAFAs often have customer boards that lack similar business experience, further compounding the problem. Additionally, the senior officials supervising DAFAs do not have the authority to make cross-DAFA trades, as this only occurs at the deputy secretary of defense level.

It should be noted that the missions of DAFAs are widely diverse, ranging from operating a DoD secondary dependent school system to running the worldwide healthcare system that includes battlefield care, to providing missile defense against growing threats to our homeland. The DAFAs, with their large government and contractor employment base, also enjoy considerable support in Congress, where any suggestions for savings are always challenged. For example, a former chairman of the Senate Armed Service Committee once included a study of how to make the commissary system less dependent on taxpayer subsidies but was immediately blocked by the full Senate, illustrating Congress's resistance to even studying how to improve the business operations in the Pentagon.

This cost immunity is underscored by what happened in September 2020 when the DoD was considering saving $2.5 billion in health care costs. Immediately, both former Vice President Joe Biden and President Donald Trump tweeted in opposition to this plan. Soon after, President Trump directed the department to back off any plans aimed at reducing health care costs. This was not the first time the DoD has received pushback for similar efforts. For example, Secretary Robert Gates requested Congress to implement a $5 increase per month in TRICARE for Life co-pays for working-age retirees, resulting in a similar outcry and opposition, despite the fact that co-pays had not increased in 16 years while retiree pay with annual cost-of-living increases had doubled in the same timeframe. Health care is not the only area that is met with resistance; attempts at reducing the annual appropriated subsidy to the defense commissary system, which today measures $1.4 billion annually, have been denied.

Despite the pushback, Congress is aware of these growing expenses and has been working to address them without substantial success. For example, the FY17

NDAA forced greater consolidation under the DHA. Here, the Pentagon sought to consolidate health facilities under DHA so the services' health commands could better focus on providing care itself. Additionally, seeking to control costs associated with uniformed service members in non-warfighting positions, the DoD recently announced plans to convert some 18,000 military physicians, dentists, nurses, corpsmen, medics, and administrative staff to civilian positions.

However, a DHA spokesman pointed out that none of the proposed reductions would come from DHA itself, possibly stating the obvious for an agency with a formal headcount of only 1,700. Additionally, as recent congressional remarks and concerns have demonstrated, there is speculation as to whether these personnel reductions will even occur at all, especially in a COVID-19 environment. Moreover, the leaders in the military departments continue to pushback against DHA consolidation, making the implementation of these changes appear even less likely.

Tracking DAFA Performance

Throughout the majority of their existence, there has been no consistent structure or process to assess DAFA performance. Additionally, there has also been a lack of written performance objectives. However, despite this history, Secretary of Defense Mark Esper and Deputy Secretary of Defense David Norquist sought to direct a major review of the DAFAs in 2020. In addition, the DBB recommended the SecDef to conduct a major assessment of the management options for the DAFAs along with a major review of the Defense Working Capital Funds (DWCFs), which also need improvements.

It is clear that the senior DoD leadership needs an effective and robust way to improve DAFA performance levels, create efficiencies, reduce costs, and establish benchmarks and outputs compared to China. Here, the key question focuses on centralized versus decentralized management and understanding whether a new centralized approach such as instituting a service secretary for the DAFAs would be successful or create further complications. Regardless of the management structure type, the DoD needs to ensure that any new organization would promote improved performance. In Figure 5, the DBB provides potential solutions to improve DAFA management.

FIGURE 5: DAFA MANAGEMENT OPTIONS TO CONSIDER

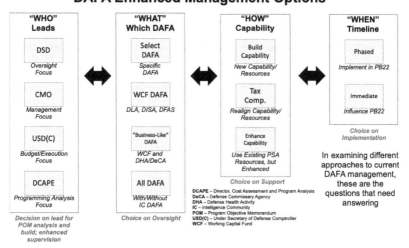

FIGURE 5 PROPOSES DIFFERENT SOLUTIONS FOR DAFA MANAGEMENT STRUCTURES.

In addition to these options, other potential solutions include adding performance contracts for the leaders of the business-orientated DAFAs, including DLA, DHA, DISA, DeCA, and others. In this scenario, DoD leadership would also need to institute trackable and enforceable performance metrics to ensure success.

Another option involves creating a DAFA oversight committee. This would be chaired by the deputy secretary of defense and consist of senior PAS leaders with DAFA oversight, who would report to the committee on a rotating basis. Additionally, the DoD should consider creating a DAFA Performance Office in a newly-established Performance Improvement Office. This would be led by the deputy secretary of defense and oversee performance metrics compliance while working with the PSAs on management training and internal consulting.

There has also been discussion around creating a DAFA service secretary. This position would possess the same standing as the other service secretaries and report directly to the secretary of defense. Most importantly, this position would have the authority, direction, and control over the directors of the 28 DAFAs. Former Secretary of Defense Mark Esper is a proponent of a single authority over the DAFAs. Such an approach would be controversial, as it would require fundamental changes to Title 10 and all existing reporting relationships. However, this change has not been formally proposed and would require serious evaluation, particularly considering the diverse nature of the DAFAs. The DAFAs are much more diverse than the scope of the responsibilities of the military department service secretaries.

Other less turbulent options include efforts to improve management of the Defense Working Capital Funds (DWCFs) that support the DAFAs with enhancement to the Under Secretary of Defense Comptroller. Another consideration involves replacing the three-star military leaders currently running the business-oriented DAFAs with successful private sector executives. In this scenario, the three-star would become the deputy and the new civilian agency head would have a performance contract. Additionally, the DoD would add oversight fiduciary boards containing a blend of private sector experts and DoD customers. Here, the lead director would come from the private sector, and independent directors would have the majority of the board seats. Former Secretary Esper recently replaced the three-star military leader as head of the Defense Security Cooperation Agency with a civilian and was known to favor a similar approach for the other business-centered DAFAs such as the Defense Logistics Agency and the Defense Information Systems Agency.

Figure 6 outlines in greater detail a range of management options ranging from least aggressive to most aggressive. These should be evaluated in a DAFA review initiated by the secretary of defense as recommended by the Defense Business Board.

FIGURE 6: DAFAs: ENHANCED MANAGEMENT OPTIONS

	Least aggressive →					Most aggressive
	Options for a Central Management Official in OSD					Outside OSD
Red = Changes between Options	Status Quo 0	Increased Visibility 1	OSD Process 2 Owners Split ADCON	DSD Process 3 owner Full ADCON	Enhanced 4 CMO OPCON/ADCON	Global 5 Business Services
Admin Mgmt ADCON	DAFA directors *All admin matters*	DAFA directors *All admin matters*	OSD Leads *Select admin matters*	DSD *All admin matters*	CMO *All admin matters*	GBS *All admin matters*
Mission Direction OPCON	PSAs	PSAs	PSAs *w/ Analysis Cells*	PSAs *w/ Analysis Cells*	CMO	GBS
POM Build	DAFA Directors *w/ PSA oversight; Individual POMs*	DAFA Directors *w/ CAPE assistance; individual POMs*	DAFA Directors *w/ CAPE assistance; Individual POMs*	DAFA Directors *w/ DSD guidance; Synchronized individual DAFA POMs*	DAFA Directors *w/ CMO ownership; single integrated DAFA POM*	GBS Directors *Single integrated GBS/DAFA POM*
POM Adjustments	Intra-DAFA only	Intra-DAFA only	Across DAFA	Across DAFA	Across DAFA	Across GBS *composed of DAFA*
DAFA Resource Competition Process	DoD-wide *PBR competition DSD decides*	DoD-wide *PBR competition w/ CMO recommendations DSD decides*	DAFA-wide *CMO-level competition w/3C's PSAs advising CMO decides*	DAFA-wide *DSD-level competition w/3C's PSAs advising DSD decides*	DAFA-wide *CMO decides*	GBS *GBS Leader decides*
			After DAFA-wide competition, DAFA enter back into DOD-wide competition			*GBS enters DoD-wide competition directly*
Thematics		Enhanced POM development SES Performance Reviews (opt) CXO council (opt)	Cells in OCMO/OUSD(C) /ODCAPE Remaining admin handled by DAFA	DSD all admin Ramped up capability and centralization	OPCON to CMO CMO "owns" DAFA PSAs maintain policy oversight	New element: "Mil-Dep for Fourth Estate" - like
Additional choices	DAFA merged by category e.g., WCF, CSA, Intel - potential for organizational efficiencies by selected DAFA mergers DAFA included/excluded by category e.g., Intel, CSA, Business included vs Financial excluded					

FIGURE 6 ILLUSTRATES A VARIETY OF POTENTIAL MANAGEMENT OPTIONS FOR DAFAs.

DEFENSE WORKING CAPITAL FUNDS (DWCFs)

Any efforts to improve management of the DAFAs would need to include performance improvements to the DWCFs. These funds are integral to the DAFA workings as outlined in Figure 2, depicting funding support to the DAFAs.

The DWCF is used for "customers" to purchase the goods and services they need from the DAFAs. The FY20 working capital funds included $62 billion in the defense-wide area and $71 billion in service-specific funds. Within the $62 billion for defense, DLA measured $43 billion, DISA at $12 billion, DFAS at $1.4 billion, and DeCA at $6 billion. In the military departments, the Navy working capital funds for FY20 is $30 billion, $36 billion for the Air Force, and $15 billion for the Army.

DWCFs are essentially revolving funds that charge for what you need to purchase. For example, DLA purchases a part from a supplier. Then, when someone in the field needs that part, DLA sells it and uses the profit to cover the cost of acquiring, storing, and delivering the part. As indicated earlier, the volume of sales and the manpower involved in these purchases is massive. The profit for these actions are closely controlled and limited by WCF review boards; however, the active management of the WCF oversight has atrophied in recent years.

DWCFs are used to provide the DoD with a number of advantages, including decreased costs by purchasing goods and procuring services in bulk rather than individually – think of it like a Costco or Sam's Club membership. Other benefits include less duplication of effort, price transparency, and price stability. However, there is worry that DWCFs do not always realize these advantages to the fullest extent. Specific concerns include the way overhead costs have grown with size, and their costs to customers are higher than necessary.

There are a variety of options for DWCF improvements, including maintaining the status quo given the flattening of DoD budgets and the downward pressures on force structure and operations. However, as volume of sales decrease, overhead rates could rise as fixed costs would be spread over a smaller base. Other potential solutions involve increasing the number of DoD activities that utilize DWCFs, such as the test and evaluation efforts, and allowing customers to find better prices and purchase directly when suitable.

No matter which improvements are employed, the sub-element of the USD Comptroller that once oversaw the DWCFs (before being cut by a previous administration) should be restored. Like the need for a DAFA management review, the secretary of defense should also subject the DWCFs to inspection. Given the integral nature of DAFAs and the DWCFs, these reviews should be conducted together to promote an efficient process and successful result.

IS THERE A CONCLUSION?

As demonstrated with the discussion above, the number of DAFAs has slowly been on the rise since the establishment of the modern Defense Department through the National Security Acts in 1947 and 1949 and the significantly impactful GNA. The 171,000 people working in the DAFAs oversee a shadow manpower pool of contractors, which may be as great as 50,000. The total DAFA budgets are well in excess of $115 billion a year (which does not include the intelligence agencies' budgets). The question to be considered is whether this large investment in personnel and budget is worth the effort.

Certainly, President Eisenhower's goal when establishing DARPA in 1958 has been achieved. To date, the nation has avoided falling prey to an unexpected strategic technological surprise, a success for which DARPA can take a high degree of satisfaction. And along the way, DARPA created some historic items that have become part of modern everyday life, such as the internet and the Global Positioning System (GPS). In all likelihood, there are many more items and gadgets out there, in both the military and commercial domains, with unattributed origins in DARPA-funded research. The degree of that contribution will likely never be fully known, but it is undoubtedly considerable.

It is in the second dimension, McNamara's aspiration for greater efficiency, that further study and consideration may be warranted. Is this gathered and seemingly growing number of DAFAs cost-effective and managerially efficient?

As has been seen since the trauma of *Sputnik*, when something happens that shocks the defense system, the common response has been to pull disparate elements together under one organization. In many instances, this has meant additional headquarters elements rather than a reduction of the existing service organizations. The instinct is always to add, rarely to combine.

The creation of the NSA in 1952 is a useful example. Despite the arrival of this defense-wide source for signals intelligence, it was another quarter century before the Army's ASA was disestablished. Similarly, after the formation of ARPA (now DARPA) in 1958, the Army retained its own laboratory command as a subordinate element of the Army Materiel Command (AMC) until 1992, when it was downsized and became the Army Research Lab (ARL). The Navy and Air Force also continue to operate research labs. While there is a natural division of labor between DARPA and these service organizations and clear technological innovations of interest to the Navy that will differ from those of interest to the Army, the degree to which this requires separate organizations as opposed to separate sub-units within DARPA should be a topic of careful scrutiny.

The challenge, as always, remains the effort to separate the muscle from the fat. When DHA was exploring one of its many efforts to further consolidate the defense health program, it discovered that the services quite naturally saw the needs of health somewhat differently, particularly as it pertained to medical research. Because of the environment in which it operates, the Army had a great interest in tropical diseases, whereas the Navy and Air Force were more focused on broken bones and burns, the common injuries suffered in aircraft accidents, illustrating the sometimes-disparate focuses of the different services.

At other times, when a service has had difficulty with a developmental program, OSD has stepped in to take over. This has sometimes been a successful approach, but often the OSD team has discovered that achieving the desired outcome was just too hard. In one of those instances, the Army's Theater High Altitude Air Defense (THAAD) program was simply returned to the service after it had been moved to the Ballistic Missile Defense Organization (BMDO), making OSD's involvement largely inconsequential.

When informed that OSD was sending in the metaphorical cavalry to "help" a program, a senior service official once commented, "Does help mean I get horses or jockeys?" Although perhaps somewhat frivolous, this quip captures the question to be asked when a DA is established, expanded, and sustained. Is it providing help in a manner that allows for efficiencies and overhead reductions elsewhere, or is it just another jockey weighing down the horse?

Regardless, the secretary of defense, the deputy secretary of defense, and Congress need a laser focus on changing the benchmark for the output and performance of the DAFAs and DWCFs to ensure we are better, faster, and cheaper than China. As we enter a defining decade for defense modernization, the importance of this issue cannot escape the focus of our leaders both at the Pentagon and on the Hill.

Chapter 20: Defense Acquisition: A Workforce in Progress

This chapter originates from my multi-decade expertise in acquisition and has been newly-expanded and updated exclusively for this volume. The acquisition workforce is the backbone of the nearly $400 billion DoD spends per year on goods and services, supplies, and equipment.

History of the Acquisition Workforce (AWF)

In the past 50 years, there have been no less than 50 expansive and focused studies on the Department of Defense acquisition process and over 160 studies addressing the topic in some manner. These efforts usually follow some headline-grabbing error, whether in procuring a new capability or just one of sufficient scale of lost investment or malfeasance that Congress has noted.

Some of these studies have their origins in presidential direction, such as the 1970 Blue Ribbon Defense Panel, also known as the Fitzhugh Commission, ordered by President Richard Nixon or the Grace and Packard Commissions ordered by President Ronald Reagan in the mid-1980s. Other major DoD efforts originated internally, such as the "32 Initiatives" of Deputy Defense Secretary Frank Carlucci in the early 1980s and the reform efforts of Defense Secretary

William Perry during the early 1990s. These were later followed by the Defense Acquisition Performance Assessment (DAPA) of 2006, ordered by Deputy Defense Secretary Gordon England, and the 2009 study by the Defense Science Board (DSB) that concluded, "fixing the acquisition process is a critical national security issue."

Congress has also invested considerable effort and passed legislation on the acquisition process. In 1950, as the Korean War intensified, Congress passed the Defense Procurement Act, which has been amended numerous times over the years. In the mid-1980s, running parallel with several executive branch actions, came the Competition in Contracting Act, followed by the Defense Procurement Act of 1984, followed a year later by the Defense Procurement Improvement Act. In 1986, Congress passed the landmark Goldwater-Nichols Act along with the Packard Commission's acquisition reform recommendations, legislation that was followed by the Federal Acquisition Streamlining Act in 1994. In 2009, as a result of efforts spearheaded by Senators Carl Levin and McCain, Congress passed the Weapons Systems Acquisition Reform Act. Furthermore, in the FY17 National Defense Authorization Act (NDAA), Congress directed DoD to break up the Under Secretary for Acquisition, Technology, and Logistics into two positions: an Under Secretary for Research and Engineering (R&E) and an Under Secretary for Acquisition and Sustainment (A&S). However, despite broad consensus on the need for reform and legislative shifts of a profound nature, the history of constant adjusting shows how each proposed improvement has never fully satisfied all requirements and needed improvements.

Many of these acts focused either directly or indirectly on a continuing challenge in defense procurement practices: the quality of the defense AWF overseeing the massive effort required for acquiring defense capabilities. In a significant review on the history of defense procurement efforts, Harvard Business School Professor J. Ronald Fox noted:

> The acquisition process has a number of built-in, even cultural aspects
> that resist change. These include a workforce frequently with too little

training, experience, and stable tenure to monitor and manage huge defense acquisition programs; the short tenure of senior politically appointed acquisition officials, averaging a mere eighteen months in office; an irregular and erratic flow of weapons systems appropriations; the very nature of cutting-edge, highly risky research and development; an ill-informed requirements process that virtually mandates changes to contracts as requirements are added or changed; and the many financial incentives that reward lowball contractor bids and provide negative sanctions for failing to spend all allocated funds.

This summation thoroughly captures what many of the reports and studies had previously concluded. Namely, that the defense AWF was not adequately trained or structured to manage huge acquisition efforts. Accordingly, in 1990, Congress passed a major piece of legislation entitled the Defense Acquisition Workforce Improvement Act (DAWIA). I was the Staff Director of the Senate Armed Services Committee when this legislation was drafted and passed. This was a landmark piece of legislation that has contributed significantly to professionalizing the AWF. Its dictums have structured and organized the acquisition workforce, established clear specialties and career paths, created an institution dedicated to acquisition training and education, and set aside funding to provide acquisition organizations access to that training.

Though DAWIA has not served as a cure-all, and efforts to improve the AWF continue, they are now largely on the margins. Thus, what DAWIA has accomplished is worthy of comment in three areas.

First, DAWIA's purpose was to require the Department of Defense to develop and manage a highly-skilled professional acquisition workforce that "has the technical expertise and business skills to ensure the department receives the best value for the expenditure of public resources."

Second, to achieve this objective, DAWIA directed several steps. The DoD was to establish education and training standards, requirements, and courses for both the civilian and military acquisition workforces. The act charged the secretary of defense with establishing "policies and procedures for the effective management (including accession, education, training, and career development) of persons serving in acquisition positions in the Department of Defense," and designated those positions requiring appropriately trained and experienced managers.

Lastly, in order to provide the instruction mandated, DAWIA directed the establishment of the Defense Acquisition University (DAU). The act placed the oversight responsibility for the AWF under the Under Secretary of Defense for Acquisition, Technology, and Logistics (AT&L), recently renamed Acquisition and Sustainment (A&S).

The legislation specified that only an individual who was a "properly qualified member" of either the armed forces or the DoD civilian workforce could fill the key acquisition leadership roles, defined as:

1. Program executive officer

2. Deputy program executive officer

3. Program manager

4. Deputy program manager

5. Senior contracting official

6. Chief developmental tester

7. Program lead product support manager

8. Program lead systems engineer

9. Program lead cost estimator

10. Program lead contracting officer

11. Program lead business financial manager

12. Program lead production, quality, and manufacturing

13. Program lead information technology

The designation of these key acquisition leadership positions, along with the requirement that they be filled by individuals with adequate experience and qualifications, improved program management and helped professionalize the AWF itself. The then-USD (AT&L) further strengthened the AWF by identifying 15 career fields that comprised the acquisition effort and that required specialized training. These career fields were:

1. Auditing

2. Business – Cost Estimating (CE)

3. Business – Financial Management (FM)

4. Contracting

5. Engineering

6. Facilities Engineering

7. Information Technology (IT)

8. Life Cycle Logistics

9. Production, Quality, and Manufacturing

10. Program Management

11. Property

12. Purchasing

13. Science and Technology Management (S&T)

14. Small Business

15. Test & Evaluation

AWF DEMOGRAPHICS

Since the DAWIA's reforms in 1990, the AWF end-strength has greatly fluctuated. Driven by the end of the Cold War and the subsequent reduction of DoD personnel, the AWF's numbers decreased significantly. This trend continued until 9/11, when the AWF began to grow again in order to support American interventions in Afghanistan and Iraq. While the AWF has shown variation similar to that seen elsewhere in government, its contemporary size is unduly large: The AWF currently accounts for nearly a fifth of all DoD civilian employees worldwide.

As shown in Figure 1, the AWF's roughly 175,000 members represent a significant portion of the overall DoD workforce. Within the AWF, the majority of employees are civilians. Moreover, in the past decade alone, the AWF's size has increased by nearly 40%, despite the fact that the number of uniformed AWF employees has stayed consistent around 15,000, and the size of the active duty warfighting forces has decreased by over 1 million since the Reagan era. We also need to determine if having 175,000 government employees with almost 32,000 contracting officials is necessary, because these personnel are in the "tail" of the DoD rather than the "tooth." This trend is contributing to the "ever-shrinking fighting force."

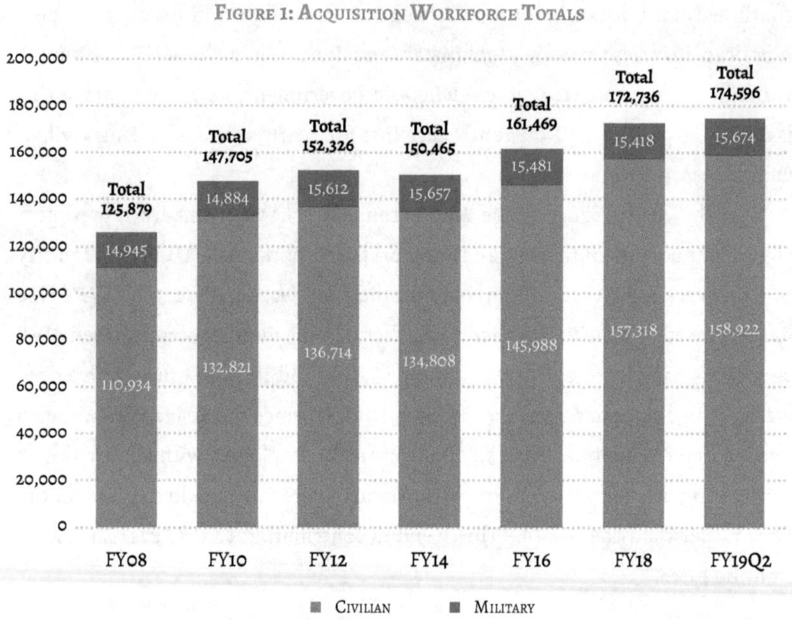

FIGURE 1: ACQUISITION WORKFORCE TOTALS

FIGURE 1 ILLUSTRATES THE SIGNIFICANT SIZE OF THE CIVILIAN SECTOR WITHIN THE AWF.

A portion of this increase, particularly in the facilities engineering sub-specialty, appears to be driven by the increase in positions now designated as acquisition. As shown in Figure 2, this subfield varies enormously by service.

Figure 2: Acquisition Workforce by Service and Career

FY19 Q2	Army	Navy	Marine Corps	Air Force	4th Estate	Totals	% Total
Auditing	-	-	-	-	4,082	4,082	2.3%
Business - CE	254	555	35	517	92	1,453	0.8%
Business - FM	1,775	2,194	179	2,218	604	6,970	4.0%
Contracting	8,045	6,250	538	8,170	8,205	31,208	17.9%
Engineering	9,094	23,608	325	9,652	2,146	44,825	25.7%
Facilities Engineering	5,954	5,871	32	701	95	12,653	7.2%
Information Technology	1,860	3,477	226	1,422	1,071	8,056	4.6%
Life Cycles Logistics	6,941	6,451	705	3,762	3,435	21,294	12.2%
Production, Quality and Manufacturing	1,368	3,804	43	472	5,553	11,240	6.4%
Program Management	3,334	5,780	761	6,417	1,906	18,198	10.4%
Property	50	71	-	14	277	412	0.2%
Purchasing	273	373	37	47	474	1,204	0.7%
S&T Manager	489	518	4	2,854	135	4,000	2.3%
Test and Evaluation	1,930	3,292	142	3,265	354	8,983	5.1%
Unknown/Other	7	2	1	-	8	18	0.0%
Totals	41,374	62,246	3,028	39,511	28,437	174,596	
Component %	23.7%	35.7%	1.7%	22.6%	16.3%		

FIGURE 2 PROVIDES A DETAILED BREAKDOWN OF THE AWF MAKEUP BY SERVICE BRANCH AND CAREER FIELD.

While the overall AWF consists of both military and civilian personnel, civilians account for nearly 90% of the AWF's total growth. While rapid growth in some sectors, such as the Information Technology branch, is easily understood given the acceleration of technology development, other areas are harder to understand. For example, S&T Management has grown by over 700% in recent years.

FIGURE 3: BREAKING DOWN THE ACQUISITION WORKFORCE

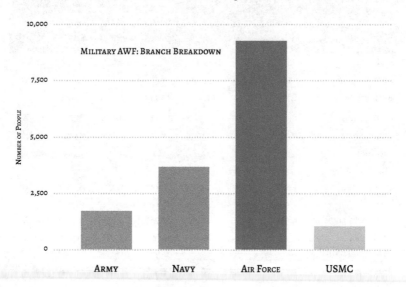

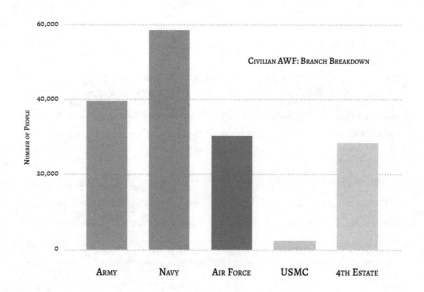

DoD AWF: Civilian v. Military Makeup

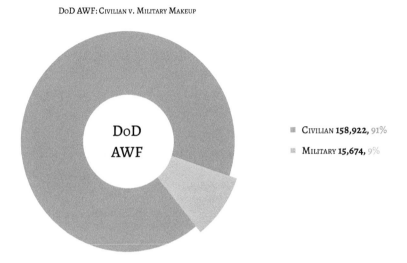

DoD
AWF

- Civilian **158,922,** 91%
- Military **15,674,** 9%

Figure 3 provides greater insight into the service and military/civilian makeup of the acquisition workforce.

DAWIA's reforms required substantial AWF data in order to be effective. Despite this need, Congress spent the first decade of DAWIA's existence arguing what constituted as an acquisition post, an important designation as acquisition posts are subject to the training and education requirements required by both the law and the DoD's implementation regulations. These debates were compounded by drawdowns in military and civilian positions in the Pentagon and the slashing of the modernization budget. It was not until 2004 that lawmakers and defense officials reached a consensus on this matter.

However, the complications did not abate, and many curiosities concerning the AWF's distribution still exist. For example, the largest component of the military – the Army – maintains the smallest modernization effort. For the FY20 budget submission, Army's requested modernization funding accounts for only 16% of the DoD total. Looking to history, this is not unusual, as the Army is a labor-intensive organization whose personnel appropriation accounts for over

40% of the DoD total. By comparison, the two capital-intensive services – the Navy and Air Force –possess modernization balances representing 33% and 39% of the DoD modernization accounts. However, these significant variances are not reflected in the services' acquisition workforces.

The Army AWF numbers more than 41,000 military and civilian personnel, making up 23% of DoD's total AWF. This number is larger than the Air Force, which measures an AWF of 39,000. This is interesting, given the fact that Air Force's modernization effort is 2.5 times larger than the Army's, yet the AF manages a smaller AWF. The Army has a similar relational comparison with the Navy, which has the largest service AWF at over 62,000. In this case, although the Army AWF equals 66% of the Navy's AWF size, its modernization accounts equal only 43%.

There may be reasonable explanations for these observations. Obviously, ships and high-performance aircraft are complex and expensive items, but the government orders a relatively small number of them. It may be that the Army needs a large AWF as it has a larger number of contracts that cover less sophisticated capabilities, such as trucks, and many other items that are, in essence, commodities. Although Army trucks—acquisitions often managed for the other services—must have certain unique qualities for global operations and survivability in the current environment, they are not as technologically challenging as the Joint Strike Fighter or an Arleigh Burke destroyer. However, Army systems are often bought in large quantities, meaning those in the Army AWF in the Contracting and Life Cycle Logistics sub-specialties are roughly equal in number to their Navy and Air Force counterparts.

Another interesting distinction exists between the military officers involved in acquisition. As mentioned earlier, the numbers of military officials working in acquisition has held rather steady over the past decade, as clearly shown in Figure 1. However, the Air Force assigns significantly more officers to acquisition duties – over 15,000 officers working in acquisition, a number accounting for nearly 60% of all military officers working in the overall AWF. The Army, with less than 1,700 officers and accounting for 11% of the total, is by far the smallest.

The Air Force's heavy AWF domination may be explained by the service's decision to commission officers directly into an acquisition specialty. In this model, an officer can spend his or her entire career within their specialty. By contrast, the Army and Navy place officers in acquisition roles later in their careers, typically after they have served assignments in the more traditional specialties such as artillery and aviation. However, this practice could change in the future. This is especially true for the Army, where, despite its historical labor-intensity, it finds itself relying more on technological developments than in the past. This is particularly true in advanced technology areas such as aviation, networking, unmanned surveillance, and missile defense.

Engineering is the defense AWF's single largest career field, accounting for over 25% of roles within the total acquisition workforce (see Figure 2). Several years ago, Dr. Ash Carter, while serving as the USD (AT&L), commented to an industry group that he was well aware that, "I don't make anything. I write checks that pay other people to make things."

In the aftermath of WWII, the defense industry was heavily privatized. Because of this, few products are actually made in-house by the DoD. For an example, let's look at shipyards. During WWII, the U.S. government owned and operated 13 shipyards, such as the famous Brooklyn Navy Yard responsible for the USS *Arizona* and the USS *Missouri*. Today, the government only operates four shipyards, and these only perform maintenance and overhauls. This begs the question – why does the AWF possess such a large engineering staff?

The answer is rather straightforward. Even though the government largely outsources its own design and construction, it still needs a large number of engineers to assist in the development of requirements and then to evaluate proposals that are received.

Training the AWF

The government acquisition agencies are largely responsible for identifying workers and establishing paths for them to receive the necessary training and education for certification. As dictated by the DAWIA, the DAU serves as the major hub for acquisition training. DAWIA's section 1746 states:

> The President of the Defense Acquisition University shall work with the relevant professional schools and degree-granting institutions of the Department of Defense and military departments to ensure that best practices are used in curriculum development to support acquisition workforce positions.

To meet this mission assignment, the DAU has evolved into an expansive operation that has received numerous recognitions for the instruction it provides. Like a traditional university, DAU offers courses ranging from the 100 to 400 levels. DAU also has five campuses across the United States, better helping to meet the needs of its acquisition customers. In 2018, DAU conducted 2.4 million classroom hours of instruction and graduated 44,000 resident students. In addition, the university graduated an additional 874,000 students through online instruction. For online students, graduation means completing a designated course or curriculum. Interestingly, DAU does *not* issue certification to those completing the courses. That power is held by each student's home office. This means that, while all the workers-turned-students are trained centrally, they are not necessarily graded against the same centralized standard.

In addition to these important acquisition contributions, DAU also provides numerous other services to the AWF. In 2018, the university provided mission assistance to over 400 programs and projects and invested over 465,000 instruction hours while conducting 533 workshops. In addition, DAU invites defense industry employees to participate in courses. This allows industry workers to gain valuable Pentagon and policy insight while also establishing cooperative connections with important industrial partners.

Over the past three decades, DAWIA and other pieces of legislation have contributed to the structure, education, and training of the defense AWF. This helps ensure the AWF is well-versed and equipped to manage the complexities of system acquisition. The AWF needs to possess capabilities that range from developing high-performance aircraft to supplying broadly-used commodity items such as canteen cups. An area of continuing concern is the government is essentially teaching and training other government employees, and there is little insertion of world-class business experiences into the system.

In the past, there has been a tendency to ascribe the complexity and problems of the acquisition system to the AWF itself. However, this is a misplaced criticism, as the AWF does not make the rules. Rather, regulations emanate from legislative statutes and the various DoD and service implementation regulations, some of which interpret statutes in an overly-restrictive manner.

CONCLUSION

Today, we need to approach acquisition management with broad thinking and innovative approaches. This is especially important in order to shorten the acquisition cycle and accelerate the pace at which capabilities are placed into the hands of warfighters, a mission that is only increasingly imperative in today's era of rapid technological advances.

However, accelerating the acquisition cycle is, and will remain, largely dependent on simplifying complex and cumbersome processes that have become increasingly risk-averse. Both the AWF and legislators in Congress and in the executive branch detest program failures. Despite this aversion, decision makers must muster an increased tolerance for risk. Otherwise, the desire for greater speed in a period of increasing technological complexity will be impossible to fulfill. Therein lies a major challenge for all parties represented in the acquisition enterprise.

Chapter 21: Implications of the Current Configuration of the Defense Industry

I created this analysis about the need to strengthen the defense industrial base based on my time as a guest lecturer at major business schools and industry functions and involvement for over four decades in the national security field. This analysis discusses the need to strengthen the defense industrial base. In 2018, I first provided this paper to industry and government leaders and have updated it for industry leaders, the Biden administration, and this book.

The defense industrial base (DIB) is markedly different from the one that existed three decades ago, but this fundamental structural change is largely unrecognized by the contemporary acquisition community, most of whom entered the acquisition workforce well after the consolidations of the mid-1990s. In general, the DoD acquisition community views the defense industry as a set of providers rather than private sector participants in a marketplace. Over time, the defense ecosystem, which includes the DoD, industry, and Congress, has evolved in ways that are not conducive for achieving the cost, schedule, or technological innovation objectives desired by the department.

There needs to be a recognition among senior DoD leaders that today's DIB is much smaller, much more concentrated, and ironically much more distributed toward small business suppliers than is commonly recognized. In addition, today's major firms are managed for, and internally measured by, financial performance, which was not the case in the 1950s when the industry first formed. These are changes with significant implications, and the more broadly these changes are recognized, the better the prospects will be for achieving major DoD acquisition objectives.

As chairman of the National Defense Industrial Association (NDIA), Maj. Gen. Arnold Punaro, USMC, Ret. presents former Secretary of Defense Leon Panetta with the NDIA's Eisenhower Award in 2015 for his sustained leadership in maintaining a strong national defense.

History

In his farewell address to the nation on January 17, 1961, President Eisenhower famously offered a caution: "In the councils of government, we must guard against the acquisition of unwarranted influence, whether sought or unsought, by the *military-industrial complex*. The potential for the disastrous rise of misplaced power exists and will persist" (emphasis added).

Gen. Andrew J. Goodpaster, President's Eisenhower's executive secretary to the National Security Council who had served in the White House since 1954, played a major role in drafting the speech. He would comment in later years that he felt Eisenhower would be disappointed to learn that the speech was primarily remembered for the "military-industrial complex" phrase, as that was not intended to be the speech's major message.

Nonetheless, although the phrase "military-industrial complex" has persisted, the sprawling complex of defense companies has not. As the Cold War was ending, a meeting was held at the department in July 1993 with the 15 largest defense contractors. Referred to by industry followers as the "last supper," that meeting provided guidance that firms were cleared to begin merging to reduce redundant capacity and increase efficiency. The resulting consolidations trimmed the DIB of competition to a staggering degree, as hundreds of defense companies merged into today's five major defense contractors. Figure 1 illustrates this trend over time.

FIGURE 1: 20 YEARS OF INDUSTRY CONSOLIDATION

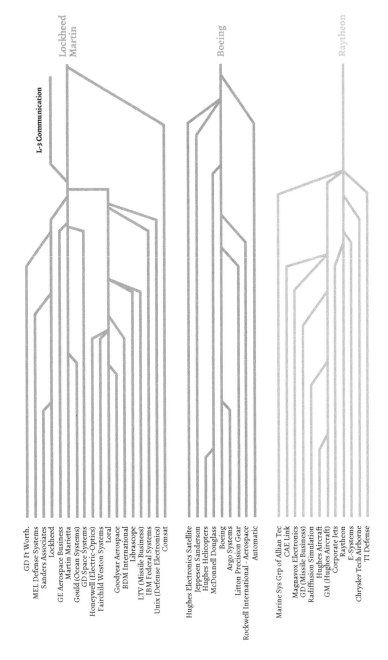

FIGURE 1: 20 YEARS OF INDUSTRY CONSOLIDATION CONTINUED

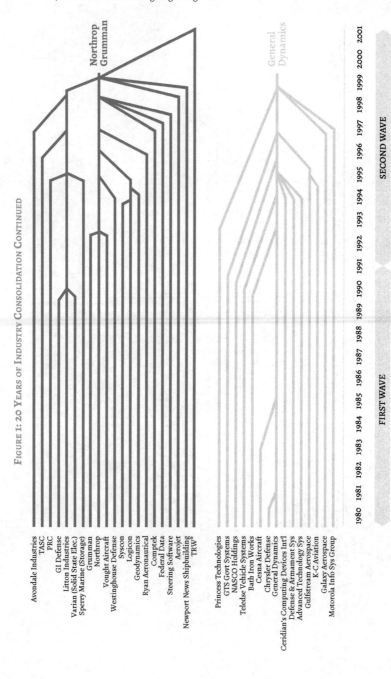

FIGURE 1 ILLUSTRATES THE CONSOLIDATION OF THE DEFENSE INDUSTRY OVER THE LAST TWO DECADES.

Rather than growing the industry, the consolidations (particularly, the second wave in the late 1990s) were a response to a shrinking market. The laissez faire policy was effectively halted for major transactions in 1998 with the rejection of the proposed merger of Lockheed Martin and Northrop Grumman, as well as the proposed merger of General Dynamics and Newport News Shipbuilding. A more nuanced, if far less clear, policy has prevailed since then. Many important lessons are embedded below in Figure 2, drawn from data contained in the historical database of *Fortune* magazine's Fortune 500. The chart focuses on the top 100 companies of the Fortune 500.

FIGURE 2: U.S. DEFENSE INDUSTRY, 1961-2018

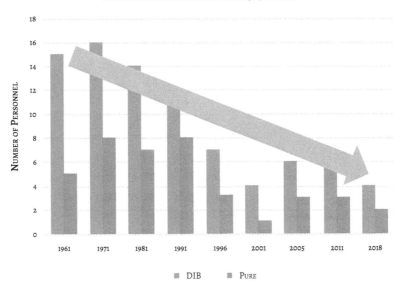

FIGURE 2 ILLUSTRATES THE DECLINE IN THE NUMBER OF DEFENSE
INDUSTRY PERSONNEL FROM 1961-2018.

In 1961, when Eisenhower delivered his speech, approximately 15 of the top 100 companies were significantly engaged in the defense industrial effort, five of them almost exclusively. The largest was General Dynamics, which in 1961 was ranked seventh.

Furthermore, those in the defense market in 1961 accounted for nearly 30% of the revenue generated by the top 100. In other words, these 15 companies were generating economic activity almost double their numbers. This would account, in some way, for President Eisenhower's observation about the size and economic power of companies in this newly-formed defense market.

However, what President Eisenhower did not note in his address was that, as a group, these companies were operating at a loss. They were either not making money or, if they were profitable, were not making much. This is not an unusual situation for a new business sector as costs become more fully appreciated and the competitive landscape of the market more fully developed. But in the long term, this is unsustainable.

In the 2020 release of the Fortune 500, only five companies in the top 100 were categorized as "Aerospace and Defense" (A&D) firms, of which one was not even a "pure" defense company – defined as 70% of gross revenue derived from the defense market. The largest of this group, ranked 39th, was Raytheon Technologies Corp (RTX), which came about after the 2019 merger of United Technologies and Raytheon. United Technologies spun off most of its commercial activities, such as Carrier and Otis, before the merger, leaving Raytheon Technologies with a wide array of defense activities including aircraft and missile defense systems.

Second on the list at 40th is Boeing. Boeing's defense activities come primarily from its 1997 acquisition of McDonnell Douglas along with other smaller activities, including Boeing's own units, and other acquisitions such as North American Rockwell. Prior to 2020, Boeing topped the Fortune 500 A&D firms, but fell behind due to the crashes and subsequent grounding of its 737 MAX jet and the COVID-19 pandemic's disastrous effects on travel.

Third was Lockheed Martin, ranked 57th, and the most profitable of the A&D firms thanks in part to the success of the F-35 program and a new contract from the Pentagon for Patriot missiles.

Fourth was General Dynamics, ranked 83rd, the largest defense company in 1961, which had somewhat diversified with its purchase of Gulfstream Aviation in 1999. This step was seen by GD senior management as providing a "counter-cyclical" countering of expected fluctuation in defense spending.

Fifth was Northrop Grumman, ranked at 96th and entering the top 100 for the first time in almost a decade. In 2019, the company had been ranked 108th. Northrop benefited greatly from its 2018 purchase of Orbital ATK, a rocket engine manufacturer, and after Boeing dropped out of a missile contract competition for the Air Force, Northrop became the de facto winner.

The DIB is perceived as an enormous entity by both DoD and Congress—some believe it to be larger than ever—but when compared to truly large companies and industries, its actual size can be seen as very modest. On the full Fortune 500, there are only 11 companies categorized as A&D. It must be appreciated that all the companies on the Fortune 500 list account for nearly $14 trillion of economic activity, which is two-thirds of the American GDP. The National Defense Industrial Association (NDIA), the largest of the DIB associations, has over 1,700 member companies. This means that the vast majority of companies in the contemporary DIB are second, third, and even lower-tier suppliers to the five major integrators. This would suggest that the contemporary DIB is not only much smaller, but much more fragile than widely perceived.

Other metrics are also of interest regarding the contemporary DIB. As Figure 3 shows, the combined annual revenue of the top five defense contractors (Raytheon, Boeing, Lockheed Martin, General Dynamics, and Northrop Grumman) in 2020 was less than half the annual revenue of top-ranked Walmart.

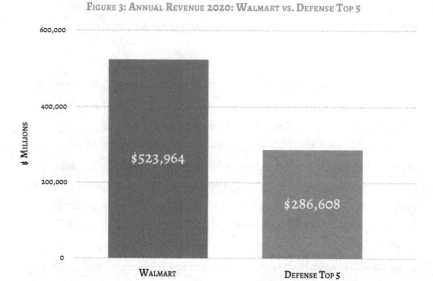

FIGURE 3: ANNUAL REVENUE 2020: WALMART VS. DEFENSE TOP 5

FIGURE 3 ILLUSTRATES HOW THE COMBINED REVENUE OF THE TOP FIVE DEFENSE AGENCIES
COMPARES TO THE REVENUE OF WALMART, THE U.S.'s LARGEST COMPANY.

An additional view of the compact size of the industry is to compare its cash to market cap ratio to the ratios of other large companies. Figure 4 shows the combined market cap (shares outstanding multiplied by current share price) of the top tier defense companies compared to cash holding and the near-term convertible assets of fourth-ranked Apple as reported in its recent annual report.

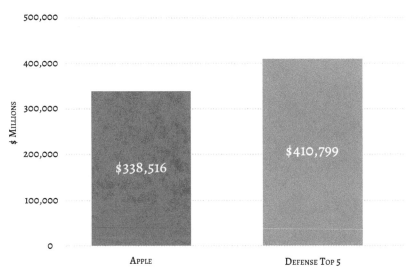

FIGURE 4: ASSETS: APPLE VS. DEFENSE TOP 5

FIGURE 4 DEPICTS THE DIFFERENCE IN ASSETS BETWEEN
THE TOP FIVE DEFENSE COMPANIES AND APPLE.

This comparison shows Apple could essentially buy the DIB top tier and seek only a modest amount of financing. However, this would not occur for two obvious reasons. First, neither DoD nor the Department of Justice would ever allow such an acquisition; and second, Apple would never desire such an acquisition.

Apple records an annual profit margin of nearly 40%, well in excess of anything that would be achievable, or even permitted, in defense. In addition, Apple would never accept the demands for access to its intellectual property, the examinations of its supply chain, and the audit of its cost structure that the government routinely asks of its defense contractors.

National Defense Industrial Association (NDIA) Chairman Arnold Punaro presents Gary Sinise with the Eisenhower Award from the NDIA for his work supporting the military and their families (2014). Sinise, of "Lieutenant Dan" fame from the movie Forrest Gump, *was described by Punaro as the "Bob Hope of today's era," for his unmatched continuing support for the troops and their families.*

UNDERSTANDING THE DEFENSE MARKETPLACE

When Eisenhower became president in 1953, the transformation of the American DIB from the largely publicly-owned "arsenal system" to the privately-owned, corporate-based industry we have today was underway. Eisenhower recognized this change. He seemingly understood that to oversee it, he would need a defense secretary who was experienced in this new realm in a way the president was not.

Accordingly, his first two defense secretaries came from the business world: Charles Wilson, a former chairman and CEO of General Motors and Neil McElroy, the former president of Procter and Gamble. President Kennedy followed this approach in 1961 by selecting Robert McNamara, the president of Ford. All three of these men made a mark on DoD. McNamara's development and installation of the Planning, Programming, and Budgeting System (PPBS) structure was most notable. Wilson, McElroy, and McNamara understood that the companies that provide equipment operate in a defense marketplace; like participants in any market, their continued participation is determined by the health and vibrancy of the market. Current leaders need to understand this as well.

The ideal market, as originally described by the famous Scottish economist Adam Smith in his seminal work *The Wealth of Nations* in 1777, has several fundamental components:

- It has many buyers (seeking products) and many sellers (competing for market share).
- There is little, if any, government regulation.
- There are low barriers to entry.
- There is perfect information available to both buyers and sellers on comparative price and cons.

The defense market, as it has evolved over the past seven decades, is largely the antithesis of Smith's model market as shown in Figure 5 and is now (in economic terms) highly distorted.

FIGURE 5: THE DISTORTED DEFENSE MARKET

- MONOPSONISTIC:
  - ONE BUYER: DoD
  - HANDFUL OF SELLERS
- BUYER IS ALSO THE REGULATOR
- BUYER IS A VERY INTRUSIVE AUDITOR
- SIGNIFICANT BARRIERS TO ENTRY
- FRAGMENTED INFORMATION
- AND... THEN THERE'S THE CONGRESS

FIGURE 5 ILLUSTRATES IRREGULAR FACTORS WITHIN THE DEFENSE MARKET.

The market is very "monopsonistic"—a term that many in the acquisition workforce are unfamiliar with. This means it basically has one buyer – the Defense Department – and only a handful of sellers, at least on the product side.

The DIB also faces extensive regulation. Former Under Secretary of Defense for Acquisition Dr. Jacques Gansler often stated that over the past 20 years the number of pages of acquisition regulations has nearly doubled, growing from about 100,000 to 180,000.

In a twist that's unique to the defense marketplace, the buyer is also the regulator. Unlike normal market buyers who can shop for the best value product that exists on the market demand curve at a price point the buyer finds attractive, the defense buyer can regulate both prices and, to no small degree, costs. And there are other significant barriers to entry to the defense market. In order to enter and compete, a company must be willing to accept and comply with the onerous demands from the regulator-customer. Dr. Gansler also estimated that the major defense providers over the past 15 years have paid nearly $1 trillion in compliance costs. This is a burden most companies, particularly those in fast-moving Silicon Valley, are unwilling to accept.

The defense market operates with highly-fragmented information. In some cases, this is the natural consequence of security classifications on specific programs. In others, it is the result of a sometimes equally secretive requirements process where needs are developed in the absence of technological understanding. This leaves many providers unsure about requirements and whether existing technologies are adequate to meet them.

Distorted markets are, in general, unattractive to business. The distortion of the current defense market, a condition that has accumulated over years, is the fundamental explanation for the decline in the companies participating in today's market. Consider, for example, that in 1981 when President Reagan restarted the B-1 bomber program, there were 14 companies that could design, manufacture, field, and sustain high performance aircraft. Today, there are three. And had Northrop Grumman not been awarded the Air Force Long-Range

Strike Bomber (LRS-B), it would have likely exited the aircraft business, leaving just two: Boeing and Lockheed.

The early defense market also differed from today's in how it viewed profit. As a group, those companies were operating at a loss. This lack of focus on financial performance is perhaps because nearly all of them were managed by engineers motivated by the technological challenges being addressed. Over time, these managers were replaced by a new, business-savvy generation more motivated by financial performance than technological innovation. Nothing illustrates this evolution better than the "tale of two Jacks," about two industry giants who embody their respective eras.

Jack Northrop founded the Northrop Company in 1939 following an early career as a technical draftsman in the Lockheed Company. Northrop was famously innovative and in 1947 designed a tail-less aircraft that in later years would inspire the Northrop B-2 bomber. Like most pioneers in A&D, Jack Northrop's passion for engineering meant he was more interested in how to thwart the technological challenges of his time than on how his company performed financially.

Jack Welch—legendary chairman and CEO of General Electric and voted by *Fortune Magazine* in 1999 as "The Manager of the Century"—typifies the other end of the spectrum. Relentlessly focused on financial performance, Welch authored the concept of "Shareholder Value," stating it to be the only objective of business. Since the consolidations of the 1990s, the senior management of the A&D sector has steadily seen its traditional engineering impetus replaced by the pursuit of shareholder value. As one former major defense company CEO put it: "If today's defense company CEOs are not well-grounded in the financial portion of the job, they'll have a very lonely life in the C-suite."

Companies today take after Jack Welch. They are motivated by financial performance and its indicators: earnings and earnings per share (EPS). Since we live in a time of high shareholder expectations and shareholder activism, senior management must have this focus to successfully compete for equity and necessary support in financial markets. This translates, in a period of flat

422 | The Ever-Shrinking Fighting Force

revenue, to efforts that increase margins and EPS, commonly at the expense of other important activities such as independent research and development (IRAD) and capital expenditures (CAPEX).

The effort to meet financial expectations is difficult in a sector that is comparatively low-margin and faces barriers to offering its products overseas, where margins are usually higher. Whereas most large American companies, such as Exxon or Caterpillar, operate extensively overseas, the defense industry is—necessarily but often frustratingly—highly-regulated regarding its international activities. Processing a foreign sale involves navigating a lengthy and complex set of procedures for either foreign military sales (FMS) or direct commercial sales (DCS). These processes involve coordination between three executive agencies—Defense, State, and Commerce—and eventually congressional acquiescence as well. In other words, a market segment that is exploited by commercial firms is only narrowly available to defense firms, thus adding another barrier to entry.

*As executive vice president of Science Applications International Cooperation (SAIC),
Arnold Punaro welcomes then-Governor Tim Kaine of Virginia at a ceremony
commemorating the SAIC corporate headquarters move from La Jolla, California, to
McLean, Virginia, in 2009.*

FINAL THOUGHTS

At a 2016 event hosted by the Center for Strategic and International Studies
(CSIS), its President and CEO Dr. John Hamre, a former deputy defense secretary,
stated:

> I never understood when I was in government what it meant to be in the
> business of being a defense business, other than the government rela-
> tions part of it. These are private entities who have to compete for capital
> in the global markets. They are valued by global investors, and we just
> don't understand this dynamic in the Defense Department.

The reality of the contemporary defense industry is appreciably different from the way the Pentagon believes it to be. The defense marketplace is distorted, and today's industry—one that produces increasingly sophisticated equipment in increasingly small quantities—now has more in common with Ferrari than Ford. Defense Secretary Ashton Carter, while serving as the Under Secretary for Acquisition, Technology, and Logistics (AT&L), once commented that a vibrant national defense industry is "not a God-given right," and that the defense industry is best seen as "part of the force structure." These are accurate observations, and the more they are recognized and translated into policy, the more likely that the defense sector will function as the cost-competitive, innovative industry it needs to be.

At an event in Washington in late 2015, former Defense Secretary William J. Perry was asked if the post Cold War defense industry consolidation had turned out as he had envisioned. Perry's view was that it had not, and the result has been an "unnecessary, undesirable consolidation of the defense industry." He added that the industry has become less competitive and, because of the regulatory burden, continued to possess high overhead. He concluded, "We would have been better off with more, smaller firms than with a few large ones."

The only way to strengthen and increase competition in the DIB is to make the marketplace more attractive. This is an enduring challenge for all administrations.

The U.S. can only maintain the world's finest military when it continues to recruit and retain the highest quality military personnel, provide troops with realistic and constant training against present and future threats, and ensure we have a DIB that provides the technological advantages on any battlefield, as we never want our military to enter into a fair fight. Without the defense industry, we cannot provide our warfighters with the necessary training, skills, and technology they deserve. The leaders in the Pentagon need to ensure we protect, preserve, and grow the defense industrial base. Just like the decline of the fighting force, we are currently experiencing an "ever—shrinking industrial base" – a trend that must be reversed.

Maj. Gen. Arnold Punaro, USMC, Ret. receives the 2019 James Forrestal Industry Leadership award from the National Defense Industrial Association (NDIA). The award is presented to an industry executive pioneer who embodies vision, leadership, and support of a strong national security industrial base, comparable to then-Secretary Forrestal's leadership during the WWII era. From left: Sid Ashworth, NDIA chair; Punaro; and General Hawk Carlisle, NDIA CEO & president. Punaro served as NDIA chair from 2013 to 2015 and began a second two-year term as NDIA chair in October 2020.

CHAPTER 22: A BRIEF HISTORY OF THE SENATE ARMED SERVICES COMMITTEE

All the remaining chapters in this final section trace their origins to 1987. As control of the Senate flipped that year, my boss, Senator Sam Nunn, became chairman of the Senate Armed Services Committee (SASC) and chose me as his staff director, as I had previously served as minority staff director. In this capacity, on top of running the committee staff on a day-to-day basis, I was asked for my recommendations for restructuring the committee and redesigning its role in guiding America's national security. The outcome was a collective product of the SASC staff. I have augmented, updated, and refined the numerous white papers over the years for every incoming SASC chairman, including Senator McCain in 2015 and, most recently, Senator Inhofe in 2018. I also plan to share them with Senator Reed in 2021.

The SASC met for the first time in January 1947. Created by the Legislative Reorganization Act of 1946, SASC replaced the Naval Affairs and Military Affairs Committees. The new committee was granted broad powers with jurisdiction over many areas of national defense, making it directly responsible for providing the legislative basis for all policies, programs, and personnel of the armed forces.

This realignment and re-designation of the congressional committees focused on national security occurred as the Department of War and the

426

Department of the Navy were merging into the newly-established National Military Establishment (NME). These changes were initiated by the 1947 National Security Act signed by President Harry Truman. In addition to starting the unification of the armed services, the 1947 Act also codified the U.S. Air Force as a separate service with its own military department, established the Central Intelligence Agency (which had evolved from the Office of Strategic Service in World War II), established the National Security Council (NSC) in the Office of the President, and codified the Joint Chiefs of Staff (JCS), although it initially gave them a very narrow role.

The act was amended two years later in 1949, renaming the NME to the Department of Defense, expanding the powers of the secretary of defense, more clearly subordinating the three service departments under the secretary of defense, and creating the position of Chairman of the Joint Chiefs of Staff (CJCS). Other major organizational changes came through legislation in 1958, 1980, and 1987, with a series of updates in 2016 and 2017, all under the SASC jurisdiction.

The SASC, like other Senate authorization committees, was intended to focus on matters of broad policy. For defense, this would include such areas as strategy, force structure, defense organizational issues, acquisition policy, personnel policies, and confirmations for presidential appointees and senior military officers. The committee has had notable impacts over the years, including its role in establishing officer personnel policy in the Defense Officer Personnel Management Act (DOPMA) of 1980, clarifying command relationships and service governing authority (such as in the Goldwater-Nichols Act (GNA) of 1986), implementing the Packard Commission recommendations, creating the Special Operations Command, and playing an integral role to any Senate consideration of arms control legislation. From the authorization for the use of force prior to *Operation Desert Storm* in 1991, to the invaluable guidance it provided in the post-Cold War drawdown after 1992, to its regular role in the military operations following 9/11, to recent major legislation related to acquisition, personnel, and operations, SASC has played and continues to play a leading role in American security.

However, over time the committee has lost some focus on broad issues of policy development and oversight and instead has become more focused on the thousands of authorization lines contained in the annual defense budget. In assuming this role, the function of the SASC increasingly commingled with the Senate Appropriations Subcommittee on Defense (SAC-D), as did the HASC and House Appropriations Subcommittee on Defense (HAC-D). Given the broader role played by the SASC, including their involvement in the confirmation process, the changing nature of the Senate workweek, and the leadership's involvement in all matters, the committee's workload inevitably resulted in its authorization process lagging behind that of the appropriators in some years. In years when the SASC took on very controversial policy matters, floor consideration of the bill was delayed further still. Some have observed that the SASC should not relinquish its role as an independent source of strategy, evaluation, and oversight in favor of detailed budget scrubbing at the line-item level.

The authorization and appropriations processes today are certainly less distinct and more duplicative than in the SASC's early years, notwithstanding Senator Richard Russell's requirement starting in 1960 for a prior authorization in advance of an appropriation.

A more realistic explanation of how the authorization and appropriations processes have converged can be found in the recognition that the SASC (and to no small degree the HASC) simply lost sight of its original purpose during the post-Cold War drawdown. During this time, the authorization committees, lacking a well-articulated strategic construct from the administrations in power, found themselves overseeing a miniaturization of the services consistent with reduced budgets, rather than a restructuring of the military conforming to a new strategic environment.

Today's security problems require an integrated effort of all instruments of national power. This requires an overarching national security strategy. The requirement for the president to submit a formal National Security Strategy (NSS) originated in the SASC's work on the GNA. In early 1987, the SASC started its hearing process with 16 hearings on strategy. Chairman Sam Nunn explained the reason for this priority:

> The Committee has decided to focus its initial series of hearings on U.S. national security strategy and its military strategy component because strategy is the only logical starting point for both the development and consideration of security policy and programs and budgets. Without an understanding of strategy there can be no comprehensive context in which to evaluate our military needs and our budgetary priorities.

Senator Nunn also saw in these hearings an opportunity to move away from micromanagement of the defense budget request:

> These strategy hearings also represent an important element of the committee's plans for shifting the focus, to the extent that we can, away from an excessively detailed line-item review and scrub of the defense budget and more toward consideration of the fundamental issues of national defense.

There will be an opportunity as the new administration revisits the NSS, National Defense Strategy (NDS), and National Military Strategy (NMS) to reestablish the key link and to ensure that budgets follow strategy and that the administration has the right strategy, threat prioritization, and programmatics. This would be a major undertaking but is consistent with the core mission of the SASC.

Over time, this absence of a defined strategy created some bad habits that continue to linger and has caused the authorization committees to focus less on strategy and defense policy. A few years back, during the frantic rush to complete the Senate authorization bill, a SASC staffer complained that, "Getting the defense budget finalized is hard because all of these policy issues get in the way." The staffer making the comment, who went on to be a senior DoD budget official, had somehow missed the point that "policy issues" were actually the SASC's natural turf.

The SASC also exercises the Senate's advice and consent power through its role in the confirmation process of senior civilian and military nominees. The SASC has jurisdiction over 61 civilian positions within DoD, from the secretary of defense down to assistant secretaries, as well as a handful of civilians within the Department of Energy's National Nuclear Security Administration (NNSA). The committee also has jurisdiction over all military promotions above the rank of captain (0-3) and on the nominations of service chiefs, combatant commanders (COCOMs), and judges to the Court of Military Appeals.

The SASC has used its confirmation authority as an extension of its oversight—and occasionally policy—focus. After the 1991 Tailhook sexual harassment scandal, for example, the committee scrutinized every single military promotion for their involvement in the scandal. Out of 35,000 nominations processed during this time frame, the Senate did not confirm eight officers because of their involvement in Tailhook, despite the fact they had been cleared by the service promotion boards. Chairmen have also used the nomination process as leverage against administrations. Most recently, Senator McCain held up nominees in both the Obama and Trump administrations because he was dissatisfied with the administrations' policies or strategies, or their perceived lack of respect for Congress's role in national security. The nomination process is another powerful tool in the SASC's arsenal to keep the Department of Defense accountable.

However, the time has come for the SASC and HASC to redouble their traditional focus on strategy, policy, and—in the SASC's case—the confirmation of senior personnel. This should require the SASC to reduce time spent on appropriation budget line items. Both authorization committees have made pretensions toward taking steps to return to "first principles," but both need to make further progress in this direction.

Past Areas of Focus by the Senate Armed Services Committee

Early Years

1947-1948: Chandler Gurney (R-South Dakota)

The major accomplishments during this time included the examination and passage of the National Security Act of 1947, consideration of universal military training, and passage of the Selective Service Act of 1948. A watchdog subcommittee was established for oversight of armed services and agencies.

1949-1950: Millard Tydings (D-Maryland)
1951-1952: Richard Russell (D-Georgia)

During Senator Tydings's chairmanship, the National Security Act of 1949 was passed, creating the Department of Defense. Additionally, the Korean War and the loss of China to communism resulted in greater partisanship on the committee. In 1950, the Preparedness Investigating Subcommittee, patterned after the Watchdog Subcommittee, was established and led by Lyndon Johnson. SASC also held joint hearings with the Foreign Relations Committee on the Truman administration's plan to permanently base troops in Europe to support NATO, and also conducted the MacArthur hearings after his dismissal by Truman.

1953-1954: Leverett Saltonstall (R-Massachusetts)

The committee size grew from 13 to 15 permanent members and began to hold DoD nominees to a high standard on conflicts of interest that still exists in 2021.

Russell Era

1955-1968: Richard Russell (D-Georgia)

During his second tenure as chairman, Russell established the Real Estate and Military Construction Subcommittee led by John Stennis, the Subcommittee on the Central Intelligence Agency led by himself, the National Stockpile and Naval Petroleum Reserves Subcommittee led by Stuart Symington, and the Status of Forces Subcommittee led by Samuel Ervin. Each of these committees had legislative responsibilities but were notable for their administrative and quasi-judicial functions which greatly expanded the power of the committee. A "temporary" subcommittee on the Air Force was created as well. This directly challenged Eisenhower's New Look defense policies and concluded that U.S. airpower was declining relative to the Soviets, marking the first time that the committee became an advocate of specific military policies and strategies at odds with the president's. The committee grew to 17 members in 1959. The Russell Amendment prevented the appropriation of funds unless those funds had already been authorized. This was the beginning of defense authorization legislation and fundamentally changed the role of the committee.

Stennis Era

1969-1980: John Stennis (D-Mississippi)

During Stennis's chairmanship, the SASC ended the draft and heralded the beginning of the all-volunteer force (AVF). Personnel costs began to increase significantly, leading the committee to create a new Manpower and Personnel Subcommittee led by Sam Nunn. SASC also passed the War Powers Resolution in response to the Vietnam War. The committee also granted sequential referral over intelligence matters to the Senate Intelligence Committee when it was formed in 1975. Additionally, the creation of the Budget Committee and Congressional Budget Office (CBO) adjusted the committee's operations with respect to the annual defense authorization bills as they wanted to conform to the required spending targets.

Senate Resolution 60 passed, authorizing committee members to hire an additional three personal staff members to focus on the members' committee work. This affected the chairman's authority by creating a cadre of staffers not directly responsible to him. During this time, the committee was known for having members who cared about defense issues and worked on those issues to such a degree that they became their personal hallmarks. Committee members such as Sam Nunn, Henry Jackson, and John Tower drove the committee's efforts to fulfill its oversight obligations with a number of wide-ranging investigations at the subcommittee and personal staff level.

After many years of post-Vietnam smaller defense budgets, the end of the decade saw the committee leading the drive to rebuild national defense. However, a number of issues began to tear at the fabric of bipartisanship that had ruled the committee since its inception: divisiveness over the Vietnam War, a Congress that was more willing to challenge the executive branch rather than accept its policies at face value, and the aforementioned congressional reforms that led a more decentralized committee.

In 1977, the Senate passed Senate Resolution 4, curtailing the ability of committee chairmen to form ad hoc subcommittees and allowing junior senators a greater opportunity to chair subcommittees. Over the course of Stennis's chairmanship, the committee staff increased from 15 to 30. Senate Resolution 4 also provided that the committee staff should "reflect the relative number of majority and minority members of the committee." In 1977, John Tower, as ranking member, held the first separate Republican caucus over major policy differences in the committee. As a result, Tower proposed the formation of a separate staff to represent the minority exclusively.

A New Era

1981-1984: John Tower (R-Texas)

For the first time since 1954, Republicans directed the committee. Chairman Tower led a majority composed mainly of junior senators. Tower reorganized the subcommittees by arranging the committees along mission-oriented lines, as opposed to the functional orientation they previously held. The new subcommittee structure sought to assess the capabilities of the military to perform its missions. New subcommittees included the Strategic and Theater Nuclear Forces Subcommittee, Tactical Warfare Subcommittee, and Seapower and Force Projection Subcommittee, though functional subcommittees on military construction and manpower and personnel remained.

For the first time, the committee reviewed the operations and maintenance portion of the defense budget as part of the defense authorization bill. As a result, Senator Tower created a new functional Preparedness Subcommittee. Additionally, the appointment of Christine Cowart as chief clerk marked the beginning of a full-time administrative section who sought to run the committee "on a purely business basis." The defense authorization process also changed drastically by expanding the scope to cover the entire defense budget and placing a greater emphasis on the budgetary context.

1985-1986: Barry Goldwater (R-Arizona)

The committee's sole focus during this time was defense reorganization led by the chairman, Barry Goldwater, and the ranking member, Senator Sam Nunn, which led to the passage of the landmark Goldwater-Nichols defense reorganization.

1987-1994: Sam Nunn (D-Georgia)

During the years spanning the end of the Cold War, the Senate became increasingly concerned with deficit reduction at the expense of defense needs. Nunn further reorganized the committees, building on Tower's changes with the Strategic Forces and Nuclear Deterrence Subcommittee replacing the Strategic and Theater Nuclear Forces Subcommittee and the Conventional Forces and Alliance Defense Subcommittee replacing the Tactical Warfare Subcommittee. The Projection Forces and Regional Defense Subcommittee focused on the military mission of defending regions where the U.S. stationed troops abroad in peacetime. The Defense Industry and Technology Subcommittee focused on the defense industrial base. The two functional subcommittees—Readiness, Sustainability, and Support and Manpower and Personnel—remained, though Nunn redirected their agendas so that they were guided by mission.

The SASC held a series of hearings on U.S. national security strategy, specifically highlighting the disconnect between accumulating commitments and the forces to back up those commitments. As a result, the committee created the Base Realignment and Closure Commission in the FY89 Defense Authorization bill. The committee held hearings that resulted in the "Don't Ask, Don't Tell" provision of the FY93 Defense Authorization bill. The committee also enhanced the confirmation process, establishing the procedures still in place today.

Senator Nunn and his ranking member, Senator Warner, worked in a complete bipartisan fashion. This collegiality was mirrored by the professional staff relationships. Furthermore, when Senator Thurmond became ranking member, the same bipartisan approach was followed.

The members of the SASC from the 101st Congress (1990) pose in the SASC formal hearing room in Russell 212. Seated left to right: Sens. Jeff Bingaman, Ted Kennedy, Carl Levin, Jim Exon, Chairman Sam Nunn, Ranking Member John Warner, Strom Thurmond, Bill Cohen, John McCain. Standing left to right: Sens. Robert Byrd, Dick Shelby, Tim Wirth, Al Gore, John Glenn, Alan Dixon, Staff Director Arnold Punaro, Minority Staff Director Pat Tucker, Sens. Malcolm Wallop, Slade Gorton, Trent Lott, and Dan Coats.

1995-1998: Strom Thurmond (R-South Carolina)

Under Senator Thurmond, the committee was focused on retaining a strong voice on national security and defense matters that its predecessors had championed. The Republican-controlled Congress frequently clashed with Democratic President Bill Clinton, leading to a government shutdown and a veto over the FY96 NDAA. Thurmond also rearranged the subcommittee structure to include the Strategic Forces Subcommittee, Readiness Subcommittee, Personnel Subcommittee, Acquisition and Technology Subcommittee, Seapower Subcommittee, and Airland Subcommittee. Senator Nunn was Senator Thurmond's ranking member from 1995-1996, and he replicated the approach Senator Warner had taken when Senator Nunn was chairman.

Post 9/11

1999-2001: John Warner (R-Virginia)

2001: Carl Levin (D-Michigan)

2001: John Warner

2001-2002: Carl Levin

2003-2006: John Warner

2007-2015: Carl Levin

Senators Warner and Levin led the committee concurrently through this transition from the Cold War to the post-9/11 environment. During this time, both Senator McCain and Senator Inhofe served as ranking member during Senator Levin's chairmanship. Throughout their tenures, both chairman and ranking member exemplified strong models of bipartisanship, a characteristic still present in Senator Inhofe and Senator Jack Reed's relationship today. Before 9/11, Warner formed the Emerging Threats and Capabilities Subcommittee. However, following the 9/11 attacks, the committee primarily focused on overseeing DoD as engaged with the Global War on Terrorism (GWOT) in Iraq, Afghanistan, and other countries. The committee's major issues included wartime contracting, detentions and the military justice process for terrorists caught on the battlefield, and interrogation techniques. The committee passed the Weapon Systems Acquisition Reform Act in 2009. In the same year, Cyber Command was added as a COCOM under STRATCOM. "Don't Ask, Don't Tell" was repealed in 2010. In 2011, the Budget Control Act (BCA) was signed into law, triggering automatic spending cuts to the department.

2015-2018: John McCain (R-Arizona)

With the drawdowns in Iraq and Afghanistan underway and the budget restrictions in place, the focus of the committee pivoted toward major defense reforms. Chairman McCain, with his Ranking Member Senator Carl Levin and then Senator Jack Reed, began a multi-year process of reconsidering and updating the Goldwater-Nichols Act. The 2017 NDAA led to major changes at DoD, including splitting the Under Secretary for Acquisition, Technology, and Logistics (AT&L) into two positions and reforming the defense acquisition system. It also increased focus on cyber warfare, including the creation of the Cybersecurity Subcommittee and the elevation of CYBERCOM to a full COCOM. Personnel reforms were also a major focus, including reforms allowing transgender individuals to serve in the military, as well as sexual assault and harassment reforms and suicide prevention. As a whole, McCain strongly enforced the committee's oversight role and was critical of both the Obama and Trump administrations' policies and strategies. Several times throughout his chairmanship, McCain emphasized the importance of retaining a strong relationship with the Pentagon and made clear that he would not accept any encroachments on the committee's oversight responsibilities.

2018-2021: Jim Inhofe (R-Oklahoma)

Taking over after the passing of Senator McCain, Senator Inhofe sought to maintain productive relationships with DoD, the White House, and Senator Jack Reed (D-RI). Senator Inhofe championed the increases in defense spending coming out of the sequester and the promotion of the new National Defense Strategy (NDS) focusing on great power competition. He was able to ensure passage of the annual NDAA even with a divided Congress beginning in 2018 including successfully overriding President Trump's veto of the NDAA in late 2020. In early 2021, Senator Jack Reed assumed the role of SASC Chairman.

CHAPTER 23: SENATE APPROPRIATIONS AND SENATE ARMED SERVICES COMMITTEES

Early History

For its first 130 years, the United States bounced between various decentralized ⸱approaches when it came to appropriating government expenditures pursuant to Congress's constitutional power of the purse. No central responsibility existed for budgetary matters. Instead, eight different committees pursued their own agendas, with several different committees handling appropriations for a single executive department.

However, in 1921, President Warren Harding signed the Budget and Accounting Act (BAA), fundamentally changing the appropriations process. The legislation sought to give Congress greater control over the budgetary process and establish a more cohesive approach to financial policy in both the executive and legislative branches. For the first time, "the financial operation of the Government was to be brought within a centralized system." The BBA also required the president to submit an annual budget proposal to Congress.

439

The new budgeting procedure was not compatible with the Senate's previous method of assigning appropriations bills to the relevant legislative committee with jurisdiction over the department whose funds were in question. Prior to 1921, authorizations and appropriations were handled within the committee of jurisdiction. Thus, the Senate made a change to the rules that coalesced singular authority for appropriations bills within the Appropriations Committee. The committee, in turn, formed subcommittees to oversee the executive departments, including its Subcommittee on Defense Appropriations (SAC-D).

The Senate Armed Services Committee (SASC) did not come into being until 1947. Created by the Legislative Reorganization Act of 1946, Armed Services merged the Naval Affairs and Military Affairs Committees, which had both been established in 1816. SASC became responsible for oversight of "the common defense." However, since SASC lacked both the jurisdiction to appropriate funds and the ability to authorize their use, the DoD did not submit authorization requests. In the early 1950s, Ralph Flanders (R-Vermont) of Armed Services proposed an amendment that would rectify this weakened oversight power. As Senator Flanders saw it, SASC was "elaborately and exhaustively" briefed by military officials but "to no constructive end, for no authorization is asked or given." Moreover, the only Armed Services Committee members who were able to make effective use of the DoD information were those senators who also sat on the Appropriations Committee, which was a very small group.

SASC under Russell, Stennis, and Tower

Naturally, this did not provide Congress with a satisfactory grasp of U.S. defense programs and policies. The Flanders amendment required the executive to submit a program to Congress for authorization "in the same way that other activities of the administration are authorized." Such an authorization process would allow the Armed Services Committee to more clearly understand the appropriations bill that would follow. Though the original Flanders amendment failed, Chairman Richard Russell (D-Georgia) successfully attached a similar amendment to the 1959 military construction bill; the first defense authorization requirement went into effect in 1961.

Initially, the authorization was limited to the procurement of aircraft, missiles, and naval vessels, but was expanded to include three more budget categories by the end of the Russell era in 1968. Under Senator Stennis's chairmanship, the review was broadened yet again to include seven more categories. These expansions were incremental and occurred over a 20-year period. Moreover, Senators Russell and Stennis were both members of the Appropriations Committee. This was an enormous benefit as the annual authorization was based on an accommodation with the Appropriations members to authorize a limited number of items in the defense budget, which the appropriators would then fund. Without any formal agreement, however, this arrangement depended on the "self-restraint of the Armed Services Committee to limit the scope of the annual authorization."

Both Senators Russell and Stennis viewed the Armed Services–Appropriations relationship as a complementary one. Even as Armed Services expanded its authority, the two committees still had a rough division of labor and did not encroach too much on each other. Moreover, they each had different strengths. Appropriations, for example, had a greater capacity for budget scrubbing with direct links into the comptrollers of the DoD. Armed Services, on the other hand, had a long tradition and refined infrastructure for handling strategic policy, arms control, major weapons systems, and other major policy issues.

But perhaps one of the greatest reasons that the relationship between the two committees remained relatively benign was that, from 1955-1980, when Senators Russell and Stennis served as chairmen of Armed Services, they were also senior members of the Appropriations Defense Subcommittee. At one point, Senator Stennis chaired both the Armed Services Committee and the Appropriations Subcommittee on Defense. Moreover, commenting on the committee relationships, Senator Russell once famously observed that, "Appropriations are the saucer that cools the legislative tea."

Compared to his two predecessors, John Tower's (R-Texas) leadership of Armed Services (1981-1984) was short, but the changes he initiated had an equally long-lasting impact on the committee and also marked a turning point in the committee's relationship with Appropriations. Senator Tower fundamentally altered the defense authorization process to ensure it was the Senate's lead voice on national security matters. First, he reorganized the subcommittees in a way that "changed the decision-making structure of annual authorization and forced the panelists, the staff, and the Pentagon to look at annual authorization as a means for reviewing military missions." Second, he expanded the scope of the authorization process to cover virtually the entire defense budget, adding operations and maintenance for the first time.

Senator Tower broke with his two predecessors, both of whom viewed the authorization bills as the guidance provided to the Appropriations Committee on annual defense funding decisions. In contrast, Senator Tower believed the authorization bill was the Senate's comprehensive and definitive statement on the nation's defense requirements. In effect, Armed Services now covered in the annual authorization process every single item covered in the appropriation bill. He also believed that the Appropriations Committee should follow the SASC lead and mirror-image the SASC bill. In Chairman Tower's view, the defense appropriators should not make changes in what was authorized either at the macro level or at the program, project, and activity level.

These developments changed the traditional relationship that stretched back to the formation of the Armed Services Committee in 1947. None of this sat well with Ted Stevens (R-Alaska), who had been chairman of the Defense Appropriations Subcommittee since 1981. Senator Stevens viewed his subcommittee as having the final word on defense. Consequently, the naturally tense relationship between defense authorizers and appropriators became increasingly strained.

Though it existed prior to Senator Tower's chairmanship, the second factor contributing to the heightened tension was the 1977 cessation of appointing three Armed Services members as ex officio members of Appropriations. Then, in an effort to keep power from accumulating into only a few hands, senators were barred from serving on both Armed Services and Appropriations except for those grandfathered in, including Senator Stennis and later Robert Byrd (D-West Virginia). By the middle of 1986, the relationship between the committees had deteriorated to the point that the leadership of SASC and SAC-D felt compelled to create a formal Memorandum of Agreement (MOA) in the interest of reducing tensions.

ATTEMPTS AT RECONCILIATION

The MOA, agreed to on June 5, 1986, by Chairman Barry Goldwater (R-Arizona), set out to institutionalize processes and procedures for a productive working relationship. The prominent features of the MOA included appointing the leadership of the two committees as ex officio members of each other, thus reestablishing an important mollifier in their relationship. The MOA also provided the same markup materials to each other's leadership as to their own committee members, cutting down on unpleasant surprises. Appropriations agreed to resist including legislative provisions and reversing the position of Armed Services while Armed Services agreed to avoid legislating constraints in terms of financing adjustments. The two committees further agreed to meet and discuss the feasibility of a combined authorization/appropriations bill.

While a positive development, the MOA was short-lived; it was only in effect through FY88. Additionally, the committees adhered to it with only mixed success. While markup materials were provided to the other committee on time, and both leaderships participated in the markup, the two committees continued to encroach on each other's responsibilities. The authorization bills contained provisions that were tantamount to appropriations (floors) and the appropriations bills contained legislative provisions and often violated the authorization ceilings.

An appropriation is authorized or unauthorized depending on the breadth of a given authority drawn in law. An "authorized" appropriation can be made in response to a broad authority or a highly specific program authorization made to a dollar amount. An appropriation is considered "unauthorized" when it clearly contravenes some limit on appropriated funds made in law or when the law does not provide a broad authority covering the purposes for which appropriations were made. In both the House and Senate, the rule against unauthorized appropriations is enforced by points of order, with the application of the Senate's rule being much more relaxed than that of the House.

When the Democrats won control of the Senate after the 1986 elections, incoming Armed Services Chairman Sam Nunn's staff, of which I was part, were hopeful that the relationship could be repaired and considered several avenues for effecting change. Since control of the Senate was going to change, many options were discussed, including a formal change to Senate rules that would formally reestablish the practice of appointing Armed Services members as ex officio members of Appropriations. Another option was renewing the MOA, for there was some uncertainty over its status since control of the Senate was changing hands. Lastly, Nunn's staff noted that the Armed Services Committee could enact several unilateral actions that would foster closer collaboration between the committees. By focusing less on micromanaged budget scrubbing and instead on the larger, underlying policy questions, Armed Services could disengage from some redundancy between the committees. The previous MOA was considered by both committees to still be in effect, but its effectiveness would erode over time.

Chairman Senator Sam Nunn, Staff Director Arnold Punaro, Minority Staff Director Pat Tucker, and Senator John Warner strategize during a SASC hearing in 1987.

One of the reasons Armed Services was willing to tolerate the discrepancies between the two bills was that DoD agreed to withhold spending funds on "unauthorized appropriations" until retroactively approved by the Armed Services Committee. This was an informal practice in which DoD would go through the tables in each bill and provide a list of the appropriated programs, projects, or activities (line items), which were not authorized. Armed Services would subsequently review and, for the most part, approve them. The SASC would use the confirmation process for key senior civilians and military leaders to get them to agree to continue this practice as part of gaining the SASC approval of their nomination.

However, Appropriations felt this process, which had weak legal standing, continued to undermine their authority. The Government Accountability Office (GAO), which has the final voice on appropriation law, ruled that an appropriation is an authorization of budgetary authority. This informal arrangement gradually deteriorated over a three- to four-year period under Secretary of Defense Dick Cheney, who opposed it and only reluctantly agreed in the first place. This pattern further continued under House Armed Services Committee (HASC) Chairman Les Aspin, who did not want to enforce the unauthorized appropriations agreement at the expense of his relationship with HAC-D Chairman Jack Murtha.

MODERN DAY

Currently, absent any MOAs and any recognition of unauthorized appropriations, the defense appropriation bill has become the final voice at the program, project, and activity level. Today, one of the largest threats to authorizing power is timeliness; the authorization process frequently runs late. During the mid-1980s through the late 1990s, the SASC/HASC bill typically solved key program and policy discrepancies between House and Senate. The authorization set the ceiling for the appropriation to follow. For many years, the appropriation had to wait for the authorization to finish due to the complexity of the issues. However, this practice has lapsed, given the frequent tardiness of the authorization conference.

It should also be noted that the appropriations process does not always meet deadlines, and lengthy continuing resolutions (CRs) have become the norm here as well. However, in the years when a full defense appropriation bill is passed, it has contained both legislative provisions and funding amounts that breach the authorization ceilings at both the account and program, project, and activity levels. If the authorization bill is neither a ceiling nor a floor, then it has no relevance. It is important for the authorization process to reestablish its standing as both the policy driver and the authorization ceiling.

RECOMMENDATIONS

There exist three main options for the future: consider a new MOA, ensure the authorization bill is completed ahead of the appropriations cycle, and revisit unauthorized appropriations with the DoD. While larger, more comprehensive congressional reforms should include the institution of two-year budgets, the first three recommendations remain more realistic for now.

CHAPTER 24: ALIGNING CONGRESS'S AUTHORIZING AND APPROPRIATING RESPONSIBILITIES

Article I, Section 9 of the Constitution establishes that "No Money shall be drawn from the Treasury, but in Consequence of Appropriations made by Law." Separating these authorities and responsibilities establishes the essential boundaries between the Armed Services and Appropriations Committees. Unfortunately, as discussed previously, those clear lines drawn by the Constitution have been blurred over time. For Congress to efficiently and effectively discharge its constitutional role, the chairmen and ranking members of the four congressional defense committees should seek a return to a stricter adherence to their enumerated constitutional roles.

It is a common perception among close observers of the Defense Department, Congress, and the defense budget process that the authorizers' deep entanglement in controversial policy issues (such as "Don't Ask Don't Tell," women in the military, hate crimes, Guantanamo, and interrogation practices) has led the authorization process to become the catch-up act in many years to the Appropriations Committee. In some years, these controversial matters were so all-consuming that the full Senate failed to pass an authorization bill and instead used the SASC-marked bill as the basis for conference. Over time, the inefficiencies of this construct have become quite pronounced for both authorizers and appropriators.

As noted by Todd Harrison of the Center for Strategic and International Studies (CSIS), the Defense Department has started the fiscal year with an approved budget in only nine of the past 50 years. The other 41 years began with a continuing resolution (CR), a trend that has only worsened in recent years. Although CRs became the norm many decades ago, they were only utilized for an average of 33 days between 1977 and 2009. However, since 2010, the Pentagon has operated under CRs for an average of 128 days at a time. The FY17 budget set an unfortunate modern era record at 217 days for operating under a CR. Then-USD Comptroller David Norquist called this trend "just another sign of fall," saying, "The kids go back to school, football season begins, and the federal government operates under a CR."

In only 11 of the past 30 years has the National Defense Authorization Act (NDAA) been completed and signed into law before the Defense Appropriations Act, with most of those "successes" occurring after 2010. However, seven of the appropriations bills were part of omnibus acts, nearly all of which were passed late—sometimes by eight months—as a result of partisan feuding over spending levels, not because the SASC got its work done early. In a number of years, the SASC has been unable to pass their bill in the Senate and instead was only able to achieve success through an authorization conference using a "virtual" process. This is not a condition peculiar to the SASC; the authorization process for domestic objectives as regular order in the appropriations process has largely disappeared across the Senate and House. Figure 1 provides an in-depth look at the history of NDAA tardiness over the past 30 years.

Figure 1: Days NDAA was in Advance of Appropriations			
Fiscal Year	NDAA Signed	Defense Appropriations Act Signed	Days NDAA was In Advance of Appropriations
1990	11/29/89	11/21/89	-8
1991	11/5/90	11/5/90	0
1992	12/5/91	11/26/91	-9
1993	10/23/92	10/6/92	-17
1994	11/30/93	11/11/93	-19
1995	10/5/94	9/30/94	-5
1996	2/10/96	12/1/95	-71
1997	9/23/96	9/30/96	7
1998	11/18/97	10/8/97	-41
1999	10/17/98	10/17/98	0
2000	10/5/99	10/25/99	20
2001	10/30/00	8/9/00	-82
2002	12/28/01	1/10/02	13
2003	12/2/02	10/23/02	-40
2004	11/24/03	9/30/03	-55
2005	10/28/04	8/5/04	-84
2006	1/6/06	12/30/05	-7
2007	10/17/06	9/26/06	-21

2008	1/28/08	11/13/07	-76
2009	10/14/08	9/30/08	-14
2010	10/28/09	12/19/09	52
2011	1/7/11	4/15/11	98
2012	12/31/11	12/23/11	-8
2013	1/2/13	3/26/13	83
2014	12/26/13	1/17/14	22
2015	12/19/14	12/16/14	-3
2016	11/25/15	12/18/15	23
2017	12/23/16	5/5/17	133
2018	12/12/17	3/23/18	101
2019	8/13/18	9/28/18	46

Source: Congress.gov, The Punaro Group

FIGURE 1 EXAMINES THE TIMELINESS OF THE NDAA FROM 1990-2019.

As Defense Secretary Robert McNamara once commented, a defense budget should be "the quantification of a strategic concept." Indeed, McNamara's Planning, Programming, and Budgeting System (PPBS) was meant to provide a management structure for moving from strategic concept to budget stratification. Since McNamara, along with assistance from RAND Corporation analyst and defense Comptroller Charles Hitch, installed this process in the Pentagon, much progress has been made. But still, there are mission, operational, and even tactical areas where the services do not have a fully coordinated approach.

To illustrate with an example, let's examine what criteria the Pentagon uses to decide the correct numbers for the stockpile of anti-tank munitions and systems. In this situation, each service has its own weapons, such as the TOW,

Hellfire, SLAM, and Maverick missiles. After several efforts, the current joint program being pursued is the Joint Air-Ground Missile (JAGM), which replaced the canceled Joint Common Missile program. While the services' joint weapons collaboration is a step in the right direction, the question remains on what methodology the services used to determine the necessary inventory of weapons. This is especially intriguing as the worldwide threat of armored vehicles declines and the use of drones increases.

In the past, each service has developed its own approach to determining anti-tank (and mobile target) needs. This individualized process has resulted in the services purchasing multiple systems to address the same target set. There has been little discussion across services reconciling the actual needs, despite some efforts to do so through the joint efforts of the Joint Requirements Oversight Council (JROC). However, if the authorization and appropriations committees jointly committed to eliminating this redundancy, then the DoD would be forced to discuss program needs from its own joint perspective. Additionally, this would also make DoD identify how it uses its Major Force Program (MFP) structure—supposedly the key central element of the Planning, Programming, Budgeting, and Execution (PPBE) process connecting strategies and plans to budgets—to determine budget levels.

It may be useful to hold a small number of joint hearings with the Senate Appropriations Subcommittee on Defense (SAC-D), where DoD has to crosswalk the budget submission (arrayed by appropriations) with the MFP mission areas. Moreover, a unified front would compel the Pentagon to offer explanations on how it has crafted its resource requests in a manner focused on overall output as opposed to service-specific input. It might also serve to better sequence the congressional process by focusing on how the National Security Strategy (NSS) is reflected in programming and displayed in the resultant defense budget. To further this outcome, two clear steps should be considered and are discussed in detail below.

Step 1: Refocus the Armed Services Committees on Policy

As the authorizing committees for matters of national defense, the House Armed Services Committee (HASC) and Senate Armed Services Committee

(SASC) have the authority to establish, continue, or modify an agency, program, or activity for a fixed or indefinite period of time. The two committees may set forth or restrict a variety of components related to agencies and programs, including its organizational structure and responsibilities.

The House rules lay out the different areas where the committee has jurisdiction, from "common defense generally" to force structure levels, pay and benefits, and all matters of "policy." However, nothing in the rules describes the authority, much less the need, to authorize specific levels of funding along with establishing broader policy authorities. Still, the language in the rules of each chamber is broad enough that the Armed Services Committees are not prevented from authorizing specific funding levels as part of their responsibility in each respective area. The text of the bill language generally authorizes funding at the appropriation account level, such as "military personnel, Army." The tables in the reports (which accompany the bill) enumerate the line-item funding at the program, project, and activity level. The department continues to follow the program, project, and activity specificity as contained in the tables versus the broader appropriation accounts.

If the Armed Services Committees transition away from authorizing every line-item and instead return to focusing on broad matters of policy and strategy, their role in deciding the actual outcome of spending decisions will actually be strengthened. Rather than spending precious time on budget justification matters, which are the primary responsibility and authority of the Appropriations Committees (and, in accordance with John Quincy Adams's vision, their essential purpose), the HASC and SASC should assume broader and more strategic views on national defense and military matters. This can involve examining the country's national defense needs and assessing whether our military forces are organized, trained, equipped, and operating in such a way to bring about the desires of the Congress and the directions of the president.

Limiting the committees' authorized spending levels would not inhibit the HASC and SASC their tasks, including freezing, reversing, or otherwise modifying force structure decisions, establishing end strength levels, directing policy on issues such as enemy combatants and prisoners of war, military personnel and health care, authorizing military force, naval fleet strength, or military pay raises. Rather, by reallocating the time and effort currently devoted to line-item spending, the committees will actually have a greater ability to assume a more strategic approach in congressional defense policymaking.

Where the HASC and SASC establish matters of policy with significant funding implications, the committees should take pains to discover and record the likely budgetary impacts of those changes in order to establish military policy within the constraints of budget realism. This stipulation would not mean authorizing line-item spending, but instead working closely with the Appropriations Committees and the Congressional Budget Office (CBO) to understand the impact of funding certain policies. For example, the authorizers make decisions on matters like the strategic nuclear deterrent's modernization and whether to move to a sixth generation fighter or a future vertical lift program. The Armed Services Committees should continue overseeing these programs, but they should allow the Appropriations Committees to determine the annual amounts.

Step 2: Refocus the Appropriations Committee on Spending

In a similar vein, the Appropriations Committees need to focus on their main task: appropriations. These committees should not be deeply involved in questions of defense policy; this would risk undermining the appropriations process by injecting matters of contentious policy best handled in other pieces of legislation. Furthermore, given the extent the Authorization Committee is entrusted with determining highly-specific appropriations to government line-item activities, any foray into defense policy risks becoming an unnecessary and dangerous distraction from evaluating the cost, schedule, and performance of programs of record and presidential requests for funding in other areas.

While the appropriators should eschew policy, they should make funding decisions within the parameters established in permanent authorities by the Armed Services Committees in their annual defense authorization bill. In this respect, both authorizers and appropriators employ their authorities most effectively when they exercise their unique roles with respect to the function of the other committee. Furthermore, if the authorizers create mandates that the appropriators refuse to fund, or vice versa, the committees can risk destabilizing our national security.

The appropriators should focus on funding and meeting the October 1 fiscal year start. Rather than seeking to establish broad matters of policy through appropriated funding, appropriators can increase or decrease specific accounts based on cost, schedule, and performance considerations or the prerogatives of its committee members. The Armed Services Committees do not enjoy these prerogatives, but instead, SASC and HASC are granted the prerogative of setting the defense policy of the United States. Both authorizers and appropriators should be satisfied with their roles: The Armed Services Committees with the strategy of funding, and the appropriators with its tactics.

WORKING TOGETHER

Once the committees have established the working parameters of these authorities and responsibilities, the four committees can very effectively work together to properly guide and oversee the Department of Defense.

Both the HASC and SASC hold a variety of informative hearings throughout the year. These hearings focus on a wide array of subjects, including national security matters and DoD budgetary hearings. They also feature members from the services and combatant commands (COCOMs), think tanks and industry, and the department itself. All of this provides an enormous amount of insight into the defense policy of the United States.

On the other hand, the Appropriations Committee should limit itself to hearings and briefings on the specifics of programmed funding levels. This limitation should not be viewed adversely. Rather, to properly set specific funding levels, the committees require a significant amount of highly-specific information to exercise their prerogatives. Both the House and Senate Appropriations and Armed Services Committees should hold occasional joint hearings or meetings to hammer out questions that fall in the space between policy and funding.

Specifically, without encroaching on each other's jurisdictions, the committees should consider the following options to increase communication and oversight:

- Joint hearings, meetings, and briefings for members and staff.
- Increased leadership and member-to-member dialogue.
- Joint, closed-door meetings with members and department officials.

Increasing the joint activities of the authorizers and appropriators has benefits and drawbacks. Not every hearing, meeting, or briefing taken by either committee must involve the other, and making these decisions is clearly the prerogative of the chairmen. Nonetheless, at the staff level, the committees must work together to help members identify the spending impacts of desired policy changes made in the NDAA.

Future leaders of the Senate and House Armed Services and Appropriations Committees should seek to restore historical and constitutional norms. When the committees focus on their respective authorities, responsibilities, and strengths, they face less friction and improve collaboration and outcomes. Additionally, when it comes to oversight, the committees will be able to better identify and rollback ill-advised policies advanced by the Pentagon before they take effect and cost lives or taxpayer dollars.

Numerous studies conducted on the Pentagon's Planning, Programming, Budgeting, and Execution (PPBE) process have identified the planning phase—the initial effort that seeks to determine immediate and future defense directions and suggest necessary priorities regarding programs and spending—as the weakest portion of the system. To no small degree, the authorization committees' focus on budget lines rather than strategy and policy has contributed to this weakness. In order to remedy this and bring forth the numerous benefits discussed above, the authorizers and appropriators should seriously consider refocusing on their original problem areas. Simply put, the authorizers need to focus on strategy and policy (and oversee the confirmation of those who formulate them) and leave the budget line-item scrubbing to the appropriators. Similarly, the appropriators should steer clear of broad strategy and policy matters and rely on the authorizing committees to successfully fulfill their proper roles.

In a perfect world, the three overlapping processes: budget, authorization, and appropriation should be collapsed into two—budget and a joint authorization/

appropriations committee. The members of the budget committee would be the chairs and ranking members of the combined authorization/appropriations committees. And thus, the trade-offs could be made at the outset of the budget year. We should also move to a two-year budget where the combined Authorization/Appropriation Committees spend the first year determining the levels and specifics of a two-year budget and the second year providing oversight of its implementation.

Simply put, we need to apply the "shrinking force" to the proliferation of congressional committees, subcommittees, and associated organizations and staff. A leaner approach would also allow these groups to produce results in a timelier fashion.

CHAPTER 25: A RECONSIDERATION OF EXISTING SASC SUBCOMMITTEES

Every two years, Congress convenes a new session, and every six years, the entirety of the Senate has either been reconfirmed or replaced. For the Senate Armed Services Committee (SASC), these changes may simply result in a new Congress or even a new chairman. These transition years are often a time for reexamination of the status quo, especially the existing roster of subcommittees and consideration of alternative approaches. As Senate rules do not restrict the number of subcommittees within the SASC, evaluating existing methods require asking key questions, including:

- Are the subcommittees too focused on resource inputs rather than mission outputs and other outcomes?

- Do the subcommittees have a sufficient focus on world regions?

- Would the work of the SASC benefit more by adding subcommittees that could give a greater focus to priority topics, or is it better to refocus the existing subcommittees, given Senate norms on the number of subcommittees?

- Are the subcommittees too large to effectively and efficiently perform their responsibilities?
- Would additional subcommittees enable the SASC to better perform its authorization and oversight responsibilities?

CURRENT SUBCOMMITTEES

In the 117th Congress, the SASC organized seven subcommittees. These align rather well with the seven subcommittees of the House Armed Services Committee (HASC), which had previously shifted from appropriation accounts to approximate the earlier changes in the SASC.

FIGURE 1: CURRENT SASC AND HASC SUBCOMMITTEES

SASC Subcommittees:	HASC Subcommittees:
Airland	Tactical Air and Land Forces
Cybersecurity	Cyber, Innovative Technologies and Information Systems
Emerging Threats and Capabilities	Intelligence and Special Operations
Personnel	Military Personnel
Readiness and Management Support	Readiness
Seapower	Seapower and Projection Forces
Strategic Forces	Strategic Forces

FIGURE 1 SHOWS HOW THE SASC AND HASC SUBCOMMITTEES ALIGN.

460 | The Ever-Shrinking Fighting Force

Although the subcommittees have had different names over the years, the SASC subcommittee structure has not changed much over the last 40 years since Chairman Tower reorganized the subcommittees to be mission-focused rather than functionally oriented around procurement, research and development (R&D), operations and maintenance (O&M), and personnel.

Mission and Outcome Orientation

For the SASC, realizing an effective and traceable linkage between strategy, policy, and missions with the requested programs and budgets can prove challenging. The responsibilities of the existing subcommittees seldom list missions or outcomes. Given that the defense budget request is organized around inputs rather than missions or outcomes, this is not surprising. By focusing solely on input, the budget request often fails to link the big picture. Additionally, this setup contributes to the committees' tendency to micromanage, as it creates a focus on minuscule budget request line-item details rather than the budget's fundamental strategic direction.

The 1986 SASC report, *Defense Organization: The Need for Change*, cited the consequences of this input focus:

> This pattern of reviewing programs within artificial categories of inputs means that Congress rarely obtains a comprehensive picture of current defense capabilities, or of the progress being made toward a major defense commitment or national policy objective.

This section presents ideas for strengthening the orientation of each subcommittee to missions and outcomes. Five subcommittees are candidates for stronger mission orientations: Airland, Cybersecurity, Emerging Threats and Capabilities, Seapower, and Strategic Forces. The two other subcommittees—Personnel as well as Readiness and Management Support—are candidates for improved business outcome orientations.

MISSIONS

The plethora of strategy documents produced by the Pentagon presents a challenge for the committees. Most analyses tend to be more descriptive of the international environment than prescriptive on how to address it. While the Trump administration published its National Security Strategy (NSS) and National Defense Strategy (NDS) in 2018, other documents that guide their implementation and generally provide more details are typically updated on an annual basis. The primary objectives for U.S. armed forces, as outlined in the NDS, include:

1. Defending the homeland from attack;

2. Sustaining joint force military advantages;

3. Deterring adversaries from aggression;

4. Enabling U.S. interagency counterparts to advance U.S. influence and interests;

5. Maintaining favorable regional balances of power in the Indo-Pacific, Europe, Middle East, and Western Hemisphere;

6. Defending allies from military aggression and bolstering partners against coercion;

7. Dissuading, preventing, or deterring state adversaries and non-state actors from acquiring, proliferating, or using weapons of mass destruction;

8. Preventing terrorists from directing or supporting external operations against the homeland;

9. Ensuring common domains remain open and free;

10. Continually delivering performance with affordability and speed;

11. Establishing an unmatched 21st century national security innovation base.

Of the five subcommittees with potential for a stronger mission orientation, five of these 11 primary military objectives in the NDS are listed as a responsibility:

- Airland: One objective listed—sustaining joint force military advantages

- Cybersecurity: One objective listed—ensure common domains remain open and free

- Emerging Threats and Capabilities: Three objectives listed—defending homeland, counter WMDs, counterterrorism

- Seapower: One objective listed—sustaining joint force military advantages

- Strategic Forces: No direct objective listed

To provide for a strategic approach and to ensure the results match the strategy, the SASC and HASC should consider adapting a subcommittee structure reflecting the strategic outcomes expected by (and of) the DoD. While the subcommittees' alignment with the Pentagon's missions may not be perfect, the SASC and HASC should seek to implement a subcommittee structure that prioritizes strategic planning and reflects some degree of outcome alignment.

BUSINESS OUTCOMES

The past few secretaries of defense have consistently listed business reforms as one of their top three priorities. DoD's *Strategic Management Plan FY2014-FY2015* presents the "strategy for delivering effective business operations to support and enable the warfighter." The plan has four goals, each with its own desired outcomes.

The first goal is optimizing DoD's personnel readiness posture. "Readiness" has been a buzzword in recent years, but its ubiquity belies the extremely important and interdependent outcomes of full readiness. Maintaining a highly-skilled military and civilian workforce shaped for today's and tomorrow's needs—a goal of any large organization—will also strengthen individual and mission readiness and family support and will promote well-being. Managing health care costs while delivering quality health care and improving medical readiness is a central part of providing the benefits and health care critical to retaining the best force. This mission also continues after a service member's active duty, as we support our veterans and care for our wounded warriors to ensure our service members are confident they can achieve their personal goals, whether that be through employment, higher education, or small business success.

The second goal focuses on strengthening DoD's financial management. In order to effectively and efficiently use DoD's resources in full compliance with oversight laws, we need to better align those resources to prioritized activities. To get there, the department needs interoperability among business systems to provide better financial information. This is linked to the third goal: building agile yet well-protected information capabilities. This will improve mission effectiveness, cybersecurity, and overall efficiency.

Last but not least, the fourth goal seeks to strengthen DoD's acquisition process. As I've written in previous chapters, improving the acquisition process would allow for greater efficiencies (especially for the installation and environmental aspects of sustainment) and ultimately allow for more focus, in both time and dollars, on the warfighter. Additionally, streamlining the acquisition process would reduce transportation costs and excess inventory, further adding to the positive benefits.

As for the SASC, the first goal and its outcomes, or appropriate revisions of the goal and outcomes, could be the focus of the Personnel Subcommittee. The second and fourth goals and part of the third goal could be the focus of the Readiness and Management Support Subcommittees. The third goal's outcome on cybersecurity would be the responsibility of the Cybersecurity Subcommittee.

ESTABLISHING A REGIONAL FOCUS

The DoD implements a significant amount of its national defense policy on a regional basis through its regional combatant commands (COCOMs). The Pentagon is also aligning more of its forces with regions, particularly in regard to the Special Operations Command (SOCOM). Within the SASC, the only mention of a regional focus is the Emerging Threats and Capabilities Subcommittee, which provides oversight of the U.S. Northern Command (NORTHCOM).

It would seem useful to have mission-oriented subcommittees also focus on those regions where assigned and identified missions have greatest application. Under Chairman Tower, the SASC was the first committee to begin the practice of calling combatant commanders (then known as CINCs) to testify. The Goldwater-Nichols Act (GNA) amended Title 10, making the military departments responsible for organizing, training, and equipping their forces in support of COCOM requirements. However, the committee has not forced the military departments to justify their programs in the context of how they support the COCOMs using this required link.

A senior officer in the former Joint Forces Command once commented that not a single service program originated from an articulated requirement of the COCOMs. To some degree, this might be expected, as the combatant commanders focus on the near term, and the service chiefs, who must construct a Future Years Defense Program (FYDP), must focus on the long term. Nonetheless, a linkage must be made between near-term requirements and longer-term programs. U.S. forces in Korea have the motto "ready to fight tonight." If we are to accomplish that mission, near-term requirements must be met in terms of readiness, maintenance, sustainment, and training. Congress must have a high degree of visibility on how effectively this linkage is made.

SUBCOMMITTEE CONSIDERATIONS

During a public appearance in the late 1990s, then-Senator Dan Coats (R-IN) was asked by a uniformed military officer, "After the Pentagon submits a defense budget that is tightly tailored to meet all of its needs and requirements, why does the Congress insist on making so many changes?"

Senator Coats reflected for a few moments and then replied:

I have yet to see a defense budget that clearly and tightly ties strategic needs to budget lines. What I actually see is internal Pentagon 'pork-barreling' between the services. So, unless you come and give us an explanation of this tight strategic connection, don't blame us for 'pork-barreling.' That's our job, not yours.

Senator Coats was much closer to the mark than perhaps he even realized. Secretary McNamara and Comptroller Hitch's PPBS process was meant to tie together programs, budgets, and strategies. To facilitate this, the Major Force Programs (MFPs) of the original FYDP were created and a lengthy list of program elements (PEs) were identified that aligned with one of the MFPs.

The PEs were intended to contain all resources regardless of the color of money involved. For example, if there were PEs under the Strategic Forces MFP for ballistic missile submarines, it would be expected to contain funds for personnel (the crews), research and development (for ongoing or expected modification), acquisition funds (SCN – shipbuilding), operations and maintenance (for on-station and patrol costs), and installations for basing (including military construction). For budget submission, the appropriations within each PE would be collated and sent to Congress as the budget request; but, within the Pentagon, the programs were intended to align with the MFPs, each having objectives and metrics attached to them reflecting strategic intent.

Regrettably, within the Pentagon, this concept has largely atrophied over the years, and the MFPs are rarely—if ever—used to reflect strategy and for developing programmatic objectives. Their lack of utilization for their intended function is reflected in the basic fact that the MFPs have hardly changed since McNamara and Hitch first established them in 1961. Meanwhile, the same period has seen an enormous change in how the DoD is structured and managed, and the strategic environment in which it operates. For example, there has been a shift to an all-volunteer force (AVF), at least two technological revolutions, the collapse of the Soviet Union, 9/11 and the elevation of counterterrorism in national strategy, the expanded reliance on Special Operations Forces, and the enormous decline in the global base structure, and now the pivot toward great power competition. And those are just the headlines.

A useful approach to reorganizing subcommittees would involve structuring them in a manner roughly reflecting the FYDP MFPs. From here, it would be wise to use this structure to explore issues that bridge the divide between strategy, programs, and budgets with senior defense officials during testimony and hearings. For example:

1. Why do the current MFPs exist?

2. What purpose do they serve?

3. What program and budget lines are contained in each?

4. What metrics are being used, and how were they developed?

5. Are the resources distributed to each MFP appropriate? How do we know?

This dialogue could result in reconfiguring the existing MFPs into ones more consistent with current strategic demands and the current managerial demands of the Pentagon. For instance, an updated FYDP/MFP structure that roughly divides mission areas into those that support combat forces and those aligned with contemporary support functions might look like Figure 2.

FIGURE 2: A NEW FYDP STRUCTURE (BREAKING OUT MILITARY SERVICE PROGRAMS INTO MISSION AREAS)

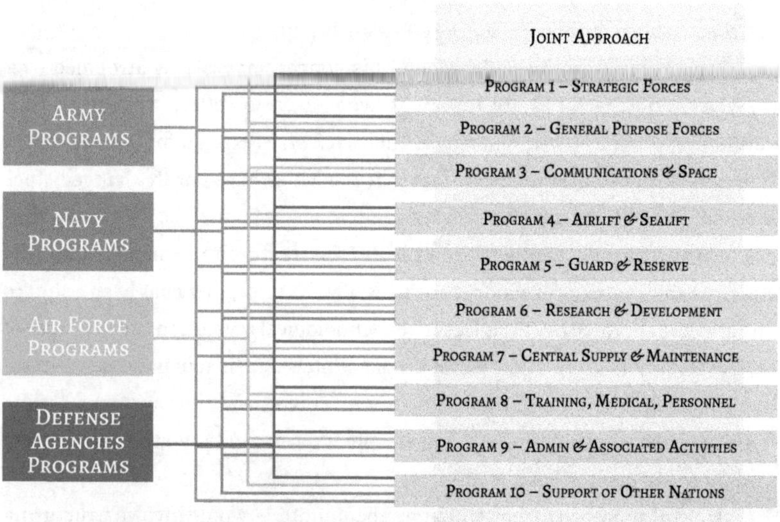

JOINT APPROACH

ARMY PROGRAMS
NAVY PROGRAMS
AIR FORCE PROGRAMS
DEFENSE AGENCIES PROGRAMS

PROGRAM 1 – STRATEGIC FORCES
PROGRAM 2 – GENERAL PURPOSE FORCES
PROGRAM 3 – COMMUNICATIONS & SPACE
PROGRAM 4 – AIRLIFT & SEALIFT
PROGRAM 5 – GUARD & RESERVE
PROGRAM 6 – RESEARCH & DEVELOPMENT
PROGRAM 7 – CENTRAL SUPPLY & MAINTENANCE
PROGRAM 8 – TRAINING, MEDICAL, PERSONNEL
PROGRAM 9 – ADMIN & ASSOCIATED ACTIVITIES
PROGRAM 10 – SUPPORT OF OTHER NATIONS

FIGURE 2 ILLUSTRATES THE STRUCTURE OF THE NEW FYDP GRID.

With this as a new structure within the Pentagon, for determining strategic objectives and allocating resources, congressional oversight could then be conducted by establishing a subcommittee structure that roughly paralleled it, perhaps as shown here:

1. Strategic Forces (MFP 1)

2. Major Theater War Forces (MFP 2)

3. Intervention, Presence, and SO Forces (MFP 4)

4. Strategic Mobility Forces (MFP 5)

5. Intelligence, C4I, and R&D (MFP 3 & 6)

6. Medical, Supply, Maintenance, and Sustainment (MFP 7 & 8)

7. Personnel, Training, and Manpower Development (MFP 9)

MFP 10 and a potential MFP 11, International Programs, might lend themselves to being an area of joint committee interest with the Senate Foreign Relations Committee (SFRC). Joint hearings with the SFRC were held in the early 1950s during the SASC chairmanship of Senator Russell, demonstrating that precedent exists for such a joint effort. This effort, in addition to providing oversight of foreign aid efforts and military support to foreign countries, might also stimulate improving interagency activities between the Pentagon and State Department.

Specifically, one area that might lend itself to exploration and discussion could be the internal organizations of the two departments and the possibility of better aligning the various bureaus of State (such as Near Eastern Affairs) with the operational commands of DoD (such as Central Command). The current alignment is rather loose, stemming from decades of each department defining the international area in its own terms and resulting in COCOMs dealing with several assistant secretaries of state on issues that fall within one section of DoD but several for State. The reverse is equally common. Adjustments to the Pentagon's Unified Command Plan would be easier than the long-standing structure of the State Department, but a closer alignment would facilitate better coordination and reduce the complexity of existing planning and crisis response actions.

A restructuring of the SASC subcommittees around clearly defined and output-oriented missions of the Pentagon would serve several important functions. First, this would force the DoD to reconsider what its major output areas actually are and how its FYDP/MFP structure should be adjusted to address contemporary needs. Second, it would align the SASC with these missions requiring DoD submissions and hearing witnesses to talk in these terms as opposed to service-specific decisions that were made reflecting service-specific perspectives. Third, this would serve as a useful bridge to a discussion on relating strategy to budget outcomes.

Budgets ideally reflect the next year's steps leading toward a desired objective, rather than the most recent steps from where we last were. The former connects to strategy, while the latter can lead to anywhere and tends to continue programs whose initial need may have eroded, if not vanished. Testifying about strategies and strategic direction by Pentagon leaders tends to be an exercise in vague pronouncements, followed by specific assertions about how various programs follow the strategy. The missing element is always the dialogue about how one transitioned from strategy to program. A focus on developing a new set of MFPs, structuring subcommittees to roughly reflect them, and then requiring defense witnesses to explain programmatic decisions in these terms, would better make the connection that Senator Coats was seeking two decades ago.

Subcommittee Efficiency

Each member of the SASC serves on three subcommittees, except for the chairman and ranking member, who serve as ex-officio (non-voting) members of all subcommittees. With the other 24 members split among seven subcommittees, the membership of each subcommittee is large, averaging 10 members:

FIGURE 3: SASC SUBCOMMITTEE SIZE

Subcommittee	Number of Members
Airland	12
Cybersecurity	8
Emerging Threats and Capabilities	12
Personnel	6
Readiness and Management Support	10
Seapower	12
Strategic Forces	12

FIGURE 3 SHOWS THE MEMBERSHIP SIZE OF THE SASC SUBCOMMITTEES IN THE 117TH CONGRESS.

The literature on groups (committees, task forces, and teams) argues for a small membership, as a smaller group takes less time to organize, communicates more effectively, and decides more quickly. Although this research is not conclusive, a Wharton Business School paper notes that the optimal size "does tend to fall in the five-to-twelve range, though some say that five to nine is best." For many years, the SASC had six subcommittees with an average of nine members.

If the SASC continues to have 24 members serving on subcommittees, with each serving on three subcommittees, the number of subcommittees could be increased to eight with nine members on each or 10 subcommittees with seven members.

Maj. Gen. Arnold Punaro, USMC, Ret. and SASC Chairman Senator John McCain discuss defense reform prior to Punaro's testimony before the committee in 2015. Senator McCain was a leader on pushing major organizational changes in DoD to improve performance. Punaro and McCain first met in 1977 when then-Captain McCain was the head of the Navy's Senate Liaison Office and Punaro was on the Senate staff of Senator Sam Nunn. McCain became a member of the SASC in 1987 when Punaro was SASC staff director.

POTENTIAL NEW SUBCOMMITTEES

If the number of subcommittees were increased to eight or 10, new topics could address:

1. Technological superiority (or defense technology and industry):
Globalization and foreign competition in science and technology have placed American technological superiority—the foundation of U.S. defense posture for decades—at risk. A new subcommittee in this area would examine the technological base and the breadth of DoD research and development programs to determine their adequacy and to identify initiatives to maintain

U.S. technological superiority, which numerous experts, including former Under Secretaries for Acquisition, Technology, and Logistics, have said is deteriorating. This subcommittee could also add industrial base issues.

2. Defense oversight and investigations:

As chapter 26 discusses, statistics have shown a steady decline in oversight activities by Congress. Moreover, the SASC and HASC have been criticized for ineffective oversight, especially of the use of force and procurement programs. If the full committee and existing subcommittees are too busy to conduct sufficient oversight activities, it might be appropriate to establish a new subcommittee with oversight and investigations as its sole responsibility.

3. Organization and management (or institutional reform):

The full committee has traditionally addressed broad organization and management issues. Typically, the DoD has had great difficulty in addressing the need for organizational reform. Moreover, by the department's own admission, many management areas require significant reform. This workload might justify a subcommittee. In addition, such a subcommittee might give needed attention to interagency reform, in light of the failure of the executive branch to achieve whole-of-government solutions to national security problems.

4. Power projection:

Although the Seapower Subcommittee has responsibility for strategic lift programs, it does not have responsibility for the full range of capabilities to project ready military forces over great distances. Because maintaining superior power projection capabilities is a cornerstone of defense strategy, it might be useful to devote a subcommittee to oversee this area.

CONCLUSION

The organization of a committee and the setting of the agenda is largely the purview of the committee chairman. Many will work with their ranking member in determining the best subcommittee approach during the two years of each Congress. Some will take into account the expertise and interest of their members. Within their consideration, the overarching goal should be that the committee's organization, agenda, hearing, and priorities ensure that their jurisdiction is executed to provide the strongest national defense for the dollars available and one that deals with both today's and tomorrow's threats.

Chapter 26: Reinvigorating Oversight and Strategic Management

The Constitution's system of checks and balances among the legislative, executive, and judicial branches provides the foundation for congressional oversight. A 2012 Congressional Research Service (CRS) report, *Congressional Oversight*, summarized oversight as "a way for Congress to check on, and check, the executive branch." Oversight can serve a number of overlapping objectives and purposes, as outlined in the CRS report:

- Evaluate and improve the efficiency and effectiveness of governmental operations.

- Evaluate programs and performance.

- Detect and prevent poor administration, waste, abuse, arbitrary and capricious behavior, or illegal and unconstitutional conduct.

- Protect civil liberties and constitutional rights.

- Inform the general public and ensure that executive policies reflect the public interest.

- Gather information to develop new legislative proposals or to amend existing statutes.

- Ensure administrative compliance with legislative intent.

- Prevent executive encroachment on legislative authority and prerogatives.

Despite being one of the most important roles of Congress, oversight of the executive branch has steadily declined. In 2006, two noted congressional scholars, Norman Ornstein and Thomas Mann, observed in a 2006 Brookings Institution report that "Congressional oversight of the executive across a range of policies, but especially on foreign and national security policy, has virtually collapsed." The Senate Foreign Relations Committee's (SFRC) own website even admits that it has ceded too much power to the executive branch, a trend that began in the 1960s.

This is not a problem just for the SFRC. In 2010, Kay King of the Council on Foreign Relations took the two Armed Services Committees to task on oversight lapses. She argued, "The HASC and SASC must share in the responsibility for Congress's failure to sufficiently challenge the executive branch on the use of military force." King also noted:

> Critics of the defense authorization process also worry that, in their zeal to support the military, the armed services committees can be less vigilant than they should be, sometimes endorsing unwanted or bloated programs or failing to hold the Pentagon sufficiently accountable for its weapons systems and operations.

These criticisms suggest that it might be appropriate for the Senate Armed Services Committee (SASC) and the House Armed Services Committee (HASC) to establish a more rigorous approach to their oversight responsibilities, but also that the committees will likely need a concerted effort to ensure that those improvements are recognized and therefore more effective. Developing and maintaining a media profile contributes to the reputation of a committee chairman and ranking member as an opinion leader. It also can leverage the work of the committee by placing it in a broader public domain. An effective public profile benefits largely from having a coherent message and oversight agenda.

A committee oversight agenda should be made available to the public, as having such a readily identified agenda is helpful to both the public and committee members. While committee chairs give a large amount of latitude to the subcommittee chairs, subcommittee agendas that align closely with the full committee will enhance the overall unity and effectiveness of the committee's oversight.

Currently, the HASC does make its oversight agenda available on its website. Ideally, the SASC and HASC could agree on complementary agendas. However, if that is not feasible, then each committee should develop its own public document. This agenda should inform the committee's consideration (and ultimately that of the Senate or House as a whole) of the annual defense authorization bill as well as the committees' broader oversight responsibilities. It should help determine how members and staff allocate their time and resources.

The agenda should focus on the most significant issues. If too many issues are deemed high priorities, the available time and attention to each will be diluted. This is especially true when planned oversight activities will inevitably be constrained by rapidly developing events on the ground, most of which cannot be predicted. Reviews of national security issues that are not part of the oversight plan can sometimes dominate committee and staff resources at the expense of planned activities. Planning has to be done flexibly, with an understanding of the need to adapt to unforeseen circumstances.

STEP BACK AND REDUCE MICROMANAGEMENT

Prior to 1959, the Armed Services Committees authorized activities or programs on a permanent basis and let the Appropriations Committees handle annual funding. This changed in 1959 when the Armed Services Committees included a provision in the Authorization Act requiring annual authorizations for procurement of aircraft, missiles, and naval vessels. Over time, additional portions of the budget request became subject to an authorization prior to an appropriation until the 1980s when this had crept into almost every aspect of the defense budget.

During the 1960s and 1970s, the defense authorization bills became the primary means for influencing DoD policy through imposing conditions on annual spending requests. In the 1980s, the appropriations committees began to increasingly deviate from the course set out in the authorization bill, so the

Armed Services Committees began scrubbing the defense budget in even finer detail to remain relevant to the process.

Congress is intended, however, to be the nation's board of directors. Congress is best at reviewing, questioning, and where necessary revising the executive branch's plans on major issues of national importance. The Constitution intended for the Congress to engage in strategic (or macro) management, not micromanagement. Congress has become so preoccupied with micromanagement that it has all but abandoned strategic management. It adjusts thousands of line items, yet it does not deal with fundamental underlying problems. As the Armed Services Committees pursue this approach, its roles become less relevant.

The Armed Services Committee chairman and ranking member should lead through a strong and clear vision that focuses attention on the big management issues, so that scarce time and staff resources are not devoted to items of less importance. Senate oversight of government management also occurs in the Homeland Security and Governmental Affairs Committee; this bifurcated oversight exists as well on the House side where the Committee on Oversight and Government Reform has a Subcommittee on National Security. It would be ideal if the chairs of these two committees in both arms of Congress work with each other to develop a common set of management issues and joint hearings to create a more unified oversight message.

One potential macro approach is for the committees to examine whether DoD's business, administrative, and management functions really support the overall defense enterprise as they should. DoD's overarching strategic goals as laid out in the National Defense Strategy (NDS) are to restore America's competitive edge by blocking global rivals from challenging the U.S. and our allies and from throwing the international order out of balance. Its main lines of effort in working toward these goals are to build a more lethal force, strengthen alliances and attract new partners, and reform the department for greater performance and affordability.

Examining how the department is faring in terms of its highest priority business initiatives to support its other defense strategic goals should be an important focus for Armed Services Committee oversight.

The committee currently receives a report from DoD, but a focused hearing on those very issues DoD claims are important in its report would hold DoD more accountable. For example, DoD states that it has four high-priority management goals: First, optimizing DoD personnel readiness posture; second, strengthening DoD financial management; third, building agile and secure information capabilities; and fourth, strengthening DoD acquisition processes. There are several initiatives for each of these goals. This information is presented by DoD in its Strategic Management Plan (SMP) to Congress. It represents a very good baseline of information from which to ask hard-hitting questions.

Last, in spite of failed attempts in the past, it is still worth considering a two-year authorization bill that could benefit all parties. While there would still be the temptation to "tinker" in the second year, ideally, the only issues that should be addressed in the second year would be those items of absolute legislative necessity. This approach would lend itself to more macro management and allow for pursuit of the committees' agenda items in a more thorough and thoughtful manner.

Maj. Gen. Arnold Punaro, USMC, Ret. discusses major reforms to the Chief Management Office (CMO) and other elements of the Office of the Secretary of Defense (OSD) on the news program Government Matters with host Francis Rose in July 2020. Punaro, as part of the Defense Business Board, co-chaired a task force conducting an independent assessment of the CMO, as required by Congress. Recommendations from the study have been incorporated into the FY21 National Defense Authorization Bills.

THE IMPORTANCE OF BIPARTISANSHIP IN IMPROVING OVERSIGHT

Several major security policy issues also fall under the purview of various committees. To address these policy issues more effectively, committee leadership should set an example of collaboratively working with other committees through joint hearings and investigations. Such behavior will send strong signals to various federal departments and help dissuade them from taking refuge from inaction by claiming committee jurisdiction for not addressing a broader problem. As important as it is, experience suggests that making this kind of change would be a tall order. Three examples of such cross-cutting issues include:

1. The impact of fiscal insecurity on national security

How concerned should we be about our long-term debt and its impact on the security of this country? How likely is it that those countries buying our debt (such as China) might stop if they become convinced they will not be fully repaid? What are the implications of long-term fiscal scenarios for this country's security overall? This issue could inform the debate between the two camps of thought that defense should not be subject to future constraints like the Budget Control Act constraints (and possibly similar legislation in the future) and those who believe it should.

2. Balancing scarce natural resources and national security

Given natural resource trends, issues over access to natural resources in new and previously inaccessible areas amidst a changing climate will cause more conflict in the next century.

3. The relationship between the Department of Veterans Affairs (VA) and DoD medical care systems

What are the pros and cons of increased integration of the DoD and VA systems? What has been the experience to date where there has been consolidation in selected areas? Why has there been no progress on a unified medical record for service members?

Strong leadership of the Armed Services Committees could bring about engagement of the members and heads of different committees to conduct joint hearings and joint investigations on some of these issues. The outcomes of cross-committee collaboration would far outweigh the extra burden involved.

IMPORTANCE OF COMMUNICATION WITH OMB AND NSCS

Communication between the Armed Services Committees and Office of Management and Budget (OMB) does not happen very often. There are benefits to a more open communication channel, especially the significant analytic capacity and programmatic knowledge within OMB. OMB has the responsibility to run the clearance process on every legislative proposal in the administration's proposed NDAA package before it can be submitted to Congress. OMB staff also make the key recommendations to OMB and White House leadership on various pieces of legislation in addition to their principal role of preparing and transmitting the budget.

Likewise, the National Security Council Staff (NSCS), many of whom are detailees from various federal agencies, including DoD, State, the intelligence community (IC), and the National Nuclear Security Administration (NNSA), organize the administration's interagency policy process, of which OMB is also a participant. National Security Council (NSC) staffers provide a broader perspective than DoD or DoE on a variety of issues, largely because of their interagency focus and exposure.

Strengthening communication links with OMB and NSCS—especially in administrations that take a more centralized approach to decision-making, a hallmark of both the Obama and Trump White Houses—will provide the committees with another important perspective beyond just what the agencies think. Having an up-to-date sense of where the executive branch is (defined more broadly than just DoD, NSC, or IC) on various issues can only help enhance the effectiveness of Armed Services Committees leadership, all without undermining committee independence.

Working with OMB can also facilitate achievement of common goals for both committees and the administration in such areas as:

1. Facilitating inspector general (IG) investigations of fraud, waste, and abuse

Committees could leverage OMB's influence on agencies to ensure that agencies cooperate with IGs by providing needed information and data for their investigations. This has recently been a complaint from IGs.

2. Reviewing defense contracting practices

Working more collaboratively with OMB on issues such as wartime and non-wartime service contracting could enhance effectiveness. For example, priority could be given to the phasing out DoD's practice of employing private contractors to execute inherently governmental tasks, especially in the acquisition process. Another collaborative focus could be to increase the use of strategic sourcing as a way of producing savings. Strategic sourcing is a continuous, systematic, and fact-based approach for optimizing an organization's supply base and "improving the overall value proposition."

3. Achieving real acquisition reform

How can the committees work with the executive branch to improve the composition and quality of the federal acquisition workforce (a common goal of the Office of Federal Procurement Policy in OMB and the committees)? How can the committees work with OMB (and perhaps CBO and GAO) to ensure that internal DoD processes for establishing requirements for major new acquisitions have enough transparency and input from competing voices? How can a collaborative effort bring about greater efficiencies in the tens of billions spent in DoD's budget on IT, a concern recognized by DoD itself as well as OMB? One potential topic is focusing on the progress of the recently-announced restructuring of the Defense Information Systems Agency (DISA), whose goal is to make DISA more agile, more efficient, and more connected to CYBERCOM.

4. Implementing the Government Performance and Results Act (GPRA)

The GPRA Modernization Act of 2010 requires OMB to coordinate with agency efforts toward two goals. First, to establish outcome-oriented, federal government priority goals (known as cross-agency priority, or CAP, goals) with annual and quarterly performance targets and milestones. Second, to report quarterly on a single website, now known as Performance. gov, the results achieved for each CAP goal compared to the targets. Since this is legislation passed by the Congress, including members of the Armed Services Committees, they could join the Governmental Affairs Committees in reviewing both the meaningfulness of the goals and the progress to meet them. Presently, the Armed Services Committees do not become very involved at all in the implementation of this act. Yet, they have much to contribute here in terms of their background and expertise.

CONDUCTING HIGH PROFILE INVESTIGATIONS

The HASC once had an Oversight and Investigations Subcommittee that conducted studies and investigations across the jurisdiction of the committee, including inquiries into allegations of waste, fraud, abuse, and wrongdoing and inefficiencies within the DoD. Members and staff managed comprehensive oversight studies of major programs and issues and produced reports for the committee and DoD providing recommendations and improvements of these programs. This subcommittee was retired at the end of the 115th Congress in 2018.

The Senate, on the other hand, has only had a Senate Permanent Subcommittee on Investigations, which covers a broader portfolio than just DoD. The subcommittee has only focused occasionally on defense, holding hearings on various issues such as contracting and Prisoner of War (POW)/ Missing in Action (MIA) accounting. Under Senator Stennis's chairmanship in the early 1970s, the SASC had an investigations subcommittee. While there is no subcommittee on investigations within the SASC today, the chairman has the authority to set up investigative teams on selected issues and could do more of this to garner attention on significant issues. For example, Senator Levin established an investigative team to examine the treatment of detainees in U.S. custody at Guantanamo Bay and Iraq and Afghanistan. The SASC has also investigated the use and oversight of private security contractors in Afghanistan, producing a report in September 2010. In my time on the SASC, we investigated Desert One, the Beirut Barracks Bombing, the USS *Iowa* explosion, the Somalia operation, and much more.

One option is to consider taking more advantage of the analytic capacity of Congressional Budget Office (CBO), CRS, and Government Accountability Office (GAO) to amplify the committees' oversight capability. These agencies could serve as a real resource to the Armed Services Committees. Simultaneously, the hiring of large numbers of military retirees by both Armed Services Committees should be examined. To what extent do the staff separate themselves from their allegiances to their services? While there are undoubtedly exceptions to this, hiring other kinds of staff and using the capacity of CBO, CRS, and GAO would reduce at least the appearance of conflicts of interest and gain more independent analytic support. On the other hand, any officer with active duty experience will be familiar with DoD's occasional intransigence. They know when to push, when to hold the line, and when to take the Pentagon at its word – all incredibly important skills when conducting oversight.

IMPROVING THE EFFICIENCY OF THE REPROGRAMMING PROCESS

In its annual appropriations bills, Congress provides authority for DoD to move money across appropriation accounts for other uses. This authority allows DoD to move, in base and Overseas Contingency Operations (OCO) funds combined, about $8 billion to other purposes during the year of execution to reflect changing needs throughout the year. DoD takes advantage of this authority, and much time is spent developing specific and omnibus reprogramming actions for congressional approval. Subject to specific low dollar thresholds and other constraints, reprogramming of funds within appropriation accounts can occur without congressional approval.

DoD-proposed transfers or reprogramming requests that do go to Congress for approval must be submitted to OMB and then to Congress where they must be personally approved by the chairmen and ranking members of the appropriation and authorization committees. Having this flexibility is of great benefit to the department to adjust its resources to surprises and new priorities in a fluid security environment. To the frustration on both sides of the aisle, the process of compiling these requests and getting them approved often takes a long time. There may be value in having the Armed Services and Defense Appropriation Committees, jointly with DoD, reexamine how this process works. The goal should be to make the process reflect both congressional and executive branch concerns while allowing for funds to be obligated in a timely and effective manner.

Most of Congress's concerns with proposed reprogramming focus not on the purposes to which additional funds are being directed, but more often to the offsets being used to pay the bill, especially if it is a congressional interest item. Just one objection from the chair or ranking member of either appropriations or authorization committees can stop funds from being used as an offset for additional spending elsewhere. And of course, when the Trump administration used DoD money to fund the border wall, they broke the decades-long gentlemen's agreement on congressional prior approval of reprogrammings and also caused a huge setback for the cooperative working relationship.

Some possible approaches to streamlining the reprogramming process include the SASC and subcommittees initiating their review of the defense budget request with hearings on strategy in their areas of responsibility. The separate section on strategy hearings provides a rationale for doing so, a past example of strategy hearings in the committee, and an illustrative strategy hearing schedule. The subcommittees could also be given more of a mission and regional orientation. This would change the focus from inputs to missions, outcomes, and outputs and provide a strategic-management framework. The chairman could require each subcommittee to identify two strategic issues it will address during the session (and maybe two in the subsequent session to lengthen their horizon). This would elevate the subcommittees' focus. The full committee would review and approve each subcommittee's strategic issues. Lastly, the chairman could require each subcommittee to identify two oversight topics it will pursue during the session. Given the existing burdens on each subcommittee chairman and ranking member, it might be useful to assign this oversight project to a two-person, bipartisan team, possibly of the subcommittee's most junior members.

The more Congress focuses on line-item details rather than guiding policy, the less influence Congress will have on guiding the executive branch's strategy and execution. As Congress must ensure they provide for the common defense and promote the general welfare as required by our Constitution, improving oversight is key.

Chapter 27: Relations Between the SASC and the Senate Intelligence Committee

On May 19, 1976, the Senate adopted S. Res. 400, creating a separate committee with consolidated oversight, legislative, and authorization jurisdiction over the intelligence activities of the U.S. government. Congress recognized a need for such a committee as far back as the 1950s, and several temporary select committees were established to investigate abuses, illegalities, and improprieties in the CIA, FBI, and NSA. The Church Committee's recommendations for stronger oversight of the intelligence community finally led the Armed Services Committee to reluctantly propose S. Res. 400 to establish the Senate Select Committee on Intelligence (SSCI). Prior to the creation of SSCI, the Senate Armed Services Committee (SASC) maintained the authorizing jurisdiction on all intelligence matters, including the CIA. The resolution provided significant protections for the SASC's authority in these areas, since the vast majority of U.S. intelligence activities, funding, and platforms remain within the purview of the DoD. Throughout the 1980s and 1990s, SASC exercised strong involvement in all SSCI matters with its sequential referral ability.

However, much has changed over the past decade or so in the intelligence community (IC), and the same is true for the relationship between SASC and

486 | The Ever-Shrinking Fighting Force

SSCI. The 9/11 attacks underscored the need to better integrate the then-16 intelligence agencies. The Intelligence Reform and Terrorism Prevention Act of 2004 sought to achieve improved integration through the creation of the Office of the Director of National Intelligence and the National Counterterrorism Center. Over the same period, SSCI became more independent and protective of its jurisdiction. Gone are the days when SSCI automatically accommodated SASC interests. Moreover, to an outsider, it now appears that since 2004 the SASC has been much less engaged with the SSCI and does not fully exercise its legitimate prerogatives which are essential to protect DoD intelligence requirements.

Both committees should see this development as counterproductive. The SASC's inability to pass its bill on the Senate floor mirrors some of the same challenges the SSCI faced year after year with its authorization bill, which did not pass on an annual basis. This also occurred when I was the SASC staff director in the 1980s and 1990s when the SSCI bill did not come up for independent floor debate. Given the lack of formal arrangements for improving SASC-SSCI coordination, specifically that of their shared responsibilities and for protecting the SASC's intelligence interests, what might be done?

In today's complex work environments, many organizations are facing similar cross-boundary challenges. To effectively achieve their purposes, SASC and SSCI need to find informal means for working with organizations that have important expertise, capacities, and authorities. This includes creating cross-boundary teams and establishing networks. Each of these efforts depends upon a commitment to collaboration.

There are four essential steps toward collaboration, known as the collaboration continuum:

1. Communication – exchanging ideas, opinions, or information.

2. Contribution – providing assistance, giving something.

3. Coordination – connecting different organizations for a harmonious action.

4. Cooperation – different organizations with similar interests taking part in planning activities, negotiating roles, and sharing resources to achieve joint goals.

Building upon these steps, collaboration requires that organizations go beyond their individual expertise and vision to constructively explore their differences and search for common, innovative solutions. To a substantial degree, success also relies on voluntary participation, usually among relatively equal members. It is worth examining whether the work of the SASC and SSCI would benefit from a more collaborative relationship.

In this regard, six ideas are offered for consideration:

1. Ensure that the maximum benefit is achieved from the SASC members who serve on SSCI.

The SASC has two reserved seats on the SSCI, and the SASC chairman and ranking member serve as ex officio members. As of the 117th Congress, the SASC has three SSCI members: Senator Tom Cotton (R-AR), Senator Angus King (I-ME), and Senator Kirsten Gillibrand (D-NY). These crossover positions are important, as they allow members from the two committees to both share information and perspectives on important national security topics. It would be useful to prepare a one-page paper describing the responsibilities of these crossover members to both committees. This paper could be approved by both SASC and SSCI leaders.

2. Schedule meetings of SASC and SSCI leaders to discuss goals, problems, agendas, priorities, potential issues, and opportunities for collaborative work.

Given the demands on the committee leaders, these sessions would be few and far between, but they could prove quite useful. Collaboration depends upon clearly articulated goals. It is important to know what problems the two committees are trying to solve together. Then, the leaders can determine what they can do collectively. Beyond substantive discussions, these sessions could establish a collaborative tone for interactions between the two committees.

3. Increase staff-to-staff meetings and discussions.

The two majority and two minority staff directors should meet on a regular basis, possibly once each month, to ensure a continuous exchange of information, assessments of progress, and early identification of issues. When Senator Nunn was chairman of the SASC and a member of the SSCI, we identified a SASC professional staffer to support him on SSCI versus taking advantage of having his own designee on the SSCI staff.

4. Increase the scope of the Cybersecurity Subcommittee to include intelligence.

This expanded subcommittee would provide a means for increased collaboration with the SSCI. A strong argument could be made that these two topics deserve the combined and linked attention a unique subcommittee could provide. In addition, as the focus of SASC-SSCI collaboration, this subcommittee could develop effective working relationships, encourage cooperation, enhance understanding, avoid duplication, and share expertise, information, and knowledge.

5. Joint SASC-SSCI hearings.

It might be useful to identify key issues from the committees' shared responsibilities where joint hearings would contribute to better coordination and understanding. One possibility would be to invite SSCI members to the confirmation hearings of nominees for heads of defense intelligence agencies, such as the National Security Agency, Defense Intelligence Agency, National Reconnaissance Office, and the Under Secretary of Defense for Intelligence.

6. Agreement to share information.

The reluctance of SSCI to share information has troubled its relations with the SASC and other committees that share responsibilities with the SSCI.

It would be useful to draft an agreement between the two committees regarding information sharing.

CONCLUSION

The facts speak for themselves as the intelligence operations of the DoD, both in terms of people and money, dwarf those of all other agencies, including the Director of National Intelligence and the CIA. The DoD has the largest intelligence agencies, including the National Security Agency, the Defense Intelligence Agency, the National Geospatial-Intelligence Agency, the National Reconnaissance Office, and the large military intelligence organizations in each of the military services. Moreover, the U.S. Cyber Command, the U.S. Space Command, and the U.S. Strategic Command are inextricably linked to intelligence functions. Stovepipes that precluded cooperation and sharing of information were responsible for the surprise attack at Pearl Harbor in 1941 and the attacks on our homeland on 9/11. The two committees need to improve their coordination and cooperation in order to best protect our country.

CONCLUSION

"Our shared values define us more than our differences. And acknowledging those shared values can see us through our challenges today if we have the wisdom to trust in them again."

John McCain, August 2017

John McCain's vision underscores our country's historical ability to unite and work together in the face of existential threats. I believe that the national security challenges facing the United States today are some of the most serious and threatening I have seen in my lifetime. America is no longer the sole superpower. As stated in the 2018 National Defense Strategy:

> China is a strategic competitor using predatory economics to intimidate its neighbors while militarizing features in the South China Sea. Russia has violated the borders of nearby nations and pursues veto power over the economic, diplomatic, and security decisions of its neighbors.

490

Adding to these challenges, our nation's fiscal posture, massive debts, crumbling infrastructure, and hyperpartisan political environment have slowed down our ability to quickly and thoroughly address these issues. This reality must be reversed if we are to stay ahead of our adversaries in the coming years and provide the opportunities and freedoms previous generations of Americans have enjoyed.

Throughout its existence, the United States has been the global leader in advocating for democracy, a quest that has been greatly facilitated by our national security capabilities. The American experiment continues today, and our country must remain an example and inspiration to other nations desiring democratic ideals, representative government, and freedom and equality for all. While I recognize the United States has sometimes deviated from its values throughout history, I still believe in the exceptional appeal of American ideals. However, it is vital to understand that the United States cannot serve as a beacon of democracy, a model of freedom, and a place of enormous opportunity if the American national security apparatus becomes fragile and feeble.

The practice of the American experiment depends on the strength of our national defense, the capabilities of our warfighters, and the nation's ability to synchronize its soft and hard power while furthering its ideals and safeguarding its interests. As noted by the Defense Business Board's June 2020 report: "Normal 'budget cut drills,' although involving very tough choices, are not transformative and will not address the pacing threat of China." Rather, leaders in both the Pentagon and Congress will need to buckle down, make tough decisions, and institute major reforms. With this in mind, I care deeply about reshaping defense processes, DoD organizations, and defense spending practices. The future of our nation requires it. As developed in the preceding chapters in the book, these are the top 15 guiding principles essential to ensuring the strength of American security.

1. **Think Smarter, Not Richer.** Strategy must remain at the center of all decisions. The department has done a good job pivoting toward great power competition in its National Defense Strategy, taking into account the threats, goals, and objectives of our nation. Now, the department needs

to dramatically improve its acquisition process, significantly reduce its overhead, and curtail the unsustainable rate of increase in the fully burdened lifecycle costs of personnel and benefits. This is especially important in an increasingly limited budget environment, as there won't be the annual 3%-5% real growth in budgets Pentagon leaders require to truly implement the National Defense Strategy. Because of this, the department and Congress will need to think smarter, not richer, and make hard decisions.

2. Focus on Outputs, Not Inputs. The Pentagon and Congress should shift their focus from the inputs (how much we spend) to outputs (what we get for what we spend) to ensure the department gets the most bang for its buck. Just spending more money has not always resulted in better outcomes. Oversight mechanisms should be implemented to ensure funds are being spent efficiently and appropriately, as outputs need to truly increase the department's capacity and capabilities. Additionally, leaders need to take a long-term approach to solve present-day problems. Today's leaders owe it to future generations to break their myopic focus on the short term.

3. Put the Nation's Fiscal House in Order. The country must address the ever increasing deficit and accumulating debt. Politicians have consistently refused to solve or even honestly grapple with our almost $30 trillion debt. Continued deficit spending puts our long-term economic health at risk. We've neglected the foundations for too long. There needs to be a new Simpson-Bowles commission that addresses discretionary spending, entitlements, and revenues with a long-term bipartisan plan to reverse the adverse trends. This outcome will only occur if all are asked to sacrifice by constraining discretionary spending, reducing the growth of entitlements, and increasing government revenues.

4. Change the Benchmarks. The Pentagon needs to develop performance benchmarks to focus the department's output goals on being better, faster, and cheaper than China. As a whole, the Pentagon needs to become timelier and more efficient regarding technology development and implementation. Our warfighters must be able to quickly address new operational concepts and possible conflicts. China has seriously invested in new technological capabilities across the board, and we need to address and counter these advances. If we fail to do so, China will dominate us technologically and militarily within the decade, a reality noted by many leaders, including the Chairman of the Joint Chiefs of Staff, General Mark Milley.

5. Define Senior Leadership Roles. When it comes to the top leaders in the Pentagon, there are several important relationships that need to be clearly defined. The secretary should be the department's chief executive officer while the deputy secretary should act as the chief operating officer. Meanwhile, the Chairman of the Joint Chiefs of Staff should focus on operations while the vice chairman should concentrate on joint requirements, management, and technology. The service secretaries should specify the roles and responsibilities to be performed by the service chiefs, as well as better clarify the division of labor between service secretaries and the military staffs. Additionally, the SecDef should ensure that the combatant commanders coordinate all efforts, including legislative, with the Chairman of the Joint Chiefs of Staff.

6. Streamline the Office of the Secretary of Defense. The Office of the Secretary of Defense should focus on macro management rather than micromanagement. Because of the massive size, scope, and function of the Pentagon, the secretary needs to be able to focus on the department's major issues. In order to do this, the Office of the Secretary should focus on its core functions, such as macro allocation of resources, major policy formulation, and enterprise-level oversight.

7. Reduce the Tail and Increase the Tooth. Conflicts are fought and won by combat forces—not support organizations or service headquarters. Over the years, the defense overhead has increased as defense-wide spending has grown from 5% of the budget to almost 20% of the budget. Additionally, the defense agencies and DoD field activities—which started with just one in 1952 and are now up to 28 in 2020—are spending over $115 billion a year.

In the same period, the capabilities and number of our fighting forces have decreased. This trend must be reversed.

8. Challenge the Fully Burdened and Lifecycle Costs of Personnel. The ever increasing fully burdened and lifecycle costs of the military are unsustainable—especially for active duty military—as the all-in costs associated with a single service member continue to rise at an alarming rate. This trend also encompasses the post-service retirement benefits, which are also increasing at an unsustainable rate. Today's system currently pays a service member 70 years for those who retire after only 20 years of active service. For example, if someone joins the military at age 18, they can retire with full retirement benefits at age 38. Given that the average life-expectancy rate is now in the mid-80s, the department is now responsible for approximately 50 years of additional retirement costs. The department and Congress must acknowledge the fully burdened and lifecycle costs associated with adequately supporting an active duty warfighter and consider adjustments on a prospective basis rather than retroactively.

9. Reform and Improve the Authorization and Appropriations Process. Congress needs to get their work done on time—it is as simple as that. October 1 happens on the same day every year. Congress should adhere to the well-defined congressional budget process and move to a two-year budget cycle so they don't repeat the same processes every year. Additionally, Congress should consider collapsing the budget, authorization, and appropriation processes into a budget committee that sets overall guidelines for spending and revenues and a joint authorization and appropriation committee that both authorizes and appropriates in the same bill. This would reduce the duplication of efforts among the three current committees.

10. Update the Planning, Programming, Budgeting, and Execution (PPBE) System. The PPBE system should be updated and improved to match modern-day fighting needs. The Pentagon should redefine the Major Force Programs of the Future Years Defense Program, ensure the planning documents identify clear goals and objectives, and establish macro-level priorities. Additionally, the budget should be recognized as the final product of PPBE, not the first. Throughout the entire process, the Office of Management and Budget should provide oversight specifically focused on macro-level budget management.

11. Increase the Industrial Base. There needs to be better awareness of the industrial base and its relationship to the acquisition process and the needs of the warfighters. Industry is key to ensuring that our warfighters are never in a fair fight. Specifically, lawmakers and Pentagon leaders should understand that the current smaller industrial base reduces competition and the DoD's ability to leverage prices. The Pentagon should continue efforts to attract nontraditional providers into the defense marketplace while also encouraging efforts to streamline and compress the overall acquisition process.

12. Improve Industry-Government Communication. Industry and government need to improve the flow of information on matters of technology and personnel. The Pentagon should collaborate and consult with industry partners—both big and small—on a wide variety of matters from acquisition and technology to internal departmental workings. Industry leaders often bring much-needed world-class business practices to the Pentagon, which is critical considering the number of taxpayer dollars spent daily.

13. Enhance Bipartisanship in National Security. Historically, national security has been largely immune to partisan bickering and gridlock. In the past, leaders experienced the most success when they attacked the toughest issues head-on in a bipartisan fashion. These leaders let the facts and the situation on the ground drive decisions to ensure the nation attained its objectives, even if that meant political risk for an individual or the whole party.

However, like the rest of the country today, national security is suffering from increasing partisan gridlock that has resulted in less problem-solving, greater inefficiency, and overall dysfunction. Political leaders, whether in Congress, the White House, or the Pentagon, need to prioritize national security needs over partisan agendas. Even during periods of divided government, a bipartisan approach to national security must be preserved.

14. Foster Strong Relationships. A military unit draws together people of diverse backgrounds, talents, opinions, and abilities to accomplish its common mission. It's essential to victory and even survival that the unit develops mutual respect, understanding, and concern for one another. This is absolutely vital in combat, as it should be in politics. In addition to working in a bipartisan fashion whenever possible, Congress, the White House, and the Pentagon need to engage in more frequent and transparent communication. These discussions should also include the Office of Management and Budget and other key national security entities, including the intelligence community, the Department of State, and the Department of Homeland Security.

Across all groups, mutual respect, courtesy, and communication would help ensure the probability of good working relationships in spite of different opinions. Whether in politics, government, or business, there will always be another important issue, meeting, or decision—when an old enemy may become, at least temporarily, an ally. The old cliché of not burning bridges holds true. You can shake hands at the end of the day ... and be ready to solve the next problem together.

15. Lead by Example. General Colin Powell said, "The most important thing I learned is that soldiers watch what their leaders do. You can give them classes and lecture them forever, but it is your personal example they will follow." Leaders in the White House, Congress, and the Pentagon need to lead by example. They must listen to varying perspectives, base decisions on objective facts, and then take the necessary calculated and informed risks. We need politicians and defense leaders of sound moral character, who know what they stand for, and will steer the nation in the right direction.

These qualities will allow our leaders to make the necessary tough decisions in an increasingly competitive and hostile global order.

In the 1980s, against the backdrop of the ongoing Cold War, President Ronald Reagan noted:

> The dustbin of history is littered with remains of those countries that relied on diplomacy to secure their freedom. We must never forget ... in the final analysis ... that it is our military, industrial and economic strength that offers the best guarantee of peace for America in times of danger.

This sentiment certainly applies to the current challenges facing the nation today. In order to protect the pillars of American security that Reagan poignantly referred to, we need to implement common-sense reforms. This will require continued collaboration and dedication from leaders across policymaking, military, and industry sectors.

We face serious challenges that require making difficult decisions. The nation has faced serious challenges before, and we can do so again. I am confident that if we all work together and remain focused on this important mission, we will ultimately achieve a stronger and more robust national security foundation. We still have men and women inside the beltway who truly have the public interest at heart. In order to change the trend from the "ever-shrinking fighting force" to the "ever-growing fighting force," we will need to search out the best in ourselves, work across the aisle, and implement the much-needed reforms. There are few things as important, and none as unforgiving of failure, as this. The future of our country depends on it.

ACKNOWLEDGMENTS

While the views expressed in this book are my own, the creation and publication of this material would not have been possible without the help of many people, all of whom have my undying gratitude. As I have always said, collective wisdom beats individual wisdom any day.

I am thankful for the members of The Punaro Group who worked tirelessly to make *The Ever-Shrinking Fighting Force* a reality, even through the day-to-day requirements of running for-profit enterprises and handling unprecedented disruptions from the COVID-19 pandemic. Walker Marlatt, a University of Georgia School of Public and International Affairs graduate, served as the original lead on this project. Irina Plaks, a fellow UGA alumna, has been a consistent and appreciated source of guidance. Her experience with *On War and Politics: The Battle Inside Washington's Beltway*, my memoir and first published book, served as an invaluable source of guidance on this project.

Sarah Kathryn ("SK") Lasseigne arrived from the University of Georgia in June of 2020 and immediately jumped into the project. Joined by Julie Punaro Robertson, their dedication, attention to detail, and writing skills helped transform this book from a series of speeches, white papers, memos, and studies written over the past 20 years into an organized and informative work. Additionally, Anita Kayser, TPG's Executive Assistant, was also an invaluable asset throughout the entire process. I am deeply grateful to the entire team, not only for their hard work on this book but also for continuing to produce high-quality work for our other business enterprises throughout the entirety of this project. Thank you!

Ron Wielsma was an instrumental resource when it came to the numbers. *The Ever-Shrinking Fighting Force* includes a multitude of graphs, charts, and statistics, all of which were vetted and updated by Ron. His experience in both the Marine Corps and defense industry has made him an invaluable asset to The Punaro Group. Throughout the book, we include a variety of publicly available charts from the Defense Business Board, many of which were originally created by Ron years ago and subsequently updated by the board.

A colleague and friend of many years from both the military and industry, Tom Davis's contributions were paramount to the completion of the book. Kathy Peroff provided vital insight into the government budgeting process and served as an excellent resource and wonderful contributor, especially on the topic of defense budgets in transition. I am grateful to both Tom and Kathy for their work in making this book a reality.

Our design, editing, and publishing partners at Pinkston have been valuable assets throughout the entirety of the book process. Led by Christian Pinkston, we are grateful for the entire team, including Nathan Burchfiel, Sean McCabe, Wesley Fouse, Andres Mancini, Damir Čirkić, Chris Lang, Alexandra Phelps, Margeaux Van Horn, Vicki Carl, and Caitlin Groves. Additionally, our partners at VSSL Agency, led by David Tillson, did a wonderful job designing the cover of *The Ever-Shrinking Fighting Force*, just as they did the cover for my first book.

In my military, Senate, and industry careers, I was blessed to work for and with some of the most accomplished and iconic individuals. During my time in the Marines, I was fortunate to have Capt. J.K. Van Riper, USMC, as my Infantry Company Commander in Vietnam from 1969-1970. He was the epitome of professionalism, tactical competence, and leadership. Additionally, I met Major Jim Jones, USMC, during his tour in the U.S. Senate Marine liaison office in 1977. From 1999 to 2003, he served as the Commandant of the Marine Corps and I worked directly for him as a Major General. To this day, he has remained one of my closest colleagues and friends. Van Riper and Jones are two of the finest Marines to ever wear the eagle, globe, and anchor.

My concentrated push for management and business reform in the Pentagon had its beginnings when then-Secretary of Defense Bill Cohen asked me to chair a Defense Reform Task Force in 1997. Secretary Cohen was encouraged in this pursuit by his senior military advisor, now Lt. Gen. Jim Jones, USMC. Our task force included some of the most experienced and thoughtful national security experts, including Dr. David Chu, Dr. Dov Zakheim, Jim Locher, Kim Wincup, Michael Bayer, and Rhett Dawson.

When I started in the U.S. Senate in 1973, the Senate Armed Services Committee consisted of legendary members including John Stennis, John Tower, Barry Goldwater, and Henry "Scoop" Jackson, and grew to include leaders such as John McCain, John Glenn, Jack Reed, and Jim Inhofe. Here, I had the privilege of working daily for 24 years with my boss, Senator Sam Nunn, who served as ranking member and chairman, and other leaders like Chairman John Warner. Together, these leaders championed a bipartisan approach to national security and always put the country's interests over their personal ones. I feel fortunate to have worked with and learned from the best.

In industry, I learned directly from three of the most accomplished and caring CEOs – Ken Dahlberg, formerly at SAIC, Roger Krone at Leidos, and David Joyce, formerly at General Electric. To them, success was not defined by the bottom line, but rather by how well they were taking care of their "troops," both in their companies and on the battlefield.

I have also benefited greatly from the insights and mentorship of former Secretary of the Navy John Lehman. John supported both management and fiscal reforms in the DoD, starting as early as the 1980s. I am grateful for the expertise and insight he has provided while working on a number of these recommendations together over the years. The same applies to Michael Bayer, the former chairman of the Defense Business Board and a member of our 1997 Defense Reform Task Force. I am also thankful for Dick McConn, the CEO of M International Inc. and the recent chairman of the National Defense Industrial Association, for understanding and promoting common-sense changes needed to improve Pentagon output. Throughout my career, General Brent Scowcroft provided sound guidance and advice on a variety of defense reform projects. He was always extremely generous with his time, and his keen insights always strengthened and improved our work. He is greatly missed.

Lastly and most importantly, my family has been a constant source of support and encouragement throughout this process. My parents and my in-laws were part of the greatest generation that served our country during WWII. Their values of hard work, sacrifice, and always doing the right thing made a deep impression on me. Thank you to my siblings—Vincent, Michael, and Trudie. Thank you to Jan, my wife of 47 years, for being in the foxhole with me throughout my whole career. Often referred to as "Saint Jan," she has provided me with unwavering support and love throughout our marriage. Thank you for your constant patience, encouragement, and guidance. And to my children—Dan, Joe, Meghan, and Julie—I appreciate your unwavering support throughout my career. Additionally, to my nine grandchildren—Colbie, Reese, Jack, Bryce, Logan, Jordan, Blake, Nancy, and Brooke—you keep me optimistic about the future and always brighten my day. Jan and I are blessed that our entire family lives within a short distance of our home.

I would also like to thank our men and women in uniform and our patriotic civilians working in national security in the executive branch, on the Hill, and in industry. Our nation is stronger because of your interminable hard work and dedication. This book is not meant as a critique of these individuals, past or present, but rather to serve as a helpful resource for the good people battling against the bad processes so prevalent in government. Thank you for improving and strengthening our national security capabilities.

CPSIA information can be obtained
at www.ICGtesting.com
Printed in the USA
BVHW050404280721
613019BV00018B/1728/J